CAPODIMONTE
AND I VERGINI

DECUMANO MAGGIORE

SPACCANAPOLI

TOLEDO AND
CASTEL NUOVO

**CAPODIMONTE AND
I VERGINI**
Pages 90–101

DECUMANO MAGGIORE
Pages 74–89

SPACCANAPOLI
Pages 60–73

0 metres	500
0 yards	500

EYEWITNESS TRAVEL

NAPLES
& THE AMALFI COAST

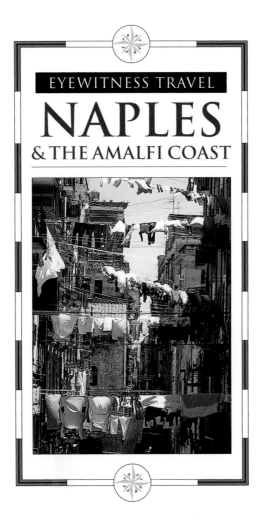

EYEWITNESS TRAVEL

NAPLES
& THE AMALFI COAST

DK

LONDON, NEW YORK,
MELBOURNE, MUNICH AND DELHI
www.dk.com

Produced by Fabio Ratti Editoria Libraria
e Multimediale Milano, Italy

PROJECT EDITOR Giovanni Francesio
EDITORS Barbara Cacciani, Giorgia Conversi, Elena Marzorati,
Michele Di Muro
DESIGNERS Paolo Gonzato, Carlotta Maderna, Stefania Testa
MAPS Paul Stafford

DK Publishing, Inc.
PROJECT EDITOR Fiona Wild
EDITORS Francesca Machiavelli, Naomi Peck, Rosalyn Thiro

CONTRIBUTORS Patrizia Antignani, Mariella Barone, Ciro Cacciola, Angela
Catello, Daniela Lepore, Emilia Marchi, Kirsi Viglione, Beatrice Vitelli
ILLUSTRATORS Giorgia Boli, Paola Spampinato, Nadia Viganò

ENGLISH TRANSLATION Richard Pierce

Reproduced by Colourscan, Singapore
Printed and bound in China by Leo Paper Products Ltd

First American Edition, 2000
11 12 13 14 10 9 8 7 6 5 4 3 2 1

Published in the United States by DK Publishing,
375 Hudson Street, New York, New York 10014

Reprinted with revisions 2003, 2005, 2007, 2009, 2011

A CATALOG RECORD FOR THIS BOOK IS AVAILABLE FROM THE LIBRARY OF CONGRESS.

ISSN 1542-1554
ISBN 978-0-75666-968-3

FLOORS ARE REFERRED TO THROUGHOUT IN ACCORDANCE WITH
EUROPEAN USAGE; IE THE "FIRST FLOOR" IS THE FLOOR ABOVE GROUND LEVEL.

Front cover main image: Faraglioni rocks, Capri, Bay of Naples

MIX
Paper from
responsible sources
FSC
www.fsc.org   FSC™ C018179

◁ **Marina Grande, Sorrento**

CONTENTS

HOW TO USE THIS
GUIDE **6**

The Farnese Hercules

INTRODUCING
NAPLES

FOUR GREAT DAYS IN
NAPLES AND THE
AMALFI COAST **10**

PUTTING NAPLES ON
THE MAP **12**

THE HISTORY
OF NAPLES **16**

NAPLES AT
A GLANCE **30**

NAPLES THROUGH
THE YEAR **40**

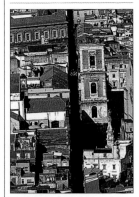

The Spaccanapoli district

Panoramic view of the Forum at Pompeii, with Vesuvius in the background

Outdoor eating, Bay of Naples

Pizza Napoletana

The church and cloisters of Santa Chiara

HOW TO USE THIS GUIDE

This guide helps you to get the most out of your visit to Naples. It provides both expert recommendations and advice as well as useful practical information. The first chapter, *Introducing Naples*, sets the city in its rich and varied geographical and historical context. *Naples at a Glance* gives you a brief overview of the main sights in the city, as well as cultural background. *Naples Through the Year* describes events and festivals season by season. *Naples Area by Area* describes the main sightseeing areas in detail, with maps, illustrations and photographs. *Pompeii and the Amalfi Coast* covers this region's splendid archaeological sites and also features an itinerary for a coastal boat trip. Information on hotels, shops, restaurants and bars is covered in *Travellers' Needs*, while the *Survival Guide* contains practical advice – for example, how to use the local transport networks.

FINDING YOUR WAY AROUND THE SIGHTSEEING SECTION

The city has been divided into six colour-coded areas, each with its own chapter. A description of the history and features of each area is followed by a Street-by-Street map focusing on the main attractions. The sights are numbered for easy reference. The most important sights in each area are described in detail in two or more pages.

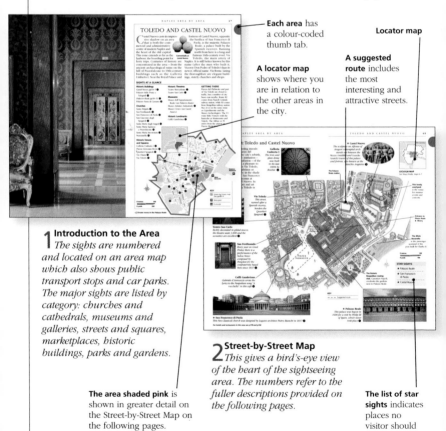

Each area has a colour-coded thumb tab.

Locator map

A locator map shows where you are in relation to the other areas in the city.

A suggested route includes the most interesting and attractive streets.

1 Introduction to the Area
The sights are numbered and located on an area map which also shows public transport stops and car parks. The major sights are listed by category: churches and cathedrals, museums and galleries, streets and squares, marketplaces, historic buildings, parks and gardens.

The area shaded pink is shown in greater detail on the Street-by-Street Map on the following pages.

2 Street-by-Street Map
This gives a bird's-eye view of the heart of the sightseeing area. The numbers refer to the fuller descriptions provided on the following pages.

The list of star sights indicates places no visitor should miss.

NAPLES AREA MAP

The coloured areas on this map *(see inside front cover)* correspond to the seven main sightseeing areas. Each area is covered in full either in the *Naples Area by Area (see pp44–129)* section or in the *Pompeii and the Amalfi Coast (see pp130–173)* chapter. The map showing the centre of Naples *(pp14–15)* also locates all of the major sights and monuments in the city.

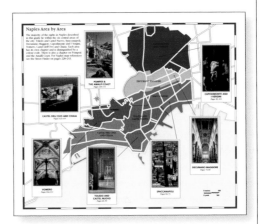

Numbers refer to each sight's position on the area map and its place in the chapter.

Practical Information provides all the information you need to visit the sights, including map references to the *Street Finder (see pp228–43).*

The Visitors' Checklist provides all the practical information needed to plan your visit.

3 Detailed Information on Each Sight

All the most important sights in Naples are described individually. They are listed in order, following the numbering on the area map, which appears at the beginning of each chapter. The key to the symbols used is shown on the back flap for easy reference.

Stars indicate the features you should not miss.

The timeline lists the most important events in the history of the building.

4 Naples' Top Sights

Historic buildings are dissected to reveal their interiors. Museums and galleries have colour-coded floorplans to help you locate the major works exhibited.

INTRODUCING NAPLES

DI NAPOLI

FOUR GREAT DAYS IN NAPLES AND THE AMALFI COAST

Visitors to Naples and the Amalfi Coast could be overwhelmed by the amount of things there are to see and do. Castles, palaces and museums, miles of breathtaking coastline, as well as plenty of culinary delights make Italy's third largest city and its surrounding area a treasure trove for travellers. These four itineraries offer a bit of

Majolica plate made in Vietri

everything, from a walk among ruins to a day exploring churches and shops, and from a drive along the spectacular coast to activities for children. All sights are cross-referenced to more information within the guide so that you can tailor the day to suit your needs. Price guidelines include the cost of public transport, food and admission charges.

The Duomo altar, Naples

CHURCHES AND SHOPPING

- **The magnificent Duomo**
- **Spaccanapoli shopping**
- **Lunch at a pizzeria**
- **Cloisters of Santa Chiara**

TWO ADULTS allow at least €40

Morning
Start on Via Duomo, at Naples' sumptuous Gothic cathedral, the **Duomo** *(see pp82–3)*. If it is the 19th September or the Saturday before the first Sunday in May, you may witness the liquefaction of San Gennaro's blood. From the Duomo, enter the **Pio Monte della Misericordia** *(see p81)*. Its walls house one of Caravaggio's master-pieces, *The Seven Acts of Mercy*. Afterwards, step into the heart of Naples' historic centre for a bit of retail therapy. Known as **Spaccanapoli** *(see pp62–3)*,

this narrow, vibrant street cuts the original Roman dimensions of the city in half and is crammed with churches, historic *palazzi*, shops and cafés. Seek out the artisan workshops on Via San Gregorio Armeno selling intriguing terracotta objects, from nativity scenes *(presepi)* and statuettes of **Pulcinella** *(see p39)* to good luck charms. Stop for lunch at one of the neighbourhood pizzerias for a classic pizza Margherita, topped with tomato, mozzarella and basil.

Afternoon
Continue along Spaccanapoli to the church of **San Domenico Maggiore** *(see p68)*. Its artworks, including Pietro Cavallini's frescoes in the Brancaccio chapel, are not to be missed. Pause for a *babà* (rum baba) at **Scaturchio** *(see p203)* before heading to Piazza del Gesù with its gaudy spire, the **Guglia dell'Immacolata** *(see p65)*. In the same piazza, the church of **Gesù Nuovo** *(see p64)* stands out for its diamond-

pointed stone façade. Across from here is the church of **Santa Chiara** *(see pp66–7)*, with its beautiful cloisters and the Museo dell'Opera di Santa Chiara, which houses parts of the church's original interior. Head for **Piazza Bellini** *(see p78)* for a look at the excavated ancient Greek walls and round off the day with a relaxing apéritif at **Intra Moenia** *(see p203)*.

A FAMILY DAY

- **The port of Mergellina**
- **Visit the oldest aquarium in Europe**
- **Ancient Castel dell'Ovo**
- **Palazzo Reale**

FAMILY OF 4 allow at least €100

Morning
Start the day by exploring the charming port of **Mergellina** *(see p119)* with its wonderful views and stop at **Chalet Ciro** *(see p203)* for some of Naples' best pastries. Head along the **Lungomare** *(see p116)* to

Boats in harbour at the port of Mergellina

◁ Historic hand drawn map of Naples

the **Villa Comunale** *(see p117)*. Built on the order of the Bourbon sovereigns in the 1700s, it is the only public park near the historic centre, so it is perenially popular with kids, and an ideal spot for a run about. Afterwards, visit the oldest aquarium in Europe, with its array of local fish, attached to the **Stazione Zoologica** *(see p117)*. Continue along the Lungomare, taking in the sun and sea, boats and bathers, until the imposing Castel dell'Ovo comes into view. Stop for lunch at any one of the many restaurants in the Borgo Marinaro.

The excavation area, Herculaneum

Afternoon
Explore Naples' oldest castle, the **Castel dell'Ovo** *(see p116)* – children love running around its ramparts – then head to Piazza del Plebiscito, to visit the extensive **Palazzo Reale** *(see pp50–51)*. After this, you'll be ready to end the day with a hot chocolate from **Caffè Gambrinus** *(see p52)*.

VIEWS OF THE AMALFI COAST

- **Majolica tiles at Vietri**
- **Lunch in Ravello**
- **Amalfi's striking cathedral**
- **Charming Positano**

TWO ADULTS allow at least €80

Morning
Begin the day's spectacular drive in **Vietri sul Mare** *(see p161)* one of Italy's largest producers of ceramic tiles, particularly painted majolica tiles. Then take the coastal road inland towards **Ravello** *(see p160)*. Verdant and tranquil, it is arguably the best known stop on the Amalfi coast tour for spellbinding views of the sea. Must-see sights here include the splendid Duomo, the church of Santa Maria a Gradillo, and the villas Rufolo and Cimbrone. Break for lunch

at **Da Salvatore** *(see p200)*, which is also justly renowned for its stunning panoramas.

Afternoon
From Ravello, head back to the coastal road. Take a moment to stop at **Amalfi** *(see p159)* to admire the magnificent Duomo di Sant' Andrea, situated just steps away from the town's only car park. Its impressive 11th-century bronze doors were brought here from Constantinople.

From Amalfi the coastal road cuts through precipitous cliffs to **Positano** *(see p158)*. Often considered to be the jewel of the Amalfi coast, it is a picture postcard of pastel houses set steep into a hillside with fishing boats dotted in the sea below. Spend an hour or so wandering the picturesque narrow alleys or browsing the many boutiques and craft shops. Then round the day off with a relaxing beachside glass of *prosecco* (sparkling wine) at sunset.

Breathtaking view of the coast from Amalfi

RUINS AND CRATERS

- **Portici villas**
- **The ruins at Herculaneum**
- **Mercato di Resina**
- **Awesome Mount Vesuvius**

TWO ADULTS allow at least €70

Morning
Take the Circumvesuviana train to **Portici** *(see p140)* (alight at Via Libertà station). The town and surrounding area are famous for their abundance of 18th-century aristocratic villas, including the royal palace. Back on the Circumvesuviana, continue to the Ercolano Scavi stop and the ruins of **Herculaneum** *(see pp144–5)*. Destroyed by Vesuvius in AD 79 *(see pp18–19)*, it is a good alternative to **Pompeii** *(see pp146–9)* as its smaller scale makes a two-hour tour possible. Remaining in the town of Ercolano, next visit the colourful **Mercato di Resina** *(see p208)* – an enormous flea market known for its antique costumes. For a picnic lunch, head to the town centre and grab a sandwich from **Viva Lo Re** *(see p198)* then take the bus up to **Vesuvius** *(see pp142–3)*.

Afternoon
Continue on foot for the 20-minute hike to the crater of the volcano. Afterwards, take the Circumvesuviana to **Torre del Greco** *(see p141)* and end the day shopping for the famous coral jewellery produced and sold here.

Putting Naples on the Map

Naples is the third largest city in Italy after Milan and Rome, and the largest city in Southern Italy. The population of the city proper *(see pp14–15)* is around one million, rising to almost three million when the suburbs are taken into account. The city faces the great sweep of the splendid Bay of Naples, extends into the fertile Campania plain, and occupies high ground and hollows formed by ancient volcanic craters.

Cassino
Campobass
Terracina
Caserta
Benevento
CAMPANI
Pozzuoli
NAPLES
Avel
Isola d'Ischia
Pompeii
Sorrento
Salerno
Isola di Capri
Battipag
Paestu

Satellite image of the Bay of Naples and Mount Vesuvius

Tyrrhenian Sea

Isole Eolie or Lipari

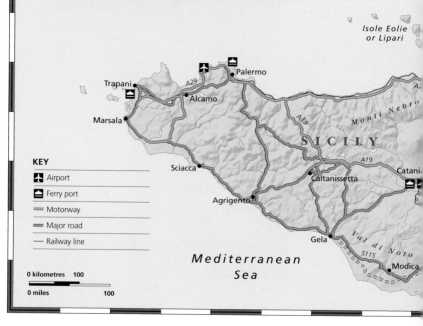

Palermo
Trapani
Alcamo
Marsala
Monti Nebro
SICILY
Sciacca
Caltanissetta
Catani
Agrigento
Gela
Val di Noto
Modica

KEY

✈	Airport
⛴	Ferry port
▬	Motorway
▬	Major road
—	Railway line

Mediterranean Sea

0 kilometres   100

0 miles   100

Foggia

A14

Barletta

Cerignola

Molfetta

A16

Bari

Le Murge   S96

Melfi

Altamura   S16   Fasano

Appennino

PUGLIA

A14

Potenza   Matera

S407

Brindisi

BASILICATA   Taranto

Penisola Salentina

Lecce

S7

Lucano   S106

Galatina

Maratea

Ionian
Sea

Sibari

Rossano

Cosenza

A3   CALABRIA

Crotone

Lamezia Terme   Catanzaro

Vibo Valentia

A3   S106

lazzo

lessina   Reggio di Calabria

Taormina

gusta

iracusa

Aerial view of Naples

EUROPE

NORWAY   FINLAND

SWEDEN

ESTONIA
RUSSIAN
FED
DENMARK   LATVIA
LITHUANIA

REP. OF
IRELAND   GREAT
BRITAIN   NETHERLANDS   POLAND   BELARUS

BELGIUM   GERMANY
CZECH
REPUBLIC   SLOVAKIA   UKRAINE

FRANCE   AUSTRIA   HUNGARY
SWITZ.   ROMANIA
CROATIA
ITALY   SERBIA   BULGARIA
MONTENEGRO KOSOVO
Rome

Naples   GREECE
SPAIN

PORTUGAL

ALGERIA   TUNISIA

Central Naples

The old town is divided into six distinct areas. From the 16th century on, the administrative and commercial centre of Naples developed around Toledo and Castel Nuovo. The old city centre is described in the chapters on Spaccanapoli and Decumano Maggiore. The Vergini district, immediately north of the Foria gorge, leads to the park of Capodimonte with its Royal Palace. The Certosa di San Martino and Castel Sant'Elmo dominate the Vomero hill. In the Chiaia area, a few steps from the most elegant shops in Naples, places such as Castel dell'Ovo and Mergellina are surrounded by greenery and the sea. To the west are the lovely inlets and villas of Posillipo.

The Certosa di San Martino, on the Vomero

The Cappella Caracciolo di Vico in San Giovanni a Carbonara

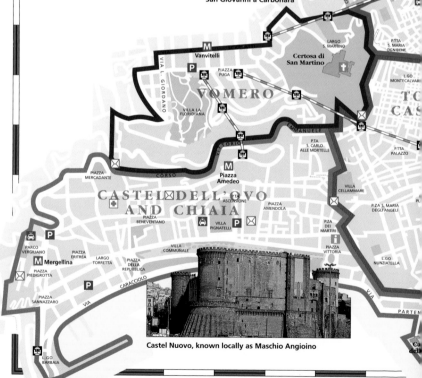

Castel Nuovo, known locally as Maschio Angioino

The tiled cloister of Santa Chiara

The fountain of *Christ and the Samaritan* in the cloister of the convent of San Gregorio Armeno

Castel dell'Ovo, seen from the bay

KEY

▢	Major sight
M	Metro station
⚓	Ferry port
🚠	Funicular
P	Car park
🛈	Tourist information
✚	Hospital with casualty unit
🚓	Police station
✝	Church
⊠	Post office

0 metres 500

0 yards 500

THE HISTORY OF NAPLES

In Greek mythology, Naples was built where the Siren Parthenope was washed ashore after she had been rejected by Odysseus. Greek colonists founded a settlement overlooking the Bay of Naples as early as the 4th century BC, calling it Parthenope. As the settlement continued to expand, they established *Neapolis* (new city) next to the *Palaeopolis*, or old city. Neapolis was a leading commercial centre, and the Greek language and customs survived even during the Roman period, when this was a favourite area of the elite.

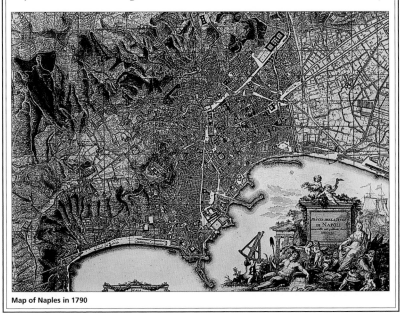

Gorgon, 6th-century BC Cumaean antefix

After the fall of the Roman Empire and a wave of invasions, the city, though it retained some independence, came under Byzantine influence and went through a period of rebirth. In the 12th century, the invading Normans succeeded in conquering the whole of Southern Italy, a kingdom initially ruled from Palermo, under Roger II. In 1266, Charles of Anjou was crowned King of the Two Sicilies, an event that began the Angevin (French) and Aragonese (Spanish) dynasties. Naples itself became a capital, and the court began to attract famous artists. The 1400s were a golden era for Naples, but there followed two centuries of direct rule by Spain. The Spanish viceroys were oppressive rulers and the era is remembered for unjust taxation, the Inquisition, the plague, overpopulation and the rebellion of Masaniello. Creativity flowered, however, despite the widespread poverty.

In 1734 King Charles began the period of Bourbon hegemony. With the exception of the short-lived republican government in 1799 and the subsequent decade of French dominion, the Bourbons ruled Naples until 1860.

Since the unification of Italy the city's problems have become national issues – for example the markedly different level of development between Northern and Southern Italy.

Map of Naples in 1790

◁ *Paquius Proculus and His Wife*, 1st-century AD wall painting from Pompeii

Greco-Roman Naples

Pompeiian cameo

By the 8th century BC, Greeks had founded a settlement at Cumae, one of the earliest Greek colonies in Italy. From there they established a new town on Pizzofalcone hill, known as Parthenope, and trade prospered. Population growth led to the founding of Neapolis, or new city, nearby, and victory over the Etruscans in 474 BC brought further expansion. Neapolis came into contact with the growing power of Rome during the latter's protracted wars with the Samnites, and in the 4th century BC the citizens agreed to become an "allied city" of Rome. In AD 79 an erupting Vesuvius buried a number of ancient Roman cities, including Pompeii.

EXTENT OF THE CITY

▨ 8 BC	▢ Today

Bedrooms and living rooms

Temple of the Dioscuri
This 16th-century print shows the Roman temple that once stood on the site of San Paolo Maggiore (see p79). The temple façade collapsed in the 1688 earthquake.

Atrium

Via Anticaglia
The "street of ruins" acquired its name from the brick arches connecting the Ancient Roman bath house and the theatre (see p84).

Ornamental basin (impluvium)

TIMELINE

900 BC	600 BC		100 BC
1000–900 BC According to Greek myth, city of Parthenope founded	**328 BC** War with Rome; Naples is defeated but a treaty sanctions the city's freedom	**90–89 BC** People o Campania become Roman citizens	
600 BC Greeks from Cumae found *Neapolis* or "new city"	*Red-figure vase (5th century BC)*	**100 BC** Tunnel built in Posillipo hill connecting city with Phlegraean Fields area and its trade and military ports	

THE HOUSES OF POMPEII

The Roman houses in Pompeii *(see pp150–51)* are among the best-preserved examples of Roman civilization in Campania. This illustration shows a typical patrician house in Pompeii, displaying characteristic features of Roman and Greek domestic architecture. The houses were generally rectangular. To ensure privacy, they faced inwards, as can be seen by the few windows on the outer walls, and the rooms were built around an atrium or courtyard, which was the focal point of domestic life. Wealthier houses were richly decorated.

The garden was surrounded by columns, known as a "peristyle".

The kitchen and dining room (*triclinium*) were in this part of the house.

The Greek Walls
Made of large tufa blocks, the city walls date from the 5th century BC. Remnants can be seen in present-day Piazza Bellini (see p78).

WHERE TO SEE GRECO-ROMAN NAPLES

Beneath the cloister *of San Lorenzo* (see p80) *layers of the ancient city are still visible.*

Although not much is left of Greco-Roman *Neapolis*, some traces are visible in Piazza Bellini *(see p78)*, around Santa Chiara *(see pp66–7)* and under the Duomo *(see pp82–3)*. Outside the city, Pompeii and Herculaneum are vivid records of ancient Roman life. The Museo Archeologico Nazionale *(see pp86–9)* in Naples houses rich finds. Amphitheatres survive at Pozzuoli *(see p136)* and Santa Maria Capua Vetere *(see p165)*, and Greek ruins at Cumae *(see p138)* and Paestum *(see pp162–3)*.

The Diadumeno Torso from Castel Capuano

Statue of Aphrodite, Museo Archeologico

305 San Gennaro decapitated in Pozzuoli; his remains are placed in the city catacombs *(see p94)*

500 Construction of first parish church, now San Giorgio Maggiore *(see p70)*

AD	AD 300	400	500

79 Vesuvius erupts; Pompeii and Herculaneum destroyed

The Siren Parthenope on a Roman coin

476 Romulus Augustulus, last Roman emperor of the West, imprisoned in the *Castrum Lucullanum* *(see p116)*

536 Byzantine General Belisarius wins Naples, entering city via the aqueduct

From Byzantine Rule to the Aragonese Dynasty

Angevin lily

In the 6th century AD, Naples became part of the Byzantine (Eastern Roman) empire. Despite incursions into Southern Italy by Goths, Lombards and Saracens, it remained a semi-independent duchy, nominally under Byzantine rule, until it became part of the Norman kingdom of Sicily in the 12th century. By the 13th century the French House of Anjou had taken over and Naples became the capital of the Angevin kingdom. Ambitious schemes were begun: land reclamation and building of new castles, churches and monasteries. In 1421 the last Angevin queen, Joan II, named Alfonso V of Aragon as her successor.

GROWTH OF THE CITY

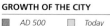

▨ AD 500　　▢ Today

Tombs in Santa Chiara
The Angevin rulers were buried in Santa Chiara, which contains superbly crafted tombs such as this one by an unknown artist (first half of the 14th century).

Louis of Anjou took vows after refusing the crown of Naples and was canonized in 1317.

Tomb of Ladislas of Durazzo
This tomb is in San Giovanni a Carbonara (see p96), chosen by Ladislas to house the tombs of the Angevin kings.

The Pietrasanta Bell Tower
This is among the few remaining examples of medieval architecture in Naples (see p78).

TIMELINE

553
Naples again under Byzantine rule

7th-century Byzantine fibula

915
After many attempts to conquer Naples, the Saracens are defeated at Gariglliano

600	700	800	900

600
Naples resists Lombard siege and remains an independent duchy

763
The duchy becomes hereditary and independent

Statue of Frederick II, Holy Roman Emperor

Frescoes of the Giotto School

Giotto lived in Naples from 1328–33. His influence can be seen in the frescoes in Santa Maria di Donnaregina Vecchia (see p84).

The crown Louis is placing on the head of his brother Robert legitimized the Angevin dynasty.

ST LOUIS OF TOULOUSE

This Gothic portrait was probably painted in 1317, after Louis of Anjou was canonized. Louis is shown as a Franciscan saint crowning his younger brother Robert King of Naples. Simone Martini's masterpiece is now in the Museo Nazionale di Capodimonte *(see pp98–101).*

Robert of Anjou

WHERE TO SEE ANGEVIN AND ARAGONESE NAPLES

Evidence of this period is everywhere in Naples, although successive reconstructions have often obscured the original architectural styles. Rather than civic buildings such as Castel Capuano *(see p81),* it was the churches that changed the face of the city: Santa Chiara *(see pp66–7),* San Lorenzo *(see p80),* San Domenico Maggiore *(see p68),* and Santa Maria di Donnaregina Vecchia *(see p84)* with its wonderful cycle of frescoes painted by the school of Giotto.

Castel Nuovo, *originally Angevin, also has Aragonese elements (see pp54–5).*

King Roger II

The Norman king of Naples is depicted in one of the eight statues placed in the niches of the Palazzo Reale façade in 1888 (see pp50–51).

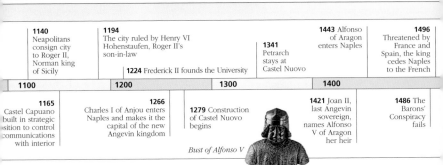

1140 Neapolitans consign city to Roger II, Norman king of Sicily	1194 The city ruled by Henry VI Hohenstaufen, Roger II's son-in-law		1341 Petrarch stays at Castel Nuovo	1443 Alfonso of Aragon enters Naples	1496 Threatened by France and Spain, the king cedes Naples to the French
		1224 Frederick II founds the University			

1100	1200	1300	1400

1165 Castel Capuano built in strategic position to control communications with interior	1266 Charles I of Anjou enters Naples and makes it the capital of the new Angevin kingdom	1279 Construction of Castel Nuovo begins	1421 Joan II, last Angevin sovereign, names Alfonso V of Aragon her heir	1486 The Barons' Conspiracy fails

Bust of Alfonso V

The Spanish Viceroyalty

Masaniello

In 1503 Naples ceased to be an independent kingdom, and became a colony of Spain, ruled by a viceroy. The city began to expand unchecked in the suburbs and beyond the walls. Palazzo Reale was built near Castel Nuovo, and courts assembled at Castel Capuano. With the construction of Via Toledo and the restructuring of Via Chiaia in the mid-1500s, the focus of city development shifted: aristocratic palaces were built along the Riviera and Toledo, and the need to accommodate the troops led to the building of the Quartieri Spagnoli district. New churches and monasteries were built. By now Naples was the largest city in Italy, with consequent problems of overcrowding and poverty. A famous figure in this period is Masaniello, the revolutionary who was first considered a hero, and then killed by the people who had supported him. Spanish rule came to an end in 1707 when, with the Treaty of Utrecht, the Kingdom of Naples was ceded to Austria.

GROWTH OF THE CITY

■ *1500*   □ *Today*

Santa Maria del Carmine *(see p73)*, which gave the square its name.

Don Pedro de Toledo
Don Pedro was viceroy from 1532 to 1553. He promoted new town planning, but also wanted to bring the Inquisition to Naples, triggering a revolt by the landed nobility.

Masaniello, born Tommaso Aniello in 1622, was an illiterate fisherman.

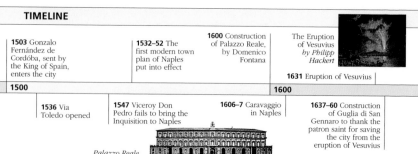

TIMELINE

1503 Gonzalo Fernández de Córdoba, sent by the King of Spain, enters the city	**1532–52** The first modern town plan of Naples put into effect	**1600** Construction of Palazzo Reale, by Domenico Fontana	The Eruption of Vesuvius *by Philipp Hackert*
			1631 Eruption of Vesuvius
1500		**1600**	
1536 Via Toledo opened	**1547** Viceroy Don Pedro fails to bring the Inquisition to Naples	**1606–7** Caravaggio in Naples	**1637–60** Construction of Guglia di San Gennaro to thank the patron saint for saving the city from the eruption of Vesuvius

Palazzo Reale

Statue of San Gennaro
The Neapolitans gave their venerated patron saint credit for having stopped the eruption of Vesuvius in 1631.

This memorial stone was to record all the concessions obtained from the viceroy by Masaniello.

MASANIELLO'S UPRISING

This painting by Micco Spadaro depicts Piazza Mercato *(see p73)* during the 1647 riot. A tax levied on fruit sparked the riot, which rapidly grew into a fully fledged uprising against the aristocracy. However, the attempt was soon crushed, as the city's moderates managed to persuade people to rebel against their revolutionary leader. Masaniello was killed the same year on 16 July.

Giambattista Vico
The famous philosopher and historian, author of La Scienza Nuova (The New Science), *was born in Naples in 1668, the son of a bookseller.*

WHERE TO SEE VICEROYAL NAPLES

The original 17th-century façade of the Palazzo Reale *(see pp50–51)* has changed little over the centuries. The Cappella del Tesoro di San Gennaro *(see pp82–3)* is one of the richest Baroque monuments in Naples. A short distance from the Duomo is a small area with a wealth of 17th-century treasures: the Guglia di San Gennaro *(see p81)* and Pio Monte della Misericordia *(see p77)*, which houses the canvas that marked a turning point in 17th-century Neapolitan painting – *The Seven Acts of Mercy* by Caravaggio, who stayed in Naples in 1607.

The Certosa di San Martino (see pp108–11) *was extended and decorated in the late 1500s.*

At San Gregorio Armeno (see p80), *the cloister is decorated with this striking fountain.*

1647 Masaniello's uprising

The plague in a painting by Micco Spadaro (detail)

1707 Beginning of Austrian viceroyalty

1723 Pietro Giannone flees to Vienna after publishing his *Civic History of the Kingdom of Naples*, which is banned by the Church

1650

1700

1656 Devastating plague epidemic; Naples loses one-third of population

1688 Earthquake damages most of old city

1701 Failure of Prince of Macchia's conspiracy to overthrow Spanish rule

1697 Giambattista Vico becomes professor of rhetoric at Naples university

Bourbon Naples

Charles of Bourbon

In 1734 the much-abused Kingdom of Naples changed hands once more, with the arrival of King Charles of Bourbon, who set out to make Naples into a metropolis. He suspended church building in favour of large-scale public works and new industries. He also built a Royal Palace in Caserta modelled on Versailles, which was to be the focal point of an entire city. At the same time, art, antiquities, music and even the *lazzaroni* (street people) attracted travellers making the Grand Tour. The royal schemes lacked a coherent plan, however, and fundamental problems failed to be addressed. Bourbon rule ended in 1860, when Garibaldi arrived in Naples, having won over Sicily and Calabria. In the same year Naples became part of the new Kingdom of Italy.

GROWTH OF THE CITY

▨ *1700*   ▢ *Today*

The Palace of Capodimonte

Charles's Porcelain
The king founded a porcelain factory in 1743 (see p101). After Charles returned to Spain his son, Ferdinand, opened his own factory.

The Beheading of Ettore Carafa
This relief in the Museo di San Martino depicts the execution of one of the martyrs of the Parthenopean Republic on 17 August 1799.

Antonio Genovesi (1713–69)
A leading figure in the Neapolitan Enlightenment movement, he became the first professor of political economics in Italy in 1754.

TIMELINE

Statuette found in Herculaneum

Ancient finds at Herculaneum transferred to Palazzo degli Studi

1700			1750	

1734 King Charles establishes the Bourbon dynasty in Naples

1738 Beginning of excavations at Herculaneum

1740 Church building suspended

1759 Charles returns to Spain; his son Ferdinand becomes king

1777 The university moves to the Jesuit College, now a banished society. Ferdinando Fuga turns Palazzo degli Studi into a museum

Cappella di San Gennaro

19th-century Neapolitan painting often featured landscapes and picturesque settings – as seen in this work by Gigante (1806– 76), showing the chapel of San Gennaro – as well as the rural scenes of Palizzi (1818–88) and the realism of Morelli (1826–1901).

WHERE TO SEE BOURBON NAPLES

The most important architectural achievements of the Bourbons are the Teatro San Carlo *(see p53)*, the Palace of Capodimonte *(see pp98–101)* and the Albergo dei Poveri *(see p97)*. Urban projects such as the Foro Carolino and the Villa Reale at Chiaia also date from the Bourbon period. The passion for antiquity inspired collecting and the setting up of the Museo Archeologico *(see pp86–9)*. But Bourbon influence is mainly to be seen outside the city, where kings built hunting lodges as well as royal palaces, such as Caserta *(see pp166–7)*.

The Bourbon court *on a shoot in a painting by Jakob Philipp Hackert (1783)*

THE DUKE OF NOJA'S MAP

This was the first modern relief map, the work of Duke Giovanni Carafa di Noja in 1775. The map shows the full extent of the city of Naples and the monumental buildings in the newly developed districts. In this detail the impressive Royal Palace of Capodimonte dominates the city skyline.

Naples appears as a chaotic muddle of buildings here.

The Naples-Portici Railway

The first Italian railway was inaugurated in 1839, when the Bayard locomotive took 9 minutes 30 seconds to travel about 7.5 km (4.5 miles). This painting of the Vesuvio by Fergola is in the Museo di San Martino.

1806 Napoleon gives the role of king of Naples to his brother Joseph Bonaparte

1808 Bonaparte goes to Spain and is replaced by Joachim Murat. The French promote great public works and administrative reforms

1848 Popular revolt restores constitution but it is annulled by Parliament in 1849

Giuseppe Garibaldi

1800

1850

1799 Birth of Neapolitan Republic, overthrown six months later by the counter-revolution. Its leaders are executed in Piazza Mercato

1820 Constitution granted but is repealed the following year

1815 Murat executed at Pizzo Castle, in Calabria. Ferdinand returns to throne as King of the Two Sicilies

1839 First railway in Italy, Naples–Portici, inaugurated

1860 Garibaldi enters city on 7 September; after plebiscite, Naples becomes part of newly united Kingdom of Italy

Naples after Unification

In a crowded, densely populated city, the 1884 cholera epidemic brought ancient problems to a head. An attempt to face them was made with the Urban Renewal Plan. Slum clearance was carried out around the port and new districts were created in the centre and towards the hills. However, the Plan failed to solve

The philosopher Benedetto Croce

many basic problems, work took much longer than expected, and triggered a wave of corruption. The Fascist regime contented itself with a new series of public works and the creation of more built-up areas. A leading local figure of the time was the philosopher Benedetto Croce, one of the few Italian intellectuals who openly opposed Fascism.

GROWTH OF THE CITY

☐ *1850*   ☐ *Today*

Santa Chiara
After being damaged in the 1943 bombardments, Santa Chiara was restored to its presumed original appearance.

THE ILVA STEELWORKS IN BAGNOLI
This plant, later known as Italsider, was built near the beach and the ancient hot springs in 1907 *(see p136)*. Renovated for the last time in 1987 and now closed, it has become a symbol of modern development carried out with total disregard for the natural context and scenic beauty of the area.

Matilde Serao (1856–1927)
"Naples must be gutted" declared the prominent author on the eve of the Renewal Plan. A few years later, disappointed by the results, she described Corso Umberto I as a "screen" concealing old and new misery.

TIMELINE

1880 Inauguration of Vesuvius funicular, which inspires the famous song *Funiculì Funiculà*

The Mount Vesuvius funicular

1891 First city funicular connecting Vomero with centre becomes operative

1860	1880	1890

1868 Via Duomo begun with first city demolition and finished in late 1800s as part of Urban Renewal Plan

1885 Special law for Urban Renewal Plan: demolition of slum areas begins

1884 Cholera epidemic

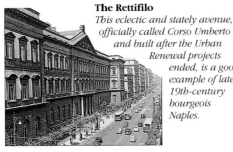

The Rettifilo
This eclectic and stately avenue, officially called Corso Umberto I and built after the Urban Renewal projects ended, is a good example of late 19th-century bourgeois Naples.

WHERE TO SEE POST-UNIFICATION NAPLES

The Caffè Gambrinus (*see p52*) was the haunt of Italian avant-garde artists, like the Futurists, as well as such illustrious visitors as Oscar Wilde. During the Urban Renewal period that changed the face of civic Naples, the Art Nouveau style prevailed in the new residential districts and the small villas in Chiaia (*see pp112–19*) and Vomero (*see pp102–11*). Monumental Fascist architecture is represented by the Palazzo delle Poste e Telegrafi (*see p57*) and the Stazione Marittima (the port). Via Toledo (*see p53*) boasts an important Novecento-style building constructed in 1939 to house the main offices of the Banco di Napoli.

The Caffè Gambrinus *was popular in the early 1900s.*

The Mostra delle Terre d'Oltremare
This huge exhibition and recreational complex was one of the Fascist regime's most notable architectural achievements. Work on the site began in 1937 after the demolition of the Fuorigrotta quarter.

1901 Saredo judicial inquiry reveals government–Camorra rapport

1925–7 Naples incorporates surrounding towns, formerly independent

1940 Mostra delle Terre d'Oltremare – a huge exhibition, recreational and sports complex built by the Fascist regime – opens

Entrance to Mostra d'Oltremare

1900

1920

1945

Benito Mussolini

1899 First stretch of Cumana railway built

1922 On October 24, Fascists meet in Naples on eve of "March on Rome"

1928–41 Rione Carità district replaces old San Giuseppe quarter

1944 Last eruption of Vesuvius

1943 *"Quattro giornate"* uprising: Germans driven out of Naples

Present-day Naples

Eduardo De Filippo

At the end of World War II the city had to cope with the appalling damage inflicted by all the bombardments. The 1950s and 1960s were marked by the large-scale, indiscriminate building activity promoted by politicians seeking short-term gain. The closure of some large factories in the 1980s aggravated the acute unemployment problem. However, Naples has always distinguished itself by its irrepressible vitality and creativity, especially in the fields of music and theatre. Today the city is rediscovering its past, and there is a commitment to city regeneration, as well as a resurgence of cultural programmes and the creation of contemporary art galleries.

GROWTH OF THE CITY

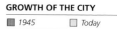
■ *1945*   □ *Today*

Vesuvius
This work by Andy Warhol was produced in 1985 for an exhibition held at the Museo di Capodimonte, where the canvas is now on display. It is the American artist's tribute to the most recurrent artistic motif relating to Naples – an erupting Vesuvius.

San Paolo Stadium
Built in the 1960s, this football stadium has a seating capacity of 60,000. Famous players for Naples include Dino Zoff and Diego Maradona.

TIMELINE

1945 Eduardo De Filippo writes *Napoli milionaria.* Town council approves reconstruction project

1952 Shipowner Achille Lauro, leader of the monarchist party, becomes mayor. Period of building speculation begins

1963 Francesco Rosi directs film *Hands over the City (see p37)*

1975 Inauguration of bypass road for fast traffic at edge of old town

1950   **1960**   **1970**   **1980**

1949 Curzio Malaparte's novel *La Pelle,* set in Naples, causes a scandal with its raw descriptions

Achille Lauro

1962 Centre-left coalition governs city

1972 Town-planning regulations (still partly in force) protect historic old town

1980 The earthquake in Campania and Basilicata also causes damage in Naples. Reconstruction includes a plan to revive the outskirts

Posillipo Today

Among the many examples of building malpractice in Naples, Posillipo is one of the most tragic. The hill, known the world over for its ancient history and lovely scenery, has been defaced by unchecked and unscrupulous development.

pedestrian avenue is between the buildings: cars use underground roads.

Skyscrapers are a novelty in Neapolitan architecture.

CENTRO DIREZIONALE

This district of futuristic administrative office buildings in the heart of the city, near the central railway station, is an example of "rational" modernization. The original plan dates from the 1960s, but in 1982 the famous Japanese architect Kenzo Tange began a new design. The layout of the area is such that traffic, which runs along underground streets, is separated from pedestrians.

The planting of trees softens the stark modern aesthetic and improves the environment for workers.

Montagna di Sale

Mimmo Paladino's Salt Mountain was installed in Piazza del Plebiscito for New Year's Day 1996. The square, restored for the G7 summit and now a pedestrian zone, has become a symbol of the new Naples.

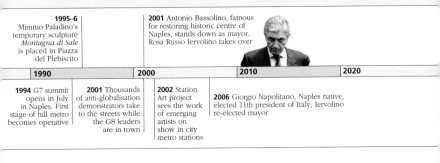

1995–6 Mimmo Paladino's temporary sculpture *Montagna di Sale* is placed in Piazza del Plebiscito

2001 Antonio Bassolino, famous for restoring historic centre of Naples, stands down as mayor. Rosa Russo Iervolino takes over

| 1990 | 2000 | 2010 | 2020 |

1994 G7 summit opens in July in Naples. First stage of hill metro becomes operative

2001 Thousands of anti-globalisation demonstrators take to the streets while the G8 leaders are in town

2002 Station Art project sees the work of emerging artists on show in city metro stations

2006 Giorgio Napolitano, Naples native, elected 11th president of Italy; Iervolino re-elected mayor

NAPLES AT A GLANCE

Naples is filled with evidence of many centuries of occupation blended into the fabric of the present-day city. This complex heritage, from ancient Greeks and Romans to the dukes, kings and queens of the Middle Ages and beyond, has contributed to a rich store of galleries and museums, ancient amphitheatres and ruins, as well as churches, monasteries, royal palaces and monuments. While the *Area by Area* section *(pp44–129)* describes the various places of interest in detail, the following ten pages will provide some background and cultural context. Each corner of Naples has something different to offer, but below is a selection of attractions that no visitor to the city should miss.

NAPLES' TOP TOURIST ATTRACTIONS

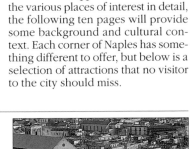

Castel Nuovo *See pp54–5*

Santa Chiara *See pp66–7*

Museo di Capodimonte
See pp98–101

Certosa di San Martino *See pp108–11*

Mergellina *See p119*

Castel dell'Ovo *See p116*

Museo Archeologico Nazionale
See pp86–9

Posillipo
See pp124–9

◁ The seafront with its historic hotels, Castel dell'Ovo and the Borgo Marinaro

Naples and the Bay

The Faraglioni of Capri

Formed by an immense crater, the Bay of Naples is both sheltered and exposed; sheltered by the curve of hills to the east which create a natural semi-circular amphitheatre, but open to the sea. The zone is volcanic, shaped by cones and craters of all ages, some submerged, some still bubbling with thermal springs and jets of steam. Now that Vesuvius is quiet (the last smoke trail was seen in 1944), the most active crater in the region is the Solfatara at Pozzuoli *(see p137)*. The living, breathing quality of the land led Homer to choose the coastline as the setting for parts of the *Odyssey*. Chaotic development along the coast has not deterred visitors from seeking out and appreciating the beauty of the bay.

Ischia *has small sandy beaches that are a great tourist attraction.*

Gaiola *is the largest of the three islands facing the Gaiola quarter. The coastline is rocky and precipitous with natural caves.*

Posillipo

Castel dell'Ovo

THE BAY OF NAPLES

Mount Vesuvius stands guard over a bay which owes its beauty and characteristic curves to the violent and often deadly explosions of a series of volcanoes. The conical shape of Monte Epomeo on Ischia still shows its volcanic origin; one submerged crater now does service as the port of Ischia and hot springs abound. Capri, once joined to the mainland, is geologically an extension of the Sorrento peninsula; time has carved beautiful caves along the island's precipitous coastline. Just beyond Punta Campanella are islands known to Homer as the home of the Sirens.

THE BAY FROM MERGELLINA

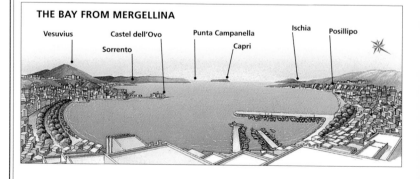

Vesuvius   Castel dell'Ovo   Punta Campanella   Ischia   Posillipo

Sorrento   Capri

The port of Naples, *once a disembarkation point for transatlantic ships, is now the centre of intense ship, ferry and hydrofoil traffic for tourists along the coast and to the islands of Capri, Ischia and Procida. The Angioino wharf is also important commercially.*

The fertility of the soil *in Naples was proverbial in ancient times. To this day you can still find unexpected pockets of terrace cultivation in built-up areas.*

Riviera di Chiaia

San Francesco di Paola

Palazzo Reale

The pebble beaches *under Castel dell'Ovo and Palazzo Reale serve as small marinas for all kinds of boats, especially leisure craft.*

The natural grottoes *of Sorrento, with their original shapes produced by water erosion, are a characteristic feature of the southern stretch of the bay.*

The Architecture of Naples

One feature of the architecture of Naples is the way in which traces of various epochs and styles can be seen in one short section of street, from Roman foundations and remains to the turn-of-the-century galleria made of iron and glass. Little remains within Naples of its Greek heritage, yet in the heart of the city you can still discern the regular grid layout adopted in 5th-century BC Neapolis: the three main streets going east–west – present-day Via Anticaglia *(see p84)*, Via Tribunali *(see pp76–7)* and Via San Biagio dei Librai – and the north–south roads that intersect them at right angles. Along the waterfront (Lungomare) and the Riviera di Chiaia, more modern buildings can be found, elegant palazzi alternating with villas and splendid luxury hotels.

The ancient grid layout of Neapolis (red lines) over a plan of the modern city

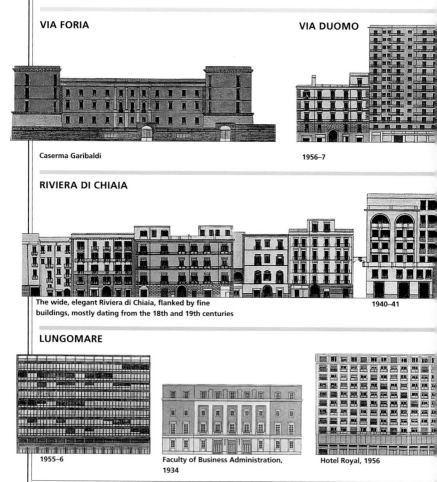

VIA FORIA

Caserma Garibaldi

VIA DUOMO

1956–7

RIVIERA DI CHIAIA

The wide, elegant Riviera di Chiaia, flanked by fine buildings, mostly dating from the 18th and 19th centuries

1940–41

LUNGOMARE

1955–6

Faculty of Business Administration, 1934

Hotel Royal, 1956

A MULTI-LAYERED CITY

San Lorenzo Maggiore *(see p80)* is one example of a layered building. Remains of the ancient city are visible under the monastery. The church itself is also the result of a series of reconstructions; the Angevin basilica, built over the ruins of a 6th-century church, was completely rebuilt in the 1700s, and then restored to its original medieval state in the last century. The 18th-century façade still has the original 14th-century wooden doorway.

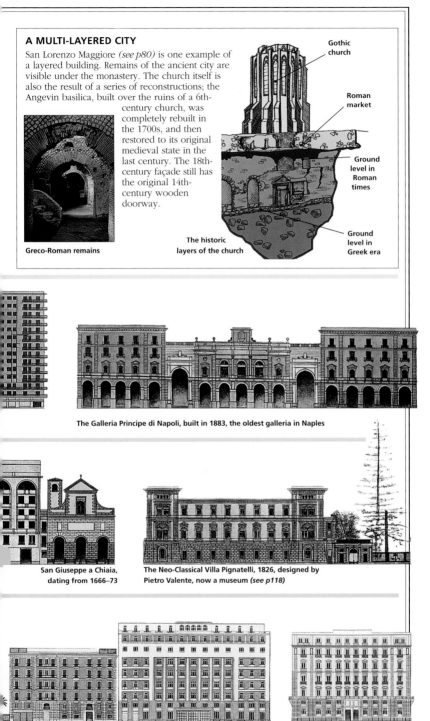

Gothic church

Roman market

Ground level in Roman times

Ground level in Greek era

Greco-Roman remains

The historic layers of the church

The Galleria Principe di Napoli, built in 1883, the oldest galleria in Naples

San Giuseppe a Chiaia, dating from 1666–73

The Neo-Classical Villa Pignatelli, 1826, designed by Pietro Valente, now a museum *(see p118)*

Hotel Continental

Hotel Vesuvio (reconstruction), 1948

Santa Lucia, 1902

Writers in Naples

The beauty of the Bay of Naples and the fascination of Vesuvius have inspired writers and artists for over 2,000 years. The Greeks wove stories around the landscape, seeing in it a variety of mythological creatures; volcanic activity was regarded as the work of the gods. The poet Virgil so loved Naples that he spent his last years there while writing the *Georgics* and the *Aeneid*. The city's rich Classical inheritance again attracted travellers with the advent of the Grand Tour, over 17 centuries later, when no young man could be considered well educated without a visit to Italy.

Bust of Virgil

Portrait of Giacomo Leopardi

FROM CLASSICAL WRITERS TO THE RENAISSANCE

Before the eruption in AD 79 Vesuvius had been quiet for 1,200 years, but inhabitants were nonetheless aware of the living nature of the land. Pliny the Elder, author of *Naturalis Historia*, died at Pompeii; his curiosity tempted him to go closer to the volcano and he was suffocated by the fumes. His nephew, Pliny the Younger, provides in his letters an eyewitness account of the eruption.

The Renaissance brought a revival of interest in Greek and Latin culture. In the 14th century writers and artists including Boccaccio, Giotto and the great lyric poet and scholar Petrarch were attracted to the court of

Petrarch

Robert of Anjou. Torquato Tasso, a native of Sorrento, worked on his epic poetry at the monastery of Monteoliveto at the end of the 1500s.

TRAVELLERS AND THE GRAND TOUR

The Grand Tour first became a custom in the 16th century and by the 18th century it was English fashion. Young aristocrats were expected to study Europe's Classical past to complete their education and the Tour took them to Rome and Naples. Excavations at Herculaneum in 1711 and at Pompeii in 1733 added to the enormous appeal of this part of Italy. Sir William Hamilton, an archaeologist, collector and envoy to Naples from 1764, entertained Grand Tour travellers at the embassy. The Tour inspired journals, letters and guide books and Goethe, overwhelmed by his visit to the city in 1775 with the painter Tischbein, wrote of Naples in *Italian Journey*.

ROMANTIC NAPLES

Stendhal departed Naples in 1817 smitten with Toledo and Teatro San Carlo, the glories of the "most beautiful city in the universe". In 1812 Alphonse de Lamartine recalled his experiences of Naples in *Graziella*, which featured a girl from Procida,

Tischbein, *Goethe in the Country* (Museo di San Martino)

and the *Gulf of Baia*. In 1828 the American author James Fenimore Cooper was so taken by the city he managed to find good qualities even in its negative aspects. In his description of the Castel Nuovo area he declares: "This was the area of the *lazzaroni*; and it is no easy task to find lovelier or happier vagabonds than the ones here". Charles Dickens' 1844 observations were published in the *Daily News* and in his book, *Pictures from Italy*. The end of Bourbon rule, the unification of Italy and the cholera epidemic of 1884 brought about a decline in the number of visitors to Naples. The foreign traveller remained enchanted by Naples and its Bay, but set off for Pompeii and Paestum, and later, Capri.

TO THE 20TH CENTURY

Poet Giacomo Leopardi (1798–1837) spent the last years of his life in Naples. Neapolitan Matilde Serao wrote vividly of the hectic city and hopes and passions inspired by the lottery in *Il Paese di Cuccagna* (1891). Curzio Malaparte, whose red villa is a landmark on Capri (*see p169*), wrote in *La Pelle* (1948): "Naples is the most mysterious city in Europe. It is the only city of the ancient world that has not perished. ...It is not a city: it is a world – the ancient pre-Christian world – which has survived intact on the surface of the modern world".

Naples and the Arts

Silent film stars of 1914

Naples was famous in the 19th century for its spectacular operas and the magnetism of its popular songs, and in more recent times, Neapolitan performers such as Eduardo De Filippo, Totò and Sophia Loren, have all gained worldwide acclaim. The arts scene is still alive today, with creative experiments ranging from variations on the *sceneggiata* to avant-garde theatre, and from traditional song to modern cinema.

Eduardo De Filippo and Totò

OPERA AND THEATRE

Opera may be the preserve of the elite elsewhere, but in Naples passion for opera knows no social boundaries and even permeates street life. Historic Teatro San Carlo *(see p53)* is one of Italy's most prestigious opera houses. The season is well subscribed and performances often sell out. Rossini's opera *Otello* was first performed at the San Carlo, as were two other of his world premieres: *Mosè in Egitto* (1818) and *La Donna del Lago* (1819), based on Sir Walter Scott's *The Lady of the Lake*. Donizetti's *Lucia di Lammermoor* made its debut at the San Carlo in 1835.

Gioacchino Rossini

Theatre has a broad popularity in Naples. Cinemas forced to close because of dwindling attendance have even been reborn as theatres. Neapolitans are proud of their dialect, used to great effect by beloved comic actors like Eduardo Scarpetta (1853–1925), Totò (1898–1967) and Eduardo De Filippo (1900–84). Comedies by actor-playwrights De Filippo and Raffaele Viviani (1888–1950) affectionately expose the ironies and petty concerns of daily life. They are performed as much today as when they were written.

Experimental theatre has been active in Naples since the establishment of the "Falso Movimento" in 1979. Its founders are now involved in the Teatri Uniti, staging avant-garde plays at the Teatro Nuovo and Galleria Toledo.

THE SCENEGGIATA

The *sceneggiata* (popular Neapolitan melo-drama) dates from the turn of the 20th century. Simple plots and characters embroiled in tragedy and farce delighted audiences that cheered heroes and booed villains. Music played a vital part in the show and there was always a rousing title song, the *pezzo forte*. This lively genre temporarily fell into disfavour, but was revived in the 1970s and is still performed today.

NEAPOLITAN SONGS

Enrico Caruso remains Naples' most famous tenor, though opera singers from far and wide are lured by the beauty, power and melancholy of Neapolitan songs. The songs' romantic melodies have had a profound influence on the development of Italian music

Massimo Troisi on the set of *Ricomincio da Tre* (1981)

and are familiar worldwide. Best known of all is *O Sole Mio*, composed in 1898 (and modified for Elvis Presley's *It's Now or Never*). Present-day masters of the tradition include Sergio Bruni, who achieved fame with *Carmela*, and Roberto Murolo.

Less well-known traditional forms include the *macchietta* (a comic song routine) and *tammorriate* (dances accompanied by songs).

CINEMA

Although Lombardo Film was founded in the Vomero district in the early 1900s, the first major film produced in Naples was *Assunta Spina* (1915). More familiar however are the films made in the 1950s. Neapolitan stage actors that made the crossover into film included Eduardo De Filippo and Totò. Pozzuoli native Sophia Loren starred in *The Gold of Naples* (1954) and *Marriage Italian Style* (1964). Roberto Rossellini's portrait of the city in *Viaggio in Italia* (1954) is unsentimental, while in the 1960s Francesco Rosi attacked corrupt politicians and developers in *Mani sulla Città*. Despite its flaws, Naples is not easy to leave, as Massimo Troisi showed in *Ricomincio da Tre* and Mario Martone in *L'Amore Molesto*. More recently, Caserta's Royal Palace *(see pp166–7)* was the setting for Star Wars: Episode I (1999) and II (2002), and *Mission Impossible III* (2006).

Symbols of the City

Naples is a city that defies rational explanation, yet visitors have always found a wealth of sights and sounds that sum up aspects of its character. Some are positive: the beauty of the bay, the romantic melodies of Neapolitan songs, the craftsmanship of the cribs in the churches. Others are quite the opposite. Northern Europeans (and Northern Italians) are often shocked by the contrast between the city's general air of *dolce far niente* and its widespread poverty and superstition. All these things have become clichés, making it even harder to distinguish the true nature of Naples.

The pazzariello and his band

THE PAZZARIELLO

A curious and unique figure, sadly now defunct, the *pazzariello* could be seen dressed in an old-fashioned military uniform, wielding a long ceremonial baton with a gold pommel at one end and leading a small marching band. The amusing and immensely popular character, he was originally a town crier, but his duties were later extended to include leading parades on local feast days and advertising goods for sale in a new shop. The *pazzariello* was immortalized by Totò in Vittorio De Sica's film *The Gold of Naples (see p37).*

Street life: colourful stalls in a city market

FIRST IMPRESSIONS

Naples has always been famous for the vivacity of its alleyways, streets and squares. The zest for life in the Toledo district amazed foreign visitors such as Goethe and Stendhal *(see p36).* The *lazzaroni* (ruffians) lounging around on street corners made such a strong impression on foreign visitors to Naples in the 18th and 19th centuries, that they became more or less synonymous with the city. Ferdinand I, King of the Two Sicilies from 1759 to 1825, was even nicknamed the *Re Lazzarone*.

Today, many people are struck by the ubiquitous street pedlars. There have been many attempts to regulate their activities, but most have come to nothing.

THE WATER-SELLER

The Neapolitan water-seller *(l'acquaiolo)* was once a very common sight on the streets of the city, offering refreshing drinks to passers-by on torrid summer afternoons. The water often came from the sulphurous springs of Chiatamone, which used to rise near the church of Santa Lucia *(see p116).* It was kept cool in clay jugs, known

Old water-seller's marble stand

as *lummare*. If you paid extra, you could have lemon or orange juice added to make a *spremuta*. In some parts of the old city you can still spot a *banco dell'acqua* or water stand with its solid marble counter and decorative citrus fruit. Most, however, have been modernized by the addition of stainless steel and sell cans of Coca-Cola as well as traditional drinks.

THE SCUGNIZZO

The stereotype of the cheeky, but basically good, street urchin, plays a major part in the folklore of the city. Living by his wits, ready to run errands for anybody who would give him money or food, he made an indelible impression on American troops based in Naples during World War II. The true *scugnizzo* no longer really exists. Yet one can perhaps sense his streetwise spirit in the many small boys who now whizz about the city on mopeds.

A scugnizzo

PULCINELLA

The character of Pulcinella, stupid, yet at the same time cunning, dogged by chronic bad luck and always hungry, is the stock comic figure of a Neapolitan. One can never be quite sure, as the philosopher Benedetto Croce remarked, whether he represents a faithful portrait, a caricature or an ideal to which Neapolitans aspire. Either as a puppet (he was the model for the English Mr Punch) or in the theatre, Pulcinella has always made people laugh. With his crazy schemes, wild grimaces and the comic effects of his permanently empty stomach, he personifies the city's age-old scourge of famine.

The character of Pulcinella, as we know him today, first appeared in about 1600, but he may well have had a Classical ancestor in the equally hungry Macchus, a character from the ancient farces of Atella, a town northeast of Naples.

Pulcinella

The greatest interpreters of the role within living memory were naturally the two actors who most fully represented the spirit of Naples – Eduardo De Filippo and Totò *(see p37)*. Their performances were especially poignant in the period of famine during and after World War II.

THE CHRISTMAS CRIB

Nobody knows when the custom of representing the nativity of Christ in a sculpted tableau began. One of the earliest examples is the 13th-century sculpture by Arnolfo di Cambio at the Basilica of Santa Maria Maggiore in Rome, but the tradition may well be much older. In Naples it became such an important feature of the Christmas celebrations that people came to think

Detail of historic crib scene at the Museo di San Martino *(see p111)*

of the crib *(il presepe)* as a Neapolitan institution. The traditional local craftsmen, who, in many cases, have produced magnificent works of art *(see p111)*, do not limit themselves to the central figures of the nativity grouped around the baby Jesus in the manger. The scene expands to become a miniature representation of the whole of Naples, with all its characteristic sights and personalities. Look closely at the figures in a modern crib scene and you may spot Pulcinella, Totò or even reality show contestants and unpopular politicians.

THE LOTTERY

The drawing of the lottery, in which a blindfolded child extracts the winning numbers, has remained unchanged, but the lottery is not quite the force it once was. Founded by Ferdinand I

in 1774, *il lotto* can be said, without exaggeration, to have ruled the lives of many 19th-century Neapolitans. It is still very popular and *La Smorfia*, a book that claims to interpret dreams and events to help you choose the winning numbers, has been reprinted many times *(see p71)*.

PIZZA AND PASTA

Ingredients for the topping of a pizza Margherita

The gastronomic symbols of Naples, pizza and pasta, were not always the city's staple foods. Before the population explosion of the 1600s, the poor lived mainly on cabbage and other vegetables. These were then replaced as the staple food by wheat flour, which was less perishable, and the Neapolitans acquired the nickname "macaroni eaters".

Pizza, in its present form, dates from the end of the 18th century. It may not have been a Neapolitan invention, but it was Naples that gave the world the napoletana and the Margherita, its two most enduring varieties.

Period print showing the traditional lottery drawing ceremony

NAPLES THROUGH THE YEAR

There is no single ideal season for visiting Naples; the temperate climate means a pleasant stay at any time of year. However, every season has its particular attractions. In May, more churches and monuments are open to the public; while July and August are perfect for the beach. The miracle of the city's patron saint San Gennaro is celebrated in May and September. In December, craftsmen create traditional Christmas crib scenes. Events in Naples are sometimes changed or cancelled at short notice due to a lack of funds or organizational problems so check at local tourist offices.

SPRING

The mild spring climate is perfect for enjoying drinks at an outdoor café, walking around the town centre, or visiting the surrounding countryside, which is relatively uncrowded during this season compared with summertime. At Easter it may be warm enough to swim in the sea, although traditionally 1 May marks the beginning of the bathing season. The months of March and April can be unsettled, however, and a brief spell of fine weather may be interrupted by a cold snap or even hailstorms. According to a local proverb, the weather experienced in Naples on 4 April will continue for the following 40 days.

San Giuseppe's day *zeppole*

MARCH

Feast of San Giuseppe (19 March). A bird festival is held in Via Medina, with *zeppole* (doughnuts) in every bar, bakery and home. At one time the festival marked the change from winter clothes to the spring wardrobe.

EASTER

In many outlying districts and in some quarters of Naples there are **Good Friday** processions. One of the most

Madonna dell'Arco, Easter Monday

interesting takes place on the island of Procida. The cortege of priests and parishioners leaves at dawn from the top of Terra Murata and ends up at Marina Grande.

Easter Monday, or "Pasquetta" is the day for outings, when the whole family goes for a meal in a trattoria out of town. For the more traditional, a ceremony is held at the sanctuary of Madonna dell'Arco, near Sant'Anastasia, 15 km (9 miles) east of the city. Barefooted men, known as *fuijenti*, ask for alms, and a statue of the Madonna is carried on flower-laden carts into the countryside. Here the occasion turns into a lively "pagan" feast.

Trotting races at the Agnano racetrack

APRIL

The Agnano racetrack hosts trotting races for the **Gran Premio della Lotteria di Agnano** in April.

MAY

One of the two annual celebrations of the miracle of **San Gennaro** *(see p83)* takes place on the Saturday before the first Sunday in May. The procession starts off at the cathedral with the statue of San Gennaro, the patron saint of Naples, being carried from the church. The procession is known locally as the *Inghirlandata* (garlanding) because it was traditionally accompanied by flowered decorations, and the faithful would throw rose petals over the saint's statue.

The *Inghirlandata* ceremony

During May visitors can make the most of the **Maggio dei Monumenti**, when buildings and churches which are normally closed are open to the public. Some offer special tours or concerts too. The scheme, also known as *Napoli Porte Aperte*, was started in 1992 by the Fondazione Napoli '99. Since 1995 it has been sponsored by the Naples city council to encourage the "rediscovery" of historic Naples. May is also the month of the **Vela Longa** regatta, open to any type of sailing boat.

AVERAGE DAILY HOURS OF SUNSHINE

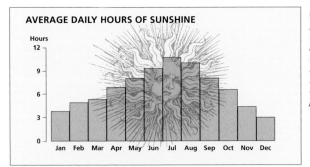

Hours

Sunshine Hours
Naples is famous for its light. The longest days fall in July, when the midday heat can be intense. In autumn the sun can still be quite hot, particularly in the middle of the day.

The Vela Longa regatta is held every May

SUMMER

This season can be quite muggy, especially in July, when the temperature sometimes exceeds 40°C (104°F). However, after mid-August the heat is sometimes interrupted by a brief, heavy and often violent thunderstorm that is known all along the coast as the *tropea*.

Summer nights in the city can be spent at the **Estate a Napoli** festival, which from late July to September features various performance art events and films. The week of the Assumption, or *Ferragosto* (15 Aug), is ideal for those who prefer a semi-deserted, if hot, city.

Outside Naples, interesting cultural events are held at the Pompeii amphitheatre *(see p148)*, and the Vesuvian villas *(see p140)* also host various events. For music-lovers, there are the **Estate Musicale Sorrentina** at Sorrento, and the well-known **Ravello Festival**, which takes place at Villa Rufolo in Ravello *(see p212)*.

JUNE

The feast of **San Giovanni** (24 Jun), linked to the summer solstice, used to be celebrated with magicians and feasting, and night bathing. Out in the countryside people still gather walnuts to make the traditional walnut liqueur called *nocino* that will be ready by late autumn.

From late June to mid-July, the Mostra d'Oltremare *(see p25)* features the **Fiera della Casa**, when furniture, interior furnishings and local handicrafts are on sale or simply on display. The *fiera* gives you the chance to join the busy crowds and makes a change from sightseeing.

JULY

Piazza Mercato *(see p73)* plays host to the feast of the **Madonna del Carmine** (16 Jul), an ancient tradition. The *Madonna Bruna* is kept inside the church of Santa Maria del Carmine: according to legend she miraculously saved the bell tower from a fire.

Fireworks are used to re-enact the miracle wrought by the Madonna; the ceremony ends with the so-called "burning" of the bell tower.

Sant'Anna is celebrated in Ischia on 26 July with a night procession of illuminated boats and a firework display.

AUGUST

August is the traditional holiday month in Italy and you may find many city restaurants, as well as shops, local services and bars, closed until September. Throughout the region the traditional "fast" held on the Eve of the Assumption (the night of 14–15 August) is helped along by helpings of watermelon, eaten on the beach. At Positano, a ceremony in period costume celebrates the landing of the Saracens.

Feast of the Madonna del Carmine

AVERAGE MONTHLY RAINFALL

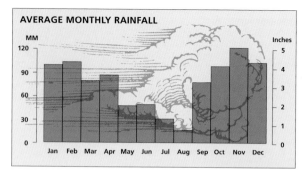

	Jan	Feb	Mar	Apr	May	Jun	Jul	Aug	Sep	Oct	Nov	Dec

Rainfall

The wettest months of the year are November and February. The rainfall does not last for long, but it comes in brief, violent downpours. The driest month is August, but this can also be interrupted by heavy thunderstorms near the end of the month.

AUTUMN

Autumn in Naples is quite mild; with September and October perfect for outings and long hikes in the countryside. The sea is warm enough for swimming well into October and even in early November. Nature lovers and amateur photographers will enjoy the splendid soft autumn light and clear days. Then there are popular local feast days, known as *sagre*, in nearby towns, such as the famous wine festivals (*sagra del vino*), that coincide with the harvesting of the grapes.

Naples itself also comes back to life after the quiet and empty summer months. From September onwards football fans can spend Sunday afternoons in the stadium, following the Neapolitans' favourite sport.

SEPTEMBER

The **Madonna di Piedigrotta** feast is held in the first half of the month. The ancient cave next to the sanctuary (*see p118*), which has been closed for many years, was once the venue for popular rituals. Today, the festival has once again become fashionable. According to an old proverb, the date of the festival of Piedigrotta marks the beginning of the rainy season.

An increasingly popular festival is the **Settembrata Anacaprese**. Throughout the month of September, shows, games and gastronomic contests are held in Anacapri, Capri's second town.

The Piedigrotta feast in a 1930s photograph

The 19th marks the second celebration of the miracle of the blood of **San Gennaro** in Naples' Duomo. For centuries this ceremony, in which the congealed blood of the saint becomes liquid, has attracted scholars, tourists, local worshippers and city authorities.

Also held in September is the **Pizza Fest**, which involves all the best pizza restaurants and a competition is held to decide which is the best pizza.

OCTOBER

The **Classical music season** begins at the Teatro San Carlo.

NOVEMBER

On **All Souls' Day** (1 Nov), also called the Day of the Dead, families take flowers to the graves of their loved ones. This was traditionally followed by a family meal at a trattoria outside town. This is the time of year when confectioners make the delicious *torrone dei morti* almond nougat.

Aerial view of the San Paolo football stadium

AVERAGE MONTHLY TEMPERATURE

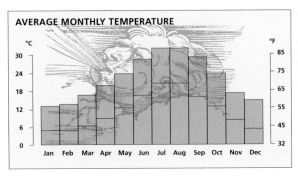

°C
30
24
18
12
6
0

°F
85
75
65
55
45
32

Jan Feb Mar Apr May Jun Jul Aug Sep Oct Nov Dec

Temperature
This chart gives the average minimum and maximum temperatures for each month. July and August are the hottest months, February the coldest. During the winter, relatively cold days may alternate with a spell of very mild and sunny days.

WINTER

The month of December and the holiday season is rarely accompanied by any snow (except on the mountaintops). However, December and January are not usually cold, and the days can be bright and sunny. February sometimes brings rain and cold. Although the rainfall is not persistent, heavy showers may occur. The "land of the sun" is not in fact warm all year around, as many think, and the few cold days can be really cold.

DECEMBER

The day of the **Immacolata** (Immaculate Conception, 8 Dec) opens the Christmas holiday season.

A bagpipe player, a tradition at Christmas

People prepare the *presepe* (nativity scene) in their homes with moss and statuettes of figures such as Mary, the ox and donkey, the Wise Men and Jesus in the crib. The Cardinal and Mayor of the city lay wreaths on the Guglia dell'Immacolata *(see p65)*.

Christmas is celebrated with dinner and presents on Christmas Eve followed by midnight mass. The streets are illuminated and the stands on Via San Gregorio Armeno have crib figures on display *(see p39)*. A few days before New Year's Day the fireworks stalls start to appear and the traditional bagpipers add colour to the street scene.

JANUARY

New Year's Eve is celebrated with an impressive display of fireworks. For an enjoyable midnight outdoors, go and join in the merrymaking in the central Piazza del Plebiscito.

Traditionally the year begins with **Sant'Antuono** (Sant' Antonio Abate, 17 Jan) and in the old centre *cippi* or old things are thrown in bonfires.

On **Epiphany** (6 Jan) the Befana witch arrives in Piazza del Plebiscito. This is a feast for children and stalls sell sweets and "gifts from the Befana", particularly in Via Foria. Naughty children are brought (sweet) "lumps of coal".

FEBRUARY

Masked festivities for **Shrove Tuesday** and **Carnival** are accompanied by lasagna dishes. The **Galassia Gutenberg** book and multimedia fair opens, and the **Mostra d'Oltremare** offers exhibits, lectures and cultural events.

Pulcinella, the protagonist of the Naples Carnival

PUBLIC HOLIDAYS

New Year's Day (1 Jan)
Epiphany (6 Jan)
Easter Sunday and Monday
Liberation Day (25 Apr)
Labour Day (1 May)
Republic Day (2 Jun)
Ferragosto (15 Aug)
All Saints' Day (1 Nov)
Immaculate Conception (8 Dec)
Christmas Day (25 Dec)
Santo Stefano (26 Dec)

A Christmas feast in a square illuminated with fairy lights

NAPLES AREA BY AREA

TOLEDO AND CASTEL NUOVO

astel Nuovo casts its impressive shadow on an area that is both the commercial and administrative centre of modern Naples and the heart of the old capital. This zone extends as far as the harbour, the boarding point for ferry trips. Centuries of history are concentrated in the area – from the ancient archaeological ruins on the hill of Pizzofalcone to 19th-century buildings such as the Galleria Umberto I. Near the Royal Palace and

Cannonballs at Castel Nuovo

fortress of Castel Nuovo, opposite the basilica of San Francesco di Paola, is the majestic Palazzo Reale, a palace built by the Spanish viceroys. Running north from here is a long and famous 16th-century road, Via Toledo, the main artery of Naples. It is still better known by this name (after the man who built it, Viceroy Don Pedro of Toledo) than its newer, official name, Via Roma. Lining the thoroughfare are elegant buildings, stately churches and shops.

SIGHTS AT A GLANCE

Historic Buildings
Castel Nuovo pp54–5 ❽
Palazzo delle Poste
 e Telegrafi ⓮
Palazzo Reale pp50–51 ❶
Palazzo Serra di Cassano ⓳

Churches
Basilica di San Francesco
 di Paola ❷
Nunziatella ⓴
Santa Brigida ⓬
San Ferdinando ❹
San Giacomo degli
 Spagnoli ⓫
Santa Maria degli Angeli ⓱
Santa Maria Egiziaca
 a Pizzofalcone ⓲
Santa Maria Incoronata ❿

**Historic Streets
and Squares**
Galleria Umberto I ❻
Piazza Giovanni
 Bovio ⓯
Quartieri
 Spagnoli ⓭
Via Chiaia ⓰
Via Toledo ❺

Historic Theatres
Teatro Mercadante ❾
Teatro San Carlo ❼

Museums
Museo dell'Appartamento
 Reale (see Palazzo Reale)
Museo Artistico Industriale ㉑
Museo Civico (see Castel
 Nuovo)

Historic Landmarks
Caffè Gambrinus ❸

GETTING THERE
Piazza del Plebiscito and part of Via Toledo are closed to traffic, but a number of city buses run nearby. Route R2 comes from Napoli Centrale railway station and R3 from Mergellina railway station. Bus C63 is on the same route as Capodimonte and the Museo Archeologico. The V1 route links Vomero with the funicular at Montesanto and Toledo. The Alibus or 3S arrive from the airport at Piazza Municipio.

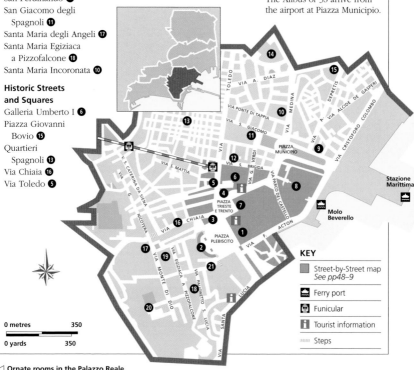

KEY

▨ Street-by-Street map
 See pp48–9

⛴ Ferry port

🚡 Funicular

ℹ Tourist information

▦ Steps

0 metres 350
0 yards 350

◁ Ornate rooms in the Palazzo Reale

Street-by-Street: Toledo and Castel Nuovo

Naples is a city of contrasting moods:
the quiet solemnity of Piazza del
Plebiscito, a symbol of the city's rebirth,
is very different from the animation –
you might even call it confusion – of
the surrounding streets. It is a pleasure
to mingle with the crowd in Via Toledo,
drop in at the Caffè Gambrinus or
Galleria Umberto I, pause in the shade
of the historic church of San Francesco
di Paola, or visit the museums at
Palazzo Reale and Castel Nuovo.
In addition to the rich history and
art treasures in this area, Via Toledo
is good for shopping.

**Galleria
Umberto I**
*The iron and
glass dome
was built
in the late
1800s by
Boubée* ⑥

Via Toledo
*This street,
named after a
Spanish viceroy,
borders the
Quartieri
Spagnoli* ⑤

★ Teatro San Carlo
*Richly decorated in gilded stucco,
the theatre seats 3,000 and the
acoustics are excellent* ⑦

San Ferdinando
*Every year on Good
Friday there is a
performance of
the* Stabat Mater
*composed by
Pergolesi for the
confraternity based
here since 1837* ④

Caffè Gambrinus
*Gabriele d'Annunzio wrote the
lyrics to the Neapolitan song
"A vucchella" in this café* ③

PIAZZA
TRIESTE
TRENT

PIAZZA
PLEBISCITO

Basilica di San Francesco di Paola
This Neo-Classical church was designed by Lugano architect Pietro Bianchi in 1817 ②

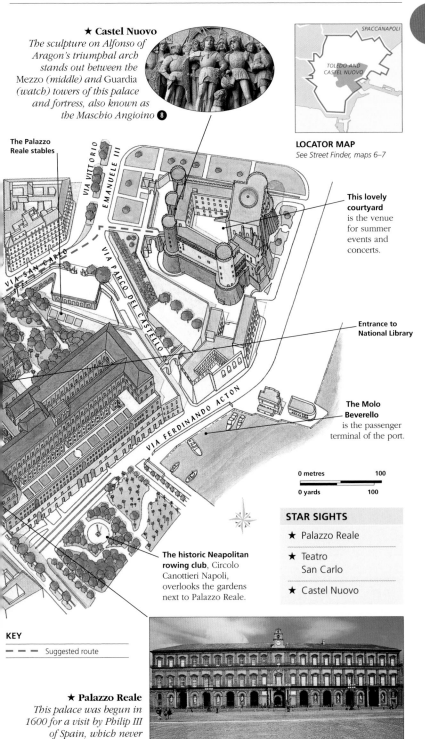

★ Castel Nuovo
The sculpture on Alfonso of Aragon's triumphal arch stands out between the Mezzo (middle) and Guardia (watch) towers of this palace and fortress, also known as the Maschio Angioino **⑧**

The Palazzo Reale stables

LOCATOR MAP
See Street Finder, maps 6–7

SPACCANAPOLI

TOLEDO AND CASTEL NUOVO

VIA VITTORIO EMANUELE III

VIA SAN CARLO

VIA PARCO DEL CASTELLO

VIA FERDINANDO ACTON

This lovely courtyard is the venue for summer events and concerts.

Entrance to National Library

The Molo Beverello is the passenger terminal of the port.

| 0 metres | 100 |
| 0 yards | 100 |

STAR SIGHTS

★ Palazzo Reale

★ Teatro San Carlo

★ Castel Nuovo

The historic Neapolitan rowing club, Circolo Canottieri Napoli, overlooks the gardens next to Palazzo Reale.

KEY

– – – Suggested route

★ Palazzo Reale
This palace was begun in 1600 for a visit by Philip III of Spain, which never took place **①**

Palazzo Reale ❶

The layout and size of the Palazzo Reale befit its role as one of the most important royal courts in the Mediterranean. Designed by Domenico Fontana at the request of the viceroy Fernández Ruiz de Castro, construction began in 1600. Building continued for centuries and the palace was only finished in 1843 by Gaetano Genovese. The Ala delle Feste wing, used in the 19th century for entertaining, now houses the Biblioteca Nazionale, the library named after King Vittorio Emanuele III, who donated the wing.

Teatro San Carlo
(see p53)

Maria Carolina's Revolving Lectern
This unusual Neo-Classical piece is based on models from monastery libraries.

The façade, 169 m (555 ft) long, was altered in the 18th century by Luigi Vanvitelli, who created the niches that now house statues of Neapolitan kings.

Teatrino di Corte
The court theatre was built in 1768 for Maria Carolina of Hapsburg's wedding to Ferdinand IV, and decorated with papier-mâché sculpture.

Main Entrance

Public Chambers

MUSEUM OF THE ROYAL APARTMENTS

The 30 rooms in the first-floor Museum of the Royal Apartments (Museo dell' Appartamento Reale) are arranged around a central courtyard. In the west wing are the Court Theatre and the public chambers; in the south are the private chambers. The east wing houses the Cappella Palatina and the Sala di Ercole. The sumptuous decoration, objets d'art and interior furnishings are of the highest quality. The rooms in the State Rooms house 16th- to 19th-century paintings.

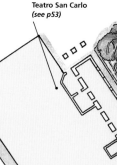

A mirror in the Museo

State Rooms

STAR FEATURES

★ Biblioteca Nazionale

★ Sala di Ercole

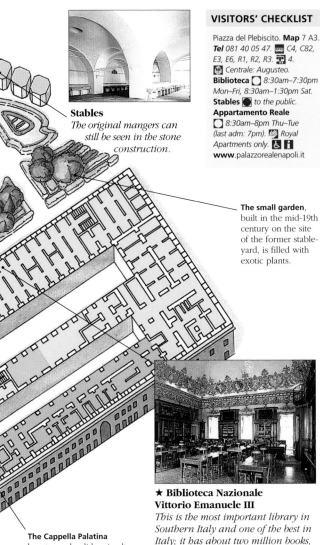

Stables
*The original mangers can
still be seen in the stone
construction.*

The small garden,
built in the mid-19th
century on the site
of the former stable-
yard, is filled with
exotic plants.

**★ Biblioteca Nazionale
Vittorio Emanuele III**
*This is the most important library in
Southern Italy and one of the best in
Italy; it has about two million books,
including manuscripts that pre-date
1500 and a collection of papyrus
scrolls from Herculaneum.*

The Cappella Palatina
boasts a splendid main altar
created by Dionisio Lazzari
in the 17th century.

★ Sala di Ercole
*This hall was named
after the plaster copies of
statues in the Real Museo
Borbonico (now the Museo
Archeologico Nazionale) –
including the Farnese
Hercules (see p87) –
which were placed here
in the 19th century.*

KEY

☐	Royal Apartments (first floor)
☐	Teatro San Carlo
☐	Ala delle Feste
☐	Coach house
☐	Stables
☐	Non-exhibition space

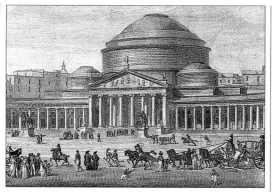

19th-century print of a riding competition at San Francesco di Paola

Basilica di San Francesco di Paola ❷

Piazza del Plebiscito. **Map** 7 A3.
Tel 081 764 51 33. C4, C82, E3, E6, R1, R2, R3. Centrale: Augusteo.
8am–noon, 3:30–7pm Mon–Sat; 8:30am–1pm, 4–7pm Sun.
www.basilicaplebiscito.it

Joachim Murat, Napoleon's brother-in-law, ruled the city of Naples from 1808 to 1815. Dissatisfied with the chaotic jumble of buildings opposite the Palazzo Reale, he decided to rebuild the whole area. The Largo di Palazzo, now called the Piazza del Plebiscito, was meant to play a major role in city life and was used for festivities, ceremonies and military parades. The first buildings to go up were the palace built for the Prince of Salerno, and the palazzo that is now the home of the Prefecture. Both were laid out symmetrically. Murat did not see the final results of his scheme, only managing to see Leopoldo Laperuta's design for the Doric colonnade and the initial construction work before the French were driven out of Naples.

In 1815 Ferdinand of Bourbon was reinstated to the throne and set about completing the project begun by Murat. He commissioned the architect Pietro Bianchi to design the central royal basilica, which was dedicated to San Francesco di Paola. Inspired by the Pantheon in Rome, the church has a circular plan with radiating chapels, a large cupola 53 m (174 ft) high and 34m (112 ft) wide, complete with rosettes.

The sculpture and paintings inside the church are mostly Neo-Classical except for the high altar, which was re-built in 1835 with semi-precious stones and multi-coloured marble, and lapis lazuli taken from a 17th-century altar in the church of Santi Apostoli (see p96). The cool, formal interior can have a rather chilling effect on visitors. According to architectural historian Renato De Fusco: "Despite the large size of the interior and the rich marble, stucco and garlanding decoration, the overall impression is not that of Neo-Classical rigour, but rather a lack of harmony between man and the setting, a funereal coldness compared to the exterior". The sobering effect is soon dispelled by emerging into the lovely open space of Piazza del Plebiscito, which is pedestrianized. The two equestrian statues of Charles III and Ferdinand I are the work of Antonio Canova and Antonio Calì.

Statue of Charles III by Canova

Caffè Gambrinus ❸

P.za Trieste e Trento. **Map** 7 A3.
Tel 081 41 75 82. C4, C82, E3, E6, R1, R2, R3. Centrale: Augusteo.
7am–1am daily (to 2am Fri, to 3am Sat). www.caffegambrinus.com

The café dates from 1860; its walls decorated by the leading Neapolitan painters of the time. It soon became the haunt of politicians, artists and writers, including Guy de Maupassant and Oscar Wilde, as well as the local composers Roberto Murolo and Giovanni Bovio. When the literary café also became popular with opponents of the Fascist regime, the prefect closed it down, initiating a long period of decline and neglect. Fortunately, its lavish Belle Epoque decor has been restored and this historic landmark is once again a favourite. Neapolitans drop in for coffee and cakes, or for iced tea and ice cream.

Interior of the historic Caffè Gambrinus

For hotels and restaurants in this area see p178 and p192

San Ferdinando ❹

Piazza Trieste e Trento 5. **Map** 7 A3.
Tel 081 40 05 43. ▦ C4, C82, E3,
E6, R1, R2, R3. ▦ Centrale:
Augusteo. ◯ 8am–noon daily (also
4:30–6pm Sat). ⛪

This church was founded
in 1665 as San Francesco
Saverio. In 1769 Ferdinand I
dedicated it to his namesake
saint. The Baroque interior
contains frescoes by Paolo
De Matteis and sculptures by
Vaccaro as well as the tomb of
Lucia Migliaccio, the Duchess
of Floridia. Ferdinand gave
her his estate on the Vomero
hill, which became Villa
Floridiana (see p106). Until
1919 the square was called
Piazza San Ferdinando.

Gay Odin shop in Via Toledo

Via Toledo ❺

Map 3 A5, 7 A1 (9 B4).
▦ C5, E3, E6, R1, R4, 201.
▦ Centrale: Augusteo.

Commissioned by the Spanish
viceroy Don Pedro de
Toledo in 1536, this 1.2-km
(0.75-mile) long street boasts
many famous buildings with
rich histories. Inside Palazzo
Cirella (No. 228), for example,
artists planned an insurrection
against the Bourbon king
in 1848, while Gioacchino
Rossini (see p37) lived at
the Palazzo di Domenico
Barbaja (No. 205).

Shopping in Via Toledo
caters to all tastes and
budgets. Locals stop at Gay
Odin for home-made choco-
lates and at Pintauro's for the
excellent sfogliatelle pastry.

The marble floor of the Galleria Umberto I

Galleria Umberto I ❻

Via San Carlo, Via Verdi, Via Santa
Brigida, Via Toledo. **Map** 7 A2.
▦ C4, C82, E3, E6, R1, R2, R3.
▦ Centrale: Augusteo.

The galleria was built as part
of the Urban Renewal plan,
drawn up after the cholera
epidemic which struck the
city in 1885 (see pp26–7).
The impressive iron and glass
roof and elegant patterned
marble pavement fill the
large open space with light.
The arcade soon became the
favourite haunt of local
composers and musicians.
From the galleria it was
possible to gain entry to
the Salone Margherita, which,
until 1912, was a famous café
chantant, and considered
the heart of cabaret entertainment in Naples.

Teatro San Carlo ❼

Via San Carlo 98d. **Map** 7 A3.
Tel 081 553 45 65. ▦ C4, C82,
E3, E6, R1, R2, R3. ▦ Centrale:
Augusteo. ▦ 10am–5:30pm Mon–
Sat, by appointment Sun. ▦
Season Oct–Jun. ▦ See
Entertainment in Naples p210,
p213. **www**.teatrosancarlo.it

This is one of the oldest
remaining opera houses
in the world. Designed by
Giovanni Antonio Medrano
for the Bourbon King Charles,
it was built in a few months
and officially opened on
4 November 1737, 40 years

before La Scala in Milan,
on the king's saint's day.
It soon became one of the
most important opera houses
in Europe, known for its
magnificent architecture and
excellent productions. For
many years, a performance at
the San Carlo was considered
the high point in the career of
a singer or composer.

A fire in 1816 severely
damaged the interior, which
was immediately rebuilt by
Antonio Niccolini, the architect who a few years earlier
had modified the façade by
adding the foyer and balcony.
The focal point of the
magnificent auditorium, with
its six tiers of 184 boxes, is
the royal box, surmounted
by the crown of the Kingdom
of the Two Sicilies.

Many great musical figures,
including Gioacchino Rossini
and Gaetano Donizetti, were
at one time artistic directors
here. The world premieres
of Donizetti's Lucia di
Lammermoor and Rossini's
Mosè were performed here.
Founded in 1812, the San
Carlo ballet school vies with
La Scala for the title of the
oldest ballet school in Italy.

The Teatro San Carlo façade,
remodelled by Niccolini in 1816

Castel Nuovo ❽

The castle, also known as Maschio Angioino, was called *nuovo* (new) to distinguish it from two earlier ones, dell'Ovo and Capuano *(see pp116 and 81)*, which were too small to accommodate the entire Angevin court. Charles I of Anjou began construction in 1279, but the Cappella Palatina is the only part remaining of the original building. Alfonso V of Aragon (who later became Alfonso I, King of Naples and Sicily) began to rebuild it completely in 1443, the year that marked his triumphant entry into Naples. To celebrate this event, he later ordered the construction of the superb Arco di Trionfo, one of the most significant expressions of early Renaissance culture in Southern Italy. The castle, with its five cylindrical towers, is designed on a trapezoidal plan facing onto a central courtyard. From here you can gain access to the most famous chamber in the castle, the Sala dei Baroni (Barons' Hall), now used by the town council. Since 1990 a small but fine art collection, the Museo Civico, has occupied part of the west wing.

The Renaissance doorway of the Cappella Palatina

Cappella Palatina

This is the only surviving part of the 13th-century building. An elegant Renaissance doorway leads to the chapel, which is dedicated to St Barbara. The portal itself is crowned with an elaborate rose window typical of the Catalan style of its creators. The portal is also adorned with a Madonna executed by Francesco Laurana (c.1430–1502) in 1474.

The walls inside the chapel were once decorated with frescoes by Giotto and his workshop; today, only small fragments on the splays of the lofty Gothic windows remain.

Sala dei Baroni

Next to the chapel, the Barons' Hall, which is reached by means of an outer stairway, owes its name to the grim events that took place there in 1486. Then, the great barons who had plotted a conspiracy against Ferdinand I of Aragon, were arrested and subsequently executed.

The imposing Castel Nuovo, with its stunning Renaissance triumphal arch

TIMELINE

1279 Charles I of Anjou begins construction of Castel Nuovo	**1443** Alfonso V's total rebuilding plan	**1443–68** Building of Arco di Trionfo	**1547** Popular revolt against the Inquisition	**1647** Signing of pact between the viceroy and Masaniello after popular uprising	
1200	**1300**	**1400**	**1500**	**1600**	**1700**	**1800**
	1329 Giotto and his assistants paint the Cappella Palatina frescoes	**1486** The Barons' conspiracy	**1509–37** Reconstruction of the defence system with new battlements and moats		The Barricades at San Ferdinando during the 1848 uprisings *(detail of a painting in the Museo Civico)*

Sala dei Baroni: the splendid Spanish Gothic vault

This elegant, yet grand and austere hall, 26 m (85 ft) wide and 28 m (92 ft) high, was built by the Spanish craftsman Guglielmo Sagrera, who was summoned to Naples for the purpose in 1446. It is now the main meeting room of the town council. Its principal features are the magnificent Catalan-inspired ribbed vault with intersecting ribs in the shape of a huge star, the monumental fireplace, and the large rectangular "cross windows".

19th-century Neapolitan painting, Museo Civico

Museo Civico

A large part of the south wing of Castel Nuovo and part of the Cappella Palatina are occupied by the Museo Civico (civic museum). Before visiting the museum, do not miss the opportunity to take in the splendid panoramic views of the Bay of Naples and Mount Vesuvius from the upper floors of the castle.

The museum houses paintings, sculptures and objets d'art that come from the castle itself, from neighbouring churches and other Neapolitan monuments. These works date from the 14th to the 19th century, but by far the largest section consists of 19th-century Neapolitan paintings. Some of these – such as Vincenzo

Caprile's *Vecchia Napoli* (Old Naples), depicting the famous Zizze fountain in its original state – offer views of a city that no longer exists.

Arco di Trionfo

The combination of white marble against the grey volcanic stone of Castel Nuovo is immediately striking to the visitor, as is the contrast between the ornamental reliefs and the severe geometric form of the towers. The structure, with its two superimposed arches, takes its inspiration from ancient Roman architecture.

The monumental gateway of the *Arco di Trionfo* (Triumphal Arch) was built in 1443 in honour of Alfonso V of Aragon. The bas relief depicting the *Trionfo di Alfonso* (Triumph of Alfonso) lies above the lower section, while the upper arch, which was once intended to house a statue of the sovereign, now holds allegorical figures representing the Four Virtues (looking from left to right, Temperance, Justice, Fortitude and Magnanimity). On the tympanum, supporting two large symbolic statues of rivers, stands a figure

VISITORS' CHECKLIST

Piazza Municipio. **Map** 7 B2.
Tel 081 420 12 41. C4, C82, R1–R4, 111N, 111R, 201, 202, 256. Centrale: Augusteo.
9am–6pm Mon–Sat.
see attendants for assistance.

Upper section of Arco di Trionfo

of the archangel St Michael. A number of Italian artists contributed to the final building of the arch, the most significant among them being the Neapolitan artist Francesco Laurana, who also worked on the Cappella Palatina and sculpted the statues of Justice and the bas relief of Alfonso I on his chariot. Another artist of note was Laurana's pupil and assistant Domenico Gagini.

Castel Nuovo in a painting by Antonio Joli

Mercadante, Teatro Stabile ⓷

Piazza Municipio 74. **Map** 7 B2.
Tel 081 551 03 36. 🚌 R2, R3, R4,
111N, 111R, 201, 202. 🚇 Centrale:
Augusteo. See **Entertainment in
Naples**, p210, p213.

Built in 1778 to a design by
Francesco Securo, this theatre
was originally known as *"del
Fondo"* because money for
its construction came from a
fund created by the sale of
confiscated Jesuit property.
The three-tier façade, with
eight caryatids supporting the
cornice, dates from 1892. The
theatre opened in 1779 with
L'Infedeltà Fedele by Cimarosa,
a Neapolitan composer.

**Late 19th-century façade of the
Mercadante, Teatro Stabile**

Santa Maria Incoronata ⓪

Via Medina 19. **Map** 7 B2. 🚌 R1,
R2, R3, R4, 111N, 111R, 201, 202,
256. 🚇 Centrale: Augusteo.
◯ 8am–5:30pm Mon–Sat.

It is immediately obvious that
this deconsecrated church is
at a lower level than Via
Medina. The reason goes
back to the 16th century,
when Charles V built the
new moats for Castel Nuovo.
Earth had been dug out
to make room for the
ditches and when it was
tipped nearby it partially
buried this small mid-
14th-century church.
Santa Maria Incoronata
was built to celebrate
the coronation of
Joan I of Anjou in
1352. The two fresco
cycles in the first bay
of the main nave, for
years attributed to
Giotto, are in fact the
work of his pupil
Roberto Oderisi.

Detail of the portico of Santa Maria Incoronata

San Giacomo degli Spagnoli ⓺

Piazza Municipio. **Map** 7 B2.
🚌 R2, R3, R4, 111N, 111R, 201,
202. 🚇 Centrale: Augusteo.
◯ limited during restoration. ✝ ◯

Part of the 19th-century
Palazzo San Giacomo (now
the town hall), the church
of San Giacomo dominates
Piazza Municipio. In 1540
Don Pedro Alvarez de Toledo,
the viceroy responsible for
the present appearance of the
city centre, built the church
and adjoining hospital for
the Spanish community. This
was the church of the local
aristocracy and although
rebuilt in 1741, it still belongs
to the Real Hermandad de
Nobles Hespanoles de
Santiago, a confraternity
founded more than four
centuries ago.
San Giacomo contains tombs
of Spanish nobles, including
that of Don Pedro and his
wife Maria. They were never
buried in their sumptuous
tomb, however: Don Pedro
died in Florence and is buried
there in the cathedral.

**The marble tomb of Don Pedro Alvarez de
Toledo in San Giacomo degli Spagnoli**

Santa Brigida ⓬

Via Santa Brigida 72. **Map** 7 A2.
Tel 081 552 37 93. 🚌 C4, C82, R1,
R2, R3. 🚇 Centrale: Augusteo. ◯
7:15am–1pm, 4:30–8pm daily. ✝ ◯

The curious aspect of this
17th-century church is the
dome, which could not be
more than 9 m (30 ft) high
because it would have
obstructed artillery fire from
Castel Nuovo. However, the
fresco of a vivid sky created by
Luca Giordano (1634–1705)
on the cupola makes the
most of boldly conceived
perspective and creates a
feeling of immense space.
The artist, nicknamed Luca
Fapresto (Luca the Swift)
because he worked so rapidly,
painted the dome in exchange
for his tomb, which can be
found in the left transept.

Quartieri Spagnoli ⓭

Map 7 A2. 🚌 E3.
🚇 Centrale: Augusteo.

The Spanish Quarter is one
of the city's working-class
districts; densely populated
and rather run-down (tourists
should take care when visiting
the area). Built in the 16th
century to the west of Via
Toledo to house Spanish
troops, its origins live on in the
name, but today it is difficult
to appreciate the original grid
layout. Alleys are festooned
with laundry, shielding the
streets from the light.
Despite the state of neglect,
there is still some fine architecture, such as the church
of Montecalvario (founded

A stall laden with fish in the atmospheric 17th-century Quartieri Spagnoli district

in 1560), which gives its name to one of the area's districts, and Santa Maria della Concezione, a Baroque masterpiece by Domenico Antonio Vaccaro.

The great Italian poet Leopardi once lived at No. 24 Via Santa Maria Ognibene, and the local playwright Eduardo De Filippo *(see p37)* used the area as a setting for his plays.

Entrance to the Palazzo delle Poste e Telegrafi

Palazzo delle Poste e Telegrafi ⑭

Piazza Matteotti 2. **Map** 7 B1 (9 B5). *Tel* 081 551 14 56. ▭ C57, E2, E3, R1, R3, R4, 111N, 111R, 201, 202, 256. ◯ 8am–6:30pm Mon–Fri, 8am–12:30pm Sat.

The post office building was designed in 1935 by Giuseppe Vaccaro as part of an Urban Renewal and Development plan that resulted in the demolition of the San Giuseppe quarter. The bombastic style of the civic architecture of this

period (also found in the police headquarters, the tax office and the provincial administration building) is typical of buildings constructed during the Fascist era. The Post Office combines these emphatic features with other innovative elements of the European Modern Movement.

The curvilinear façade and broad staircase make this one of the most interesting examples of 20th-century Neapolitan architecture. In striking contrast to the Post Office is the nearby cloister of Monteoliveto *(see p64)*, sadly now dilapidated.

Piazza Giovanni Bovio ⑮

Map 7 B1 (9 C5). ▭ C25, C55, R1, R2, R4.

Neapolitans call this square Piazza della Borsa after the former Stock Exchange *(Borsa)* that dominates it. Built in 1895 when taste was eclectic, the old exchange is reminiscent of 16th-century

buildings in the Veneto. It is now the home of the Chamber of Commerce. Incorporated into the left side of this building is the small church of Sant'Aspreno al Porto, originally medieval but totally rebuilt in the 1600s.

The square marks the beginning of Corso Umberto I, also known as the *Rettifilo.* This grand avenue was built after slum clearance around the harbour, to connect the city centre and the central railway station, giving a new look to early 20th-century Naples *(see pp28–9)*. The 17th-century Fountain of Neptune has been moved, temporarily, to the corner of Piazza Municipie and Via Medina. Frequently altered, the fountain was moved several times before finding its final home in Piazza Bovio in 1898. It was the work of three artists: the statue of Neptune was sculpted by Michelangelo Naccherino, the balusters and lions were by Cosimo Fanzago, and the monsters at the base by Pietro Bernini.

The Fountain of Neptune

Via Chiaia 🔟

Map 6 F2, 7A3. 🚎 *E3, E6.*

In Neapolitan dialect, *chiaia* means "beach", and in fact this street was opened in the 16th century to connect Largo di Palazzo (now Piazza del Plebiscito) with the coast. Together with Via Toledo (*see p53*), Via dei Mille and Via Calabritto, this is one of Naples' smartest shopping streets. While browsing, it is worth stopping to see the Ponte di Chiaia, a 17th-century gateway restored in the 1800s. Nearby is Palazzo Cellamare, built in the 16th century and enlarged in the 18th century, when it became known for the magnificent banquets and receptions held there. The impressive portal was designed by Ferdinando Fuga. Near the Ponte, a lift affords easy access to Piazza Santa Maria degli Angeli and the Pizzofalcone hill.

The portal of the church of Santa Maria degli Angeli

Santa Maria degli Angeli 🔟

Piazza Santa Maria degli Angeli. **Map** 6 F2. **Tel** 081 764 49 74. 🚎 *E3, E6.* 🕐 *7:30–11am, 5–7pm Mon–Sat, 8:30am–1:30pm Sun.* 🚹 🅾

Construction of this church began in the 17th century on land donated to the devout Theatine religious order by Donna Costanza del Carretto Dira, the Princess of Melfi. The building was designed by the Theatine cleric Francesco Grimaldi, and it is clearly visible from any point overlooking the city. The three-nave interior is so well designed that

Via Chiaia and Ponte di Chiaia

Francesco Milizia, the author of an 18th-century guide to Naples, said that it "is perhaps the most well-proportioned church in the city".

The frescoes on the vaults, which depict episodes from the life of the Virgin Mary, are the work of Giovan Battista Beinaschi (1638–88).

Santa Maria Egiziaca a Pizzofalcone 🔟

Via Egiziaca a Pizzofalcone 30. **Map** 7 A3. **Tel** 081 764 51 99. 🚎 *E3, E6.* 🕐 *9–11am, 5:30–7:30pm Tue–Sun.* 🚹 🅾

The portal on Via Egiziaca opens out onto the area in front of this Baroque church.

Its construction began in 1661 at the request of the nuns who lived nearby in the Sant'Agostino convent. The building's design was entrusted to Cosimo Fanzago (1593–1678), a Lombard architect and sculptor who was to become one of the most prestigious creators of the local Baroque style. Its octagonal plan was greatly admired by his contemporaries. The paintings in the main chapels are by Paolo De Matteis (1662–1728), while the sculptures are by Nicola Fumo (1647–1725). The high altar is in pure Rococo style.

Palazzo Serra di Cassano 🔟

Via Monte di Dio 14–15. **Map** 6 F2. **Tel** 081 764 26 52. 🚎 *E3, E6.* 🕐 *by appointment.* 🅾

The main doorway to Prince Aloisio Serra di Cassano's palace is no longer the main entrance to one of the most beautiful examples of 18th-century Neapolitan civic architecture. To express his grief over the execution of his son Gennaro – one of the leaders of the 1799 revolution in Naples – the prince ordered the original entrance (at No. 67 Via Egiziaca) to be

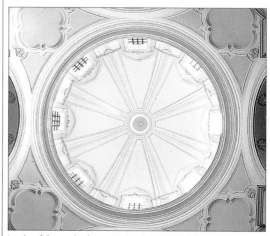

Interior of the cupola of Santa Maria Egiziaca a Pizzofalcone

The impressive double staircase in Palazzo Serra di Cassano

closed that same year. The originality of this building, which was designed by one of the leading architects of the time, Ferdinando Sanfelice (1675–1748), lies in the majestic staircase with its double flight of steps *(see p94)*. Set in the entrance hall that opens on to the courtyard, it is decorated with white marble that contrasts beautifully with the building's imposing, grey volcanic stone.

The *piano nobile* (upper floor) of the palazzo is now the home of the Istituto Italiano per gli Studi Filosofici, a leading international cultural institution.

Nunziatella ⑳

Via Generale Parisi 16. **Map** 6 F2. **Tel** 081 764 15 20. ▦ E3, E6. ◯ 9–10am for occasional Mass, by appt at other times. ◪ phone Mon–Fri and ask for Secretaria to book. ✚ ⬛

The façades of the church and former convent of the Nunziatella, which has been occupied since 1787 by the military college of the same name, converge at a right angle to form a beautiful little square. At the beginning of the 18th century, the Jesuits at the Nunziatella asked architect Ferdinando Sanfelice – who was working on the nearby Palazzo Serra di Cassano – to build the church and restore the convent, which

Scroll decoration on the Nunziatella façade

dates from the 16th century. Entering the little church, visitors are struck by the harmonious balance between the architectural space and the pictorial and sculptural decorative elements. The most important frescoes were painted by Neapolitan artist Francesco de Mura (1696–1782); in the apse is the *Adoration of the Magi*, the *Assumption of the Virgin* is on the ceiling, and on the inside of the façade is *Rest during the Flight to Egypt*. The altar, by Giuseppe Sanmartino (1720–93), is one of the main examples of Neapolitan Baroque in existence.

Museo Artistico Industriale ㉑

Piazza Demetrio Salazar 6 (off Via Solitaria). **Map** 7 A3. **Tel** 081 764 74 71. ▦ E3, E6. ◯ by appt only. ◪ ask at Art Institute. ⬛ ♿

Founded in 1882 by Gaetano Filangieri, who also founded the Filangieri Civic Museum *(see p70)*, and Demetrio Salazar, this school started out as workshops to train young

people in applied arts such as pottery, cabinet-making, goldsmithery and metalwork. The museum now houses over 6,000 works of art. The most important are the ceramics, including two large tile panels designed by the 19th-century Neapolitan artists Domenico Morelli and Filippo Palizzi.

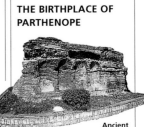

Façade of the Museo Artistico with its decorative tiles

THE BIRTHPLACE OF PARTHENOPE

Ancient ruins on Pizzofalcone

In the 7th century BC, Greek colonists from Rhodes founded the first urban settlement in Naples on the hill of Pizzofalcone: Parthenope, renamed Palaepolis (old city) three centuries later when Neapolis (new city) was founded to the east. The old city was later abandoned and by the Middle Ages the area had reverted to farmland. The site of ancient Naples was revived however in the 16th century, when it became a residential neighbourhood favoured by aristocrats and important officials, who were attracted by the beauty of the site and its proximity to the Royal Palace. In the 18th century Via Monte di Dio was one of the most important residential streets in Naples, and to this day it retains some of its original character.

SPACCANAPOLI

The straight street called Spaccanapoli corresponds to the lower *decumanus*, one of the three main thoroughfares in Greco-Roman Naples; the other two being present-day Via Anticaglia *(see p84)* and Via dei Tribunali *(see pp76–7)*. At the end of the 13th century, after the construction of Castel Nuovo *(see pp54–5)*, the administrative hub of the city began to shift towards the seafront. Commercial activity developed in the Piazza Mercato zone,

Bust-reliquary of San Bartolomeo, Santa Chiara

while in the old centre there was a concentration of churches and convents, notably Santa Chiara. When the city expanded around the newly built Via Toledo *(see p53)* during the era of the Spanish viceroyalty, the area which is now Piazza del Gesù Nuovo became the junction point between the old and modern cities. Subsequent development in the 19th century, including the opening up of Corso Umberto I, led to the demolition of part of the city's medieval fabric.

SIGHTS AT A GLANCE

Historic Buildings
Archivio di Stato ⓱
Monte di Pietà ⓮
Palazzo Carafa Santangelo ⓭
Palazzo Filomarino ❼

Churches
Cappella Sansevero ❿
Gesù Nuovo ❸
Gesù Vecchio ⓴
Sant'Angelo a Nilo ⓫
Sant'Anna dei Lombardi ❷
Santissima Annunziata ㉓
Santa Chiara *pp66–7* ❺
San Domenico Maggiore ❾
Sant'Eligio Maggiore ㉕
San Giorgio Maggiore ⓯
San Giovanni dei
    Pappacoda ㉒
Santi Marcellino e Festo ⓳
Santa Maria del Carmine ㉔
Santa Maria La Nova ❶
Santa Marta ❻
Santi Severino e Sossio ⓲

Historic Streets and Squares
Corso Umberto I ㉑
Piazza San Domenico
    Maggiore ❽

Spires and Statues
Guglia dell'Immacolata ❹
Statue of the Nile ⓬

Museums
Museo Civico Filangieri ⓰

GETTING THERE
Spaccanapoli is partly closed to traffic. The red bus lines R1 (from Vomero), R2 (from the central railway station), R3 (from the Mergellina station) and R4 (from Capodimonte) stop in Via Toledo and Piazza Dante, a short walk away from the district. The E1 electric bus stops in Piazza del Gesù and Via Santa Chiara. Piazza Mercato can be reached by tram 4. You can also get to Spaccanapoli by underground (Montesanto, Dante and Cavour/Museo stations) and, from Vomero, via the Centrale and Montesanto funicular railways.

KEY

▨	Street-by-Street map See pp62–3
Ⓜ	Metro station
▣	Funicular
ℹ	Tourist information

◁ **View over Spaccanapoli, once a major thoroughfare in ancient Naples**

Street-by-Street: Spaccanapoli

The long street commonly known as Spaccanapoli is divided into seven sections bearing different names. Because of its rich array of churches, squares and historic buildings it has been called an "open-air museum", like nearby Via dei Tribunali. It is also one of the most lively and atmospheric places in Naples, with shops, crafts and cafés. Piazza San Domenico Maggiore, near the University, is always crowded with young people. Those with a sweet tooth can enjoy the excellent pastries at the Scaturchio pasticceria.

Piazza San Domenico Maggiore
A siren with two tails is sculpted on the base of the spire **8**

San Domenico Maggiore
This church was built in 1283 by Charles I of Anjou **9**

★ **Gesù Nuovo**
The rusticated façade of the church was once part of Palazzo Sanseverino **3**

Sant'Angelo a Nilo
The interior houses the tomb of Cardinal Brancaccio, sculpted by Donatello and Michelozzo **11**

Palazzo Filomarino
The philosopher Benedetto Croce died here in 1952 **7**

Guglia dell'Immacolata
Erected in the 1700s, this spire was named after the statue of the Virgin at its pinnacle **4**

Santa Marta
This small church dates from the 15th century **6**

★ **Santa Chiara**
Robert of Anjou was responsible for building this church. The tiled cloister was designed by Domenico Antonio Vaccaro between 1739 and 1742 **5**

★ Cappella Sansevero
This moving Veiled Christ *sculpture by Neapolitan artist Giuseppe Sanmartino is in the di Sangro family chapel* ⑩

LOCATOR MAP
See Street Finder, maps 4, 5, 7

DECUMANO MAGGIORE

SPACCANAPOLI

TOLEDO AND CASTEL NUOVO

Statue of the Nile
This statue, erected in honour of the Egyptian god Nile, gives its name to the square in which it stands ⑫

Ospedale delle Bambole, the dolls' hospital, is a unique place where dolls and puppets are repaired.

Palazzo Marigliano

San Nicola a Nilo

VIA S. BIAGIO DEI LIBRAI

VIA GRANDE ARCHIVIO

VIA PALADINO

Palazzo Carafa Santangelo
Diomede Carafa designed this palazzo in the 15th century ⑬

Archivio di Stato
The state archive contains documents dating back to the Angevin period ⑰

Museo Civico Filangieri
Prince Filangieri's art collection in elegant Palazzo Como includes detailed mosaic floor tiles like these ⑯

Monte di Pietà
This majestic building and the adjoining chapel were designed by Giovan Battista Cavagna ⑭

| 0 metres | 100 |
| 0 yards | 100 |

KEY

– – – Suggested route

STAR SIGHTS

★ Gesù Nuovo

★ Santa Chiara

★ Cappella Sansevero

Santa Maria La Nova ❶

Piazza Santa Maria La Nova 44.
Map 7 B1 (9 C5). **Tel** 081 552
15 97. 🚌 C82, E1, R2, R3, R4.
🚇 Montesanto. Ⓜ Dante.
🕐 9am–noon Mon–Fri. **Cloisters**
🕐 9am–5pm Mon–Fri. 📷

In order to make room for
Castel Nuovo (see pp54–5),
a Franciscan church devoted
to the Virgin Mary had to be
demolished. In exchange,
Charles I of Anjou had a
new church built at his
own expense, Santa
Maria La Nova. The
richly decorated
wooden ceiling
was painted by
the leading artists
of the time (such
as Imparato and
Corenzio), creating
a gallery of 16th-
and 17th-century
Neapolitan painting.
In the fourth chapel
on the right is
Giovanni da Nola's
(1488–1558) altarpiece
of Sant'Eustachio.
Other chapels contain works
by Caracciolo, Teodoro
d'Errico and Santacroce.
In the former monastery,
now the seat of the provincial
government, there are two
cloisters; the smaller one

(No. 44) has Renaissance
frescoes and marble tombs,
while the other (No. 43)
contains a garden.

Sant'Anna dei Lombardi ❷

Piazza Monteoliveto. **Map** 7 A1
(9 B5). **Tel** 081 551 33 33. 🚌 CS,
E1, R1, R4, 201. 🚇 Montesanto.
Ⓜ Dante. 🕐 9am–1pm, 4–6pm
Mon–Sat, 11am Sun (for Mass and
free tour). 🚻

Founded in 1411 as Santa
Maria di Monte-
oliveto, this
was the favourite
church of the
Aragonese
kings, who
summoned the
leading artists
of the time to
decorate it. Its
name changed
when it was
assigned to the
Confraternity of
Lombards (to
whom it still
belongs), whose
church had
collapsed in the 1805
earthquake. The roof was
damaged during World
War II and has not been
restored, but the interior
contains some examples
of Renaissance sculpture.

**Dancing angels, Sant'
Anna dei Lombardi**

The amazingly realistic
sculptural tableau
*Lamentation over the Dead
Christ* was created by Guido
Mazzoni (1450–1518) in
1492. It displays seven life-
size terracotta figures leaning
over the body of Christ in
mourning. Their grief-stricken
faces are said to be modelled
on those of the Aragonese
kings. In the Vasari Sacristy,
the stunning ceiling frescoes
were painted by the Tuscan
artist Giorgio Vasari (1511–74)
in 1545; while the Tolosa
Chapel was decorated by
the della Robbia workshop
in Florence. The church also
contains the tomb of the
architect Domenico Fontana.
At No. 3 Via Monteoliveto
is the 16th-century Palazzo
Gravina, now occupied by
the Faculty of Architecture.

**Detail of the reliquary in
Gesù Nuovo**

Gesù Nuovo ❸

Piazza del Gesù Nuovo 2. **Map** 3 B5
(9 B4). **Tel** 081 557 81 11. 🚌 E1.
Ⓜ Dante. 🚇 Montesanto.
🕐 7am–1pm, 4–7:15pm daily. 🚻

The façade, covered in
diamond-point rustication, was
once part of a 15th-century
palazzo. It was retained by
the Jesuits when they bought
the building and in 1584 transformed it into the large church
seen today. The 17th-century
doorway incorporates the
original Renaissance entrance
to the palazzo. The Baroque
interior is richly decorated with
multi-coloured marbles and
ornate works of art, including
statues, a reliquary and vivid
frescoes. In the chapel of St
Ignatius of Loyola, founder of
the Society of Jesus, are two

The smaller cloister in the former monastery of Santa Maria La Nova

of Cosimo Fanzago's finest works: the sculptures of *David* and *Jeremiah*. The cupola, frescoed by Lanfranco, collapsed in the 1688 earthquake; the only survivors were the corbels showing the four Evangelists in flight. Above the main entrance is Francesco Solimena's huge fresco, *Expulsion of Heliodorus from the Temple* (1725). The statue of the Virgin, on a lapis lazuli globe above the altar, dates from the mid-1800s. The second chapel on the right houses the remains of the physician San Giuseppe Moscati. On its walls are silver images of specific body parts, which were purchased by worshippers wishing to be healed.

Façade of Gesù Nuovo

Guglia dell'Immacolata ④

Piazza del Gesù Nuovo. **Map** 3 B5 (9 B4). 🚋 *E1.* Ⓜ *Dante.* 🚌 *Montesanto.*

The Jesuits commissioned this gigantic marble spire as a symbol of devotion to the Virgin Mary, and as a tangible sign of their power. The monument, modelled on ancient Egyptian obelisks and designed by Giuseppe Genoino, was begun in 1747. The complex stone ornamentation, depicting the Jesuit saints and stories of Mary, was sculpted by Francesco Pagano and Matteo Bottigliero and is regarded as a key work of 18th-century Neapolitan sculpture. The statue of the Madonna is the centre of festivities on the Feast of Immaculate Conception.

Guglia dell'Immacolata

Santa Chiara ⑤

See pp66–7.

Santa Marta ⑥

Via San Sebastiano 42. **Map** 3 B5 (9 B3). 🚋 *E1.* Ⓜ *Dante, Cavour-Museo.* 🚌 *Montesanto.* ◯ *occasionally.*

This small church was founded by Margherita di Durazzo in the 15th century and became the headquarters of one of the city's most important confraternities, whose members included kings, viceroys and high-ranking officials. The church stands opposite the bell tower of Santa Chiara *(see pp66–7).* The doorway still retains its original depressed arch structure. On the high altar is a painting by Andrea and Nicola Vaccaro (1670), depicting Santa Marta, to whom the church is dedicated. The *Codice di Santa Marta (Codex of St Martha),* with its valuable miniatures, came from this church and is now kept in the Archivio di Stato, or state archive *(see p70).* You can get to the underground cemetery from the room next to the sacristy. Santa Marta is usually closed to the public, but it does open its doors from time to time.

Palazzo Filomarino ⑦

Via Benedetto Croce 12. **Map** 3 B5 (9 C4). *Tel 081 551 71 59.* 🚋 *E1.* Ⓜ *Dante.* 🚌 *Montesanto.* **Library** ◯ *9am–1pm Mon–Fri.*

This is the first of many noble buildings you will see in the Spaccanapoli and Decumano Maggiore areas. These mansions and palaces are often in a bad state of preservation yet have retained an air of splendour and stateliness, and still bear traces of the lives of the generations of aristocrats who built and lived in them. The original Palazzo Filomarino dates back to the 14th century, but the building was substantially altered in the 16th century. It then underwent restoration in the following century after being damaged during Masaniello's uprising *(see p23).* The 18th-century doorway is the work of the architect Sanfelice. The philosopher Benedetto Croce, a leading figure in Italian culture and politics in the first half of the 20th century *(see p26),* lived in this palazzo in the latter part of his life. The Italian Institute of Historical Studies, founded by Croce, takes up the whole of the first floor with its 40,000-volume library. Croce's apartment and personal library, however, are closed to the public.

The library of philosopher Benedetto Croce on the first floor of Palazzo Filomarino

Santa Chiara ❺

In 1310 Robert of Anjou laid the first stone of the
convent and church that the Angevin rulers later
chose as the site for their tombs. Santa Chiara was
where the kingdom's assemblies were held, as well as
ceremonies, such as the one celebrating the miracle of
San Gennaro's blood *(see p40)*. In the mid-1700s, the
church's Gothic lines were obscured by the addition
of elaborate Baroque ornamentation. After the church
was totally destroyed by fire in 1943, restoration work
tried to recover as much as possible of the original;
the present interior is simple and austere, typical of a
Franciscan church. Near the apse are the fine sculpture
groups of the royal Angevin tombs; a beautiful wooden
14th-century crucifix executed by an unknown artist
is on the altar. The lovely cloisters are an oasis of
calm and a convenient meeting place for Neapolitans.

Poor Clares' Choir
*Built by Leonardo Di Vito,
this choir is a great example
of Neapolitan Gothic. It was
frescoed by Giotto and his
assistants, but only fragments
of the original remain. The
choir is closed to the public.*

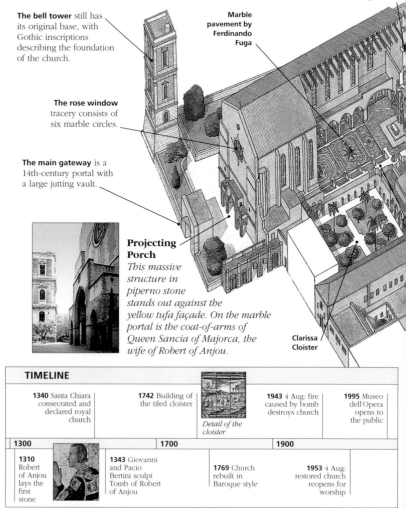

The bell tower still has
its original base, with
Gothic inscriptions
describing the foundation
of the church.

**Marble
pavement by
Ferdinando
Fuga**

The rose window
tracery consists of
six marble circles.

The main gateway is a
14th-century portal with
a large jutting vault.

**Projecting
Porch**
*This massive
structure in
piperno stone
stands out against the
yellow tufa façade. On the marble
portal is the coat-of-arms of
Queen Sancia of Majorca, the
wife of Robert of Anjou.*

**Clarissa
Cloister**

TIMELINE

1340 Santa Chiara consecrated and declared royal church	**1742** Building of the tiled cloister	**1943** 4 Aug: fire caused by bomb destroys church	**1995** Museo dell'Opera opens to the public

Detail of the cloister

1300	1700	1900
1310 Robert of Anjou lays the first stone	**1343** Giovanni and Pacio Bertini sculpt Tomb of Robert of Anjou	**1769** Church rebuilt in Baroque style **1953** 4 Aug: restored church reopens for worship

★ **Royal Tombs**
The tombs of Charles of Calabria (shown here) and his wife Mary of Valois are by Tino da Camaino (c.1285–1337). In the centre of the rear wall is the tomb of Robert of Anjou, one of Italy's greatest medieval funerary monuments.

★ **Museo dell'Opera**
This museum houses objects, decorative ornaments and sculptures from Santa Chiara. In the section devoted to archaeology, you can see the ruins of a Roman bathhouse that extend outside the museum. There are also sections on History, Ancient Marbles and Reliquaries. This last boasts Giovanni da Nola's Ecce Homo *(1519).*

The Roman baths, which once marked the city's western limit, lie between the first two rooms of the Museo dell'Opera and the outer courtyard.

The tomb of Philip of Bourbon, the idiot son of King Charles who died in 1777, is found in the last chapel on the right. Designed by Ferdinando Fuga, it is one of the few 18th-century works that survived the fire in 1943.

★ **Tiled Cloister**
The simple arches of the 14th-century cloister frame the garden redesigned by Domenico Antonio Vaccaro in 1739–42. The 72 octagonal pillars are punctuated by seats at intervals, and every surface is decorated with majolica tiles painted by Donato and Giuseppe Massa.

STAR FEATURES

★ Royal Tombs

★ Tiled Cloister

★ Museo dell'Opera

Guglia di San Domenico

Piazza San Domenico Maggiore ❽

Map 3 B5 (9 C3). 🚎 E1. Ⓜ Dante, Cavour-Museo, Montesanto. 🚇 Montesanto.

This piazza was the result of a rare Renaissance town-planning project in Naples. In the 1500s the area, once crossed by the Greek city walls, was still being used for kitchen gardens. Rebuilding by the Aragonese rulers transformed the zone into a setting appropriate for the church of San Domenico, which had been chosen to house the royal tombs. They also wanted to improve the area around the statue of the Nile, the aristocratic residential district. The top of the piazza is dominated by the apse of San Domenico. Imposing buildings line the other sides of the square. Opposite the church (at No. 17) is the 17th-century Palazzo Sangro di Casalenda; to the left (No. 3) is Palazzo Petrucci, with its 15th-century portal; to the right (Nos. 12 and 9) are Palazzo Corigliano, now home to the Oriental Studies department of the University of Naples, and Palazzo Sangro di Sansevero. In the centre stands the Guglia di San Domenico, built in gratitude for release from the plague of 1656. The spire was designed by Cosimo Fanzago and finished only in 1737 by Domenico Antonio Vaccaro.

San Domenico Maggiore ❾

Vico San Domenico Maggiore 18. **Map** 3 B5 (9 C3). **Tel** 081 45 91 88. 🚎 E1. Ⓜ Dante, Cavour-Museo, Montesanto. 🚇 Montesanto. 🕐 9am–noon, 4:30–7pm Mon–Sat; 9am–1pm, 4:30–7pm Sun. 🚻

In 1283 Charles I of Anjou ordered the construction of a new church and monastery for the Dominican order. The Gothic three-nave building was built onto the pre-existing church of Sant'Arcangelo a Morfisa, which was the original seat of Naples' University of Theology, headed by Saint Thomas Aquinas. A relic of the saint's arm is said to be kept inside the monastery. In 1850–53 Federico Travaglini rebuilt the interior in Neo-Gothic style, removing much of the original spirit of the building. In the second chapel are some 14th-century frescoes ascribed to Pietro Cavallini, a pupil of Giotto. The sacristy houses 42 coffins arranged along the balcony. Some contain the

Corradini's _Modesty_ in the Cappella Sansevero

Fresco by Francesco Solimena in the sacristy of San Domenico Maggiore

embalmed corpses of the Aragonese kings, including Alphonse and Ferdinand I. The ceiling fresco was painted by Francesco Solimena in 1707.

Cappella Sansevero ❿

Via Francesco de Sanctis 19 (off Via San Severo). **Map** 3 B5 (9 C3). **Tel** 081 551 84 70. 🚎 E1. Ⓜ Dante, Cavour-Museo, Montesanto. 🚇 Montesanto. 🕐 10am–5:40pm Mon, Wed–Sat; 10am–1:10pm Sun. 📷 🚫 ♿ limited. **www**.museosansevero.it

The lavish decoration in the family chapel was planned by Raimondo di Sangro, Prince of Sansevero, in the second half of the 18th century. In each sculpture group a member of the powerful family is represented by an allegorical figure. Antonio Corradini's _Modesty_ (to the left of the altar) is set on the tomb of the prince's mother. On the tomb of his father, said to be a dissolute man who later repented his ways, is Francesco Queirolo's _Deception_ (to the right of the altar). The chapel's focal point is the extraordinary _Veiled Christ_, the masterpiece of Neapolitan sculptor Giuseppe Sanmartino (1720–93). Sculpted from a single block of marble, the recumbent figure of Christ is draped with a translucent veil. In the chapel crypt are two "anatomical machines", perhaps creations of the mysterious di Sangro himself. The stories about the famous prince – inventor, alchemist, lover of science and the occult, and Masonic Grand Master – have engendered legends depicting him as a demon or a sorcerer.

Sant'Angelo a Nilo ⓫

Piazzetta Nilo. **Map** 3 B5 (9 C3).
CS, E1. Ⓜ *Dante, Cavour-Museo, Montesanto.* Montesanto.
9am–1pm, 4–6pm Mon–Sat, 9am–1pm Sun.

Built in the early 15th century by Cardinal Brancaccio next to his family palace, this church was remodelled four centuries later by Arcangelo Guglielminelli. It houses the earliest Renaissance work in Naples: the cardinal's funerary monument, sculpted in Pisa by Donatello and Michelozzo in 1426–7 and sent to Naples by ship. On the front of the sarcophagus, in the bas relief representing the *Assumption of the Virgin*, Donatello created one of the first examples of his revolutionary "stiacciato" technique – the relief receding gradually from the foreground to give the illusion of depth. From the church you can visit the courtyard of Palazzo Brancaccio where, thanks to the family's patronage, the first public library in Naples was founded in 1690.

Statue of the Nile ⓬

Largo Corpo di Napoli (off Via Nilo). **Map** 3 B5. CS, E1. Ⓜ *Dante, Cavour-Museo, Montesanto.* Montesanto.

An 18th-century inscription informs the reader that the Alexandrian merchants who worked in this area of the Greco-Roman city had this statue sculpted in honour of the Egyptian god Nile. The statue disappeared after the merchants left Naples; and although it was found in the 1400s, its head was missing. At that time the recumbent putti next to the god, symbols of the many tributaries of the river god, were interpreted as babies at their mother's breast, so the sculpture

The frescoed ceiling in the Monte di Pietà chapel

was called "the Body of Naples", the mother-city suckling her children. The statue has kept this name despite the addition of a bearded head in the 17th century.

Palazzo Carafa Santangelo ⓭

Via San Biagio dei Librai 121. **Map** 3 C5 (10 D3). CS, E1. Ⓜ *Dante, Cavour-Museo, Montesanto.* Montesanto.
7am–1pm, 4–7pm Mon–Sat *(courtyard only).*

This important example of Neapolitan Renaissance architecture is known as Palazzo della Capa di Cavallo because of the terracotta copy of a horse's head (now in the courtyard). This was a gift from Lorenzo de' Medici to his friend Diomede Carafa in 1471 to embellish his new palace. The original sculpture, a Roman bronze, has been in the Museo Archeologico *(see pp86–9)* since 1809.

Statue of the Egyptian god Nile, known as the "Body of Naples"

The marble portal, similar to that of Palazzo Petrucci in Piazza San Domenico *(see p68)*, and the façade with its shallow rustication are examples of the new Renaissance style. In late 15th-century Naples this look merged with the late Gothic style, as can be seen in the form of the arches and pilasters and the inlay in the wooden doors with the Carafa family coats of arms. Opposite the palace is the animated Baroque façade of the church of San Nicola a Nilo, which is also the site of a second-hand dealer's stall.

Monte di Pietà ⓮

Palazzo Carafa, Via San Biagio dei Librai 114. **Map** 3 C5 (10 D3). **Tel** 081 580 71 11. CS, E1. Ⓜ *Dante, Cavour-Museo, Montesanto.* Montesanto.
9am–7pm Sat, 9am–2pm Sun.

This majestic building was built in the late 1500s for the charitable institute set up to grant loans to people in debt to moneylenders. The Cappella della Pietà at the end of the courtyard has a late Renaissance façade with sculptures by Pietro Bernini (at the sides of the entrance) and Michelangelo Naccherino (on the tympanum). The church interior was frescoed by Belisario Corenzio and the young Battistello in the early 1600s.

San Giorgio Maggiore ⑮

Via Duomo 237a. **Map** 3 C5
(10 E3). **Tel** 081 28 79 32. ▦ CS,
E1, R2. ☐ 9am–noon, 5–8pm
Mon–Sat, 9am–noon Sun. ✚

San Giorgio Maggiore,
originally an early Christian
basilica, is one of the city's
oldest churches. It was
completely rebuilt in the
mid-1600s to a design by
Cosimo Fanzago. The only
surviving part of the original
church is the semi-circular
apse with Corinthian columns
at the entrance of the 17th-
century church, originally
built facing a different
direction. The right-hand nave
of the rebuilt church was
demolished in the late 19th
century to make room for the
extended Via Duomo. The
frescoes in the third chapel
are by Francesco Solimena.
Before visiting the church,
pause for a moment at
Palazzo Marigliano (at No.
39 Via Duomo). Though
run-down, it is one of the
most important examples
of 16th-century Neapolitan
civic architecture.

Museo Civico Filangieri ⑯

Via Duomo 288. **Map** 3 C5 (10 E3).
Tel 081 20 31 75. ▦ CS, E1.
◑ for restoration.

The building now occupied
by the Civic Museum was
built in the late 15th century
as the Como family residence
in the Florentine Renaissance

One of the cloisters in the Archivio di Stato

style. It became a monastery
in the late 1500s, was demolished during work on Via
Duomo (1879) and then
faithfully rebuilt 20 m (66 ft)
from its original site.
   In 1882 Prince Gaetano
Filangieri established his
fine art collection there and
donated it to the city in 1888.
Much of the collection was
scattered during World War II
and was reassembled through
private donations. Today it
consists of objects from
various sources, including
weapons, furniture, paintings,
medallions, porcelain, coins
and costumes. The spiral
staircase leads from the
ground floor to the Sala Agata
(named after the founder's
mother), which in turn leads
to the prince's library via a
suspended passageway.

Archivio di Stato ⑰

Piazzetta del Grande Archivio 5.
Map 3 C5 (10 D3). **Tel** 081 563
81 11. ▦ CS, E1, R2, 202, 256.
☐ 9am–1pm Mon–Sat.
www.archiviodistatonapoli.it

In 1835 Ferdinand II decided
to use the former Benedictine
monastery of Santi Severino e
Sossio to house the enormous
quantity of documents relating
to the administration of the
kingdom that had accumulated
since the Angevin period. The
old monastery, built in the 9th
century and enlarged in 1494,
was remodelled to allow for
its new function.
   The huge complex has four
cloisters and a number of
rooms containing numerous
works of art. One cloister is
known as the *Chiostro del
platano*, named after an
ancient plane tree (felled in
1959 because it was dying)
which, according to tradition,
had been planted by St
Benedict himself. The
mid-16th century frescoes
depicting the life of the saint
are the work of Antonio
Solario, known as Lo Zingaro
or "gypsy". The State Archive
contains over a million files,
registers, documents and
parchments, and is one of the
most important in Europe.
   By the entrance to the
former monastery is the 17th-
century Fontana della Selleria.

The Sala Agata in the Museo Civico Filangieri, Palazzo Como

Santi Severino e Sossio ⑱

Via Bartolomeo Capasso 22. **Map** 3 C5 (10 D4). ▦ *CS, E1, R2*. ⬤ *by appt, call Curia di Napoli on 081 557 41 11 or 081 554 97 11*. ⛪

Marco Pino, *Adoration of the Magi*

Founded in the 9th century together with the adjoining monastery (which became the Royal Archives in 1835), this church was rebuilt from the late 1400s on, and finished in 1571. The façade is the result of restoration effected after the 1731 earthquake. In the interior there are some excellent works of art. Among the paintings are beautiful canvases by the Sienese painter Marco Pino (first, third and sixth chapels on the right). The sculptures include the tomb of Andrea Bonifacio (who died at the age of six), a masterpiece by the Spanish sculptor Bartol-omeo Ordoñez, in the vestibule of the sacristy. The cloister opening times vary slightly and they are not open on Sundays.

Santi Marcellino e Festo ⑲

Largo San Marcellino 10. **Map** 3 C5 (10 D4). ▦ *CS, E1, R2*. **Monastery** *Tel 081 253 72 31*. ⬤ *9am–1:30pm Mon & Wed*. **Museum** *Tel 081 253 75 16*. ⬤ *9am–1:30pm Mon–Fri (also 3–5pm Mon & Thu)*. ♿

The two adjacent monasteries of Santi Marcellino e Pietro and of Santi Festo e Desiderio

---

A NUMBER FOR EVERY OCCASION

At noon every Saturday life stands still for a few minutes in the streets and alleyways of Old Naples in anticipation of an important event – the lottery draw. In the hall of the lottery office (Ufficio Lotto e Lotterie) at No. 17 Via del Grande Archivio, a crowd will be waiting impatiently for the result. Devised in Genoa in the 16th century, the lottery was legalized the following century and grew rapidly in popularity in the 1800s. Neapolitans were immediately hooked. As Matilde Serao wrote in the late 19th century: "Even Neapolitans who can't read know *La Smorfia* by heart

The lottery in a 19th-century print

and immediately apply it to any dream or real-life event whatsoever". *La Smorfia* is a guide to the significance of numbers and is the lottery "bible". It can be found in any Lotto office. There are about 60,000 entries in alphabetical order, and each entry has a corresponding number. The book was first published in the 19th century and is regularly updated in order to offer readers interpretations of even the most modern events and dreams. For example, should you dream of owning a computer, you will find that the number to choose is 45.

---

date from the 8th century. In the mid-15th century they were combined to create a single large complex. The church, built the following century, is adorned with refined 18th-century marble inlay. The building is now used as a congress centre. The spacious cloister with piperno stone arches has a pretty garden in the centre; from the

south-facing side there is a splendid panoramic view of the Bay of Naples. By royal decree, the complex became the property of the University of Naples in 1907. The building next to the church is open to the public. It is occupied by the Museum of Palaeontology, which has a fine painted majolica floor and more than 50,000 artifacts on display.

The airy cloister of the San Marcellino monastery

Courtyard of Gesù Vecchio, part of the University of Naples

Gesù Vecchio ⓴

Via Giovanni Paladino 39. **Map** 3
C5 (10 D4). 🚌 *CD, CS, E1, R2.*
🕐 *9am–6.45pm Mon–Fri.*
Church 🕐 *7:30am–noon, 3:30–6pm
daily.* **Anthropology Museum,
Zoology Museum, Mineralogy
Museum Library Tel** *081 253 75
16.* **Museums** 🕐 *9am–1:30pm
Mon–Fri (also 3–5pm Mon & Thu),
9am–1pm Sat & Sun.* 📷
www.musei.unina.it

The home of the University
of Naples since 1777, this
late 16th-century building
was the first Jesuit college
in the city. In the late 19th
century, thanks to the Urban
Renewal plan *(see pp26–7)*,
the University expanded
with the addition of a large
factory building looking
out over Corso Umberto I.
One part remaining of the
original college are the
rooms occupied by the
university library since
1808, and home to 1 million
volumes. In 1801 the large

hall that was once the Jesuits'
library was turned over to
the Mineralogy Museum, the
most important in Italy and
one of the most famous in
the world. Other sections
house the Anthropology
Museum and the Zoology
Museum, founded in 1811.

Back in Via Paladino, look
out for the sumptuous Baroque
interior of the college church
(at No. 38), begun in 1564,
and containing works by
Solimena and Fanzago.

Corso Umberto I ㉑

Map 4 D5 & 7 C1 (10 D5/E4/F3).
🚌 *CS, E1, R2, 111N, 111R, 202, 256.*

This wide straight street,
known to Neapolitans as
the Rettifilo, connects the
central railway station
(Stazione Centrale) with
the city centre. It was built
in the late 19th century as
part of the Urban Renewal
plan *(see pp26–7)*. The
most important building
on Corso Umberto I is
the University of Naples,
featuring an impressive
Neo-Renaissance façade.

Cappella
Pappacoda ㉒

Largo San Giovanni Maggiore.
Map 7 B1 (9 C4). 🚌 *E1, R2.*
🕐 *8am–2:30pm Mon–Fri.*
🔴 *Aug.*

In the early 15th century
Artusio Pappacoda, Grand
Seneschal and councillor
in the Angevin court,
founded this small church.

The original late Gothic
doorway, like marble
embroidery on the austere
tufa façade, is the work of
Antonio Baboccio (1351–
1435), a sculptor, architect
and goldsmith who also
sculpted the main portal of
the cathedral *(see pp82–3)*.
The campanile is particularly
interesting because of the
colour contrast created by
the different materials. The
church is now deconsecrated
and is used as the Great Hall
by the nearby Istituto
Universitario Orientale
(Oriental Institute).

Portal of Cappella Pappacoda

Santissima
Annunziata ㉓

Via dell'Annunziata 34. **Map** 4 D4
(10 F3). **Tel** *081 28 90 32.* 🚌 *152,
171, 175, 194, 195, 203, 254, 256.*
Ⓜ *Piazza Garibaldi.* 🕐 *8am–noon,
5–7:30pm Mon–Sat, 8am–1:30pm
Sun.* ✝ ♿

The Santa Casa dell'Annunziata
was a charitable institution

The façade of the University in Corso Umberto I after expansion of the site

Painting of the Madonna Bruna in Santa Maria del Carmine

that existed as long ago as the early 1300s to offer help to abandoned children. The church was destroyed by fire in 1757 and rebuilt by Luigi and Carlo Vanvitelli, who designed the cupola and one-nave interior with 44 Corinthian columns and three chapels on each side. Among the parts untouched by the fire is the sacristy, with frescoes by Corenzio (1605) and 16th-century inlaid wooden cupboards. To the left of the church, an impressive marble doorway leads to the former foundling hospital, now used as a hospital.

Santa Maria del Carmine **㉔**

Piazza del Carmine. **Map** 4 E5.
🚉 2. 🚌 C82. ⬜ 7:30am–noon, 4:30–7:30pm Mon–Sat; 7am–1pm, 4:30–7:30pm Sun. ⛪

Neapolitans are devoted to this church because of its many works of art, but in particular because of the *Madonna Bruna*, a 14th-century painting kept behind the altar. This famous effigy, the object of deeply felt veneration, is celebrated annually on 16 July at the feast of the Madonna del Carmine *(see p41)*, during which the miracle of the Madonna is re-enacted.

Except for the cross dome in the presbytery, little remains of the original Angevin construction. Instead the church displays typical 18th-century architectural forms both inside and out.

PIAZZA MERCATO

Thanks to their position near the harbour, the churches of Sant'Eligio and Santa Maria del Carmine and the area around them became the focal point of commercial life in late 13th-century Angevin Naples. The lively market quarter around Piazza Mercato in the heart of Naples was also the setting for significant events in the city's history. In 1268, Corradino, the last Hohenstaufen king of Naples, was beheaded at the tender age of 16 in front of the Carmine church and the new Angevin rulers decreed that in future all executions were to be carried out in the square. In 1647 the uprising against the Spanish headed by Tommaso Aniello d'Amalfi, known as Masaniello *(see pp22–3)*, began here. Ten years on, the square was used for the graves of those who had died during the plague epidemic. But the most dramatic events occurred in 1799, when the short-lived, glorious Parthenopean Republic was crushed and all its leaders were executed in Piazza Mercato.

View of Piazza Mercato, with Santa Maria del Carmine

The interior was decorated by Tagliacozzi Canale; the ceiling, destroyed in World War II, has been completely rebuilt in keeping with the original. To the left of the nave is the tomb of Corradino, Duke of Swabia, who was beheaded in 1268 in Piazza Mercato opposite the church *(see above)*. The medieval wooden crucifix placed in a tabernacle under the triumphal arch is also the object of devout worship. There are frescoes and canvases by Solimena in the wings of the transept. The 75-m (246-ft) campanile, completed by Fra Nuvolo in 1631, is the tallest in Naples.

The campanile of Santa Maria del Carmine (1631)

Sant'Eligio Maggiore **㉕**

Via Sant'Eligio. **Map** 4 D5 (10 F4).
Tel 081 553 84 29. 🚉 1, 2. 🚌 CS, E1. ⬜ 8:30am–1pm daily. ⛪

The history of Sant'Eligio has parallels with that of Santa Chiara *(see pp66–7)*. This church, the first to be founded by the Angevin dynasty in Naples, was destroyed in World War II and in the process of reconstruction none of the later Baroque additions was restored. Go through the side doorway with the pointed arch to enter the austere Gothic three-nave interior with its impressive raised transept. The left-hand nave leads to a cross-vaulted area decorated with 14th-century frescoes by artists of the Giotto school.

DECUMANO MAGGIORE

In the heart of Greco-Roman Naples, part of the ancient grid plan with three parallel east-west roads (Roman *decumani*), intersected at right angles by the north-south *cardines*, is present-day Via dei Tribunali. It was once called Decumano Maggiore (or Massimo) because it was so vital a part of the city structure. In the late 13th and early 14th centuries the area was significant for its

One of the lions at the Duomo entrance

Gothic religious architecture. Today, the churches of San Lorenzo, San Pietro a Maiella and especially the Duomo (cathedral), reveal this past. The Duomo is a stupendous blend of art and architectural styles from the 4th to 19th centuries. Outside the city walls, past 18th-century Piazza Dante, lies the Museo Archeologico Nazionale, home of one of the world's richest Classical archaeological collections.

SIGHTS AT A GLANCE

Historic Buildings
Accademia delle Belle Arti ⑳
Castel Capuano
  and Porta Capuana ⑭
Palazzo Spinelli di Laurino ⑤
Pio Monte della Misericordia ⑬

Churches
Cappella Pontano ③
Duomo pp82–3 ⑪
Gerolamini ⑩
Santa Caterina a Formiello ⑮
San Gregorio Armeno ⑨
San Lorenzo Maggiore ⑧
Santa Maria delle Anime
  del Purgatorio ad Arco ⑥
Santa Maria di
  Donnaregina Nuova ⑰
Santa Maria Maggiore
  della Pietrasanta ④
San Paolo Maggiore ⑦
San Pietro a Maiella ②

Historic Streets and Squares
Piazza Bellini ①
Piazza Dante ㉑
Via Anticaglia ⑱

Spires
Guglia di San Gennaro ⑫

Museums
MADRE ⑯
Museo Archeologico
  Nazionale pp86–9 ⑲

GETTING THERE
Via dei Tribunali allows limited traffic and no buses cross it. The red bus lines R1 (from Vomero), R2 (from Centrale railway station), R3 (from Mergellina railway station) and R4 (from Capodimonte) stop in Via Toledo, Via Diaz and Via Monteoliveto. The R2 bus runs along Corso Umberto I, which crosses Via Duomo at Piazza Nicola Amore. R1 passes by the Museo Archeologico Nazionale. The CS, C57 and E1 pass the Duomo. You can take the Metro (Montesanto station) and, from Vomero, the Montesanto funicular. The Metro goes to the Museo Nazionale (Cavour/Museo stations) and Piazza Dante.

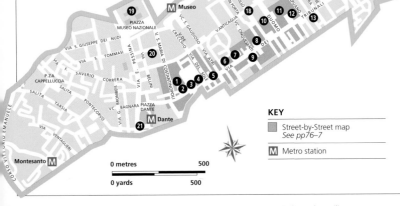

KEY

  Street-by-Street map
  See pp76–7

Ⓜ Metro station

◁ **Interior of the Duomo, with its Mannerist paintings set into the carved, gilded wooden ceiling**

Street-by-Street: Via dei Tribunali

Via dei Tribunali was named after Castel Capuano, visible in the distance at the end of this long avenue, when it became the home of the civil courts *(tribunali)* in the 1500s. One of the streets crossing the Decumano Maggiore is Via San Gregorio Armeno, among the loveliest streets in Old Naples, where art and handicrafts flourish. The craftsmen in San Gregorio Armeno still carve shepherds and other figures for the traditional Neapolitan nativity scenes *(see p39)*, just as they did four centuries ago – to the delight of visitors and Neapolitans alike.

San Paolo Maggiore
The sacristy was frescoed by Solimena in 1689–90 ❼

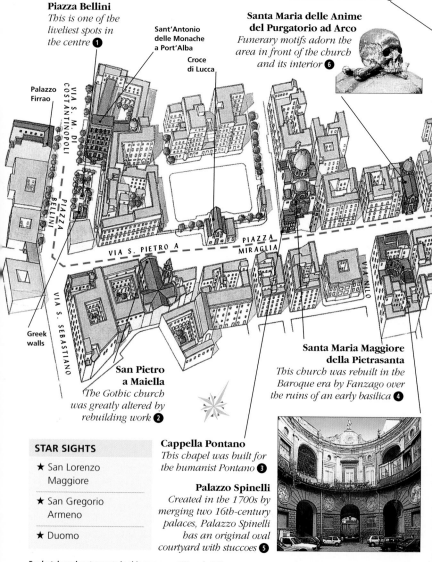

Piazza Bellini
This is one of the liveliest spots in the centre ❶

Sant'Antonio delle Monache a Port'Alba

Croce di Lucca

Santa Maria delle Anime del Purgatorio ad Arco
Funerary motifs adorn the area in front of the church and its interior ❻

Palazzo Firrao

VIA S.M. DI COSTANTINOPOLI

PIAZZA BELLINI

VIA S. PIETRO A

PIAZZA MIRAGLIA

VIA NILO

Greek walls

VIA S. SEBASTIANO

San Pietro a Maiella
The Gothic church was greatly altered by rebuilding work ❷

Santa Maria Maggiore della Pietrasanta
This church was rebuilt in the Baroque era by Fanzago over the ruins of an early basilica ❹

STAR SIGHTS

★ San Lorenzo Maggiore

★ San Gregorio Armeno

★ Duomo

Cappella Pontano
This chapel was built for the humanist Pontano ❸

Palazzo Spinelli
Created in the 1700s by merging two 16th-century palaces, Palazzo Spinelli has an original oval courtyard with stuccoes ❺

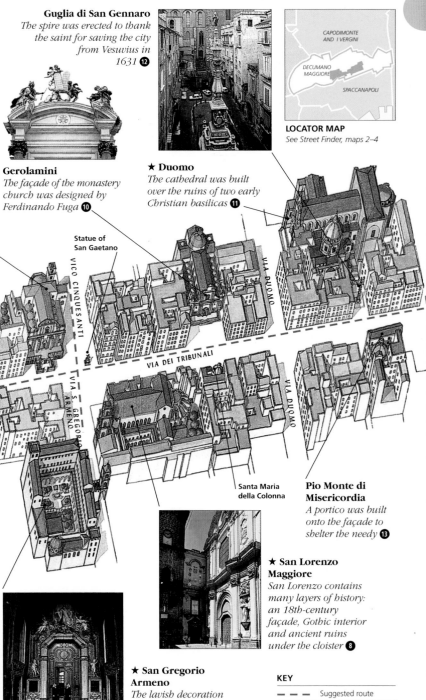

Guglia di San Gennaro
The spire was erected to thank the saint for saving the city from Vesuvius in 1631 **⑫**

LOCATOR MAP
See Street Finder, maps 2–4

CAPODIMONTE
AND I VERGINI

DECUMANO
MAGGIORE

SPACCANAPOLI

Gerolamini
The façade of the monastery church was designed by Ferdinando Fuga **⑩**

★ Duomo
The cathedral was built over the ruins of two early Christian basilicas **⑪**

Statue of
San Gaetano

VICO CINQUESANTI

VIA DUOMO

VIA DEI TRIBUNALI

VIA S. GREGORIO ARMENO

Santa Maria
della Colonna

VIA DUOMO

Pio Monte di Misericordia
A portico was built onto the façade to shelter the needy **⑬**

★ San Lorenzo Maggiore
San Lorenzo contains many layers of history: an 18th-century façade, Gothic interior and ancient ruins under the cloister **⑧**

★ San Gregorio Armeno
The lavish decoration of this monastery is immediately apparent in the vestibule **⑨**

KEY

– – – Suggested route

0 metres ———— 100

0 yards ———— 100

Piazza Bellini ❶

Map 3 B5 (9 C3). █ CS, R1, R4, 201. Ⓜ Dante, Cavour-Museo, Montesanto. ▥ Montesanto.

This square, situated at the southern end of Via Santa Maria di Costantinopoli, is one of the most interesting places in Old Naples. The area now occupied by the piazza and street lay outside the city proper until the mid-16th century, when the viceroy Pedro de Toledo extended the city walls. The remains of part of the ancient Greek walls of Neapolis were brought to light in the piazza after excavations carried out in 1954. The walls are visible in the middle of the square, at the foot of the monument to the composer Vincenzo Bellini. Overlooking the square is the monastery of Sant'Antonio a Port'Alba, which incorporates the 15th-century Palazzo Conca. The square is well known as a hip, trendy area where students and artists linger. Intra Moenia (see p203), a café-bookstore that also runs its own publishing house, is especially popular.

San Pietro a Maiella ❷

Via San Pietro a Maiella 4. **Map** 3 B5 (9 C3). █ CS, R1, R4, 201. Ⓜ Dante, Cavour-Museo, Montesanto. ▥ Montesanto. ◯ 7:30am–1:30pm Mon–Sat, 7:30am–1pm Sun. ▣

The founder of this church, the nobleman Pipino da Barletta, dedicated it to Pietro da Morrone, the hermit friar from Maiella who became Pope Celestine V in 1294. The original Gothic architecture, modified by the numerous additions over the centuries, was restored between 1888 and 1927. The restoration uncovered some 14th-century frescoes in two of the chapels. The removal of the

An outdoor café in Piazza Bellini

Baroque decoration also revealed splendid gilded wooden ceilings in the nave and transept with paintings by Mattia Preti (1656–61), regarded as among the supreme examples of 17th-century Neapolitan painting.

Since 1826 the monastery (at No. 35) annexed to the church has housed one of Italy's music conservatoires.

Cappella Pontano ❸

Piazzetta Pietrasanta 16. **Map** 3 B5 (9 C3). █ CS, R1, R4, 201. Ⓜ Dante, Cavour-Museo, Montesanto. ▥ Montesanto. ◯ 9am–1pm Mon–Sat.

The famous humanist Giovanni Pontano, secretary to King Ferdinand of Aragon, commissioned this small, elegant chapel in 1492. Based on a design for a pagan temple, the harmonious proportions make it one of the most significant works produced in Renaissance Naples. The chapel contains a frescoed triptych by Francesco Cicino da Caiazzo – restored in 1792 – and a 15th-century pavement of coloured tiles, which is in a good state of preservation. The numerous Latin epigraphs were written by Giovanni Pontano himself.

Bust of Giovanni Pontano

Santa Maria Maggiore della Pietrasanta ❹

Piazzetta Pietrasanta. **Map** 3 B5. █ CS, R1, R4. Ⓜ Cavour-Museo, Montesanto. ◯ 9am–6:30pm Mon–Sat.

The interior of Santa Maria Maggiore della Pietrasanta

A church was first erected in this location in AD 566 by Bishop Pomponio; however, the majestic, centrally-planned church that is visible today was built by Cosimo Fanzago in the 17th century. The campanile (see p20) belonged to the original basilica; it was built after the main building in the 10th century and is the sole example of early medieval architecture in Naples. In the Middle Ages the road was lower and passed under the bell tower arch. A wall of the ancient Greek city of Neapolis and a Roman villa lie directly underneath the church, as does a 3-km (2-mile) long Roman aqueduct that was used as a bomb shelter during World War II.

Palazzo Spinelli di Laurino ❺

Via Tribunali 362. **Map** 3 B5 (9 C3).
🚌 CS, E1. Ⓜ Dante, Cavour-Museo, Montesanto. 🚇 Montesanto. ⭕ 8am–7pm Mon–Sat (courtyard only).

In the 18th century, the architect Ferdinando Sanfelice carried out radical changes to this 16th-century palazzo. He also created the oval court-yard and the building beyond, where the chatter from the crowded Via dei Tribunali could be clearly heard by the dukes of Laurino. The double-flight staircase is another of Sanfelice's designs. Similar examples can be seen in the Palazzo Serra di Cassano (see p58), Palazzo dello Spagnolo and Palazzo Sanfelice (see p94).

Santa Maria delle Anime del Purgatorio ad Arco ❻

Via Tribunali 39. **Map** 3 B4 (9 C3).
Tel 081 44 68 10. 🚌 CS, E1, R4. Ⓜ Dante, Cavour-Museo, Montesanto. 🚇 Montesanto. **Church** ⭕ 9:30am–1pm Mon–Fri, 10am–4pm Sat. **Cemetery** ⭕ 10am–4pm Sat. 📷 🎫 (call 338 150 2949). ✝

This church still belongs to the confraternity of the same name founded in 1604 to collect alms to pay for the masses for the souls of the dead. Evidence of the impor-tance attached to worship of the dead in 17th-century Naples is shown by the many skulls, bones and other fune-rary motifs on and around the façade, and in the interior. The church has a single nave and lavish Baroque decora-tion. In the apse area there is a relief with a winged skull by Cosimo Fanzago, who also designed the church. Steps lead to the underground cathedral and a crypt of

Interior of the church of Purgatorio ad Arco

bones, including those of the virgin-bride Lucia, who died of consumption shortly before her wedding day in the 1700s.

San Paolo Maggiore ❼

Piazza San Gaetano. **Map** 3 C4 (10 D2). **Tel** 081 45 40 48. 🚌 CS, E1, R1, R4. Ⓜ Dante, Cavour-Museo, Montesanto. 🚇 Montesanto. ⭕ 9am–6pm Mon–Sat, 10am–1pm Sun.

In Greco-Roman Naples, present-day Piazza San Gaetano was the site of the Greek *Agora* and later, of the Roman Forum. The Romans built a Temple of the Dioscuri here, which was converted into a Christian basilica in the 8th century. This ancient church was then remodelled from 1583 to 1603 by Francesco

Grimaldi. The new church, with a three-nave Latin cross plan, also incorporated the pronaos of the pagan temple; but only two Corinthian columns of the latter survived the 1688 earthquake.

In the richly decorated interior there are fine frescoes by Massimo Stanzione on the vault over the central nave. Sadly, they were damaged by water and bombardments during World War II. The Cappella Firrao, on the left side of the apse, has many 17th-century tombs, sculptures and frescoes. The marvellous paintings in the sacristy are by Francesco Solimena (1689–90). A stairway leads down to the crypt (also accessible from outside the church).

Façade of San Paolo Maggiore

UNDERNEATH THE CITY

Underneath Naples there is another world to be explored, just as fascinating as the city above. Since its early days the city has been built out of material quarried from the ground – the local yellow tufa is excellent for building. Over the years, caves and tunnels were left in this way, and became catacombs, aqueducts, passageways, and escape and shelter areas during

Entrance to underground Naples

World War II bombing raids. The caves were extended to their current size during Spanish rule (see pp22–3), when it was forbidden to import raw material for building houses and palazzi. Today you can descend into the bowels of Naples: on the left-hand side of San Paolo Maggiore is one of the entrances to *Napoli Sotterranea (see p225).*

San Lorenzo Maggiore ❽

Via dei Tribunali 316. **Map** 3 C4
(10 D3). 🚌 *E1.* Ⓜ *Dante, Cavour-Museo, Montesanto.* 🚋 *Monte-santo.* **Church Tel** *081 45 49 48.*
🔲 *7:30am–12:30pm, 5–7:30pm daily.*
Excavations & Museum Tel *081
211 08 60.* 🔲 *9:30am–5:30pm
Mon–Sat, 9:30am–1:30pm Sun.* 🚹

The construction of one of
Naples's oldest and richest
monumental complexes began
in 1265, for Charles I of Anjou,
on the site of a 6th-century
church *(see p35).* The façade
was totally rebuilt by Sanfelice
in 1742, but the 14th-century
portal and original wooden
doors are intact. The single-
nave Gothic interior has an
apse, designed by French
architects, with nine chapels
placed around the ambulatory.
Here is the tomb of Catherine
of Austria, a fine sculpture by
Tino da Camaino (c.1323) and,
in the sixth chapel from the
right, frescoes by a Neapolitan
pupil of Giotto. It was in this
church that Boccaccio first
saw the girl he celebrated in
his writings as Fiammetta.

To the right of San Lorenzo is
the monastery, where you can
visit the cloister, the chapter-
house and the refectory,
which, from 1442, was the
assembly hall of the royal
Parliament. It also houses the
Museo dell' Opera, which has
local artifacts dating from the
3rd century BC to the 19th
century. The cloister affords
access to the excavation site
that has revealed important

The Baroque interior of the church of San Gregorio Armeno

remains of the Greco-Roman
city. These include a
macellum (market) and
evidence of other buildings.

San Gregorio Armeno ❾

Convent: Piazzetta San Gregorio
Armeno 1; **Church**: Via San
Gregorio Armeno 44. **Map** 3 C5
(10 D3). **Tel** *081 552 01 86.*
🚌 *E1.* Ⓜ *Dante, Cavour-Museo,
Montesanto.* 🚋 *Montesanto.*
Convent and Church 🔲 *9:15am–
noon daily (to 1pm Tue, Sat & Sun).*
Cloister 🚹

Located on the street known
as "Christmas Alley", where
artisans sell statuettes and
scenery for the *presepe*
(Christmas crib; *see p39),* San
Gregorio was founded in the
8th century by a group of
nuns who had fled Byzantium
with the relics of St Gregory

to escape religious
persecution. The monastery
was rebuilt in the 1500s and
enlarged during the following
century. The lovely campanile
was erected in 1716 on a
footbridge that connected two
parts of the complex. The
decoration of the sumptuous
Baroque interior – a "room of
Paradise on Earth", as Carlo
Celano wrote in his guide to
Naples – was designed in the
mid-18th century by Niccolò
Tagliacozzi Canale. Notable
works include the late 16th-
century wooden ceiling, the
two organs and, above the
entrance, Luca Giordano's
frescoes of *The Embarkation,
Journey and Arrival of the
Armenian Nuns with the
Relics of St Gregory* (1671–84).
There is a lovely fountain
in the cloister with a statue
of Christ and the Samaritan,
sculpted in 1733 *(see p23).*

Gerolamini ❿

Church: Piazza Gerolamini;
Cloisters & Gallery: Via Duomo
142; **Cappella dell'Assunta**: Via
Duomo 144. **Map** 3 C4 (10 D2). *Tel
081 44 91 39.* 🚌 *CD, E1, E3, R2, R3.*
Ⓜ *Dante, Cavour-Museo, Monte-santo.* 🚋 *Montesanto.* **Church**
🔲 *9:30am–2pm daily.* **Cloisters &
Gallery** 🔲 *9:30am–noon Mon–Sat.*
Library ⬤ *to the public.* 📷 ✏️

The monastery of the Gerolamini was founded in the late
16th century by the Oratorio di
San Filippo Neri congregation,
also called "dei Gerolamini"
because they came from San

Cloister of San Lorenzo Maggiore

The cloister in the Gerolamini

Girolamo alla Carità in Rome. The church was built in Tuscan Renaissance style; the interior was rebuilt in the early 1600s, and the façade was modified by Ferdinando Fuga in 1780. Luca Giordano, Pietro da Cortona and Guido Reni decorated the Baroque interior.

Alongside the church there are two cloisters. The first, designed by Giovanni Dosio, shares features with the cloister he created at the Certosa di San Martino *(see pp108–11)*. There are fine paintings in the Quadreria (art gallery). The 60,000-volume library has 18th-century furnishings and decoration.

Duomo **⓫**

See pp82–3.

Guglia di San Gennaro **⓬**

Piazza Riario Sforza. **Map** 3 C4 (10 E2). 🚌 CS, C57, E1. Ⓜ *Dante, Cavour-Museo.*

This sculpted marble spire is dedicated to San Gennaro, the patron saint of Naples, for having protected the city during the 1631 eruption of Vesuvius. The *guglia*, the oldest of the three spires in Naples, was designed by Cosimo Fanzago in 1636, the same artist who later worked on the Guglia di San Domenico *(see p68)*. The bronze statue at the top of the spire was sculpted by

Guglia di San Gennaro

Tommaso Montani. Behind the spire in the small square you can glimpse the stairway of the side entrance to the Duomo *(see pp82–3)* and, higher up, the dome of the Cappella di San Gennaro.

Pio Monte della Misericordia **⓭**

Via Tribunali 253. **Map** 3 C4 (10 E2). *Tel* 081 44 69 44. 🚌 CS, E1. Ⓜ *Cavour-Museo.* **Church & Gallery** ◯ 9am–2:30pm Thu–Tue. ● *Easter, 24, 25 & 31 Dec.* 📷 🎫 *by appt.* **www**.piomontedellamisericordia.it

The Seven Acts of Mercy, a masterpiece by Caravaggio

Pio Monte is one of the most important charitable institutions in Naples. It was founded in 1601 to aid the poor and ill and to free the Christian slaves in the Ottoman Empire. The entire complex was designed by Francesco Antonio Picchiatti in the second half of the 17th century. After passing through the five-arch loggia (where pilgrims could shelter) decorated with sculptures by Andrea Falcone (1666–71), you enter the church. The eye is immediately drawn to the extra-ordinary altarpiece, *The Seven Acts of Mercy*, a masterpiece by Caravaggio (1571–1610), one of Italy's greatest artists. The art gallery on the first floor of the building houses the

fine Pio Monte collection. Pio Monte is still active as a charitable institution today.

Castel Capuano and Porta Capuana **⓮**

Piazza Enrico De Nicola and Via Concezio Muzy. **Map** 4 D4 (10 F2). 🚌 C56, E1. Ⓜ *Cavour-Museo.* **Cappella Sommaria** ◯ *in May, by appt; call 081 410 72 19 (tourist office).* **www**.eptnapoli.info

A palace and fortress built by the Normans in 1165 to defend the nearby city gateway, Castel Capuano remained a royal residence for the Angevin and Aragonese rulers even after the construction of Castel Nuovo *(see pp54–5)*. In 1540 Don Pedro de Toledo turned the castle into law courts, a function it maintains to this day. On the first floor is the huge frescoed Court of Appeal, which leads to the splendid Renaissance Cappella della Sommaria, decorated by the Spanish painter Pietro Roviale.

A short distance away from the courts stands the gateway of Porta Capuana. Although much older in origin, its present appearance is the result of late 15th-century reconstruction by Giuliano da Maiano. The two towers, called Honour and Virtue, enclose the marble arch, repeating the pattern established in the Arco di Trionfo in Castel Nuovo.

The marble arch of Porta Capuana, rebuilt in the 1400s

Duomo ⑪

The bust of San Gennaro

This great cathedral was built for Charles I of Anjou in the late 1200s–early 1300s. The church incorporated older Christian buildings and has been altered substantially over the centuries. The left-hand nave leads to the early medieval basilica of Santa Restituta, radically changed in the 17th century, and the San Giovanni in Fonte baptistry. The Cappella Minutolo has retained its original Gothic structure and decoration; the mosaic pavement and 13th-century frescoes are by Montano d'Arezzo. The Crypt of the Succorpo was built under the apse in the 1500s to house the relics of San Gennaro, until then in the Montevergine sanctuary. In the early 1600s the Cappella di San Gennaro was erected after the ending of the 1527 plague epidemic.

★ Baptistry
This is the oldest baptistry in the Western world, built around AD 550. The mosaics date from the same period.

★ Santa Restituta
The structure of the early Christian basilica was changed in the Angevin period and its decoration was replaced in the late 1600s. In the last chapel on the left is the beautiful mosaic Madonna and Saints Gennaro and Restituta, executed by Lello da Orvieto in 1322.

The underground archaeological area, currently closed for restoration, reveals layers of buildings from three successive periods: Greek, Roman and early Middle Ages.

The three portals were the work of Antonio Baboccio da Piperno (1407); the middle one still bears two 14th-century lions and Tino da Camaino's *Virgin and Child* in the lunette.

Font
The basin is made of Egyptian basalt. The right-hand nave also has Greek sculptures and a 14th-century episcopal throne.

TIMELINE

c.450 The Santa Restituta and Santa Stefania basilicas built	**1300** Duomo built on the site of the two basilicas	**1497** Work begins on crypt to house relics of San Gennaro		**1876** The façade is rebuilt in Neo-Gothic style	**1969** Digs begin in archaeological area
400	**1300**	**1500**	**1600**		**1900**
	c.550 The San Giovanni in Fonte baptistry added to Santa Restituta	**1349** An earthquake destroys the façade of the Duomo	**1608–37** Cappella di San Gennaro erected	**1621** Old ceiling replaced by present-day one in gilded wood	

VISITORS' CHECKLIST

Via Duomo 147. **Map** 3 C4. **Tel**
081 44 90 97. CS, C57, E1, R2.
Cavour. 8am–12:30pm,
4:30–7pm Mon–Sat; 8am–
1:30pm, 5–7:30pm Sun. **Museo
Tel** *081 29 49 80.* 9:30am–
5pm Tue–Sat, 9am–2:30pm Sun.
Santa Restituta
8:30am–noon, 4:30–6:30pm
Mon–Sat; 8:30am–1pm Sun.

The Crypt of the Succorpo was
decorated by Tommaso Malvito
and assistants. San Gennaro's
remains are kept here.

Cappella Minutolo

Over 100 ancient columns
are used as facing for the
nave pillars.

MIRACLE OF THE BLOOD

On the Saturday preceding the first
Sunday in May and on 19 September
(see p40 and p42), the blood of San
Gennaro, kept in two phials, turns to
liquid. This ritual dates from the late
1300s and in Naples is the equivalent
of an oracle: if the miracle does not
occur, catastrophes are imminent.

**Guglia di San
Gennaro** *(see p81)*

★ Cappella
di San Gennaro
*The dome, with its depiction
of Paradise, was frescoed by
Lanfranco in 1641–3. The
reliquary bust of San Gennaro,
a masterpiece of Gothic craftsmanship, is also here.*

STAR FEATURES

★ Cappella di
  San Gennaro

★ Baptistry

★ Santa Restituta

The monumental façade of Santa Maria di Donnaregina Nuova

Santa Caterina a Formiello ⓯

Piazza Enrico De Nicola 49.
Map 4 D4 (10 F1). **Tel** 081 44 42
97. 🚌 C83, E1, 203. Ⓜ Cavour-
Museo. 🔵 8am–6pm Mon–Sat,
8:30am–1pm Sun.

The dome of Santa Caterina
a Formiello dominates the
surrounding area. The church
was called *formiello* because
it was built next to *formali*,
the ancient city aqueducts.
The 16th-century building
has delightful Baroque
decoration in the interior.
Luigi Garzi and Guglielmo
Borremans executed the
frescoes (1695–1709). The
marble tombs of the Spinelli
family are in the apse area.

MADRE ⓰

Via Settembrini 79. **Map** 3 C4
(10 D1). **Tel** 081 29 28 33. 🚌 CS,
C47, C51, C52, C57, E1, 182, 184,
201, 203. Ⓜ Cavour-Museo.
🔵 10am–9pm Mon, Wed–Fri;
10am–midnight Sat, Sun. 🎫 (free
Mon). 🖥 📷 www.museomadre.it

Opened in 2005, the Museo
d'Arte Contemporanea Donna
Regina Napoli (MADRE)
houses a remarkable
collection by artists such
as Andy Warhol, Robert
Rauschenberg, Mimmo

Paladino, Claes Olderburg,
Robert Mapplethorpe and
Roy Lichtenstein among
others. The first floor has a
library and a children's area,
while the third floor is used
for temporary exhibitions.
The museum often hosts
special events such as cinema
screenings, concerts and
theatrical performances.

The back of the museum
is also the entrance to the
8th-century church of Santa
Maria di Donnaregina
Vecchia, rebuilt in 1293
at the request of Marie of
Hungary, wife of Charles II
of Anjou. The church, with
a single nave ending in a
pentagonal apse, contains
the marble tomb of the
queen, sculpted by Tino
da Camaino in 1325–6.

Santa Maria di Donnaregina Nuova ⓱

Largo Donnaregina 7. **Map** 3 C4
(10 D2). **Tel** 081 557 13 65.
🚌 CS, C57, E1. Ⓜ Cavour-Museo.
🔵 9:30am–4:30pm Mon, Wed–Sat;
9:30am–2pm Sun. 🎫
www.museodiocesanonapoli.it

The single-nave interior of
this Baroque church built in
the early 1600s for the Poor
Clares is splendidly decorated
in multi-coloured marble.
Fine frescoes by Francesco
Solimena (1657–1747) can
be admired in the nuns'
choir. The second floor
houses the Diocesan Museum
of Naples, which boasts
two hallways of paintings,
including *St Paul's Landing
in Pozzuoli* by Giovanni
Lanfranco (1582–1647). Other
artists featured along these
corridors include Vaccaro, De
Matteis and several Neapolitan
painters from the 16th to the
19th centuries. Between the
two hallways, a lookout point
provides breathtaking views
of the church.

Via Anticaglia ⓲

Map 3 C4 (10 D2). 🚌 CS, C52, E1,
R2, 201. Ⓜ Cavour-Museo.

The third, northernmost
decumanus (east–west
major road) in Greco-Roman
Naples today has four
official sections (Via Sapienza,
Via Pisanelli, Via Anticaglia
and Via Santi Apostoli),

The elegant interior of the pharmacy in the Ospedale degli Incurabili

For hotels and restaurants in this area see p179 and p193

Foro Carolino, present-day Piazza Dante, the 18th-century palace and hemicycle designed by Luigi Vanvitelli

as does Spaccanapoli, the lower *decumanus (see p61)*.

The name "Anticaglia", meaning ruins, derives from the remains of the brick walls of a Roman building in this stretch of the street. These walls connected the ancient theatre, on the left as you go towards Via Santa Maria di Costantinopoli, and the bath-house on the opposite side of the street. The theatre, where Emperor Nero is known to have acted, had a seating capacity of about 8,000. Nearby was the *odeion*, or ancient roofed theatre, used for concerts and poetry readings.

On the corner of Via Duomo and the third *decumanus*, there is a fine marble and piperno double stairway – from here you can visit the atrium of the church of San Giuseppe dei Ruffi, which was added in the early 18th century. Once past the Roman ruins, a right-hand turn at Via Armanni takes you to the Ospedale degli Incurabili. Inside is the unusual *Farmacia* (pharmacy) with about 400 brightly coloured majolica vases on shelves of inlaid wood – a positive art gallery of Neapolitan ceramics. However, visits are allowed only during the month of May for the "Maggio dei Monumenti" *(see p40)*.

Museo Archeologico Nazionale ⑲

See pp86–9.

Accademia delle Belle Arti ⑳

Via Vincenzo Bellini 36. **Map** 3 B4 (9 B2). **Tel** 081 44 18 88. 🚌 CS, R1, R4, 201. Ⓜ Dante, Cavour-Museo, Montesanto. ⭕ 10am–2pm Tue–Thu, Sat; 2–6pm Fri. 🈳 **www**.accademiadinapoli.it

Architect Enrico Alvino transformed the 18th-century convent of San Giovanni delle Monache into the Academy of Fine Arts in the 1840s. The Neo-Renaissance style reflects the prevailing fashion of the time. A broad staircase with plaster casts of ancient sculptures leads to the first floor. There is an important collection of modern painting, especially works by 19th-century Neapolitan and southern Italian artists.

The Accademia delle Belle Arti staircase

Piazza Dante ㉑

Map 3 A5 (9 B3). 🚌 CS, R1, R4, 201. 🚋 Ⓜ Dante.

Until the 1700s this square lay outside the city walls and was used as a marketplace, hence the name Largo del Mercatello. In the second half of the 18th century it took on its present form and was called Foro

18th-century print of Largo del Mercatello

Carolino, after King Charles, who commissioned the new layout. The square is now lined with book shops all the way up to Via Port'Alba.

The semicircular façade with its colossal columns was designed by Luigi Vanvitelli as a setting for the king's statue, which was intended for the central niche but was never sculpted. The 26 figures on the cornice are allegories of the sovereign's qualities. Following the unification of Italy, a statue of Dante was placed in the middle of the square, hence its present name. To the left of the piazza is Port'Alba, the gateway built in 1625 to connect the city with outlying districts.

Museo Archeologico Nazionale ⑲

This building, housing one of the world's most important archaeological museums, started life in the late 1500s as the home of the royal cavalry and was rebuilt in the early 17th century as the seat of Naples university. In 1777, when Ferdinand IV transferred the university to the former monastery of Gesù Vecchio *(see p72)*, the building was again adapted to house the Real Museo Borbonico and library. In 1860 it became public property. Restoration and reorganization of exhibits still continue in the museum.

Blue Vase
This wine vessel found in a Pompeii tomb was made with the so-called glass-cameo technique: a layer of opaque white paste was placed over coloured glass and then engraved with decorative motifs.

Bust of "Seneca"
Found in the Villa dei Papiri (see p144) in Herculaneum, this 1st-century BC bronze head was long thought to represent the philosopher Seneca the Elder. Today, however, its identity is less certain.

★ The Battle of Alexander
The splendid mosaic from the House of the Faun in Pompeii (see p150) depicts Alexander the Great's battle against the Persian emperor Darius III (333 BC).

The Secret Cabinet
The erotic works from Pompeii and Herculaneum housed here caused embarrassment at the time of the Bourbons. Currently closed, the Secret Cabinet is due to reopen in 2012.

KEY TO FLOORPLAN

☐ Basement

☐ Ground floor

☐ Mezzanine

☐ First floor

☐ Non-exhibition space

Key to Symbols *see back flap*

Sacrifice of Iphigenia
*In this Pompeiian fresco,
Iphigenia, daughter of
Agamemnon, is about
to be sacrificed to Artemis,
who saves her by
taking a deer instead.*

VISITORS' CHECKLIST

P.za Museo 19. **Map** 3 B4 (9 B2).
Tel 081 442 21 49. Ⓜ Cavour-
Museo. CS, C47, C51, C52,
C53, E1, R1 and others. 9am–
7:30pm Wed–Mon. 1 Jan, 1
May, 25 Dec.

Spring Fresco
*This fresco removed from the
Villa Ariana in the Campo
Varano is a masterpiece
of grace and elegance; the
female figure is rendered
with soft, delicate colours.*

Stairs down to
Egyptian Collection

★ Farnese Bull
*Excavated in the Baths of
Caracalla in Rome, this
is the largest sculptural
group (c.200 BC) to
have survived from
antiquity. It shows the
punishment of Dirce who,
having ill-treated Antiope,
was tied to an enraged bull
by the latter's sons.
The Farnese Bull hall is
currently undergoing
restoration with no end
date known at present.*

Entrance

★ Farnese Hercules
*Made by Glykon of Athens,
this statue is an enlarged
copy of a sculpture by the
Greek master Lysippus.
Napoleon is said to have
regretted leaving it behind
when he removed his booty
from Italy in 1797.*

STAR EXHIBITS

★ The Battle
of Alexander

★ Farnese Hercules

★ Farnese Bull

Exploring the Museo Archeologico

The real Museo Borbonico, as the museum was known, held the Farnese Collection of paintings, ancient artifacts and books, and archaeological finds from sites in Campania and Southern Italy. In 1925 the books moved to the Palazzo Reale *(see pp50–51)* and in 1957 the Farnese Collection paintings returned to Capodimonte *(see pp98–101)*. The remaining material consisted of ancient finds, and the museum became the Archaeological Museum.

Wild goat from Edessa

The impressive Farnese Collection and sculpture from Herculaneum, Pompeii and other Campanian cities can be seen on the ground floor, the mezzanine level, and the first floor. Pompeiian mosaics, on the mezzanine level, and domestic items, weapons and murals, on the first floor, show daily life in the ancient cities. A lower ground floor level houses the Egyptian Collection. The arrangement aims to display the exhibits in context.

Funerary stela of the scribe Huy

SCULPTURE

The fine collection of Greco-Roman sculpture consists mostly of works found in excavations around Vesuvius and the Phlegraean Fields, as well as the treasures from the Farnese Collection. The sculptures – most of which are the only existing Roman copies of lost Greek originals – are displayed on the ground floor. Among the numerous fine works are the statues of *Harmodios and Aristogeiton*, or the "tyrannicides", young Athenians who killed the 6th-century BC tyrant, Hipparchos, and the bronze and alabaster *Artemis of Ephesos*, whose many breasts symbolize fertility. The *Doryphoros* carrying a spear is a copy of a famous Greek original, as is the impressive *Farnese Hercules*. The *Farnese Atlas*, holding up the world, is a Hellenistic statue, while the huge *Dioscuri* statues, discovered in the Roman baths of Baia *(see p137)*, and the harmonious *Farnese Flora* are copies by Roman sculptors.

The Farnese Flora

Cameo with Dionysus and satyr

INCISED GEMS

This precious collection, begun by Cosimo de' Medici, contains Greek, Roman and Renaissance gems. The highlight is the veined sardonyx *Farnese Cup*, a large and beautiful cameo carved in Egypt around the 2nd and 1st centuries BC. Another stunning agate and sardonyx cameo shows the infant Dionysus playing with a satyr.

THE EGYPTIAN COLLECTION

Valuable works of Egyptian art from the Ancient Kingdom (2700–2200 BC) to the Roman age are exhibited here. The black basalt *Farnese Naophorous*

represents a kneeling official. These were the intermediaries between men and gods. The limestone funerary stela of Huy (1320–1200 BC) retains some of its original colouring.

As well as human and animal mummies, the Egyptian section includes Canopic vases, containers for the internal organs of the deceased with lids in the shape of animal heads. The collection of *shabti* comprises wood, stone and faience statuettes representing workers for the deceased in the afterlife.

MOSAICS

The majority of the mosaics on display in the museum come from Pompeii, Stabiae, Herculaneum and Boscoreale and date from the 2nd century BC to AD 79. The realistic images, such as the female portraits from Pompeii, are particularly fascinating.

Mosaic of a female from Pompeii

For hotels and restaurants in this area see p179 and p193

Among the many pavement mosaics made of tiny tesserae and often derived from Greek paintings, is *La Fattucchiera* (the Sorceress). This interesting example of the Hellenistic tradition depicts a scene from *Synaristoi*, a comedy by the Greek playwright Aristophanes. Another masterpiece is the *Battle of Alexander* found at Pompeii. This large, detailed mosaic was based on a Hellenistic painting and depicts Alexander the Great leading his cavalry against Darius III, the Persian Emperor, seen fleeing in his chariot.

Some rooms in the museum have reconstructions of large mosaic paved floors.

observatory. A large sundial *(meridiana)*, decorated with the signs of the zodiac, was created for the spacious hall which had originally been destined to be the Bourbon library (Biblioteca Borbonica).

The idea of the observatory, however, was discarded when experts realized that the location of the building meant that it was impossible to have a total view of the sky. A few years later the observatory was built elsewhere *(see p97)*. As originally planned, the Salone della Meridiana was opened to the public in 1804 as a library.

There are also numerous fragments of frescoes which depict landscapes, portraits and mythological scenes and characters, such as the *Sacrifice of Iphigenia*. These show the variety and quality of Roman painting from this period.

TEMPLE OF ISIS

The paintings, sculptures and furnishings from the Temple of Isis in Pompeii are presented in such a way as to recreate the sanctuary as it appeared to the first archaeologists in 1764. *The Portrait of*

Head of Isis

Io at Canopos was uncovered on 18 November of the same year in the presence of King Ferdinand IV, and shows the nymph Io being welcomed to Egypt by Isis. The marble head of the goddess, to whom the temple was dedicated, dates from the 1st century AD.

VILLA DEI PAPIRI

This villa in Herculaneum *(see p140)*, still partly buried today, was an art gallery in its own right. The rich array of artworks found here during the excavations in 1750–61 are exceptional: this ancient private collection has been handed down to us intact. A map of the villa shows where every object was found.

Statue of a faun, Villa dei Papiri

Among the pieces on display are life-size statues and small sculptures in marble and bronze, such as the *Dancing Faun* which greeted visitors in the atrium of the villa. Most of the pieces were inspired by Greek figurative art. A vast library of around 1,800 papyrus scrolls was also found in the villa. An apparatus used to unroll the charred scrolls is on display. The original scrolls are now kept in the Biblioteca Nazionale *(see p51)*.

SALONE DELLA MERIDIANA

When the building was being reorganized and fitted out as a museum in the late 18th century, the architects had the idea of adding an

FRESCOES

Most of the frescoes in the collection were removed from buildings in cities buried by the eruptions of Vesuvius, and assembled here from the mid-1700s onwards. The most important came from the Basilica in Herculaneum (such as the painting of *Achilles and Chiron*). Others were taken from the Villa di Fannio Sinistore at Boscoreale, where one wall was decorated with illusionistic architectural perspective, and from the extensive landed property of Julia Felix in Pompeii. The frieze from her house, with a still life of apples and grapes and scenes from the forum, gives a fascinating glimpse of everyday life in a 1st-century AD city.

The famous fresco *Achilles and Chiron* from Herculaneum

THE MODEL OF POMPEII

Model of Pompeii

Paper, cork and wood were all used in the making of this extensive scale model of the Pompeii excavations. The archaeologist Giuseppe Fiorelli had the original idea and the model was constructed in various stages between 1861 to 1879. The extraordinarily exact reproduction of every detail found in the ruins (including paintings and mosaics done in watercolour), make this an extremely important historical document. In some cases, when detailed records of Pompeiian decoration are needed, this model is the only useful source that remains.

CAPODIMONTE AND I VERGINI

Although the Spanish viceroys had forbidden construction outside the city walls, from the 17th century onwards suburban development continued. In the early 19th century, building began in the northern suburbs. The avenue leading to the Capodimonte palace, now the home of one of Europe's most important museums, was created as an extension of Via Toledo. The

Porcelain at Capodimonte

square next to the Museo Archeologico was redesigned and Via Foria, on which the Botanic Garden and, from 1751, the huge Albergo dei Poveri were being built, was widened. The old Sanità, Vergini and Fontanelle districts are a lively working quarter in which visitors need to exercise caution. On the streets leading to the early Christian cemeteries, tenements alternate with historic churches and buildings.

SIGHTS AT A GLANCE

Churches and Cemeteries
Cimitero delle Fontanelle ⑥
Santi Apostoli ⑧
San Gennaro Catacombs ④
San Giovanni a Carbonara ⑦
Santa Maria degli Angeli
    alle Croci ⑨
Santa Maria della Sanità and
    San Gaudioso Catacombs ⑤

Historic Buildings
Albergo dei Poveri ⑪
Osservatorio Astronomico ⑭
Palazzo Sanfelice ③
Palazzo dello Spagnolo ②
Torre del Palasciano ⑫

Historic Gate
Porta San Gennaro ①

Museums and Galleries
Museo Nazionale and Park of
Capodimonte pp98–101 ⑬

Parks and Gardens
Orto Botanico ⑩

GETTING THERE
For the Catacombs of San Gennaro, take bus R4, starting from Piazza del Municipio. The R4 also serves Capodimonte, as do the 2M bus, from the Museo Archeologico, and the C63 and C66. For the Vergini and Sanità districts, use the Metro station at Piazza Cavour or Museo. Bus C51 serves the Fontanelle.

| 0 metres | 250 |
| 0 yards | 250 |

KEY

Street-by-Street map
See pp92–3

Ⓜ Metro station

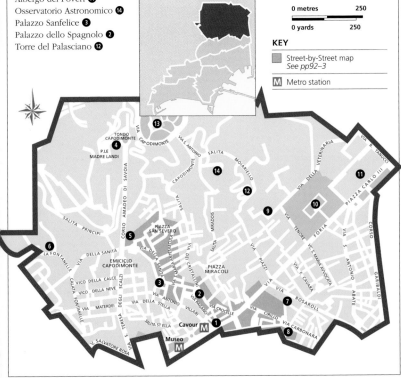

◁ Caravaggio's *Flagellation of Christ* (1610), on display in the Museo di Capodimonte

Street-by-Street: North of the Ancient Walls

The area north of the city walls has been used for
burials and worship of the dead since it was first
inhabited. A visit to the catacombs (which were underground cemeteries and not hiding places), first created
in the early Christian era, is an unforgettable experience.
The area outside the walls was also used to dump
rubbish. The district known today as Via San Giovanni
a Carbonara was once called the Fosso Carbonario
(literally, "coal ditch"), and this is how the street and
the beautiful 14th-century church acquired their
current names.

**The church of
Santa Maria dai
Vergini**, built in the
14th century, was
badly damaged in
World War II.

**The church of
San Severo**
was built on
the burial site
of St Severus,
Bishop of
Naples
from 364
to 410.

Palazzo Sanfelice
*This staircase in the smaller
courtyard was the prototype
for another one designed by
Ferdinando Sanfelice in
San Giovanni a
Carbonara (see p96)* ❸

VIA S. SEVERO A CAPODIMONTE

VICO MARESCA

VIA SANTA MARIA ANTESAECULA

VIA DELLA SANITÀ

PIAZZA DELLA SANITÀ

VIA ARENA DELLA SANITÀ

VIA S. NICANDRO

GRADINI S. NICANDRO

LA
VER

★ **Santa Maria
della Sanità**
*The high altar was built
in a raised position so
that the entrance to the
San Gaudioso catacombs
could be seen* ❺

★ **Palazzo dello Spagnolo**
*This monumental
gateway is one entrance
to the double-flight
staircase, the highlight
of this palazzo* ❷

KEY

– – – Suggested route

| 0 metres | 50 |
| 0 yards | 50 |

★ **San Giovanni a Carbonara**
The double-flight winding staircase here was designed by Ferdinando Sanfelice. The magnificent sculptures inside make this one of the most important churches in Naples ⑦

LOCATOR MAP
See Street Finder, maps 2–4

The Padri della Missione Church was designed by Vanvitelli.

San Carlo all'Arena is so-named because in the 1600s the street nearby was covered in sand *(arena)*.

Santi Apostoli
This church was founded in the 5th century, perhaps on the site of an ancient temple. It was rebuilt from the late 1500s to the mid-1600s. The Paradise in the dome was painted by Giovanni Battista Beinaschi in 1680 ⑧

Santa Maria Succurre Miseris was founded in the 14th century and rebuilt in the 1700s by Ferdinando Sanfelice, using Baroque motifs throughout.

Porta San Gennaro
In the mid-15th century the city walls were extended and this gateway was rebuilt in its present location ①

STAR SIGHTS

★ Palazzo dello Spagnolo

★ Santa Maria della Sanità and San Gaudioso Catacombs

★ San Giovanni a Carbonara

The double-flight staircase in Palazzo dello Spagnolo

Porta San Gennaro ❶

Map 3 C3 (10 D1). 🚌 C47, C51, C52, E1, 182, 184, 201, 203. Ⓜ Cavour-Museo.

This gateway was named after San Gennaro, the patron saint of Naples, because it marked the beginning of the street that leads to the catacombs where he was buried. After the plague of 1656, Mattia Preti painted a fresco on each city gate as an *ex voto* from those who survived. Porta San Gennaro is the only one that still has traces of the artist's work. On the inner façade is a bust of San Gaetano with a dedication and the date – 1658.

Palazzo dello Spagnolo ❷

Via Vergini 19. **Map** 3 B3 (9 C1). 🚌 C47, C51, C52, E1, 182, 184, 201, 203. Ⓜ Cavour-Museo. ◯ courtyard only.

This palace, built in 1738 for the Marquis Nicola Moscati, is said to have been designed by Ferdinando Sanfelice (1675–1748). The architect's name does not appear in any of the notary deeds; however, since Sanfelice built his own

palazzo just a few blocks away, it is likely that he consulted and advised on this building too. Indeed, once through the majestic doorway of the Palazzo dello Spagnolo, you will notice a feature taken from Palazzo Sanfelice: the double-flight external staircase, which effectively separates the main courtyard from the smaller one.

Moscati ran into massive debt during the construction and was forced to sell the building to the Marquis of Livardi. In 1813, the Spanish nobleman Tommaso Atienza bought the property, which has since been called the "Palace of the Spaniard".

Palazzo Sanfelice ❸

Via Sanità 2–6. **Map** 3 B3 (9 C1). 🚌 C51, C52. Ⓜ Cavour-Museo. ◯ courtyard only.

The famous Neapolitan architect Ferdinando Sanfelice built this large palazzo for his own family in 1728. Despite being in a very dilapidated state now, the building was once considered to be one of the finest *palazzi* in Naples. It was here that Sanfelice first created the unusual external staircase that was subsequently adopted, with some variations, in the Palazzo dello Spagnolo. This type of strikingly original staircase became Sanfelice's trademark. His contemporaries likened the design to a large bird with outspread wings, and it became known as a stair *ad ali di falco* – a "falcon's wing" staircase.

The best way to grasp the beauty of the design is to walk up the steps. On the far side of the second courtyard (at Via Sanità No. 2), which has unfortunately lost its original decoration, there is yet another elliptical staircase.

San Gennaro Catacombs ❹

Via Tondo di Capodimonte 13. **Map** 3 A1. **Tel** 081 554 13 05. 🚌 C63, C67, R4, 2M, 178. 🕐 9am, 10am, 11am, noon, 2pm, 3pm Tue–Sun. 🎦 📷 www.catacombedinapoli.it

The original nucleus of this large subterranean cemetery may have been the tomb of a pagan aristocrat donated in the 2nd century to the Christian community. The catacombs grew in importance in the 3rd century after acquiring the tomb of Sant'Agrippino, but it was as the burial site of the saint, bishop and martyr Gennaro, brought here in the 5th century, that they became famous. The cemetery also housed the tombs of Neapolitan bishops up to the 11th century. The vast size and two-level layout of this holy site distinguish it from other catacombs of the same era, making it the most important complex in Southern Italy. Remains of 2nd- to 10th-century mosaics and frescoes (including the oldest known portrayal of San Gennaro, dating from the 5th century) adorn the catacombs' walls. Don't miss the Bishops' Crypt on the upper floor and the Sant'Agrippino Oratory and baptistry on the lower level. The basilica of San Gennaro extra Moenia was erected over the catacombs in the 5th century but greatly modified in the 11th century and in 1932.

Fresco of Saint Gennaro and Saint Peter, San Gennaro Catacombs

Central nave of Santa Maria della Sanità

Santa Maria della Sanità and San Gaudioso Catacombs ❺

Piazza Sanità 124. **Map** 3 A2.
Tel *081 544 13 05.* 🚌 *C51, C52.*
⭕ *10am–1pm daily.* 🔶
Catacombs 📷 *every 45 mins 9:30–12:30pm daily.* 🎫
www.catacombedinapoli.it

View of Santa Maria Sanità from the Ponte della Sanità

The heart of the working-class Sanità quarter is the basilica of Santa Maria. Confusingly, the church is also known as the church of San Vincenzo because it houses a much revered image of the popular saint, known locally as *'o munacone* (the big monk). Designed by Fra Nuvolo, the church was built on a Greek cross plan in 1603–13, with 24 columns supporting one central dome and 12 lateral domes (a reference to Christ and the Apostles). The central tiled dome is overlooked by the 19th-century Ponte della Sanità, linking the city centre to Capodimonte.

Inside, the main altar was raised to allow worshippers to see the space that serves as a kind of atrium for the underground cemetery. The entrance to the catacombs can be clearly seen.

Tradition has it that in 452, the African bishop Settimio Celio Gaudioso died in exile in Naples, and was buried in the Sanità valley. The catacombs grew up around his tomb and were named after him. The many corridors still bear traces of frescoes and mosaics (4th–6th centuries AD). Later, the Dominicans added their own macabre artistic sense to the crypt, embedding the skulls of the deceased into the tufa stone.

Cimitero delle Fontanelle ❻

Via Fontanelle 77. **Map** 3 A3.
🚌 *C52.* ⭕ *to the public except for occasional tours in May (ask at tourist office).*

A walk along Via Fontanelle, through a poor area that is more like a country village than a city district, leads to the church of Maria Santissima del Carmine. Tours sometimes run to the nearby Fontanelle cemetery (*cimitero*). The huge rock-hewn caverns on the hill of Materdei were already being used as the city ossuary when they were chosen as the final resting place for the victims of the 1836 cholera epidemic.

Some people may find the place upsetting, as did the tourist played by Ingrid Bergman in Rossellini's film *Viaggio in Italia*, which made the cemetery famous. Controversy over "adoptions" of skulls to bring good luck has made this a sensitive site.

The ossuary of the Fontanelle Cemetery

San Giovanni a Carbonara ❼

Via San G a Carbonara 5. **Map** 3 C3 (10 E1). 🚌 *C83, E1, 203.* Ⓜ *Cavour-Museo.* ◯ *9am–6pm Mon–Sat.*

Cappella Caracciolo di Vico, San Giovanni a Carbonara

The imaginative double-flight staircase designed by Ferdinando Sanfelice in the early 1700s leads to the 14th-century Chapel of Santa Monica. Left of the chapel is the doorway to San Giovanni a Carbonara. Founded in 1343 by Augustinian monks, this church was restored and enlarged at the end of the century by King Ladislas to make it a worthy burial site for the Angevin rulers.

When the king died in 1414, his tomb, the work of anonymous Tuscan and Lombard sculptors *(see p20),* was erected at the request of his sister, Joan II, who succeeded him to the throne. The grandiose funerary monument, with seated statues of Ladislas and Joan, dominates the single-nave interior. Through a small doorway beneath the monument is the circular Cappella Caracciolo del Sole, built in 1427 and paved with coloured Tuscan tiles. Behind the altar is the tomb of Ser Gianni Caracciolo, Joan's lover and Grand Seneschal at the court, who died in 1432.

To the left of the presbytery is the harmonious Cappella Caracciolo di Vico, built in the Renaissance style in 1517 by Giovan Tommaso Malvito following a design by Bramante. Another work by Malvito is the richly decorated tomb of the Miroballo family opposite the entrance of the church.

Santi Apostoli ❽

Via Santi Apostoli 8. **Map** 3 C4 (10 E1). 🚌 *C83, E1, 203.* Ⓜ *Cavour-Museo.* ◯ *9am–12:45pm daily.*

To reach the church of Santi Apostoli you have to go along a short stretch of Via Pisanelli, which turns into Via Anticaglia *(see p84).* The church was founded in the 5th century and restructured at the beginning of the 17th century by Francesco Grimaldi (1610) and, after 1627, by Giovanni Conforto. The church is best known for a wonderful fresco cycle by Giovanni Lanfranco (1638–46). This masterpiece influenced artistic development in Naples. The artist also frescoed the cupola of the Cappella del Tesoro di San Gennaro *(see pp82–3).*

Santa Maria degli Angeli alle Croci ❾

Via Veterinaria 2. **Map** 3 C2. **Tel** *081 44 07 56.* 🚌 *12.* Ⓜ *Cavour-Museo.* ◯ *8–11am, 5–7:15pm Mon–Sat; 8–11am Sun.* 🚫

The name of this church refers to the Stations of the Cross, once marked by wooden crosses *(croci)* alongside the ascent to the church. Santa Maria was founded at the end of the 16th century by Franciscans and rebuilt in 1638 by Cosimo Fanzago. The façade is simply decorated with white and grey marble.

The white and grey marble façade of Santa Maria degli Angeli alle Croci

This plain design was a daring shift from the usually lavish architecture of Neapolitan Baroque. The interior houses a magnificent marble pulpit sculpted by Cosimo Fanzago. The eagle supporting it symbolizes St John the Evangelist. The extraordinary bas relief of the dead Christ on the altar was sculpted by Carlo Fanzago, Cosimo's son.

Cactus plants in the Orto Botanico

Orto Botanico ❿

Via Foria 223. **Map** 4 D2. **Tel** *081 44 97 59.* 🚌 *C47, C83, 12, 182, 184, 201, 203.* Ⓜ *Cavour-Museo.* ◯ *9am–1:30pm Mon–Fri (May: also Sun).*

Established in 1807 by Joseph Bonaparte, the "Royal Plant Garden" is today one of the leading Italian botanical gardens for the high quality of its collections as well as its sheer size, covering 12 hectares (30 acres). It has a rich stock of tree and shrub specimens from all latitudes and examples of many plant species, as well as several glass-houses with varying climatic conditions. The temperate house is an early 19th-century Neo-Classical building. The collections of citrus trees, desert plants and tree ferns are particularly interesting. A walk along the paths of this green oasis, in the heart of one of the busiest areas in Naples, can make a very pleasant break from the city. Ring the bell at the gate, and the custodian will let you in.

Albergo dei Poveri ⓫

Piazza Carlo III. **Map** 4 E2.
🚌 *C47, C83, 182, 184, 201, 203.*
Ⓜ *Cavour-Museo.*

The enormous building visible today is only one-fifth of the large-scale complex that King Charles wanted to build to provide a refuge for "the poor of the entire kingdom". Construction of the "Hotel of the Poor" began in 1751 according to a design by Ferdinando Fuga. Work continued until 1829. In reality, the building was hated by the poor, including orphans, who were compelled to live and work there, without hope of leaving. In 1981 a wing of the building collapsed as a result of earthquake damage. After many years in a state of neglect, restoration work is now under way.

Torre del Palasciano ⓬

Salita Moiariello 65. **Map** 3 C2.
🚌 *C63, C66.* 🚫 *to the public.*

Located just behind the observatory, and inspired by the Palazzo della Signoria in Florence, this dwelling was commissioned and owned by the physician and surgeon Ferdinando Palasciano (1815–91). He became famous for providing medical care to the wounded of both sides

The Neo-Classical façade of the Osservatorio Astronomico

in Messina during the popular revolts of 1848. For this serious act of insubordination, Palasciano was sentenced to be executed. The intervention of King Ferdinand II of Bourbon spared his life, and Palasciano's sentence was commuted to one year in prison. His case attracted a great deal of international attention, providing the starting point for the Geneva Convention of 1864, which in turn led to the creation of the Red Cross.

The architect Antonio Cipolla (1822–74) directed the construction work, and the building was completed in 1868. The grounds once included a temple, two gardens and an orchard for fruit trees. Today the area, on the hill of Capodimonte, provides a pleasant walk with great views of the city.

The Florentine-style Torre del Palasciano

Museo Nazionale and Park of Capodimonte ⓭

See pp98–101.

Osservatorio Astronomico ⓮

Salita Moiariello 16. **Map** 3 B1.
***Tel** 081 557 51 11.* 🚌 *C63, C66.*
🕐 *once a month (8:30–11pm);
call for more detailed information.*

Situated in the middle of a large park on top of the hill of Miradois, 150 m (490 ft) above sea level, the observatory benefits from a splendid vantage point, with fine panoramic views of the city and the bay. Founded in 1819 by Ferdinand IV, this was the first scientific facility of its kind in Europe. The Bourbon court had always been keenly interested in astronomic studies, and it was King Charles who established the first university chair of astronomy in Naples in 1735. The observatory was originally planned for the Museo Archeologico, and in fact construction of a new observatory began there in 1791 *(see p89)*, but the project was discarded. A few years later the elegant Neo-Classical building that now houses the observatory was built by the Gasse brothers. Today part of the observatory is occupied by a museum with a fine collection of clocks, telescopes and old scientific instruments.

Museo Nazionale and Park of Capodimonte ⑬

From the beginning Capodimonte was intended to be both a royal palace and a museum because Charles of Bourbon wanted to create a home for the works of art he had inherited from his mother Elizabeth Farnese. Construction began in 1738 under architect Antonio Medrano, but the palace was only completed a century later, despite the fact that a large part of the Farnese Collection had been on display there since 1759. The collection was dispersed after the French occupation in 1799 (see p25), but following the Bourbon restoration in 1815, it was enlarged considerably.

In 1860 Capodimonte became the property of the House of Savoy and was the residence of the Dukes of Aosta until 1947. The museum was opened to the public again in 1957.

Pietà
This painting by Annibale Carracci, which dates from around 1600, drew inspiration from Michelangelo and is one of the masterpieces of Carracci's monumental style.

The rooms in the Royal Apartments on the first floor reveal the two-fold function as royal palace and museum that Capodimonte fulfilled from the outset.

THE PARK OF CAPODIMONTE

Charles of Bourbon was drawn to Capodimonte because of hunting, his favourite pastime, and he decided to build an important hunting lodge here. The first section of this large park (over 120 hectares/300 acres), with numerous ancient trees, was laid out by Ferdinando Sanfelice in 1742 into five broad radiating roads, lined with holm-oaks. The buildings used for various court activities can be found in the woods.

Ferdinand IV at Capodimonte by Antonio Joli

KEY

- ☐ Farnese Gallery
- ☐ Borgia Collection
- ☐ De Ciccio Porcelain Collection
- ☐ Farnese and Bourbon Armoury
- ☐ Maria Amalia's Porcelain Parlour
- ☐ Royal apartments
- ☐ Non-exhibition space

Neapolitan Craftsmanship

This is a multi-purpose piece of early 19th-century furniture made in a Neapolitan factory: the lower part contains a glass bowl, which serves as an aquarium, and a table with a bird cage, which serves as a jardinière. The rotating figure of Fortune is perched on top.

VISITORS' CHECKLIST

Via Miano 2. **Map** 3 B1.
Tel 081 749 91 11. 🚌 C63, C66, 2M. **Museum** ⬜ 8:30am–7pm (last adm: 6pm) Thu–Tue. **Park** ⬜ 8am–1 hr before sunset. 🏛 museum only. 🚫 🚻 ♿ ⬜ 🛒 www.museo-capodimonte.it

★ Danaë *(c.1545)*
Golden light bathes this canvas by Titian, in which the mythical god Jupiter disguises himself as a shower of gold in order to seduce Danaë, daughter of the king of Argos.

Café

First Floor

★ Crucifixion *(1426)*
In this early Renaissance painting by Masaccio, the emotional intensity of faces and gestures emphasizes the drama. The panel was part of an altarpiece for a church in Pisa, now dismantled and scattered in various museums.

Main Entrance

★ Maria Amalia's Porcelain Parlour
This room was built in 1757–9 for the Royal Palace at Portici (see p140); then dismantled and moved here in 1866. The walls and ceiling of the queen's parlour are tiled with about 3,000 pieces of finest Capodimonte porcelain.

STAR EXHIBITS

★ Crucifixion by Masaccio

★ Danaë by Titian

★ Maria Amalia's Porcelain Parlour

Exploring the Museo di Capodimonte

The Farnese Collection, which is the core of the
Art Gallery, features the major Italian and European
schools of painting from the 15th to the 17th centuries.
When the Real Museo (now the Museo Archeologico
Nazionale, *see pp86–9*) was created in Palazzo degli
Studi in the early 1800s, the paintings were transferred
from Capodimonte and returned in 1957, along with
other works purchased since the 19th century by the
Bourbon rulers and the Italian government. The first
floor is devoted to the Farnese Collection and the Royal
Apartments, while 13th- to 18th-century Neapolitan
paintings and sculpture are on the second floor, and
19th-century art is on the third floor. The second and
third floors also have a fine collection of modern and
contemporary works.

Antea (1531–5) by Parmigianino

PAINTING FROM THE 13TH TO THE 16TH CENTURIES

The Farnese Collection did
not focus on medieval
works, so that paintings from
this period are later purchases
or come from churches in the
Naples region. For example,
the beautiful *Santa Maria de
Flumine* (c.1290) came from a
church of the same name in
Amalfi. The most important
14th-century painting is the
large altarpiece painted by
Simone Martini in 1317 on the
occasion of the canonization
of St Louis of Toulouse
(*see pp20–21*), *St Louis of
Toulouse Crowning Robert
of Anjou King of Naples*.

The 15th century is also
represented by a superb
canvas – Masaccio's
Crucifixion, actually the
upper part of a dismantled
polyptych taken from the
church of the Carmine in Pisa.
The other panels are in Pisa,
London, Berlin and Malibu.

Transfiguration by Giovanni Bellini

Giovanni Bellini's masterpiece,
Transfiguration (c.1480–85),
has been considered one of
the gems of the Farnese
Collection since the 1600s.
The *Tavola Strozzi* panel is
an extraordinary "snapshot"
of 15th-century Naples.

The focal point of the 16th-
century paintings are the
splendid Titians: *Portrait of
Pope Paul III*, *Pope Paul III
with His Grandchildren* and
Danaë (*see p99*), which
exemplify the Venetian
genius's masterly use of
colour. Artists from the region
of Emilia Romagna, the home
of the Farnese family, are
well represented. Major
works are Correggio's

masterpiece *Mystic Marriage
of St Catherine* and the *Antea*
by Parmigianino, a portrait of
a young woman with elegant
dress and a marten stole. An
important group of canvases
by the Carraccis includes
Annibale Carracci's *Pietà*,
inspired by the strong
sculptural forms of Michelangelo, and his large
allegorical work, *Hercules at
the Crossroads*, in which the
mythical hero has to choose
between pleasure and virtue.

PAINTING FROM THE 17TH TO THE 20TH CENTURIES

Among the 17th-century
works in the museum,
Bartolomeo Schedoni's
Charity (1611) is one of the
most famous, and is greatly
admired for its expressive
intensity. The myth of *Atalanta
and Hippomenes* is depicted in
Guido Reni's canvas, which the
Bourbon rulers bought in 1802
because they lacked a major
work by the Bolognese master.

The astounding *Flagellation
of Christ* by Caravaggio (*see
p90*) was painted in stages
from 1607 to 1609–10, and
hung in San Domenico
Maggiore until its move to
Capodimonte. It is regarded
as the linchpin of all 17th-
century Neapolitan painting,
which is represented here by
many leading artists, such as
Battistello Caracciolo, Luca
Giordano and Mattia Preti. No
less astounding is Artemisia
Gentileschi's painting of

The *Tavola Strozzi*, a representation of 15th-century Naples (detail)

For hotels and restaurants in this area see p179 and pp193–4

Judith and Holofernes, a subject she made her own. The artist, who favoured rather violent themes, was an exceptionally gifted painter and remarkably independent for a woman of her times.

Portrait of Ferdinand IV as a Youth was painted by the German artist Anton Raphael Mengs in 1759; the young king, whose luxurious clothes are rendered in great detail, was nine at the time. In addition, there are some fine landscapes by Ferdinand IV's court painter, Jakob-Philipp Hackert.

Capodimonte also has a large body of 19th-century Neapolitan paintings, including works by Anton Pitloo, the Dutch painter who settled in Naples *(see p36)*, and Giacinto Gigante. Don't miss the latter's famous painting of the Cappella del Tesoro in the Duomo. Among the modern works, Andy Warhol's *Mount Vesuvius (see p28)* was painted in 1985 for an exhibition at the museum in the same year.

Judith and Holofernes by Artemisia Gentileschi (1597–1651)

THE COLLECTION OF DRAWINGS AND PAINTINGS

Among the museum's huge inheritance there are about 2,500 drawings and watercolours and 22,000 prints and engravings. One of the most famous works is a cartoon (a preparatory drawing made with charcoal or chalk) made by Michelangelo around 1546. It was drawn for part of the fresco of *The Crucifixion of St Peter* in the Cappella Paolina in the

Francesco Solimena's *Study of a Young Man's Face* (1728)

Vatican. Perforations (which can still be seen) were made with a needle, and powder was sprinkled over the holes to transfer the lines to the wall where the fresco was to be painted.

Solimena's *Study of a Young Man's Face* is a charming study for a later painting. Another important cartoon is Raphael's *Moses before the Burning Bush,* a preparatory drawing for a detail of a fresco in the Stanza di Eliodoro in the Vatican.

THE DECORATIVE ARTS

The major section in the fine Decorative Arts collection is the armoury, which has about 4,000 weapons and is one of the most important of its kind. Many of the objects here

come from the Naples Royal Arms Factory, founded in 1734 by Charles III. There are also over 4,000 ceramic pieces in this part of the museum, including the De Ciccio majolica collection and examples of the superb porcelain manufactured in Naples at the instigation of Charles III. A fine example of this craftsmanship is Queen Maria Amalia's Porcelain Parlour *(see p99)*.

Other decorative arts include objects made of ivory, amber and rock crystal, as well as medallions, semi-precious stones and other pieces such as the 17th-century gilded silver table trophy of Diana by Jacob Miller.

Diana on a Deer, table trophy

THE ROYAL PORCELAIN FACTORY

King Charles of Bourbon promoted and fostered the manufacture of decorated porcelain in Naples. The "soft-paste" porcelain, produced with the aid of leading chemists and mineralogists in the Kingdom of Naples, allowed the Real Fabbrica to vie with top European manufacturers such as Meissen. A new pavilion for the Royal Factory was opened in the royal park of Capodimonte in

The Biscuit Vendor (1750–51)

1743, and the fame of Neapolitan porcelain continued to grow. By 1759, when the king returned to Spain, the factory had become so important to him that he had it dismantled and took it, as well as its staff, with him. The factory was reopened in 1771 by Ferdinand, and production of top-quality pieces began again. Today the Royal Factory is the home of the Institute for the Porcelain and Ceramics industry.

VOMERO

Detail of the cloister, Certosa di San Martino

In 1885 the Town Council of Naples approved a plan for a new district to be developed "in the rise between Castel Sant'Elmo, the village of Vomero and Antignano", which, once completed, would accommodate 30,000 inhabitants. So began the story of the district of Vomero, which soon became famous for its scenic beauty and healthy climate. These qualities have since been partly ruined (especially since World War II) by chaotic, uncontrolled property development with total disregard for the natural surroundings. Yet, some interesting areas are preserved. At the top of the hill is one of the most important monuments in Naples, the Certosa di San Martino, with its splendid Baroque church, fine museum and the elegant residence called the Quarto del Priore.

SIGHTS AT A GLANCE

Historic Buildings
Castel Sant'Elmo ❹
Certosa and Museo Nazionale di San Martino pp108–11 ❺

Parks and Gardens
Villa La Floridiana ❷

Streets and Squares
Pedamentina ❻
Via Luigia Sanfelice ❼
Via Scarlatti ❶

Museums and Galleries
Museo Nazionale della Ceramica Duca di Martina ❸

GETTING THERE
The fastest way to reach Vomero is via the funiculars: the Chiaia route from Parco Margherita, the Centrale from Via Toledo and the Montesanto from the historic centre. To get to Castel Sant'Elmo and the Certosa you can also take the circle bus line V1 from Piazza Fuga, which connects with the Centrale funicular.

KEY

Street-by-Street map
See pp104–5

Ⓜ Metro station

🚟 Funicular

Street-by-Street: Vomero

Take one of the funicular railway lines up the hill to Vomero for fine views of the city centre and the Bay of Naples. Art-lovers will find that Neapolitan masters are well represented in the museums of the Certosa di San Martino and Villa Floridiana (the Duca di Martina). Meanwhile, a walk along the atmospheric streets in the heart of the district reveals an eclectic range of shops and goods, including the Caffè Scarlatti in Via Scarlatti, selling excellent coffee and delectable cakes. In Via Luigia Sanfelice is the villa of the Neapolitan comic Eduardo Scarpetta.

Eduardo Scarpetta

Montesanto funicular

Vanvitelli

Via Scarlatti
This street is the main thoroughfare through Vomero ❶

VIA MORGHEN

PIAZZA VANVITELLI

VIA SCARLATTI

VIA BERNINI

VIA CIMAROSA

VIA L. SANFELICE

Centrale funicular

Chiaia funicular

Museo Nazionale della Ceramica Duca di Martina
This is one of Italy's most important collections of decorative arts ❸

★ **Villa Floridiana**
The villa, rebuilt by Antonio Niccolini in the early 19th century, now houses the Duca di Martina museum. It stands in a large park filled with pine, holm-oak, plane and cypress trees ❷

KEY

- - - Suggested route

For hotels and restaurants in this area see p180 and p194

LOCATOR MAP
See Street Finder, maps 1, 2, 5, 6

| 0 metres | 100 |
| 0 yards | 100 |

In Via Tito Angelini are some turn-of-the-century houses, such as Villino Maria (below), which have survived the wave of property development since World War II.

★ **Certosa and Museo Nazionale di San Martino**
After the unification of Italy, this impressive complex – built in the 14th century but drastically restructured later on – became state property and was turned into a museum ❺

The section of the Museo di San Martino given over to Neapolitan painting and sculpture of the 19th century includes Vincenzo Gemito's expressive *Head of a Peasant Woman.*

★ **Castel Sant'Elmo**
The patriots of the Parthenopean Republic (see p25) conquered the castle in 1799, but when the revolution was crushed they were imprisoned there ❹

STAR SIGHTS

★ Certosa and Museo Nazionale di San Martino

★ Villa Floridiana

★ Castel Sant'Elmo

Via Scarlatti ❶

Map 2 D5. 🚃 *Centrale: Piazza Fuga; Chiaia: Via Cimarosa.* Ⓜ *Vanvitelli.* 🚃 *V1.*

The most elegant street in Vomero is lined with tall plane trees and descends from Piazza Vanvitelli towards Via Cilea. Now closed to traffic, Via Scarlatti is the perfect place for a pleasant walk interrupted by the odd break for shopping. If you lift your gaze above the line of shops you will note the striking contrast between the 19th-century buildings and those constructed in the last 30 years in the wave of property development that has radically altered the face of Vomero.

Villa La Floridiana ❷

Via Domenico Cimarosa 77, Via A Falcone 171. **Map** 2 D5. **Tel** 081 578 84 18. 🚃 *C28, V1.* 🚃 *Centrale: Piazza Fuga; Chiaia: Via Cimarosa.* Ⓜ *Vanvitelli.* **Villa** ◯ *8:30am–2pm daily (last adm: 1:15pm).* **Park** ◯ *8:30am–1 hr before sunset daily.*

In 1817 Ferdinand I acquired an estate on the Vomero hill as a present for his second wife Lucia Migliaccio, the Duchess of Floridia, whom he had married shortly after the death of Maria Carolina of Austria. The estate, which was named La Floridiana in honour of the duchess, included a park with

a magnificent view of the city. There were two buildings on the property. The Villa Floridiana was rebuilt as a summer residence in the Neo-Classical style by Antonio Niccolini in 1817–19. It now houses the Duca di Martina Ceramics Museum *(see below)*. There was also a "Pompeiian" coffee-house, later called Villa Lucia, also designed by Niccolini, which became private property.

The Italian government purchased the Villa La Floridiana in 1919.

Museo Nazionale della Ceramica Duca di Martina ❸

Villa Floridiana, Via Domenico Cimarosa 77, Via Aniello Falcone 171. **Map** 2 D5. **Tel** 081 578 84 18. 🚃 *Centrale: Piazza Fuga; Chiaia: Via Cimarosa.* 🚃 *V1.* 🚇 *8:30am–2pm Wed–Mon (last adm: 1:15pm).* 🎨 🚫 ♿

Placido de Sangro, the Duke of Martina and member of an illustrious noble family, was an avid, passionate collector of decorative art objects, especially porcelain and ceramics. When he died in 1891, his valuable collection of about 6,000 pieces was inherited by his grandson Placido, who donated them to the city of Naples in 1911.

Since 1927 Villa La Floridiana has been the home of the Duca di Martina National Ceramics Museum, where curators aim to reproduce as closely as possible the arrangement and spirit of the collections in the De Sangro residence. The pleasant and unusual atmosphere of a home-cum-museum has remained unchanged, despite additions and later donations.

The porcelain pieces come from the most important

Interior of the Duca di Martina ceramics museum

Italian and other European factories, while the collection of Oriental art – consisting mostly of 18th- and 19th-century porcelain – is one of the best in Italy.

The museum also contains 15th-century ivory pieces, majolica, Limoges enamel, leather and tortoiseshell objects and drawings by 17th- and 18th-century Neapolitan artists, including Solimena, Giordano and De Matteis.

Castel Sant'Elmo ❹

Via Tito Angelini 20. **Map** 2 E5. **Tel** 081 558 77 08. 🚃 *V1.* 🚃 *Montesanto: Via Morghen; Centrale: Piazzetta Fuga; Chiaia: Via Cimarosa.* Ⓜ *Vanvitelli.* ◯ *9am–6:30pm Wed–Mon.* 🎨 📷 ♿ *partial.*

In the 1330s the Angevin rulers instigated a flurry of building on the Vomero hill west of Naples – the construction of the Certosa di San Martino and the enlargement and reconstruction of the nearby fortified residence of Belforte, which had been inhabited by Charles I of Anjou's family since 1275.

In the 16th century Pedro Scriba, a leading military architect of the time, completely transformed the 14th-century castle into its present six-pointed star configuration.

Because of its strategic position, Castel Sant'Elmo under viceroy Pedro de Toledo became the focal

Looking across the Floridiana park

point of the new defence system for Naples. For centuries it was used as a prison; among its illustrious "guests" were the great Renaissance philosopher Tommaso Campanella, the 1799 revolutionaries and patriots involved in the 19th-century Risorgimento.

The entrance bears Charles V's coat of arms and a fine epigraph. The complex, which also contains a large lecture hall, has been the venue for temporary exhibitions and cultural events since 1988. The castle walls offer a spectacular 360-degree view of Naples and the bay.

Castel Sant'Elmo on the top of Vomero hill

Certosa di San Martino **❺**

See pp108–11.

Pedamentina **❻**

Map 2 F5. 🚇 Montesanto: Via Morghen. 🚌 V1.

The steps connecting Castel Sant'Elmo and the city sprawling below allow you to descend "towards the sea amidst the green slopes", as old guidebooks put it, even though the landscape has changed considerably in the meantime. The 414 steps from San Martino to Corso Vittorio Emanuele offer beautiful panoramic views that change at every stage. The views of the bay are very rewarding, but be aware that the route passes by dilapidated buildings, slum housing and unsavoury neighbourhoods. Do not attempt this walk on your own and always be alert to potential dangers.

Via Luigia Sanfelice **❼**

Map 2 D5 & 2 E5. 🚇 Centrale: Piazza Fuga; Chiaia: Via Cimarosa. Ⓜ Vanvitelli. 🚌 E4.

Should you ask for the "Santarella", people will point to Via Luigia Sanfelice. The key to this riddle lies in a curve in the road where there is a villa with a curious nameplate: "Qui rido io" (this is where I laugh). This was the home, built in 1909, of the well-known Neapolitan author and comic actor Eduardo Scarpetta (the father of Eduardo De Filippo) (see p37), whose best-known work is Na santarella. In Via Luigia Sanfelice and nearby Via Filippo Palizzi there are a number of elegant houses that are interesting examples of Neo-Renaissance or Art Nouveau styles.

Nameplate at the villa of comic actor and author Eduardo Scarpetta

---

FROM THE "FERROVIA DI DELIZIA" TO THE FUNICULAR RAILWAY

In 1875 the engineers Bruno and Ferraro designed a rail system to take passengers up the Vomero hill along the Chiaia and Montesanto slopes, using two funiculars, connected so that the ascent of one line caused the descent of the other. The "train of delights",

The present-day funicular railway

as it was called, allowed travellers to admire stupendous views of the bay while crossing the hill, in those days a rural area. The initial scheme gradually evolved into two independent funicular railways which ran through a tunnel, providing a rapid and efficient means of transport between Vomero and the city centre. The Chiaia funicular was opened in 1889, Montesanto in 1891. In order to improve connections with what in the meantime had become the most rapidly expanding district in the city, the Centrale funicular was built in 1928. Centrale was the longest of the three; from its starting point in Via Toledo it reaches a point halfway between the other two. There is also a fourth line, the Mergellina funicular, which connects the seafront with Via Manzoni.

Certosa di San Martino 5

Procession tray

In 1325 Charles Duke of Calabria began construction of what is one of the richest monuments in Naples. The Carthusian monks were forward looking, and from the 16th to the 18th centuries the greatest artists of the time worked at the Certosa (charterhouse) of San Martino. The original look of San Martino was gradually altered by Mannerist and Baroque rebuilding. The most radical redecoration and enlargement was carried out by the architects Giovanni Antonio Dosio, at the end of the 16th century, and Cosimo Fanzago, who took over in 1623. The 17th and 18th centuries brought further changes.

The French deconsecrated the monastery in 1806, and since 1866 it has housed the San Martino museum, with displays of Neapolitan art and history.

Chiostro dei Procuratori
This cloister was built in the late 16th–early 17th century by Giovanni Antonio Dosio.

Nativity section

Navigation section

The Prior's garden

★ Quarto del Priore
The Prior's Residence was richly decorated and had a splendid panoramic view over the Bay of Naples (see p111).

TIMELINE

		1631–56 Complex rebuilt and redecorated by Cosimo Fanzago		
1325 Construction begun under Charles of Anjou	**1578** Decoration and enlargement by Dosio and Conforto		**1807** The last monks forced to leave the monastery	*Chain of the Order of the Two Sicilies*
1300		**1600**		**1800**
1368 Consecration of the church	**1623** Cosimo Fanzago begins work on the Chiostro Grande		**1799** Monastery damaged during Parthenopean revolution	**1866** The Certosa becomes state property and part of it is turned into a museum

★ Church and its Subsidiary Rooms

Sumptuous Baroque decoration and altera- tions such as the large round windows in the façade were successfully incorporated into the original Gothic church.

VISITORS' CHECKLIST

Piazzale San Martino 5. **Map** 2 F5.
Tel *081 229 45 89.* Montesanto:
Via Morghen. V1. 8:30am–
7:30pm Thu–Tue.

Entrance

Central Nave

In 1580 Giovanni Antonio Dosio closed the aisles and built six side chapels. The vaults of the original 14th-century nave are still visible.

Historical section

★ Chiostro Grande

The main cloister, with its 64 marble columns, was designed by Giovanni Antonio Dosio at the end of the 16th century and later remodelled by Cosimo Fanzago. The latter also designed the seven corner marble doors supporting figures of Carthusian saints.

19th-century Neapolitan art

Monks' cemetery

STAR FEATURES

★ Church and its Subsidiary Rooms

★ Chiostro Grande

★ Quarto del Priore

Exploring the Certosa di San Martino and the Museum

From the outset the Carthusian monks intended San Martino to be a storehouse for Neapolitan history and civilization. Accordingly, the collections document the rich and varied forms of artistic expression that thrived in Naples between the 15th and the 19th centuries: from paintings to coral jewellery, traditional crib scenes *(presepi)*, porcelain, sculpture and ivory carvings. There is also a fascinating collection of maps and a print library that contains over 8,000 pieces. One part of the museum is devoted to Neapolitan theatre. The minor arts section contains an interesting collection of glass from Venice and other European sources. In addition, the church, the Quarto del Priore (Prior's Residence), the cloister and the gardens contribute to making this one of the premier attractions in the city.

Detail of the inlaid wood panelling in the sacristy (1587–98)

THE CHURCH AND ITS SUBSIDIARY ROOMS

In 1568, the prior Severo Turboli set up an elaborate plan for the complete restructuring of the San Martino charterhouse. The original Angevin church was enlarged and modernized and its Gothic structure almost completely disappeared under the multitude of frescoes, stucco-work and marbles produced by leading artists of the time.

The most radical changes to the building were carried out in the 17th century by architect and sculptor Cosimo Fanzago, who worked at San Martino from 1623 to 1656. He designed the interior of the church and its lavish decoration. Coloured marble adorns the nave and chapels, such as the Cappella di San Bruno. The rooms adjacent to the church are also richly ornamented. In the sacristy the panels of the beautiful inlaid walnut wardrobes contain 56 intarsia scenes with striking perspective effects (16th century). The fresco of *The Triumph of Judith* on the vault of the brightly lit Cappella del Tesoro Nuovo was painted by Luca Giordano in 1704.

HISTORICAL SECTION

These interesting rooms are dedicated to the history of the Kingdom of Naples. Paintings, furnishings, sculptures, medallions, arms and memorabilia recreate the key moments in the political, social and cultural history of Naples, from the Aragonese to the Bourbon dynasties. The importance of this valuable collection is exemplified in two famous works that combine historical and artistic

The Cappella di San Bruno, designed by Cosimo Fanzago (1631)

Statue of Charles III of Spain (1754)

documentary significance:
The Revolt of Masaniello (see pp22–3), painted in 1647, and *Piazza del Mercatello during the 1656 Plague*, both painted by Micco Spadaro. These dramatic compositions tell the story of two important events in the history of 17th-century Naples. They are also an accurate and useful representation of what the city looked like at that time.

Panorama of Naples Viewed from the Conocchia, by Giacinto Gigante

THE NATIVITY SCENES

Only towards the end of the 19th century did the *presepe* or nativity scene start to be considered an artistic genre in its own right, worthy of a museum. This section of the San Martino museum has one of the most important public collections of its kind, with displays of entire nativity scenes as well as individual figures, such as Mary and Joseph, the Three Kings or the shepherds. Animals and accessories, such as the crib, are also displayed.

Among the most important nativity scenes is a creation by the Neapolitan playwright, Michele Cucinello. Many of the statuettes were executed by famous Neapolitan artists. *Blind Beggar with Cataracts* (c.1780), in the Perrone Collection *(see p39)*, is by the artist Giuseppe Sanmartino, who sculpted the *Veiled Christ* in the Cappella Sansevero *(see p63)*.

***Blind Beggar with Cataracts* by Giuseppe Sanmartino**

NINETEENTH-CENTURY NEAPOLITAN ART

This collection of paintings and sculpture also displays pieces that are significant from both an artistic and historical standpoint. The collection consists of purchases made by the Italian government but owes its strength primarily to donations of important private Neapolitan collections.

All the schools of painting that flourished in this area during the 19th century are represented here. A recurring theme was the Campania landscape, a favourite with local artists. The paintings usually depict a serene and beautiful landscape, such as in Giacinto Gigante's *Panorama of Naples Viewed from the Conocchia*. Among the pieces of sculpture, those by Vincenzo Gemito are not to be missed. *Il Malatiello* (The Sick Child) and *Testa della Popolana* (Head of a Peasant Woman) portray the expressive intensity characteristic of this artist's work.

THE QUARTO DEL PRIORE

The prior, the only person who was allowed contact with the outside world, governed the life of the monastery from his apartments. This was a fabulous residence, rich with artistic treasures and opening onto lush gardens overlooking Naples and the sea.

Built in the 17th century and enlarged the following century, the luxurious quarters have undergone scrupulous restoration. Originally, this part of the complex was used to exhibit the rich art collection of the Carthusian monks. Following the restoration, an attempt

Triptych by Jean Burdichon (c.1495) in the art gallery of the Quarto del Priore

has been made to recreate the Quarto del Priore as it was when inhabited by the prior, with paintings, sculpture, fabric and furniture adorning the rooms.

The art collection and high-quality furnishings reflect the refinement and great artistic sensitivity of the Carthusian monks as well as their ability to keep abreast of the latest artistic and architectural developments.

With its stunning decor, works of art and sculpture and spectacular panoramic views over the city, the Quarto del Priore is one of the highlights of a visit to the Certosa di San Martino.

The Borgo Marinaro and Castel dell[...]

SIGHTS AT A GLANCE

Historic Buildings
Castel dell'Ovo ❷

Historic Streets and Sites
Lungomare ❸
Mergellina ⓫
Piazza dei Martiri ❹
Santa Lucia ❶

Museums and Galleries
Museo Diego Aragona Pignatelli
 Cortes and Museo delle
 Carrozze in Villa Pignatelli ❼

Churches
Santa Maria del Parto ⓬
Santa Maria di
 Piedigrotta ❾
Santa Maria in Portico ❽

Parks and Gardens
Parco Vergiliano a
 Piedigrotta ❿
Villa Comunale ❺

Aquarium
Stazione Zoologica ❻

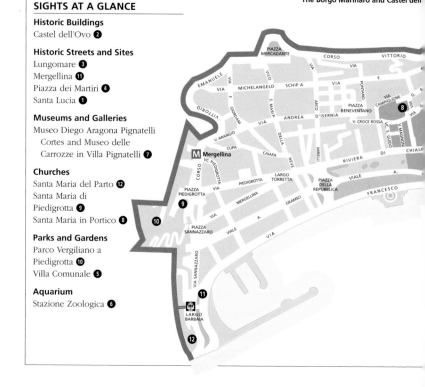

CASTEL DELL'OVO AND CHIAIA

The Chiaia area grew to its present extent in the 19th century, although there had been buildings along the seafront outside the city walls since the 16th century. In the late 18th century the construction of the Villa Reale (now called the Villa Comunale) along the Riviera di Chiaia changed the face of this part of Naples.

In the meantime, the city was becoming popular with tourists: 8,000 per year were reported by 1838 – a significant number of visitors for

Decorative detail in the Stazione Zoologica

that time. In the second half of the 19th century, the development of the Amedeo quarter and the elegant streets that radiate from Piazza Amedeo made this the favourite residential area of the upper middle class. The Chiaia area also bears traces of the distant past: Castel dell'Ovo, the fortress jutting into the sea in front of Santa Lucia, and the oldest castle in Naples, and the Parco Vergiliano a Piedigrotta in Mergellina, said to be the place where the Roman poet Virgil was buried.

GETTING THERE

The fastest way to get to this area is by metro (Mergellina station for Mergellina and the seafront area; Piazza Amedeo station for the Chiaia area). The funicular from the Parco Margarita station takes you from Chiaia to Vomero, while the Mergellina funicular takes you from Mergellina to Via Manzoni. The R3 and 152 buses run along the Riviera di Chiaia and skirt the Villa Comunale. The circular bus routes C4 and C28 link the whole area.

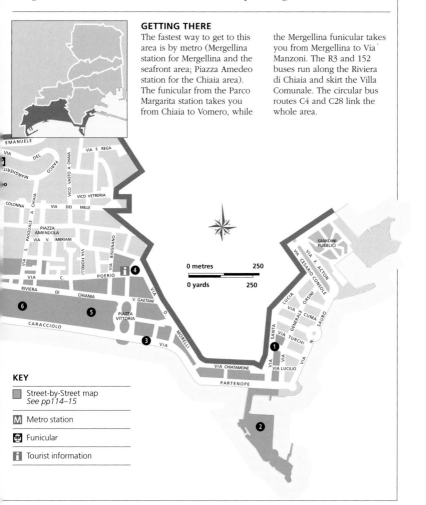

KEY

	Street-by-Street map See pp114–15
M	Metro station
	Funicular
i	Tourist information

Street-by-Street: Lungomare

Besides being a pleasant way of spending the time, walking along the seafront is a tradition handed down over generations of Neapolitans. This is one of the city's most upscale districts, with five-star hotels and restaurants once frequented by A-list celebrities, such as Sophia Loren and Salvador Dalí. Mary Shelley also visited in 1818, and some speculate that her novel *Frankenstein* was conceived during her walks along the Lungomare. At the Villa Comunale you can combine a walk in the park with a visit to Europe's oldest aquarium. Nearby Villa Pignatelli has stupendous rooms with 19th-century furnishings and decoration.

San Pasquale was built for Charles III in 1749, on the occasion of the birth of his first son.

Villa Comunale
The kiosk, known as the Cassa Armonica or sound box, was built in the gardens during the 19th-century restoration of the villa ❺

Villa Pignatelli

Stazione Zoologica
This aquarium was founded in 1872 as a centre for marine studies ❻

Santa Maria in Portico
The church is built on a Latin cross plan with one nave, and its dome is covered with multi-coloured tiles ❽

KEY

– – – Suggested route

| 0 metres | 200 |
| 0 yards | 200 |

★ **Villa Pignatelli**
Originally called Villa Acton, this house was modelled on an ancient Pompeiian design, with the side facing the sea consisting of a loggia supported by Doric columns ❼

For hotels and restaurants in this area see pp180–81 and pp194–5

Santa Lucia
There are shrines all over Naples, such as this one in Via Santa Lucia, dedicated to St Lucy ❶

LOCATOR MAP
See Street Finder, maps 5–7

Borgo Marinaro is a characteristically lively place to wander around, with its small harbour, cafés and trattorias.

Piazza dei Martiri
The lovely façade of Palazzo Calabritto enlivens this popular square ❹

★ Castel dell'Ovo
The unmistakable bulk of the castle dominates the surrounding area ❷

STAR SIGHTS

★ Castel dell'Ovo

★ Lungomare

★ Villa Pignatelli

★ Lungomare
This column, taken from a building in Via Anticaglia (see p84), is dedicated to those who died at sea ❸

Santa Lucia ❶

Map 7 A4. 🚇 C4, E6, 140, 152.

One of the most famous streets in Naples, Santa Lucia exemplifies the city's striking contrasts. Luxury hotels that were built for the elite in the 19th century and imposing buildings for the regional government rub shoulders with the Pallonetto di Santa Lucia slum area where the poor eke out a living. This quarter is named after the church at the beginning of the street, Santa Lucia a Mare, whose history goes back to the 9th century. It has been rebuilt several times. Before you reach the seafront, on the right, you will see the tall rocky face of the hill of Pizzofalcone, the site of the oldest part of Naples (see p59).

Castel dell'Ovo with its tall tufa curtain walls

appearance is the result of the rebuilding carried out after 1503, the year the fortress was almost destroyed during a siege by Ferdinand II of Spain.

Despite the rebuilding, there followed a period of decline that lasted until 1871, at which point the castle was so run-down that one urban renewal plan proposed its demolition. Thorough restoration work was begun just over a century later in 1975, and succeeded in bringing the site back to life. It is now used for cultural events. Around the castle is the picturesque Borgo Marinaro quarter, built at the end of the 19th century for the fishermen of Santa Lucia. It is a popular place with visitors because of its restaurants, cafés and lively atmosphere.

The Immacolatella Fountain

Castel dell'Ovo ❷

Borgo Marinaro. **Map** 7 A5.
Tel 081 240 00 55. 🚇 C4, 152. ⭕
8am–7pm Mon–Sat, 8am–1pm Sun.

The oldest castle in Naples is built on the islet of Megaris, once the site of a villa owned by the Roman patrician Lucullus. Later, in the 5th century, a community of monks founded the San Salvatore monastery, the only remaining part of which is the church. The oldest part of the castle dates from the 9th century. Under the Norman, Hohenstaufen, Angevin and Aragonese rulers, the castle underwent continuous changes according to the requirements of each dynasty. The present

Lungomare ❸

Map 5 & 6. 🚇 C4, C12, C18, R3, R7, 140, 152.

A walk along the road skirting the coast from Santa Lucia to Mergellina is another experience you must not miss while in Naples. The view of the city and the bay is breathtaking. The first stretch of the seafront – which corresponds to Via Nazario Sauro and Via Partenope – was built in the 19th century, as a result of reclamation along Via Santa Lucia and Via Chiatamone. The two ends of this long and pleasant seafront promenade are marked by two beautiful 17th-century fountains: the Immacolatella, which was built by Michelangelo Naccherino and Pietro Bernini in 1601, and the Sebeto fountain, which was the work of Cosimo Fanzago (1635–7).

THE LEGEND OF THE EGG

Opinions vary as to the origin of the curious name given to Castel dell'Ovo, or Castle of the Egg, which first appears in 14th-century documents. One possible explanation is the shape of the castle. However, popular tradition has it that the name derives from a magic egg hidden in the castle which determined its fate and that of the entire city: as long as the egg remained intact, both would be protected from catastrophes. The magic spell was supposed to have been originally cast on the ancient egg by the Latin poet Virgil, who, according to medieval legends, possessed supernatural powers and the gift of divination.

The castle in the 1800s

Piazza dei Martiri ❹

Map 6 F2. 🚌 *C4, E6.* 🚡 *Chiaia: Piazza Amedeo.*

The Square of Martyrs is the heart of the "chic" commercial centre of Naples. Its focal point is the Monumento ai Martiri Napoletani designed by Enrico Alvino in 1866–8, with four lions at the base symbolizing the anti-Bourbon uprisings of 1799, 1820, 1848 and 1860. Palazzo Calabritto (No. 30), built by Luigi and Carlo Vanvitelli, dominates the square on the seaward side.

Along the streets that radiate from the square, historic palazzi alternate with elegant shops and cafés. Palazzo Portanna (No. 58), built in the 18th century by Mario Gioffredo, was rebuilt by Antonio Niccolini for Lucia Migliaccio, the morganatic wife of Ferdinand IV. Among the Neo-Renaissance and Liberty style buildings along Via Filangieri and Via dei Mille, Palazzo Mannajuolo (No. 36 Via Filangieri) is worth seeing for its beautiful inner staircase. In nearby Via Poerio and Via San Pasquale are the Lutheran and Anglican churches, founded in 1861–2.

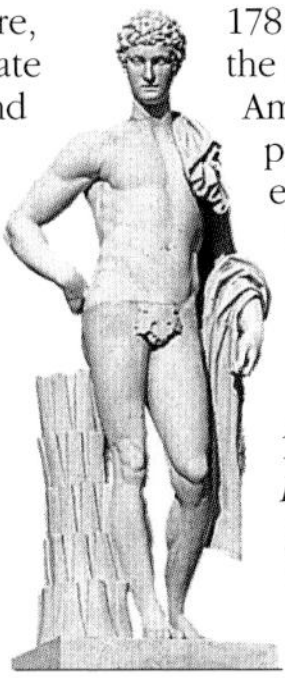

19th-century statue at the Villa entrance

Villa Comunale ❺

Via Carracciolo, Riviera di Chiaia. **Map** 6 E2. ***Tel*** *081 761 11 31.* 🚌 *C12, C18, R3, R7, 140, 152.* ◯ *May–Oct: 7am–midnight daily; Nov–Apr: 7am–10pm daily.*

The first design for this park area dates from 1697, during the rule of viceroy Luis de la Cerda, but it was Ferdinand IV who, almost a century later, asked architect Carlo Vanvitelli and landscape gardener Felice Abate to lay out the Real Passeggio di Chiaia as a public park.

The Villa Reale, later the Villa Comunale, was completed in 1781, and was enlarged in the following century.

Among the pine, monkey puzzle, palm and eucalyptus trees there are 19th- and early 20th-century sculptures and several fountains, including the so-called *Paparelle*, which in 1825 replaced the famous *Farnese Bull* sculpture group, which is now in the Museo Archeologico *(see p86)*. The park, which extends from the Riviera di Chiaia to Via Caracciolo, also boasts the Neo-Classical Stazione Zoologica and the iron and glass kiosk known as the Cassa Armonica, designed in 1877 by Enrico Alvino. Today the park hosts children's activities such as pony riding.

Façade of the Stazione Zoologica

Stazione Zoologica ❻

Villa Comunale. **Map** 6 E2. ***Tel*** *081 583 32 63.* 🚌 *C12, C18, R3, R7, 140, 152.* ◯ *Mar–Oct: 9am–5:30pm Tue–Sat, 9:30am–7pm Sun; Nov–Feb: 9am–4:30pm Tue–Sat, 9am–1:30pm Sun.* 🎟 ♿

This institute, run by the Consiglio Nazionale delle Ricerche (National Research Council), is one of the oldest and best known of its kind in the world. It was established in 1872–4 by the German scientist Anton Dohrn to study marine environments. The building, which was designed by Adolf von Hildebrandt, contains research labs, a small exhibition and the oldest aquarium in Europe, with specimens from the Bay of Naples. The frescoes depicting marine and rural scenes in the reading room of the library were painted by Hans von Marées in 1873 and can be viewed by appointment.

The park area of Villa Comunale with the Riviera di Chiaia along the seafront

Museo Diego Aragona Pignatelli Cortes and Museo delle Carrozze in Villa Pignatelli **7**

Riviera di Chiaia 200. **Map** 6 D2.
Tel 081 761 23 56. C4, C12,
C18, C28, R3, 140, 152. Chiaia:
Piazza Amedeo. 8:30am–2pm
Wed–Mon (last adm: 1pm).

The Neo-Classical villa was built in 1825 by Pietro Valente for the illustrious Acton family. The Rothschilds became the new owners 20 years later and changed the furnishings and interior. Prince Diego Aragona Pignatelli Cortes then bought the villa, which is named after him, and in 1955 his granddaughter donated it to the Italian state. The loveliest rooms are the red hall in Louis XVI style, the smoking room with leather-lined walls and the ballroom with its large mirrors and magnificent chandeliers. Villa Pignatelli is used for temporary exhibitions, concerts and other cultural events. A small building nearby is occupied by the **Museo delle Carrozze** (Carriage Museum), which has an interesting collection of 34 Italian, English and French coaches dating from the late 1800s to the early 1900s.

The façade of Santa Maria in Portico

Presbytery and apse of Santa Maria in Portico

Santa Maria in Portico **8**

Via Santa Maria in Portico 17.
Map 6 D2. **Tel** 081 76 92 94. C12,
C18, R3, R7, 140, 152. Amedeo.
Chiaia: Parco Margherita. 9–
11:30am, 5:30–8pm daily.

In 1632 the Duchess of Gravina Felice Maria Orsini donated some of her property to the Padri Lucchesi della Madre di Dio congregation so they could build a monastery and church. The name "in Portico" refers to the Roman church of Santa Maria in Campitelli al Portico d'Ottavia, where the Lucca Fathers came from. For years the façade in piperno was attributed to Cosimo Fanzago, but is now known to be the work of Arcangelo Guglielminelli. The interior is decorated with fine 18th-century canvases and stuccoes by Domenico Antonio Vaccaro, who also designed the high altar. There is a crib with 17th-century figures in the sacristy. A short walk down nearby Via Piscicelli takes you to the **Chiesa dell'Ascensione a Chiaia**, with fine paintings by Luca Giordano. The 14th-century church was rebuilt in the 1600s by Cosimo Fanzago.

Santa Maria di Piedigrotta **9**

Piazza Piedigrotta 24. **Map** 5 B3.
Tel 081 66 97 61. C4, C16.
Mergellina. 7:30am–noon,
5–8pm daily.

This church is mentioned in a letter written by Giovanni Boccaccio in Neapolitan dialect in 1339, in which he mentions the "Madonna de Pederotta". Much altered over the years, Santa Maria di Piedigrotta is commonly believed to have been built in 1353 to replace a church founded by fishermen in Mergellina. In the mid-1500s, it was rebuilt again, and this time the orientation of the church, which had faced a cave (*grotta*), was altered so that it would face the city. The present façade is the

Fresco by Belisario Corenzio in Santa Maria di Piedigrotta

result of 19th-century restoration by Enrico Alvino. Gaetano Gigante decorated the vault. Inside is the 15th-century wooden panel *Descent from the Cross*, by an unknown Neapolitan artist.

The church's great popularity is linked to a beautiful 14th-century wooden sculpture of the *Madonna and Child*, made by the Siena School, which dominates the church from a high tabernacle. The worship of the Piedigrotta Madonna culminates in the 7 September feast (see p42). In the past, even the royal family took part in the solemn procession. Worshippers, however, did not appreciate the statue's restoration in 1976 to its original state, because the Virgin's large blue mantle and luminous halo were removed.

Parco Vergiliano ❿

Via Salita Grotta 20. **Map** 5 A2.
🚌 C4, C16. Ⓜ Mergellina.
🕐 9am–1 hr before sunset.

View of the Parco Vergiliano

Myth, legend, traces of the past and natural beauty are what make this park one of Naples's most intriguing sites. It officially became a park after restoration work in 1930. In 1939 a monument to the poet Giacomo Leopardi *(see p36)* was erected, and his remains were transferred here from Recanati, his home town in the Marche.

The park is famous mostly because, according to legend, the poet Virgil is buried here. However, the so-called Tomb of Virgil is in fact an anonymous Roman funerary monument and has nothing to do with the great poet.

Another legend involving Virgil is that with a single gesture he created the *Crypta Neapolitana*, a tunnel about 700 m (2,300 ft) long; but this too is belied by historical facts: it was built by the Roman architect Cocceius in the 1st century BC to connect Neapolis and Puteoli. In the 1920s the tunnel caved in and is now inaccessible. The entrance, however, with its medieval frescoes and epigraphs, can still be seen from the park.

Mergellina ⓫

Map 5 B4. 🚌 C4, C16, C21, R3.
🚇 Mergellina.

The fishermen's quarter that developed over the inlet at the foot of Posillipo hill, and was hailed by poets and writers for its beauty, was a popular place for pleasure trips from the Angevin age onwards. The harmony of the landscape was broken by 19th-century land reclamation that extended the coastline further into the sea. However, Mergellina is still an enjoyable place for a leisurely stroll. The numerous cafés, called *chalet* by the locals, offer excellent ice cream and fresh fruit.

St Michael and the "Mergellina devil"

Santa Maria del Parto ⓬

Via Mergellina 96. **Map** 5 B4.
Tel 081 66 46 27. 🚌 C4, C16, C21, R3. 🚇 Mergellina. 🕐 8–10am Mon–Sat, 9am–1pm, 4:30–8pm Sun. 🔲

The history of the church of Santa Maria del Parto is closely linked with the figure and works of Jacopo Sannazaro (1458–1530), the famous Neapolitan humanist and poet in the service of the Angevin court. The church was built in the 1520s, upon the initiative of Sannazaro, on a plot of land donated by Frederick of Aragon and was named after one of the poet's works, *De Partu Virginis*. Behind the high altar is the tomb of the poet himself, a fine marble group sculpted by Giovan Angelo Montorsoli and Francesco del Tadda in 1537, and probably designed by Sannazaro himself. Before leaving, don't forget to look at the "Mergellina devil" depicted in a wooden panel by Leonardo da Pistoia on the right-hand altar. The panel shows St Michael, who has just vanquished the devil – the devil has assumed the guise of a beautiful woman.

The small harbour of Mergellina, filled with fishing boats and pleasure craft

TWO GUIDED WALKS

Naples is a city of contradictions: on the one side there are narrow, labyrinthine streets in the historic centre, full of revving scooters and the pungent aroma from fish stores; on the other there are wide avenues lined with chic shops, frequented by bejewelled ladies in fur coats. These two walks explore both sides of Neapolitan life. The first moves from the military district of Pizzofalcone to the elegant shopping streets of the Chiaia region, offering a complete change of atmosphere with just the short ride down the Ponte di Chiaia lift. The second walk takes you from the Fascist-era

Scroll decoration on the Nunziatella façade

buildings of Piazza Matteotti, and then through the Montesanto district and the bustling Pignasecca market with its wide variety of food and clothing stalls crammed in between rows of discount houseware shops and *tripperie* (tripe shops). Day-to-day life is on constant display here – mothers and babies, hawkers and shoppers all mingle on the streets together. Montesanto also skirts a claustrophobic but characteristic grid of tiny streets you might wish to venture into for a true experience of local life, complete with wafting cooking odours and rows of laundry flapping from balconies in the breeze.

CHOOSING A WALK

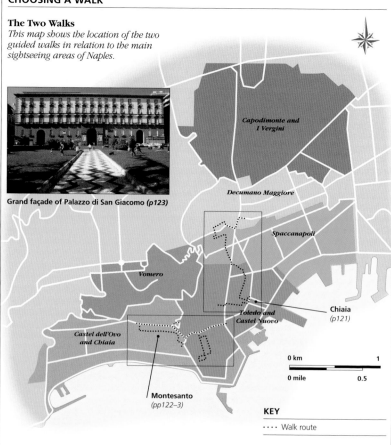

The Two Walks
This map shows the location of the two guided walks in relation to the main sightseeing areas of Naples.

Grand façade of Palazzo di San Giacomo (p123)

Capodimonte and I Vergini

Decumano Maggiore

Spaccanapoli

Vomero

Toledo and Castel Nuovo

Chiaia (p121)

Castel dell'Ovo and Chiaia

Montesanto (pp122–3)

0 km   1

0 mile   0.5

KEY

···· Walk route

A 45-Minute Walk through Chiaia

This walk balances hidden architectural gems with elegant window shopping as it winds its way through one of Naples' most glamorous neighbourhoods.

Baroque Naples

Start at Piazza Trieste e Trento ① and head west on Via Chiaia to the lift under the 17th-century Ponte di Chiaia ② *(see p58)*. Take the lift up to Piazza Santa Maria degli Angeli for the church of the same name ③ *(see p58)*. This Baroque church was erected by Francesco Grimaldi in the early 17th century and boasts frescoes by Beinaschi. Head south on Via Monte di Dio and pop into the Palazzo Serra di Cassano ④ *(see p58)*, today the home of the Italian Institute of Philosophical Studies and an example of one of Naples' many hidden architectural treasures, particularly its spectacular staircase. At the end of Via Monte di Dio, turn a short right for the Nunziatella ⑤ *(see p59)*, Italy's famous military academy. Founded in 1787 by Ferdinand IV, the Nunziatella takes its name from the nearby Annunziata, a Baroque church noted for its frescoes and paintings by Francesco de Mura as well as for its 17th-century crypts, the final resting places for the era's Neapolitan nobility.

Walk round the square until you are on back on Via Monte di Dio, turn right and then left onto Via Egiziaca a Pizzofalcone and left again on Via G. Serra, which will bring you back to the lift. Take the lift down again and continue

The double staircase in Palazzo Serra di Cassano, decorated with white marble ④

west on Via Chiaia. Follow the curve of Via Santa Caterina to the church of Santa Maria della Mercede ⑥, built in the 17th century by the Spanish Mercedari fathers. Turn right on Via Filangieri, a street full of chic

A view of Via Chiaia seen from the Ponte di Chiaia ②

painter Luca Giordano. Turn left onto Via Bausan, dotted with Spanish restaurants. Turn left onto Via Santa Teresa a Chiaia ⑪ for some window shopping at its high-class boutiques. Pass through Piazza Rodinò ⑫, then head up there to eat at the L.U.I.S.E snack bar on Piazza dei Martiri ⑬.

clothing stores. Gran Caffè Cimmino at No. 12 ⑦ is a good spot for refreshment.

Art and boutiques

Take the stairs on your right where Via Filangieri meets the elegant Via dei Mille, and walk up to Palazzo Cellamare ⑧ *(see p58)*, a Bourbon-era building once known for its royal revelries. Head back down to Via dei Mille and stroll past the Palazzo delle Arti Napoli, the contemporary art museum ⑨, to the church of Santa Teresa a Chiaia ⑩ with its two altarpieces by the Baroque

KEY

···· Walk route

Ⓜ Metro station

TIPS FOR WALKERS

Starting point: Piazza Trieste e Trento.

Length: 2 km (1 mile).

Getting there: C4, C82, E3, E5, E6, R1, R2 and R3 bus lines stop in front of Piazza Trieste e Trento.

Safety tips: Petty crime is a problem in Naples: leave valuables in your hotel safe and carry cash in a money belt.

0 metres   250
0 yards   250

A 90-Minute Walk through Montesanto

A visit to Naples would not be complete without a stroll through at least one of its fascinating open-air markets. This walk begins on the wide shopping street Via Toledo and winds its way past the imposing Fascist structures of Piazza Matteotti and through the Pignasecca in the Montesanto district. Though officially a *mercatino* (little market), the Pignasecca is a favourite among Neapolitans. In addition, several atmospheric churches here make for welcome havens from the jostling and haggling crowds.

Fish stall on Pignasecca ⑬

Renaissance to Fascism

Start the walk at the Funicolare Augusteo ①, then turn left onto Via Toledo (*see p53*) heading northwards. Turn right shortly afterwards onto Via Santa Brigida. The 17th-century church of Santa Brigida ② (*see p56*) will be ahead of you, attached to the north side of Galleria Umberto I (*see p53*). Its interior, particularly the paintings by Luca Giordano, is its real treasure. Beyond the church turn left, right and then left into Via Vittorio Emanuele III and up to Piazza Municipio (currently undergoing major work to build a new metro station). Turn right onto Via Cervantes, home to the Palazzo San Giacomo with its church of San Giacomo degli Spagnoli ③ (*see p56*), erected in 1540 by Viceroy Pedro of Toledo. The church was built in typical Mannerist style, and behind the main altar stands Giovanni da Nola's magnificent High Renaissance

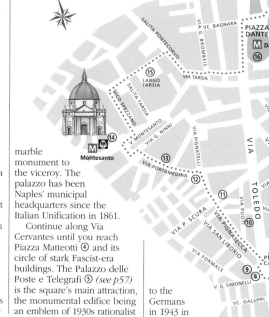

marble monument to the viceroy. The palazzo has been Naples' municipal headquarters since the Italian Unification in 1861.

Continue along Via Cervantes until you reach Piazza Matteotti ④ and its circle of stark Fascist-era buildings. The Palazzo delle Poste e Telegrafi ⑤ (*see p57*) is the square's main attraction, the monumental edifice being an emblem of 1930s rationalist architecture. Take Via C. Battisti to Piazza Carità (currently undergoing major work to build a new metro station) and the Istituto Nazionale Assicurazioni ⑥, erected in 1938. In front of the building stands the monument to Salvo d'Acquisto ⑦, the one-time Vice Brigadier of the *carabinieri* (the military arm of the Italian police) and a noted World War II hero. Born in Naples in 1920, d'Acquisto sacrificed himself

Nave of San Giacomo ③

to the Germans in 1943 in order to save the lives of 22 innocent Italians who were falsely accused of setting off a bomb that killed two German soldiers.

Art and Architecture

Across Via Toledo, still in Piazza Carità but along Via San Liborio, there are two striking 18th-century buildings, the Palazzo Mastelloni ⑧, with its fine staircase, and Palazzo Trabucco ⑨, both built by Nicolò

Imposing Piazza Dante, a popular meeting place ⑯

TIPS FOR WALKERS

Starting point: Funicolare Centrale (Augusteo station).
Length: 3 km (2 miles).
Best time for walk: Start the walk in the morning when all the churches and markets are open.

Tagliacozzi Canale, one of the three architects to renovate the beautiful Certosa of San Martino in Vomero *(see pp108–11)*. Continue north on Via Toledo until you reach the church of San Nicolà alla Carità ⑩. The highlight here is the nave that features an enormous landscape painted over two centuries by several Neapolitan artists including Francesco Solimena and Alessio d'Elia.

Turn back and walk 100 steps or so to reach Via Pignasecca. This busy and lively street is a great place to watch animated locals haggle for goods.

Stop for tasty, mostly fried snacks at Florenzano ⑪, then continue to the bustling Pignasecca *mercatino* in Piazza Pignasecca ⑫. Take the left fork onto Via Portamedina. On the right is the Ospedale Pellegrini, the courtyard of which hides the church of

Wide thoroughfare of Via Toledo

SS Trinità dei Pellegrini ⑬, built in the 16th century for religious pilgrims. Via Portamedina ends at Piazza Montesanto where the church of Santa Maria di Montesanto ⑭ stands. From the church, follow Via Montesanto and turn left onto Vico Spezzano. Turn right and walk along to the Palazzo Spinelli di Tarsia ⑮, one of Naples' largest and finest noble

residential complexes, which now houses shops on the ground floor. It was built by the architect Domenico Antonio Vaccaro for the aristocratic Spinelli family in the 1700s. The Teatro Bracco is just across the street.

Lively piazzas
Head down Via Tarsia and turn left to Piazza Dante ⑯ *(see p85)*. This square has been pedestrianized and now serves as a general meeting point for students, a rest spot for elderly Neapolitans, and an unofficial football arena for the young. The entrance to the Convitto Nazionale di Napoli Vittorio Emanuele II ⑰ can be seen on the eastern side of the square. The colonnade was designed by the architect Luigi Vanvitelli and now marks the western side of a boarding school.

Follow the road round to the right to Port'Alba and spend an hour or so at this pedestrianized lane lined with bookshops and outdoor book stalls. At the end of this street is Antica Pizzeria Port'Alba ⑱, said to be the restaurant where pizza was invented in the 18th century. The walk ends at Piazza Bellini ⑲ *(see p78)*, an ideal spot for a refreshing apéritif.

Impressive double staircase of Palazzo Mastelloni ⑧

PIAZZA MATTEOTTI
DIAZ
VIA CERVANTES DE SAAVEDRA
VIA MEDINA
VIA S. BARTOLOMEO
PIAZZA MUNICIPIO
VIA G.
VIA S. CARLO
VERDI
V. VITTORIO EMANUELE III

0 metres   200
0 yards   200

KEY

···· Walk route

Ⓜ Metro station

🚠 Funicular

TWO TRIPS AROUND POSILLIPO

The peninsula that juts into the sea, separating the Bay of Naples from Pozzuoli, was called *Pausilypon* ("respite from pain") by the ancient Greeks, because of the great beauty of the site. As can be seen by the many ruins along the coast, in Roman times a huge settlement grew up along the westernmost edge of what is now called Posillipo, and was connected to the neighbouring Phlegraean Fields *(see pp136–9)*. Posillipo was occupied by religious communities and suburban villages during the Middle Ages, and became the favourite holiday resort of the Spanish aristocracy in the 17th century, when luxurious seaside villas

Sant'Antonio campanile

and aristocratic palaces were built here. In the following century, the area began to decline, and it was only in the early 19th century that it regained its former popularity. This was partly as a result of improved access, thanks to the coastal road opened in 1812 by Joachim Murat, ruler of Naples from 1806 to 1815. However, from the 1950s on (during the era when Achille Lauro, *see pp28–9*, was mayor of Naples), the upper part of the hill between Via Orazio, Via Petrarca and Via Manzoni was overtaken by unregulated, unscrupulous property development that has sadly ruined an area of unsurpassed scenic and historic beauty.

GETTING AROUND

The best way to take in the fascination and beauty of the Posillipo coast is by boat; however, excursions can only be made in the summer (for information: **Ascultur Campania**, Via F Galiani 20, **Tel** 081 665 532). Otherwise take bus 140 down Via Posillipo and Via Santo Strato and then walk towards the sea along Via Ferdinando Russo and Via Marechiaro.

SIGHTS AT A GLANCE

Capo Posillipo ③
Grotto di Seiano/Pausylipon ⑦
Marechiaro ④
Palazzo Donn'Anna ①
Parco di Posillipo ⑥
Santa Maria del Faro ⑤
World War I Memorial ②

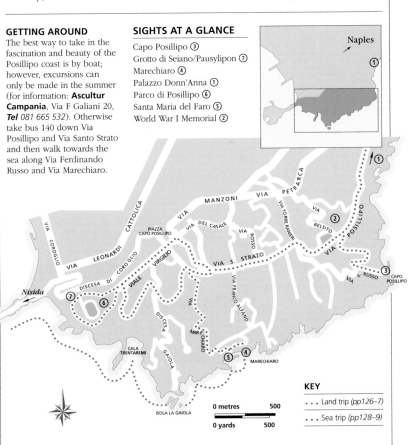

KEY

· · · Land trip *(pp126–7)*

· · · Sea trip *(pp128–9)*

0 metres　　500
0 yards　　500

Naples

Nisida

ISOLA LA GAIOLA

CALA TRENTAREMI

MARECHIARO

CAPO POSILLIPO

◁ **View of the rocky Posillipo coastline**

Posillipo by Land

If you decide to explore Posillipo by land, bear in mind that the complete itinerary shown here would make a very long walk. The best way to get around is, in the following order, by scooter, taxi (you are advised to agree on the fare beforehand), Citysightseeing Napoli tour bus *(see p224)*, bus (routes 140, C27 and C31) or, least popular because of traffic and parking problems, a rented car. Many of the old villas, which are now privately owned, are hidden from view and only a few of them can be seen from the road. However, the views are stupendous and the routes down to Capo Posillipo and Marechiaro, though demanding, are very rewarding.

Palazzo Donn'Anna ①

Palazzo Donn'Anna on the seafront

In 1637 the Spanish viceroy Ramiro Guzman, Duke of Medina, married the Neapolitan princess Anna Carafa. To celebrate, Don Ramiro asked the architect Cosimo Fanzago to build the large Palazzo Donn'Anna at the water's edge. Construction began in 1642, but the building was never completed and was never used by the couple. The viceroy returned to Spain in 1644 and Donn'Anna died soon after.

The palazzo was damaged during the 1647 uprising and again as a result of the 1688 earthquake. It was partly restored in the early 1700s but decades later it was still being described in tourist guides as a building in a state of total neglect.

Its air of mystery gave rise to the rumour that in its past the palace had been used by Queen Joan II for secret assignations with her lovers. Popular belief has it that after these men had served their purpose, they were thrown into the sea below the palace. Palazzo Donn'Anna suffered further damage in the early 19th century when part of the façade was demolished to build the Via Posillipo. In 1870 attempts were made to turn it into a hotel, but the idea was abandoned.

Despite its tormented history and the damage wrought by time and neglect, the massive tufa palace with its cavernous vaults is still majestic, and one of the city's celebrated sights.

World War I Memorial ②

From Piazza San Luigi it is clear to see how property development has spoilt the view of the hill. Beyond the piazza stands the Ara Votiva, or War Memorial, situated in a small park. The middle of the park is dominated by the large Egyptian-style mausoleum that Matteo Schilizzi began building in 1883 as a tomb for his brother Marco. This impressive monument was purchased and finished in 1923 by the Naples city council, in order to house the remains of soldiers who had died in World War I.

Capo Posillipo ③

After Piazza Salvatore di Giacomo, a square with a small garden in the middle, go down Via Ferdinando Russo towards the bay of Capo Posillipo and Villa Volpicelli. The villa, first built in the 17th century, was rebuilt in the 19th century by Raffaele Volpicelli and gives the impression of a castle floating on the sea.

The Neapolitans call the area around the Villa Volpicelli the Riva Fiorita, or flowered shore. In the summer months, the little harbour, the beach and the cliff area opposite hum with life. Cafés and restaurants lend atmosphere to this area at all times of the year. To reach the fishing village of Marechiaro, take the road that curves down to the left.

The 17th-century Villa Volpicelli, built on the water's edge

For hotels and restaurants in this area see p181 and p195

The Bay of Naples viewed from Posillipo in a 1920s photograph

Marechiaro ④

A famous song by the Neapolitan artist Salvatore di Giacomo says that this coastline is so romantic, even the fish make love in the moonlight. Going down Via Marechiaro by day, you will see elegant villas surrounded by greenery and beautiful panoramic views of the countryside.

Towards the sea is a small square with the remains of a Roman column from the so-called Temple of Fortune. Further down, in the pretty fishing village of Marechiaro, there are bars, cafés, restaurants and bathing facilities.

Santa Maria del Faro ⑤

This church, recorded in documents as far back as the 1300s, was probably built over the remains of an ancient Roman lighthouse (*faro* in Italian). It was restored by Sanfelice in the 18th century, but the façade dates from the 19th century. From here you can walk down the Calata del Ponticello, which brings you close to the sea.

Parco di Posillipo ⑥

After going back up Via Marechiaro along Via Boccaccio, you will arrive at the beautiful Parco di Posillipo, also known

as Parco Virgiliano or Parco della Rimembranza. It occupies the top of the hill overlooking the sea and offers a spectacular view from the Bay of Naples to Mount Vesuvius and the Sorrento peninsula on one side, and the Bay of Pozzuoli and the Phlegraean Fields on the other. Below are the island of Nisida, formed from an ancient volcanic crater, and the remains of the now-restored ILVA steelworks (*see pp26–7*). At sunset, the views towards Ischia are stunning.

Grotto di Seiano and Pausylipon ⑦

In Roman times, a 770-m (0.5-mile) long grotto allowed access to a vast villa, perched high on a cliff. Known as *Pausylipon* ("respite from pain"), the villa included an amphitheatre and a kitchen decorated with marble. The Bourbon kings discovered the ruins in the 1700s and fixed the tunnel to make it structurally sound again. Visits are by appointment only (call 081 575 44 65).

THE VILLAS OF POSILLIPO

The northern stretch of Via Posillipo is dominated by **Villa Doria D'Angri**, built in 1833 by Bartolomeo Grasso for Prince D'Angri and now the Istituto Santa Dorotea. Further down, on the seaward side, is 17th-century **Villa Quercia**, painted a typically

Villa Rosebery, now state property

Pompeiian red. A hunting lodge built by the Duke of Frisio in the 1700s was bought at the end of the 19th century by Count **Pavoncelli**, who gave the villa at No. 43 his name. **Villa Grottamarina** (No. 33) was the home of Maria Anna, sister of King Philip IV of Spain, in the 1630s. The French engineer Alfredo Cottreau built the **Villa Cottreau** (No. 35) in the late 1800s; several wings on different levels descend towards the sea. Pompeiian red is again the colour of the **Villa Bracale** (No. 37), whose original 17th-century structure is almost unrecognizable today. The pagoda-shaped **Villa Roccaromana** (No. 38a) was built in 1814 for Prince Caracciolo. **Villa d'Abro** (No. 46) was named after the nobleman Aslan d'Abro, who bought it in 1870 and had it

restored in Neo-Romantic style. Beyond Capo Posillipo is **Villa Rosebery** (No. 26 Via Russo), the Neapolitan residence of the President of the Italian Republic. It was here, on 9 May 1946, that King Vittorio Emanuele II abdicated and the crown passed to his son Umberto. At No. 27 Via Russo is the 17th-century **Villa Emma**, the summer residence of the German painter Jakob Philipp Hackert who depicted the excavations of Pompeii. Fringed palms give a tropical feel to the **Villa Gallotta**, built close to the water's edge.

Villa Gallotta

Viewing Posillipo from the Sea

**Neapolitan
gozzo boat**

From the sea, Naples and the bay can be viewed in all their splendour. To the west of the city, from Castel dell'Ovo north to Nisida and beyond, as far as the Phlegraean Fields, the coast is dotted with grottoes and inlets. Beyond Capo Posillipo you can see the fishing village of Marechiaro, Roman ruins, and the small islands of Gaiola and Nisida. Bars and bathing beaches lure visitors here in summer. In winter the dramatic coastline can still be admired from a hydrofoil or ferry on an excursion to Procida and Ischia *(see pp170–73)*.

Cala di Trentaremi
The tufa cliffs of Cala di Trentaremi are reflected in the sea, which gleams blue and green. This cove is particularly sheltered and is a favourite with bathers.

Nisida
The ancients called this place Nesis, or little island. It was here that Brutus and Cassius, in the former's villa, plotted to kill Caesar in 44 BC. The Angevin building that dominates the island became a prison under the Bourbons.

← Nisida

Punta
Pennata

Harbour
of Gaiola

Gaiola
The presence of ruined ancient buildings between the tufa island of Gaiola and the village of Marechiaro has led scholars to suggest that a complete Roman city once existed here.

Posillipo Park
A well-equipped sports centre is one of the attractions in the park of Posillipo, on the Coroglio summit.

Marechiaro

The original name for the water by this fishing village was Mare planum (calm sea), which was translated literally in Italian as "Marepiano". With usage it became "Marechiaro", the name now used for the area as a whole. At weekends Neapolitans love to come and eat out here (see p195).

Marinella Beach, with its parks and lido, is one of the area's most popular resorts.

Church of Santa Maria del Faro

DIRECTORY

Bagno Elena
Via Posillipo 14.
Tel 081 575 50 58.
www.bagnoelena.it

Bagno Marechiaro
Calata Ponticello di Marechiaro
31. *Tel 081 769 12 15.*
www.lidomarechiaro.it

Villa Fattorusso
Via Posillipo 68. *Tel 081 240 30 17.* **www**.donsalvatore.it

Villa Imperiale
Via Marechiaro 90.
Tel 081 575 43 44.
www.villaimperiale.eu

Palazzo degli Spiriti

The remains of the "palace of the spirits" are visible only from the sea. This name was given to the three-storey Roman ruins because of their mysterious appearance.

SWIMMING AND RELAXING

If sightseeing in Naples in midsummer becomes too much, take a break at one of the *stabilimenti balneari* (bathing spots) along the Posillipo coast. Rent a deck-chair and an umbrella and swim in the sea or the pool provided. Neapolitans started the habit in the 19th century at the **Bagno Elena**, first opened 150 years ago. For those who prefer cliffs to sand, there is the **Villa Fattorusso**, with two seawater pools; **Bagno Marechiaro**, with its restaurant overlooking the waters of the bay; and the elegant **Villa Imperiale**.

The rocks at Posillipo

The picturesque village of Atrani, Amalfi Coast ▷

POMPEII & THE AMALFI COAST

POMPEII & THE AMALFI COAST

To the north of Naples, fertile plains sweep down to the town of Santa Maria Capua Vetere, home to one of the largest remaining Roman amphitheatres in Italy. The remote hinterland to the east is wild, mountainous and lonely country. To the south is the breathtaking Amalfi coast and the dramatic seaboard of the Cilento. Buried Roman towns and Greek ruins reveal the region's ancient history.

From the 17th century onwards Naples was an increasingly crowded and often tormented metropolis. By contrast, the countryside around the city managed to retain its charm and attracted visitors, especially foreigners, many of whom made Campania their home. "A brief sojourn in Naples", the German historian Gregorovius wrote in the mid-1800s, "is enough to demonstrate that not all life is concentrated in the city but flows mightily into the surroundings".

Today, a visit to Pompeii, buried by an erupting Vesuvius in AD 79, is a high priority for tourists, but this was not always so. Travellers on the Grand Tour in the 1600s and early 1700s preferred the volcanic phenomena of the Solfatara crater and the Phlegraean Fields to the west of Naples. Even in the late 18th century Goethe described the area around Paestum, southeast of Naples, as "anything but picturesque", populated by "buffaloes that look like hippopotami, with wild, bloodshot eyes". Only when the first archaeological digs unearthed the remains of Paestum and the buried cities around Mount Vesuvius, did a tour of the ancient ruins become popular.

The beautiful colour, light and atmosphere found on the islands of Capri and Ischia, and the Sorrento peninsula began to interest landscape painters in the 19th century. The southern flank of the peninsula – the Amalfi coast – remained isolated, and regarded by many as barren, until the mid-1960s, when it attracted visitors in search of an alternative, remote lifestyle. Ironically, the Amalfi coast has since become a very popular holiday area.

Paestum, south of Naples; in the background are the temples of Neptune and Hera

◁ The fishing harbour of Corricella on the island of Procida

Exploring the Coast

The main centre from which to explore Campania is Naples itself, well situated in the middle of the bay. Road and rail links are generally good in the region, with both state railways (FS) and privately run lines serving a variety of destinations. The Circumvesuviana railway connects all the sights in the area of Vesuvius, including Pompeii. The islands in the bay are accessible by hydrofoil (half an hour) or ferry (one hour) from Mergellina and Beverello. Services also run from Sorrento, Positano, Amalfi and Salerno.

Castello Aragonese in Ischia

SIGHTS AT A GLANCE

The Amalfi Coast ⑭
Bagnoli ❶
Baia and Bacoli ❸
Capri ⑰
Caserta ⑯
Cumae ❹
Herculaneum ❾
Ischia ⑱
Paestum ⑮
Pompeii ❿
Portici and the
   Vesuvian Villas ❺
Pozzuoli ❷
Procida ⑲
Sorrento ⑫
The Sorrento Peninsula ⑪
Torre Annunziata ❻
Torre del Greco ❼
Vesuvius ❽

Tours

Along the Sorrento Coast ⑬

KEY

═══	Motorway
═══	Major road
──	Secondary road
⋯⋯	Minor road
──	Scenic road
┅┅	Main railway
──	Minor railway
△	Summit

0 kilometres   20

0 miles   20

SEE ALSO

• **Where to Stay** pp181–7

• **Where to Eat** pp195–201

• **Shopping in Campania** pp208–9

View of the Phlegraean Fields at Cumae

The impressive façade of the Royal Palace at Caserta

The Solfatara at Pozzuoli

GETTING AROUND

You can easily reach the area of the Phlegraean Fields at Pozzuoli using the Cumana railway; the metro also goes to Pozzuoli. The Circumvesuviana railway connects Naples with Pompeii, Herculaneum and other towns below Vesuvius and continues on to the Sorrento peninsula. FS (Ferrovie dello Stato) trains take you to Caserta, Paestum and Pompeii. SITA coaches go to the Amalfi coast. All the islands can be reached by ferry or hydrofoil from the port of Naples, while ferries from Pozzuoli go to Ischia and Procida, and from Sorrento they leave for Capri. In summer, boats go to the Amalfi coast towns, and from Amalfi and Positano to the islands. See also pp226–7.

The village of Positano perched on the Amalfi coast

Bagnoli ●

Road map C3. 🚌 *C1, R7.*
Ⓜ *Bagnoli.* 🚆 *Cumana: Bagnoli.*

The area west of Naples, beyond Posillipo, is called "de' Bagnoli" because of the fumaroles and hot springs there. In 1907 the ILVA steelworks was built here *(see pp26–7)*, blighting a beautiful natural setting. The factory has since been closed down. Today part of the site is taken up with the **Città della Scienza** (Science City), first opened in 1996. A series of itineraries features education through games involving science, aimed at both children and adults.

🏛 **Città della Scienza**
Via Coroglio 104. **Tel** 081 242 00 24. ⭘ 9am–5pm Tue–Sat, 10am–7pm Sun. 🈺 📷
🎫 ♿ www.cittadella scienza.it

Pozzuoli ●

Road Map B3. 🏛
77,000. 🛈 *Azienda Autonoma di Soggiorno e Turismo, Via Campi Flegrei 3.* **Tel** 081 526 66 39.
Ⓜ *Pozzuoli.* 🚆 *Cumana: Pozzuoli.*
⛴ *to Ischia & Procida.*
www.infocampiflegrei.it

The *macellum* at Pozzuoli, commonly known as the Temple of Serapis

The amphitheatre stage entrance

Around the 7th century BC, the Greek colony of Dicearchia was founded on this site overlooking the port. By 194 BC Roman Puteoli was a flourishing trade centre with luxurious villas. The town later became the Rione Terra quarter. It was evacuated in 1970 due to the effects of movement in the earth's crust. Attempts to keep the area open have failed due to a lack of money. A Roman temple can still be seen under the San Procolo cathedral. The amphitheatre, one of Italy's most ancient, shows how important the city once was.

🏛 **Anfiteatro Flavio**
Via Terracciano 75. **Tel** 081 526 60 07. ⭘ 9am–1 hr before sunset Wed–Mon. 🈺

The amphitheatre had a seating capacity of 40,000. The underground area was used for the caged animals and the equipment to lift them up to the arena, as well as a sophisticated drainage system to collect rainwater.

🏛 **Temple of Serapis**
Piazza Serapide.

The so-called Temple of Serapis (2nd century AD), actually the *macellum* or food

The Anfiteatro Flavio at Pozzuoli, with three tiers of seats

The Solfatara in Pozzuoli, known as *Forum Vulcani* in ancient times

market, is all that remains of the ancient port district.

🔥 Solfatara

Via Solfatara 161. **Tel** *081 526 23 41/74 13.* ◯ *8:30am–7pm daily.*
◫ ▣ 🏠 www.solfatara.it

A dormant volcano, the Solfatara features a mud lake bubbling at 160° Celsius (320° Fahrenheit) and two fumaroles belching sulphur fumes. Vulcan, the Roman god of fire, was thought to have his workshop here, and the Solfatara is also believed to have been the inspiration for Virgil's description of the underworld in *The Aeneid*. The Romans, whose ruins dot the western side of the area, harnessed the therapeutic waters and created mineral baths. Hi-tech equipment installed within the volcano tracks the movements of the earth's crust.

Baia and Bacoli ❸

Road Map B3. 🏙 *27,000.*
▣ *Cumana: Baia, Bacoli.*

Along the coast between Pozzuoli and Capo Miseno there are many places that were well known in antiquity. Baia boasted sumptuous Roman villas with terraces overlooking the sea, famous therapeutic springs (still in use in the Middle Ages) and an Aragonese castle, now an archaeological museum.

Bacoli lies along the coast and runs into the modern town of Miseno, which developed over the site of the Roman town of Bauli. At the time of the Emperor Augustus, the port of Miseno was connected to Lake Miseno in the interior. The port was planned so as

The Bath of Mercury at Baia

to avoid silting from volcanic movement, and replaced Porto Giulio *(see p139)*, the headquarters of the Roman navy. The Arco Felice, which in the 1st century AD was the gateway to Cumae *(see pp138–9)*, stands on the peninsula protecting the Bay of Pozzuoli.

Beaches and clubs make this area a summer favourite.

🏛 Casino Vanvitelliano del Fusaro

Via Fusaro 162, Baia. **Tel** *081 868 19 57.* ▣ *Cumana: Baia.* ◯ *summer: 4–7pm Sat, 10am–1pm, 4–7pm Sun.*
www.parcovanvitelliano.it

In 1794 Vanvitelli built a Casino or hunting lodge on an island in Lake Fusaro for Ferdinand IV. This is the only non-volcanic lake in the area.

🗝 Parco Archeologico di Baia

Via delle Terme Romane 37, Baia. **Tel** *081 868 75 92.* ▣ *Cumana: Baia.* ◯ *9am–7pm Tue–Sun.* ◫

The large domes at this site are the remains of a spa that included baths named after Venus and Mercury and the so-called Temple of Diana.

This monumental complex was built from the late 2nd century–early 1st century BC, on two levels, with terraced land descending to the sea. Some of the park lies under water, but guided dives are organized *(see p215)*.

The site is now used to exhibit excavation finds from the Phlegraean Fields area.

🏛 Museo Archeologico dei Campi Flegrei

Via Castello 39, Baia. **Tel** *081 523 37 97.* ▣ *Cumana: Baia.* ◯ *9am– 1 hr before sunset Tue–Sun (May– Sep: to 7pm).* ◫

The Castello di Baia was once an Aragonese fortress. It was totally rebuilt in the 1600s.

View of the city of Baia; in the foreground, the Roman ruins

Hall in the Museo Archeologico

It is now an Archaeological Museum, with finds from the Phlegraean Fields *(Campi Flegrei)*. Also on display are the Roman plaster casts of Greek statues found in Baia. From the northwest tower you can see the reconstructed Sacello degli Augustali, used for worship of the emperor, found near the Forum at Miseno. The zone is now partly under water.

Piscina Mirabilis
Via Piscina Mirabile, Bacoli. **Tel** 081 523 31 99. ◯ daily, by appointment. 🏛 donation.

This enormous reservoir, divided into five longitudinal sections supported by pillars, collected water brought by Roman aqueduct from the River Serino, then supplied to the fleet stationed at Miseno.

Capo Miseno
A windy, narrow stretch of road leads through a dark tunnel to the dramatic peak of Capo Miseno. Pliny the Younger watched the eruption of Vesuvius from this hill. This is also where the Roman Imperial Navy had its headquarters. You can park here and hike up a trail leading to stunning views of Naples.

The *Piscina Mirabilis* at Bacoli

Cumae ❹

Road map B3. 🚉 *Cumana: Fusaro.* 🚌 *from Fusaro (10 mins to Cumae).*

Founded in the 8th century BC, probably by Greeks stationed on Ischia, Cumae is one of the oldest colonies of Magna Graecia. A powerful port for centuries, Cumae resisted the Etruscans but succumbed to the Romans in the 3rd century BC and became a Roman colony. A village grew up over the ruins of the upper city in the 5th–6th centuries but was utterly destroyed by the Saracens in 915. The ancient settlement has not yet been completely excavated.

The tufa corridor in the Sibyl's Cave

The best-known areas are the acropolis on the rise to the northwest and the necropolis in the plain. The acropolis walls, partly rebuilt, and two huge temples are well preserved. The Temple of Apollo lies on the lower terrace, the Temple of Jupiter on the upper one; both were rebuilt in the age of Augustus and the pre-Christian era. At the foot of the acropolis is the entrance to the so-called Sibyl's Cave.

The lower city, inhabited at a later period, is still being excavated and studied. There is a forum, various baths and an amphitheatre. There are also remains of different epochs: the Samnite age forum conceals the more ancient *agora*, or Greek city centre. A sanctuary dedicated to Isis,

ARCHAEOLOGICAL PARK

Acropolis

Temple of Jupiter

destroyed with the rise of Christianity, has also been discovered in the port area.

Archaeological Park
Via Acropoli. **Tel** 081 854 30 60. ◯ 9am–1 hr before sunset.

Temple of Apollo
Most of the finds from the Temple of Apollo date from the Roman era, when a terrace overlooking the city was added on. In the early Christian period the temple was turned into a basilica and burial pits were hewn out of the ancient foundations.

Sibyl's Cave
According to myth, this was where to find the Cumaean Sibyl, the oracle consulted by Aeneas. The tufa passageway, trapezoid in section, is illuminated by narrow

View of the Archaeological Park, the site of the excavations revealing ancient Cumae

Lake Averno

⋒ Temple of Jupiter

This ancient sanctuary became an early Christian church and remains of the altar and baptistry are still visible today.

⋒ Roman Crypt

The part visible is the last stretch of a long tunnel that begins at Via Sacra and goes through the hill of Cumae.

THE PHLEGRAEAN LAKES

The wide arc of land around the bay of Pozzuoli has been known for centuries as the Campi Flegrei, or Burning Fields, because of the constant volcanic activity. Mud still bubbles from the clay bed of the Solfatara and in places the ground is still hot. Over time some of the Phlegraean craters have become lakes. **Lake Averno**, in ancient times thought to be the entrance to hell, owes its name (*a-ornon* in Greek: "without birds") to the once-suffocating vapours. At the end of the 1st century BC, its almost sacred character declined after the construction of Porto Giulio, a system of channels that connected the sea and the lakes. Ships first reached the outer port in **Lake Lucrino** and then the inner basin of Lake Averno, connected to Cumae by the tunnel through Monte Grillo. The port was abandoned when it silted up and trade was transferred to Miseno. Lake Lucrino again became a pleasure area. Its extent was greatly reduced by the 1538 eruption that created **Monte Nuovo**.

fissures and ends in a vaulted chamber. Despite its undoubted fascination, there is no proof of the tunnel ever having had a religious function. It seems more likely that the tunnel was part of a network of underground routes used for military purposes. The complex system includes the Roman crypt and the Grotto of Cocceius, which connected Cumae to Lake Averno.

Map labels:
- Roman crypt
- Temple of Apollo
- Necropolis
- Thermae
- Forum
- Arco Felice
- Sibyl's Cave
- Tomb of the Sibyl
- Amphitheatre
- To the station

0 metres — 500
0 yards — 500

Portici and the Vesuvian Villas ❺

Road Map C3. 🚶 68,000.
🚆 🚉 *Circumvesuviana: Via Libertà, Bellavista.* 🚌 *city buses.*
ℹ️ *Fondazione Ente Ville Vesuviane, Villa Campolieto, Corso Resina 283, Ercolano.* **Tel** *081 732 21 34.*
🕐 *10am–1pm Tue–Sun.*
www.villevesuviane.net

The coast east of the city, up to the foot of Mount Vesuvius, has always been dotted with rural estates, owned by the nobility but used for agriculture as much as rural retreats. The luxurious villas now known as the Ville Vesuviane were built in the early 1700s, when the value of land in the area rose because of the interest in local archaeological excavations. Prince d'Elboeuf, who discovered Herculaneum in 1709, built a villa here. A few decades later, after the building of the Royal Palace at Portici, these villas grew in number, and the road between Resina and Torre del Greco became known as the **Miglio d'Oro**, or Golden Mile. The presence of the Bourbon palace and the location of these villas, with fine views of, and often access to, the countryside and sea, made this area a favourite resort among the aristocracy. A port was built here in 1773.

There are 122 villas in all, but only a few can be visited. Some are well worth a stop, if only to see the decorations on the façade or the magnificent gardens that have survived massive urbanization.

🏛️ Reggia di Portici

Via Università 100, Portici. **Orto Botanico Tel** *081 775 51 36.* 🕐 *by appt.* **Herculanense Museum Tel** *081 580 83 90.* 🕐 *by appt.*
The Royal Palace *(reggia)* was built between 1738 and 1742 in the centre of a splendid park at the foothills of Vesuvius and overlooking the sea.

The Royal Palace in Portici

Two villas had previously occupied the site, and a road still crosses the large inner courtyard, continuing towards Herculaneum. On the site are botanical gardens and the Herculanense Museum, which houses copies of sculptures found in Herculaneum; the originals are in the museum at Capodimonte *(see p99).*
The palace did not have a mooring, so the sovereigns bought the Villa d'Elboeuf for this purpose. Designed by Ferdinando Sanfelice, the villa incorporates some splendid stucco-work and a magnificent circular staircase. The villa was separated from the sea by the Naples–Portici railway *(see p25)* in 1839.
In 1873, the Royal Palace and its park became the home of the Faculty of Agriculture of the University of Naples. Every March, it hosts an antiques fair.

🏛️ Villa Campolieto

Corso Resina 283, Ercolano.
Tel *081 732 21 34.*
🕐 *10am–1pm Tue–Sun.* 🎫
Built in 1755–75 first by Gioffredo and then by Vanvitelli, this is the only Vesuvian villa that has been completely restored. A monumental staircase links the ground floor and upper floor. Vanvitelli's elegant portico hosts the Festival delle Ville Vesuviane *(see p41)* each summer, and the villa sometimes stages events.

🏛️ Villa Favorita

Corso Resina 291, Ercolano.
🕐 *10am–1pm Tue–Sun (park only).*
This villa, set in an extensive park, was designed by Ferdinando Fuga in 1768 as a royal residence. Ferdinand IV decorated it with paintings, silk from San Leucio *(see p165)* and a mosaic removed from the Villa Jovis in Capri *(see p169).* His son Leopold supervised the layout of the stables and the park, which can be accessed from Via Gabriele D'Annunzio.

🏛️ Villa Ruggiero

Via Alessandro Rossi 40, Ercolano.
Tel *081 732 21 34.* 🕐 *10am–1pm Tue–Sun.*
Built in the first half of the 18th century, this villa has been owned by the Ruggiero family since 1863. It was occupied all year round, not just in the summer, as the rich agricultural land shows. The barn is now used for exhibitions.

Vanvitelli's curved portico in Villa Campolieto

Torre Annunziata ❻

Road Map D3. 🏛 51,000. 🛈 Pro Loco Ufficio Informazioni Turistiche: Via Sepolcri 16. **Tel** 081 862 31 63. 🚉 Circumvesuviana: Torre Annunziata.

The town was built over the ruins of ancient Oplontis, which was destroyed in the eruption of Vesuvius in AD 79. Its name derives from a watch-tower (torre) built to warn the populace of any imminent Saracen raids, and a chapel consecrated to the Annunziata (the Virgin Mary), around which the town grew up.

In the 18th century Charles III founded an arms factory here, designed by a pupil of Vanvitelli and finished by Ferdinand Fuga. In the late 1700s and early 1800s Torre Annunziata became a centre for pasta production. Towards the sea are the spas, Terme Vesuviane Nunziante, named after the general who discovered the ruins of a Roman baths complex here in 1831. He was responsible for the present-day structure, which is still in operation.

⋔ Oplontis Excavations

Via Sepolcri 1. **Tel** 081 857 53 47. ⌚ Apr–Oct: 8:30am–7:30pm daily (last adm 6pm); Nov–Mar: 8:30am–5pm daily (last adm 3:30pm). ● 1 Jan, 1 May, 25 Dec. 🎫

The excavation area includes the villas of Craxus and Poppaea (the latter was Nero's second wife). Brought to light in 1964, the complex reflects the elegant taste of its owners. As well as gardens and porticoes, the private baths of the house can also be seen, complete with *calidarium* (the hot room) and *tepidarium* (the warm room). Also interesting are the 1st century BC–1st century AD wall paintings. These depict still lifes or scenes combining architecture and figures, in some cases with illusionistic effects around the doorways or windows. Many amphoras were found in the rooms of the Villa of Craxus, which were used as storerooms or shops.

The harbour at Torre Annunziata

Torre del Greco ❼

Road Map C3. 🏛 104,000. 🛈 Via Procida 2a. **Tel** 081 881 46 76. 🚉 Circumvesuviana: Torre del Greco.

The name derives from a watch-tower built by Frederick II and from the vineyards which produce wine from a grape variety called Greco. Torre del Greco is mainly known for its fine coral manufacture. The old town, rebuilt several times after the various eruptions of Vesuvius, lines the coast, while the newer districts, with villas surrounded by gardens, lie on the slopes of the volcano itself. Don't miss Palazzo Vallelonga in Via Vittorio Emanuele and the Camaldoli alla Torre monastery, both 18th-century buildings. The poet Giacomo Leopardi lived in the Villa delle Ginestre (on a road crossing Via Nazionale) and wrote his last poems there, including *La Ginestra* (The Broom).

The imperial villa of Poppaea Sabina at Torre Annunziata

THE RED GOLD AT TORRE DEL GRECO

By the 15th century the main trade in Torre del Greco was coral fishing. Over the centuries the town became a collection point for coral, as other coastal towns followed suit. The first factories were established by foreigners during the course of the 1800s and the Bourbon rulers then set up their own. Local designs were at first inspired by classical models, and subsequently influenced by the Art Nouveau style. As well as coral, there are mother-of-pearl, turtle shell and ivory pieces. The *coralline* boats that went out to collect the coral have been modernized and re-equipped, but today most of the raw material comes from Japan. Admirers of red gold can visit the numerous workshops (see pp208–9) in town or the museum at No. 6 Piazza Palomba.

Carved piece of coral

Mount Vesuvius ⓫

Carbonized eggs from Pompeii

In ancient times Vesuvius was simply "the mountain", covered with vegetation and vines. The first person to understand its volcanic nature was the Greek geographer, Strabo (AD 19), who suggested that its rocks had been burned by fire. In AD 79 an almighty eruption smothered the cities on its foothills and greatly altered the surrounding landscape. Ash and debris showered Pompeii, and Herculaneum was buried by a landslide of thick mud. Pliny the Younger recorded the cloud of black smoke that rose "like an umbrella pine" from the mountain. His uncle, Pliny the Elder, was suffocated by the gaseous vapours that engulfed the area. Today, the volcano inspires both fear and fascination and it is constantly monitored for activity.

Layers of ash alternate with lava flow, settle on the sides of the volcano and gradually build up the cone.

Vineyards
The land around volcanoes, rich in alkali and phosphorus, is extremely fertile. On the slopes of Vesuvius, the grapes grown make Lacrima Christi, *once considered one of Italy's best wines.*

Layers of lava

HISTORY OF THE VOLCANO
These sections show the changes in the structure of Vesuvius following the most significant eruptions, from prehistoric times to the formation of the present-day cone.

First eruptions began 35,000 years ago

Further ash and lava flows built up a second cone

8th century BC: Monte Somma is a single cone

After AD 79: Monte Somma is an open caldera

Today's cone, Vesuvius, formed in the old caldera

Magma (molten rock from the earth's mantle) wells upwards and forms a reservoir beneath the earth's surface.

Vesuvius Observatory
The observatory on the slopes of Vesuvius was built by Ferdinand II in 1841–5. The Neo–Classical building has a well-stocked library and an interesting collection of minerals. There is a splendid panoramic view from the square. Today it is only used as a base for recording data; the research section has been transferred to Naples.

Volcanic Rocks

Rising magma sometimes brings fragments of solid rock from the earth's surface. These dense pieces of rock give geologists an insight into the composition of the earth's core.

Crater summit

Monte Somma is the ancient volcano crater; Vesuvius is inside.

Lava flows

GETTING THERE

Road Map D3. *Tel* 081 771 09 11. Naples–Salerno A3 motorway, Ercolano exit. Follow the signs "Vesuvio" for 13 km (8 miles) until the entrance. Proceed on foot for the crater (20 mins). **Vesuviana Mobilità** (081 963 44 20 / www.eavbus.it) leaves from Pompeii every hour (8am–2:30pm) and from Mergellina twice a day. **Busvia del Vesuvio** (www.busviadel vesuvio.com) runs daily tours (9:30am–3:30pm) from Pompeii. www.parconazionaledelvesuvio.it

Pressure forces the magma up through the main conduit.

The Cone of Mount Vesuvius

This impressive crater is an enormous cavity created by successive eruptions inside Monte Somma: it is 200 m (655 ft) deep and has a diameter of 600 m (1,970 ft).

The Funicular

The funicular dates from 1880. Two cars took visitors up to an altitude of 1180 m (3,870 ft) above sea level. After a series of accidents, however, the funicular was taken out of service in 1944.

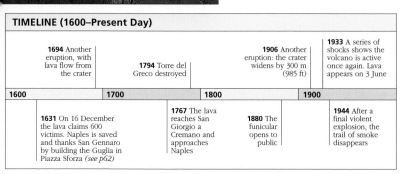

TIMELINE (1600–Present Day)

1694 Another eruption, with lava flow from the crater

1794 Torre del Greco destroyed

1906 Another eruption: the crater widens by 300 m (985 ft)

1933 A series of shocks shows the volcano is active once again. Lava appears on 3 June

1600 — 1700 — 1800 — 1900

1631 On 16 December the lava claims 600 victims. Naples is saved and thanks San Gennaro by building the Guglia in Piazza Sforza (*see p62*)

1767 The lava reaches San Giorgio a Cremano and approaches Naples

1880 The funicular opens to public

1944 After a final violent explosion, the trail of smoke disappears

Herculaneum ❾

Silver disc of Apollo

Ancient Herakleion fell under Greek influence around the 5th century BC and then under Samnite rule. In 89 BC the town became part of the Roman Empire, a residential *municipium* and resort. The town's quiet existence was brought to an abrupt halt in AD 79, when the eruption of Vesuvius that buried Pompeii covered Herculaneum with a deep layer of lava and mud. Excavations began in the 18th century, and uncovered Roman houses built around a rectangular plan. Perhaps the best known is the Villa dei Papiri, the inspiration for the J Paul Getty museum in Malibu, Los Angeles. Sculptures found in the villa are now in the Museo Archeologico Nazionale (*see pp86–9*).

The city baths, built in 10 BC, are divided into two sections. The one for men is larger and decorated, and includes a gymnasium; the women's section is smaller and better preserved.

Decumanus Maximus

★ Trellis House
A characteristic example of an inexpensive Roman multi-family dwelling, the Trellis House has wood and reed laths in the original crude tufa and lime masonry.

The House of the Gem is named after a cameo portrait from the era of Claudius that was found here.

House with the Mosaic Atrium
This house has a famous mosaic floor with geometric patterns, as well as living rooms, and a portico and terrace facing the sea.

Villa dei Papiri

★ House of the Stags
The name derives from the beautiful sculpture groups of stags found here. The house is one of the more elaborate: the inner porticoed garden connects the northern section (entrance, indoor triclinium and smaller rooms) to the southern side, which has bedrooms and an arbour with a sea view.

★ House of the Neptune and Amphitrite Mosaic

This mosaic is in the summer dining room. The building and a shop, with wooden shelves for amphoras, are among the best preserved.

VISITORS' CHECKLIST

Road Map C3. **FS** *Portici-Ercolano.* **R** *Circumvesuviana: Ercolano-Scavi.* **Tel** *081 732 43 38.* **○** *Apr–Oct: 8:30am–7:30pm (last adm: 6pm); Nov–Mar: 8:30am–5pm (last adm: 3:30pm).* **☒** **Villa dei Papiri ●** *to the public.*

Entrance

House of the Bicentenary
This patrician residence, excavated 200 years after digging began, had mosaic floors and wall paintings.

STAR SIGHTS

★ House of the Neptune and Amphitrite Mosaic

★ House of the Stags

★ Trellis House

Decumanus Inferiore

The Excavation Area
The site of ancient Herculaneum is well below the level of the modern town. The area is still being excavated. The restored Villa dei Papiri contains frescoes, mosaics and the skeleton of a horse, but is now closed to visitors.

The House of Telephus contains a 1st-century BC relief narrating the myth of Achilles and Telephus.

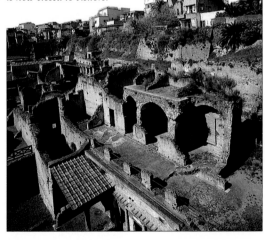

0 metres   50

0 yards   50

Pompeii ❿

"Samovar" from Pompeii

An earthquake in AD 62, which shook Pompeii and damaged some of its buildings, was merely a prelude to the tragic day in AD 79, when Vesuvius erupted, engulfing the city and its inhabitants with a terrible storm of cinders and ash. The remains of Pompeii were discovered by accident in the 1590s, but it was not until the 1750s that the site was seen as an archaeological treasure. The bodies of people were unearthed along with their houses, temples, works of art and everyday objects. The first archaeologists removed the most important finds, which became part of the royal collection and were then transferred to the Museo Archeologico Nazionale *(see pp86–9).*

The House of the Golden Cupids is named after the delightful images, reproductions of the originals, in the bedroom.

House of the Faun *(see p150)*

★ House of the Vettii
This is one of the most famous places in Pompeii (see p150). *It has rich wall decoration dating from the last Pompeiian period after AD 62. The array of themes includes Daedalus and Pasiphaë, shown here.*

The Forum
Originally the market place, the Forum (see p148) *became the focus for the most important civic functions, both political and religious.*

Temple of Apollo *(see p148)*

Porta Marina entrance

Macellum
The macellum was the covered meat and fish market. Fronted by a portico with two moneychangers' kiosks, it opened onto the Forum near the weights and measures office and the Forum Holitorium vegetable market.

Forum *(see p148)*

Basilica *(see p148)*

Temple of Venus *(see p148)*

STAR SIGHTS

★ House of the Vettii

★ Via dei Sepolcri

Fresco from the Lupanare

The Latin word lupa *means prostitute, and this* lupanare *was the best-organized of Pompeii's many brothels. Here, the walls are decorated with erotic paintings and graffiti depicting this world and the services offered by prostitutes, as well as boys, to satisfy their clients and lovers.*

VISITORS' CHECKLIST

Road Map D3. **FS** *Pompei-Scavi.* **Q** *Circumvesuviana: Pompei-Villa dei Misteri.* **Entrances:** *Porta Marina, Piazza Anfiteatro, Piazza Esedra.* **Tel** *081 857 53 47.* ☐ *Apr–Oct: 8:30am–7:30pm (last adm: 6pm); Nov–Mar: 8:30am–5pm (last adm: 3:30pm).* 🎫 ▢ 🛈 *AAST, Via Sacra 1.* **Tel** *081 850 72 55.* **www**.pompeiisites.org

Via dell'Abbondanza

This street was lined with private homes and shops selling a range of goods.

Temple of Isis

Built in the late 2nd century BC, this temple has two niches holding statues of Egyptian gods.

Plaster Casts

Since 1863, plaster cast techniques have enabled researchers to re-create body shapes. Many were killed by the toxic fumes while engaged in everyday tasks.

Small Theatre
(see p149)

The Great Theatre
(see p148) was built in the hollow of a hill for good acoustics.

Gladiators' courtyard and barracks *(see p149)*

THE ARCHAEOLOGICAL SITE

The illustration shows the western section of Pompeii. For a map of the entire area see p151.

0 metres		50
0 yards		50

★ Via dei Sepolcri

"Twenty steps wide, 500 long, the entire length still furrowed by the ancient carriage wheels, completely furnished with pavements like ours, and lined throughout, at left and right, with funerary monuments." This is how an awestruck Alexandre Dumas described Via dei Sepolcri, outside the northwest city wall, which was discovered in the first digs.

Exploring Pompeii

Thanks to its strategic position near the Sarno River, Pompeii was a centre of commerce for inland areas. The first town plan (6th century BC) was irregular but, from the 4th century BC on, building developed on a Greek-inspired grid plan. Slabs of old lava from Vesuvius were used to pave the roads. Large villas and houses of different periods and styles, made of brick, stone and cement and often richly decorated, offer an unparalleled view of ancient domestic architecture (*see pp150–51*). Furthermore, the streets, workshops and public areas are in an excellent state of preservation. Finds such as furnishings, tools, jewellery and even food and drink reveal how the people of Pompeii lived, from the ruling class down to the slaves.

The Forum viewed from the Temple of Apollo

The Basilica, Pompeii's ancient judicial seat opening onto the Forum

THE FORUM

The Forum, a rectangular paved area, was the centre of public life, and the oldest part of Pompeii, built on the highest spot. Arranged around it are a number of important administrative and religious institutions. To the south is the Basilica, or law court, while opposite are the temples of Apollo, Jupiter and Vespasian, and the Sanctuary of the Lari. The imposing Eumachia building was perhaps used by the wool merchants' guild or, more probably, for commercial transactions. On the other side of the Basilica is the site of the Temple of Venus. The goddess was the protectress of the city, but in tandem with the fate of Pompeii, her temple was badly damaged in the earthquake of AD 62, then totally devastated by Vesuvius.

FORUM BATHS

Built after 80 BC, these well-preserved baths follow the traditional sequence from dressing room to *frigidarium* (cold room), then on to *tepidarium* (warm room) and *calidarium* (hot room). Mythological figures decorate the vaults of the warm room, and the hot room contains a mammoth marble basin. Most people would use the public baths for their ablutions.

THEATRES

The Great Theatre (2nd century BC) was rebuilt several times in its history and in modern times has again been used as the venue for summer cultural events. It was built to seat about 5,000 people. The quadrangular portico behind the stage, originally designed as a space

The Forum, with Vesuvius in the background

The gladiators' barracks, part of the Great Theatre complex

pool in the middle, are in an outlying area between the Nocera and Sarno gateways. The amphitheatre, the oldest of its kind in existence, was used for gladiatorial combat and could hold 20,000 people. The stone tiers were separated into different sections for the various social classes. A cloth canopy *(velarium)* shaded spectators from the sun.

for the audience to stroll in during intermissions, was turned into a barracks for the gladiators after AD 62. Skeletons, including one of a baby, have been excavated here.

Next door is the indoor theatre, or Small Theatre, used for music concerts. Behind this is the Temple of Isis, the goddess worshipped locally.

VIA STABIANA

This avenue, passing through the Porta di Stabia, to the south, was a major thoroughfare used by carriages travelling between Pompeii and the port and coastal districts. On the west side of the avenue are the Stabian Baths (currently closed for restoration). These are the most ancient in Pompeii – the original structure dates from the 4th century BC.

Near Porta Vesuvio it is possible to see the remains of an aqueduct. This channelled water from the Serino River aqueduct, built in the era of Augustus, into three conduits that served both private homes and public fountains. The

aqueduct fell into disuse after being damaged by the earthquake of AD 62.

On the street parallel to Via Stabiana are the remains of the most organized of Pompeii's many brothels. While other such places were mostly single rooms or the top floor of a shop, this *lupanare* features five rooms on the ground floor with stone beds as well as a latrine. Erotic frescoes line the walls.

An inn in Via dell'Abbondanza

AMPHITHEATRE AND GREAT GYMNASIUM

The Amphitheatre (80 BC) and the Augustan-era Great Gymnasium, with a swimming

VIA DELL'ABBONDANZA

A public fountain in Via dell'Abbondanza

The excavations for this street lined with homes and shops *(see pp150–51)* end just to the left of the Amphitheatre. The buildings and contents present a vivid picture of everyday life, down to the cart tracks in the street. You can visit the shop of VeArecundus, who made felt and tanned hides; Stefano's well-preserved laundry, where urine was used as a cleaning agent; or the bakery run by Sotericus, where bread was baked but not sold retail. Among the inns, the most famous belonged to Asellina, whose obliging foreign waitresses are depicted in graffiti on the wall. The inn *(thermopolium)* still has the record of the proceeds of that fateful day in AD 79: 683 sesterces.

The Houses in Pompeii

Many large houses of great historical value and architectural interest are concentrated in the area between Via di Mercurio (the most elegant *cardo*, reserved for pedestrians, in the northwest of Pompeii) and Via Stabiana, and along Via dell'Abbondanza. Wealthy residents had houses with courtyards, living rooms and gardens (*see pp18–19*), often with decorated walls. A typical Pompeiian house was constructed around two open courts: the atrium, an Italic feature, and the colonnaded garden, a feature of Greek origin. The layout of suburban farmsteads was different; the Villa of the Mysteries is one of the most famous.

Bronze statue, House of the Faun

HOUSE OF THE VETTII

The lari shrine, House of the Vettii

The owners of the House of the Vettii were freedmen who had become rich merchants. The house's interior walls are adorned with splendid paintings and friezes featuring mythological themes. In the atrium of the more rustic part of the house is the altar of the lari – the deities who protected the place. This depicts the ancestral spirit of the *pater familias* with two lari and, below, a serpent.

On the north side of the house is a kitchen, with a small room decorated with erotic scenes.

The House of the Vettii is currently closed for restoration.

HOUSE OF THE FAUN

The name comes from a bronze statue in the middle of the *impluvium* (pond) in one of the atria. The original is in the Museo Archeologico Nazionale, as are many of the mosaics, including the famous *Battle of Alexander (see pp86–9)*. Built in the 2nd century BC, this is one of the largest private dwellings here.

HOUSE OF THE TRAGIC POET

The entrance has a mosaic of a dog with a "beware of the dog" inscription, but many frescoes are in the Museo Archeologico. The name derives from a mosaic showing a drama rehearsal.

HOUSE OF THE CEII

The façade of this house bears a series of inscriptions that seem to indicate an electoral campaign programme. One of the messages is signed L Ceius Secundus, who is thought to have been the owner of the house at the time of the eruption. Behind the atrium, a richly decorated garden features a back wall frescoed with hunting scenes and fountains, giving the impression of a wider space. The sides are decorated with landscapes with an Egyptian flavour, a common style in the final years of Pompeii.

HOUSE OF VENUS

This house is named after the goddess of Love because of a fresco discovered there in 1952. Located on the back wall of the garden, it portrays Venus with two cherubs in a pink seashell. The atrium of the house was damaged by a bombardment on Pompeii in 1943.

THERMOPOLIUM

Ancient Pompeiians mostly consumed lunch outside the home, in a *thermopolium*. Such places usually had a long counter on the street side, with benches and terracotta receptacles for food. A colourful fresco adorns the back wall of this shop, which belonged to Vetuvius Placidus and which is also one of the

The peristyle in the House of the Vettii

For hotels and restaurants in this region see pp181–7 and pp195–201

0 kilometres 4

0 miles 2

VISITORS' CHECKLIST

At **Positano** *you can hire a boat from* **Lucibello** *on the large beach:* **Tel** *089 87 50 32.* **www**.lucibello.it
At **Capri**, *from* **Sercomar**: *Piazza Fontana 64.* **Tel** *081 837 87 81.* **www**.capriseaservice.com

Positano

The square, pastel-coloured houses of Positano (see pp158–9) cling to the steep slopes of Monte Sant'Angelo a tre Pizzi and Monte Comune overlooking the sea. Lush gardens and bougainvillea fill the terraces of these charming houses. This is one of the most popular resorts on the Amalfi coast, famous for its bright, patterned textiles.

Isca

Just offshore is the small island of Isca, where the Neapolitan actor and playwright Eduardo De Filippo (see p37) lived. The house now belongs to his son Luca.

The Li Galli Archipelago

These islands, known as the Sirenuse until the 19th century, were once considered to be the home of the mythical Sirens who lured sailors onto the rocks. The clear water between the three crags, Gallo Lungo, La Rotonda and Castelluccia, makes swimming irresistible.

The Amalfi Coast

Portal of Amalfi Duomo

Suspended between sea, sky and earth, state road 163, which twists and turns along the full length of the Amalfi coast, offers stunning views at every corner. Until the 19th century, this stretch of the "divine coast" was isolated and could only be reached by going up difficult mountain paths on mules. By the early 1900s, this very isolation had become the main appeal and the coast began to attract travellers, artists and writers. Visitors of all kinds were drawn to steep-stepped Positano, clinging to tall cliffs; Amalfi with its glorious past as a marine republic; and Ravello, which Wagner chose as "the magic garden of Klingsor", the setting for his opera *Parsifal*. The limestone islands called Li Galli, southwest of Positano, are traditionally the home of the Sirens made famous by Homer in his accounts of the trials of Odysseus. Exploring by boat *(see pp156–7)* enables you to appreciate this astonishing coast at closer quarters.

A stretch of state road 163

NERANO

Road Map C4. ▩ Sita.

The first stop on the Amalfi coast road is the quiet village of Nerano, administratively part of Massa Lubrense. The road to Nerano goes upwards from Sorrento and cuts across the end of the peninsula near the small village of **Termini**. The sea sparkles in the distance, and the panoramic views are stunning. You can even see Capri and the rocky islands of Li Galli *(see p157)*.

Nerano is perched on a ridge; below is the beach and the town of **Marina del Cantone**, popular mostly because of its small seafront restaurants, some supported by stilts. Walkers can descend on foot among the olive trees to the bay of **Ieranto**.

POSITANO

Road Map D4. ▩ 3,900. ▩ Sita. ▦ from Capri, Naples, Salerno, Amalfi & Sorrento. ▌ AAST, Via del Saracino 4. **Tel** 089 87 50 67. www.aziendaturismopositano.it

In 1953 John Steinbeck wrote that Positano "bites deep. It is a dream place that isn't quite real when you are there and becomes beckoningly real after you have gone". The town climbs the hill in steps, with the oldest houses in the upper part of Positano, either faded red or pink, decorated with Baroque stuccoes. The traffic-free street going down to the sea, Via Pasitea, penetrates the atmospheric heart of town with its narrow stepped alleys, houses with vaulted roofs, terraces and tiny gardens that defy the

rock. The brightly coloured articles Positano is famous for – such as cloth bags and beachwear – on display inside and outside the many shops, blend well with the pastel-coloured houses, and the local craftsmen are only too happy to make sandals for you while you wait.

Near the beach is the small church of Santa Maria dell'Assunta, whose cupola is covered with yellow, blue and green majolica tiles. The descent ends at Marina Grande, a pebble beach used by fishing boats, lined with bars and restaurants.

If you want to go to inlets inaccessible by land, or to the little islands of **Li Galli**, or take a trip along the coast, boats are always available. If you prefer to go on foot, you can always swim at Ciumicello, Arienzo or take the easy path to Fornillo beach, with its two watch-towers. There are also craggy grottoes in the inlets,

Typical Amalfi scenery, with sheer cliffs overlooking the sea

For hotels and restaurants in this region see pp181–7 and pp195–201

including La Porta, where there are Palaeolithic and Mesolithic ruins. From Montepertuso, a village above Positano, you can walk along a splendid scenic path to **Nocelle**. For those who love good food, there are plenty of bars and restaurants, including Buca di Bacco *(see p199)*, which is famous for its *arancini* rice croquettes.

The beach at Marina di Praia

PRAIANO

Road map D4. 🏘 *2,000.* 🚌 *Sita.*
This fishing village is perched on the ridge of Monte Sant'Angelo and stretches towards Capo Sottile. The church of San Luca, with 16th-century paintings by Giovan Bernardo Lama, lies in the upper part. In an inlet just outside Praiano is **Marina di Praia**, a small beach surrounded by fishermen's houses. On the road from Positano there are more delightful beaches; just before Praiano is **Vettica Maggiore** and further on, Conca dei Marini. The views are splendid from the terraced square of Vettica Maggiore, by the church of San Gennaro. Before you reach Amalfi, the road widens into an open space where you can go down (by lift) to the **Grotta dello Smeraldo**, where stalagmites and stalactites merge to form great columns in the emerald-green water.

🦈 **Grotta dello Smeraldo**
State road 163, km 264 (via lift or stairs); boat from Amalfi. ◯ open daily (weather permitting). 📷

AMALFI

Road map D4. 🏘 *6,000.*
🚌 *Sita.* ℹ *AAST, Corso Repubbliche Marinare 27.*
Tel *089 87 11 07.*
Tucked in between mountains and sea, Amalfi is a perennial favourite with visitors for its scenic beauty and original archi-tecture. It also has a glorious history as a powerful maritime republic – in the 11th century Amalfi was a rival to the ports of Venice and Genoa.

Little remains to show for the colourful trading history of this small town, whose inhabitants once numbered 60,000. Amalfi's cathedral, the **Duomo di Sant'Andrea**, founded in the 9th century, was rebuilt in Romanesque style in the 11th century and then altered several times. The façade and atrium date from the late 1800s, but the carved bronze doors were cast in Constantinople around the year 1000, and the campanile (1276) is decorated with Arabic-like interlaced arches typical of southern Italian Romanesque. Left of the porch, the Chiostro del Paradiso (Paradise cloister) was built in around 1266 for Bishop Augustariccio as a

The rocky Amalfi coastline

cemetery for prominent citizens. The garden is surrounded by an ornate colonnade with interlaced arches supported by paired columns and with fragments of sculpture from different periods. Near Piazza Duomo is the Arsenal; you can still see the ruins of two naves and the vault. Heading inland from Amalfi, you can visit the Valle dei Mulini (Valley of the Mills), famous for its traditional paper production and the **Museo della Carta** or Paper Museum.

🏛 **Duomo di Sant'Andrea**
Piazza Duomo. ◯ daily. Mar–Oct: 7:30am–7:30pm; Nov & Dec: 7:30am–6:30pm; 7 Jan–28 Feb: 7:30–11:30am, 4–6:30pm.

🏛 **Museo della Carta**
Via delle Cartiere. **Tel** 089 830 45 61. ◯ Mar–Oct: 10am–6:30pm daily. **www**.museodellacarta.it

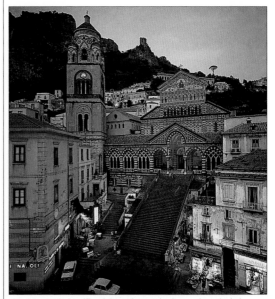

Piazza Duomo in Amalfi and the wide steps leading to the cathedral

RAVELLO

Road map D4. 🏘 *2,500.*
🚌 *Sita.* 🚌 *AAST, Via Roma
18 bis.* **Tel** *089 85 70 96.*
www.ravellotime.it

Ravello's history is entwined
with that of Amalfi: the
former became part of the
Duchy of Amalfi in the 9th
century. The period of
greatest splendour was the
13th century, when trade
with Sicily and the Orient
was at its height. Somewhat
off the beaten track, Ravello
is for those who love peace
and quiet and stupendous
coastal views.

The **Duomo** is dedicated to
San Pantaleone, the town's
patron saint, and the blood of
the saint is kept here. The
church dates from 1086 and
its bronze doors from 1179.
Inside is a splendid raised
pulpit, the work of Niccolò
di Bartolomeo da Foggia in
1272. The twisted columns,
patterned with mosaics,
rest on sculpted lions.

Walking around the town,
Moorish details are evident in
the buildings, in the inner
courtyards and gardens and
the many churches. The
narrow streets and pathways
offer occasional, often
unexpected, glimpses of
marvellous coastal views.
Two of Ravello's architectural
highlights are Villa Rufolo
and Villa Cimbrone.

The view from the terrace at Villa Cimbrone

Villa Rufolo, originally built
for the Rufolo family, is a mix-
ture of 13th- and 14th-century
constructions. It was remodelled in the 19th century by a
Scottish enthusiast, who preserved the Arabic elements. It
is famed for the courtyard with
double arches and even more
for the tropical gardens, which
inspired Wagner's *Parsifal*.
The annual Ravello Festival
stages concerts here.

On Via San Francesco,
which takes you to Villa
Cimbrone, are the churches
of San Francesco, of Gothic
origin but rebuilt in the 18th
century, and Santa Chiara, the
only one on the coast that
has retained its *gynaeceum*
(women's gallery).

Villa Cimbrone was built in
the late 1800s by the Englishman Lord Grimthorpe. A
range of ancient architectural
elements were incorporated

in the house. From the villa's
clifftop terrace there is a spellbinding view of the coast to
Punta Licosa and the Paestum
plain. Villa Cimbrone is now
a small hotel *(see p186)*.

Another place well worth
visiting is the church of San
Giovanni del Toro, in the
square of the same name,
with its three tall semicircular
apses and beautifully
decorated domes.

🔒 **Duomo**
Piazza Duomo. **Tel** *089 85 83 11.*
⏰ *9am–noon, 5:30–7pm daily.*
www.chiesaravello.it

🏛 **Villa Rufolo**
Piazza Duomo. **Tel** *089 85 76 21.*
⏰ *Summer: 9am–1 hr before
sunset.* 📷 **www**.villarufolo.it

🏛 **Villa Cimbrone**
Via Santa Chiara 26. **Tel** *089 85
74 59.* ⏰ *9am–sunset.* 📷
www.villacimbrone.com

The picturesque village of Cetara; standing out among rooftops is the dome of San Pietro

MAIORI, MINORI AND CETARA

Road map D4 & E4.
👤 *Maiori: 6,000; Minori: 3,100;
Cetara: 2,500.* 🚌 *Sita.*
ℹ️ *Maiori: AAST, Corso Regina 73.*
Tel *089 87 74 52.*
www.aziendaturismo-maiori.it
Cetara: *Pro Loco, Corso Garibaldi 15.*
www.prolococetara.it

Ancient *Reginna Minor* and *Maior* are now two popular seaside resorts with a long and noble history. **Minori**, where the Amalfi Maritime Republic arsenals were situated, dates back to Roman times. Near the seafront is the basilica of Santa Trofimena, built in the 12th–13th centuries and then rebuilt in the 1800s. The church houses the relics of the ancient patron saint of Amalfi.

Maiori is like an amphitheatre at the end of the Tramonti valley. It was founded in the 9th century but is today a modern town, rebuilt after a flood in 1954. The fine beaches and good bathing facilities have made it one of the most visited towns on the coast. The 18th-century campanile on 12th-century Santa Maria a Mare towers over the Maior stream.

After the lovely beach of Erchie, **Cetara** was the easternmost possession of Amalfi. At the end of the 9th century it was also a stronghold for the Saracens, who anchored their ships at Cala di Fuenti cove. The name perhaps derives from the Latin *cetaria*, or tunafishing net; the fish, salted and sold in ceramic pots, is a typical local product.

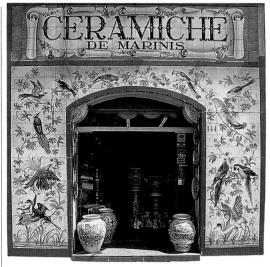

A characteristic ceramics shop in Vietri sul Mare

VIETRI SUL MARE

Road map E4. 👤 *10,000.* 🚌 *Sita.*
ℹ️ *Pro Loco, Vía O Costabile 4.*
www.prolocovietrisulmare.it

The majolica-decorated dome and bell tower of San Giovanni Battista (begun in the 11th century) have almost come to symbolize this town overlooking the Bay of Salerno. Vietri sul Mare is famous as a seaside resort and especially for its ceramics. Cooking utensils, plates, vases and tiles have been made here since the 1400s. In the mid-18th century, Vietri became known as the majolica-makers' district, a suburb of the Cava de' Tirreni (see below).

Majolica plate made in Vietri

The most original items made were the very popular tiles painted with religious subjects. You can still see these tiles in streets, private homes and churches.

Today you can find ceramics of all kinds, catering for all tastes. The green donkey used as the logo of local production is a relatively recent invention, inspired by the German artist Richard Doelker in 1922. The **Museo della Ceramica** (Ceramics Museum) features local items from the 1600s to the present.

🏛 **Museo della Ceramica**
Raito di Vietri sul Mare. **Tel** *089 21 18 35.* 🕐 *May–Sep: 9am–1pm, 4–7pm Tue–Sun; Oct–Apr: 9am–1pm, 3–6pm Tue–Sun.*

CAVA DE' TIRRENI

Road map E4. 👤 *53,000.* 🚌 *Sita.*

Lying in a valley in the interior, Cava de' Tirreni is the only town in Southern Italy to have streets lined with porticoes. Go and see the 11th-century abbey of Santissima Trinità and the old Scacciaventi quarter, whose winding streets block the wind (*scacciaventi* means "wind-chaser").

View of Vietri sul Mare, with the dome and campanile of San Giovanni

Paestum ⑮

Ancient Poseidonia, founded along the Sele River by Greek colonists from Sybaris around 600 BC, became the Roman colony of Paestum in 273 BC. The town began to decline in the 1st century BC due to malaria. Seismic distur-bance and deforestation (the

Red-figure lekythos

local pines made excellent raw material for building ships) had gradually turned the area into marshland. The inhabitants tried to combat the rising water level; they raised their streets and homes, or went to live on higher ground. It was at this time that the Temple of Hera was made into a church by the converted population. Eventually, however, Paestum was abandoned for the nearby town of Capaccio.

This ancient site was first unearthed in the 18th century during the building of a road, but most of it remained undiscovered until the 1950s.

★ Temple of Ceres
This temple was built around 500 BC and dedicated to Athena. For centuries, until a votive offering was found nearby, it had been attributed to Ceres.

Temple of Neptune
The name of this temple has been a subject of debate. It was probably dedi-cated to Apollo or Zeus, but it is commonly known as the Temple of Neptune. Built in 450 BC, it is one of the most complete Greek temples in Europe.

THE THREE TEMPLES AT PAESTUM

These plans compare the structure of the 3 main temples at Paestum. The Temple of Hera (6th century BC) has 9 front columns, 18 side columns and 2 aisles divided by a row of columns. The Temple of Ceres (6th century BC) has 6 fluted columns at the front, 13 lateral ones and an un-divided *cella*. The largest, Temple of Neptune (5th century BC), has 6 front columns, 14 side ones and its *cella* is divided into 3 aisles by 2 rows of 2-tier columns.

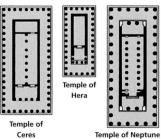

Temple of Ceres

Temple of Hera

Temple of Neptune

STAR SIGHTS

★ Temple of Ceres

★ Temple of Hera, the "Basilica"

★ Tomb of the Diver (funerary fresco in Paestum Museum)

Paestum Museum

VISITORS' CHECKLIST

Road map F5. *Via Magna Grecia.*
FS *Napoli–Salerno: Paestum.* **Site** ☐ *9am–1 hr before sunset.* **Tel** *082 872 11 13.* **Museum Tel** *082 881 10 23.* ☐ *9am–7pm daily.* ● *1st & 3rd Mon of month.* 🎫 ℹ️ *AAST, Via Magna Grecia 887.* **Tel** *082 881 10 61.* **www.**info paestum.it; **www.**paestumsites.it

Metope with Dancing Girls

This metope, on display in the Paestum Museum, comes from one of the two temples in the sanctuary of Hera Argiva at the mouth of the Sele River. Founded by the first colonists, the complex was discovered in 1934–40 after almost two centuries of searching.

The amphitheatre (1st century BC–1st century AD) has only been partly excavated.

Forum

Baths

★ Tomb of the Diver

The frescoed slab of the Tomb of the Diver, which dates from about 480 BC, was discovered in 1968 about 1 km (half a mile) from Paestum. The image of the diver on the lid symbolizes the passage to the afterlife. More unique examples of Greek funerary art can be seen in the site's museum.

★ Temple of Hera, the "Basilica"

The absence of religious features led the first archaeologists to believe this was a civic building, when in fact it is the oldest temple in Paestum, built around 530 BC.

Antonio Joli, The Temples of Paestum (1758)

Temple ruins had a profound effect on local landscape painters, who often used them in their art. Antonio Joli's painting shows the Basilica, the Temple of Neptune and, beyond, the Temple of Ceres.

0 metres   100

0 yards   100

Hoardings and shop signs in present-day Caserta

Caserta ⑯

Road map C2. 🏛 80,000.
FS *Caserta*. 🛈 *Ente Provinciale per il Turismo, Palazzo Reale.* **Tel** *0823 32 11 37.* **www**.eptcaserta.it

Caserta was once known as the village of La Torre, named after a medieval tower of the Acquaviva d'Aragona family. It was only from the mid-1700s, when Charles of Bourbon chose the plain at the foot of the Tifatini mountains as the site for his new centre of administration, that the town began to flourish and expand. It was at this time that it took the name of the nearby medieval village of Caserta Vecchia.

Present-day Caserta is a modern agricultural town that was largely rebuilt in the 1950s. A few older buildings remain, such as the church and monastery of Sant'Agostino in Via Mazzini and the former residence of the Acquaviva d'Aragona family in Piazza Vanvitelli. However, the main reason to visit Caserta is the Royal Palace (*see pp166–7*). Conceived by King Charles as the heart of his new adminis-trative centre, the palace was to be a leading European court, modelled on Versailles and linked to the capital and other cities by radial roads and protected by the fortress at Capua. This plan to move power away from the capital

Façade of the cathedral of San Michele, Caserta Vecchia

city was influenced by the apparent vulnerability of the Palazzo Reale on the Naples seafront (*see pp50–51*), a fact that came to light in 1742 when the English fleet had threatened to attack. Once this danger had passed, however, attention was turned to the style of the palace. The king summoned Luigi Vanvitelli, tech-nical adviser at the Vatican, to draw up designs. The palace and the new city were begun in 1752.

When Charles became king of Spain and returned to Madrid in 1759, construction on the Royal Palace languished. Supervision of the costly works was handed over to his son Ferdinand IV and, in par-ticular, his minister Tanucci. The new king concentrated on the magnificent park and bothered little about the unfinished palace. Some further work was carried out, but as the

two semicircular buildings at the entrance to the grounds illustrate, these were poor substitutes for the splendid buildings proposed in Vanvitelli's original designs.

ENVIRONS
🏛 Caserta Vecchia
Road map C2.

The fascination of Caserta Vecchia, 10 km (6 miles) along a winding road north-east of Caserta, does not lie in the individual monuments but the town itself, which has a remarkably well-preserved medieval character. This small hilltop town was probably founded by the Lombards in the 8th century and then came under Norman rule. When Charles III designed his new palace, activity in this lively community moved into the new town in the plains.

Caserta Vecchia revolves around the main square where the cathedral of San Michele stands. Nearby is the Gothic church of Annunziata, with a marble portal opening onto a 17th-century portico. On the eastern side of the village are the ruins of a 13th-century castle, dominated by a 30-metre (98-ft) turret.

🔒 Cathedral of San Michele
Piazza del Vescovado 1. **Tel** *0823 37 13 18.* ◯ 9am–1pm, 4–7pm daily (to 8pm Sat & Sun).
The cathedral in Caserta Vecchia was completed in 1153. The faded yellow and grey tufa façade is simple, with three marble portals. Columns on the triangular tympanum above the middle portal are supported by lions.

Caserta Vecchia, dominated by the cathedral of San Michele

The 14th-century dome has the interlaced Arabic arches often seen on Romanesque buildings in Southern Italy.

The interior of the church is lined with irregular columns and stunning majolica tiles. A starlit sky is represented in the dome, with grey stone for the night and white marble stars.

To the right of the cathedral stands the dark stone bell tower, added a century later, with an archway over the road.

₩ Belvedere Reale di San Leucio

Road map C2. **Casino del Belvedere** Via del Setificio 7. *Tel* 0823 27 31 51. ◯ 9am–5pm Wed–Mon by appt. ☒ Sat & Sun. This area, 3 km (2 miles) northwest of Caserta, was purchased by Charles of Bourbon in 1750. Five years later, Ferdinand IV built a royal lodge here, the Casino di Belvedere. In 1789, he ordered an existing building be made into a silk factory to be used by the local artisans. All that remains of the ambitious project are the workmen's dwellings and the royal lodge, which was also the residence of the silk factory management.

The Casino di Belvedere, San Leucio

₳ Basilica Benedettina di San Michele Arcangelo

Via Luigi Baia. ◯ by appt; call 0823 96 08 17. ☒ This small Romanesque church lies 10 km (6 miles) northwest of Caserta. Built on the ruins of an ancient temple to Diana, Roman goddess of the forest, it was reconstructed in 1073. Many features of the temple were incorporated into the church, such as the delicate Corinthian columns on the portico and the church floor.

Inside, a cycle of 11th-century frescoes, painted in Byzantine style by artists from the School of Montecassino, depict stories from the Bible.

THE IDEAL VILLAGE OF SAN LEUCIO

Pretty street in the village of San Leucio

San Leucio was founded in 1789 by Ferdinand IV as a village for workers of the local silk factory. The aim of this social experiment was to create a community dedicated to the pursuit of happiness instead of personal profit. The community had its own laws, attributed to the king but in fact written by Antonio Planelli. These were based on reason and morality, included compulsory education, equal inheritance rights for men and women (who, however, had to marry within the community), the abolition of the dowry and medical assistance for the aged and disabled. The 1799 revolution brought about the end of the most ambitious project of the founders, the creation of an entire model city, Ferdinandopoli, although the designs survive. San Leucio is famous for its silk manufacture and the articles produced here are still very much in demand.

₦ Roman Amphitheatre

Piazza Adriano, Santa Maria Capua Vetere. *Tel* 0823 79 88 64. ◯ 9am– 1 hr before sunset Tue–Sun. ☒ The amphitheatre at Santa Maria Capua Vetere, 6 km (4 miles) west of Caserta, dates from the 1st century BC. Second in size only to the Colosseum in Rome, it once had four storeys and subterranean passageways where wild animals were kept in cages. A museum houses artifacts and displays a life-size reproduction of the gladiatorial fights. A short drive away is an underground sanctuary dedicated to the god Mithras. It features a 1st-century BC fresco of Mithras slaying a bull.

₩ Ponti della Valle

This viaduct, 2 km (1 mile) from Maddaloni, is over 500 m (1640 ft) long and is supported by three arches. It was built between 1753 and 1762 by Vanvitelli to bring water to the Royal Palace at Caserta.

Ruins of the amphitheatre at Santa Maria Capua Vetere

Royal Palace of Caserta

Statue on a fountain

In his memoirs, the architect Vanvitelli says it was the king who designed the Royal Palace. This may have been adulation, or perhaps Charles of Bourbon knew what he wanted – to emulate his favourite models, the Buen Retiro in Madrid and Versailles in France. Vanvitelli drew inspiration from the former for this quadrangular, 1,200-room structure, which was completed 72 years after the architect's death, in 1845. The lower ground floor houses a museum, with photos and exhibits relating to the palace and Caserta culture.

First floor

★ **Eighteenth-century Royal Apartments**
The Halberdiers Hall connects the upper vestibule and the 18th-century Royal Apartments. The ceiling is adorned by Domenico Mondo's fresco The Triumph of the Bourbon Arms *(1785).*

The upper Vestibule is a grand, imposing space, with its marble-lined walls and an inlaid floor.

★ **Throne Room**
This is one of the large 19th-century salons – in contrast with the smaller 18th-century rooms – in the palace. It was decorated by Gaetano Genovese in 1844–5 and was once filled with elegant French furniture.

STAR FEATURES

★ Eighteenth-century Royal Apartments

★ Throne Room

★ Court Theatre

For hotels and restaurants in this region see pp181–7 and pp195–201

Great Staircase
The staircase is positioned to one side so as not to interrupt the splendid view of the park from the main doorway.

VISITORS' CHECKLIST

Road map C2. Via Douhet 22.
Tel 0823 44 80 84. **Apartments**
⭘ 8:30am–7:30pm Wed–Mon.
Park ⭘ 8:30am–6pm (2:30pm winter). 🚻 🍽 **www**.reggia dicaserta.beniculturali.it

KEY (UPPER FLOOR)

☐ 18th-century Royal Apartments
☐ 19th-century Royal Apartments
☐ *Terraemotus* exhibition
☐ Cappella Palatina
☐ Biblioteca Palatina
☐ Art Gallery
☐ Non-exhibition space

Art Gallery
Among the portraits in the Art Gallery is that of Maria Carolina, Ferdinand IV's wife, who occupied four elaborate rooms in the 18th-century apartments.

★ **Court Theatre**
The theatre is on the ground floor. The rear of the stage could be opened to the air, creating a natural backdrop.

THE PARK

Luigi Vanvitelli designed this famous park, one of the last examples of the fashion for a regimented garden in the Baroque style. The long central axis is designed on descending levels, creating a remarkable effect with pools and fountains ornamented with splendid sculptures. The play of flowing water culminates in the **Grande Cascata** waterfall, almost 80 m (260 ft) high, also known as the Fountain of Diana and Actaeon. Next to this is the English Garden, perhaps the first of its kind in Italy. The idea was suggested to Queen Maria Carolina by her friend Lord Hamilton and landscaping work began in 1786.

Flowing water with fountains and waterfalls, the park's central feature

Capri ⑰

Excursion taxi

The first illustrious residents in Capri were the Roman emperors Augustus and Tiberius. For the last decade of his life, Tiberius ruled Rome from Capri, and the ruins of his luxurious villa can still be seen today. Despite this noble history, the island saw few visitors until the 19th century, when a poet named August Köpisch found the Grotta Azzurra, which was known to locals but not to travellers on the Grand Tour. Tourism began to flourish, and Capri became the haunt of foreign politicians, artists and intellectuals, Alexandre Dumas and Oscar Wilde among them. The singer Gracie Fields and the writer Norman Douglas, author of *Siren Land*, made the island their home.

Marina Grande
Capri's main harbour is a colourful village with seafood restaurants and some Roman and Byzantine remains. A funicular takes you to central Capri in a few minutes.

Rocky Beaches
Sunloungers are set up among the rocks on this island with few sandy beaches.

The Grotta Azzurra, or Blue Grotto, owes its name to the blue colour of the water, the result of light refraction.

| 0 metres | 1000 |
| 0 yards | 1000 |

Anacapri
On the slopes of Monte Solaro (see p173) is the second town on the island, Anacapri. Here you can visit the church of San Michele, the Villa San Michele (home of the Swedish physician Axel Munthe), the excavations at the imperial villa of Damecuta and, of course, appreciate the magnificent view from the top of the hill.

For hotels and restaurants in this region see pp181–7 and pp195–201

Villa Jovis
The retreat built by Emperor Tiberius stands on the mountain named after him. Excavations have unearthed baths, apartments and "Tiberius's drop", from which his victims were supposedly thrown into the sea.

Writer Curzio Malaparte gave this villa, shaped like a hammer with a sickle on the roof, to the Chinese government in 1957.

I Faraglioni, Capri's most striking offshore rocks, soar up to 109 m (360 ft) out of the sea.

Tragara

The Certosa di San Giacomo, founded in 1371, is now occupied by a school and the Diefenbach Museum which has paintings and historical objects.

Marina Piccola

VISITORS' CHECKLIST

Road Map C4. 🏛 *Capri 8,000; Anacapri 5,400.* ⛴ 🚤 *from Naples & Sorrento.* ℹ *AAST:* **Capri**, *Via Marina Grande/Piazza Umberto I.* **Tel** *081 837 06 34 or 081 837 06 86;* **Anacapri**, *Via Orlandi 59.* **Tel** *081 837 15 24.*
Grotta Azzurra: ⛴ *from Marina Grande.* 🚤 *from Anacapri, 9am–1 hr before sunset.* ⬤ *if the sea is particularly rough.* 📷
Certosa di San Giacomo: *Viale della Certosa, Capri.* **Tel** *081 837 06 34 or 081 837 06 86 (AAST).* ⏰ *9am–2pm Tue–Sat, 9am–1pm Sun.* 📷
Villa Jovis: *Via A Maiuri, Capri.* ⏰ *9am–1 hr before sunset daily.* 📷
Villa San Michele: *Viale Axel Munthe 34, Anacapri.* **Tel** *081 837 14 01.* ⏰ *Nov–Feb: 9am–3:30pm daily; Mar: 9am–4:30pm daily; Apr & Oct: 9am–5pm daily; May–Sep: 9am–6pm daily.* 📷
Monte Solaro: *Anacapri. Chair lift from Via Caposcuro.* **Tel** *081 837 14 28.* ⏰ *Mar–Oct: 9:30am–4:30pm daily; Nov–Feb: 9:30am–3:30pm daily.* ⬤ *in adverse weather conditions.* 📷
www.capritourism.com

The "Piazzetta" in Capri
In the heart of town the famous "Piazzetta", officially Piazza Umberto I, is an outdoor living room, crowded day and night, packed with café tables buzzing with gossip and animated discussion. Excursions around the island also start from here. Overlooking the scene is the Baroque dome of Santo Stefano.

Via Krupp
Commissioned by the German industrialist Krupp, this famous road makes its vertiginous descent towards the sea in a series of hairpin bends.

Ischia ⑱

Bougainvillea

The hot springs on the volcanic island of Ischia were renowned in antiquity and still draw visitors today. Ancient Pithecusa was founded here in the 8th century BC by the same Greek traders who later founded Cumae on the mainland *(see pp138–9)*. Repeated attacks in the early 1300s forced people to take refuge on the small offshore island which the Aragonese later turned into a castle. A favourite with Bourbon royalty, Ischia also enchanted landscape painters and visitors such as the Irish philosopher Berkeley and the French poet Lamartine. The island is green and rugged, and each coast has a different character, offering beaches or steep hills, busy nightlife or quiet seclusion.

Fungo di Lacco Ameno
This "mushroom" rock is a prominent landmark outside Lacco Ameno, where the Greek colonists first landed.

Lacco Ameno is home to Museo di Pithecusae, where it from the Gr settlen are h

Santa Maria del Soccorso
This small sanctuary in the town of Forio combines elements of Gothic, Renaissance and Baroque, and is known for its collection of votive offerings from sailors. The English composer Sir William Walton lived just north of here, at La Mortella.

Forio

The beach at Citara is generally considered the most beautiful in Ischia.

Sant'Angelo
Originally a fishing village and now a thermal spa resort, Sant'Angelo lies west of the long Maronti beach. Here "taxi boats" can be hired to take you to coves otherwise inaccessible by land. Nearby are the Nitrodi hot springs.

0 kilometres 2

0 miles 1

Monte Epomeo
(see p173) is an extinct volcano. According to mythology, the eruptions and quakes were caused by the wails and sighs of the giant Typhoeus, imprisoned under the island.

Casamicciola Terme
Despite the damage caused by the 1883 earthquake, the spa town of Casamicciola has retained its atmosphere and some Art Nouveau architecture. The Norwegian writer Ibsen wrote Peer Gynt here.

VISITORS' CHECKLIST

Road Map A4. 🏠 *Ischia 17,000; Barano 7,800; Casamicciola Terme 6,600; Forio 11,600; Lacco Ameno 4,000; Serrara Fontana 3,000.* 🚢 🚤 *from Naples & Pozzuoli to Ischia Porto.* 🚤 *from Naples for Casamicciola Terme.* ℹ️ *AAST, Via Sogliuzzo 72, Ischia Porto.* **Tel** *081 507 42 11.* 🏛️ **Castello Aragonese Tel** *081 99 19 59.* 🕘 *9am–1 hr before sunset daily.* 📷 🏛️ **Museo di Pithecusae** *Corso A Rizzoli, Lacco Ameno.* 🕘 *9:30am–1pm, 3–7pm (4–8pm summer) Tue–Sun.* 📷 🏛️ **Giardini La Mortella** *Via F Calise 39, Forio.* 🕘 *Apr–Nov: 9am–2 hrs before sunset Tue, Thu, Sat & Sun.* 📷 **www.**infoischiaprocida.it

Ischia Porto is the island's main town where ferries dock.

Ischia Ponte
This village is connected to the small offshore island of Castello Aragonese by a causeway built in 1438.

Castello Aragonese
Different architectural styles can be seen inside the fortified walls of the island: the Angevin cathedral of the Assunta, a monastery and the church of San Pietro a Pantaniello. There is a lovely view from the Cartaromana belvedere.

Maronti beach

Procida ⓳

Road map B3. 👥 11,000.
🚢 🚢 from Naples & Pozzuoli.
ℹ️ Ufficio Informazione Comune
di Procida, Via Roma. **Tel** 081 810
19 68. Or Associazione Autonoma di
Soggiorno e Turismo, Via A Sogliuzzo
72, Ischia. **Tel** 081 507 42 11.
www.procida.it

Much smaller than Capri
and Ischia and also much
less affected by tourism, the
third island in the Bay of
Naples is a favourite with
those who love the simplicity
and traditions of the local
culture. This is the enchanting
world that author Elsa
Morante, recollecting her
many visits here, evoked in
Isola di Arturo (Arthur's
Island). Procida's economy is
sustained not only by tourism
but, to a large extent, by the
money its emigrants send
back home to their families.

Deeply rooted local
traditions are evident
in the various festivals;
for example, the Good
Friday procession *(see
p40)* that descends to the
modern port from so-called
Terra Murata – the rise
dominated by the Abbey of
San Michele – or the Graziella
celebration that takes place
in the port in mid-August.

The multi-coloured houses
resting against the tufa rock
make the island architecture

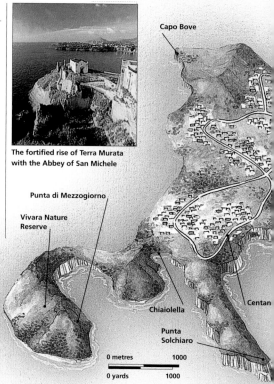

**The fortified rise of Terra Murata
with the Abbey of San Michele**

Capo Bove

Punta di Mezzogiorno

Vivara Nature
Reserve

Chiaiolella

Centan

Punta
Solchiaro

0 metres   1000

0 yards   1000

one of the most distinctive
in the region. Unique to
the island are the vaulted
buildings; originally built
as winter boat shelters and
later enlarged, acquiring
among other things façades

with arches and half-arches
that frame the doors and
windows, terraces, loggias
and long external staircases.
You can see this type of
architecture, albeit in a
partially modernized version,

View of Marina Grande

Marina
Grande
Punta della
Lingua

Marina
Corricella
Terra
Murata

Punta di
Pizzaco

Typical Procida architecture

on your arrival in Procida
in Marina Grande near the
area built up in the 17th
and 18th centuries, and at
the small, popular Chiaiolella
port on the other side of
the island. The Abbey of
San Michele, dominating
Terra Murata, dates back
to 1026, though it has
since been rebuilt. Marina
Corricella, at the foot of
Terra Murata, has been
virtually untouched by
modern times; the soil is very
fertile and the gardens here
are filled with lemon trees.

Procida also has many
splendid beaches, including
Ciraccio, across the western
shore and dotted with snack
stands; Chiaia, on the south-
eastern cove; and Pozzo
Vecchio, made famous by
the film *Il Postino*, which
was filmed there.

🏛 **Abbey of San Michele**
Via Terra Murata 89. **Tel** 081 896
76 12. ◯ 10am–12:45pm,
3–5:30pm Tue–Sat, 10am–12:45pm
Sun. www.abbaziasanmichele.it

WALKING ON THE ISLANDS

While Procida is almost flat – the highest point, Terra
Murata, is 91 m (300 ft) above sea level – Capri and
Ischia are steep-sided. On Capri (*see pp168–9*), the path
connecting Monte Solaro (589 m, 1930 ft)) to Anacapri is
delightful and practicable even for lazy visitors, though
there is always the option of the chairlift. Walkers will be
well rewarded by the striking view and the 14th-century
Santa Maria di Cetrella monastery on Marina Piccola (a
detour halfway up). Experienced hikers come back down
by the "Passetiello" path which includes a stretch directly
above the sea and leads to Capri.

The highest mountain in the bay is the extinct Epomeo
volcano (788 m, 2580 ft) on Ischia (*see pp170–71*). A climb
up the cone traditionally starts off at night from Fontana so
as to admire the view at dawn. The view takes in the island
itself, the Bay of Naples and the Tyrrhenian coast up to
Roccamonfina and the Pontine Islands. A rough dirt track
leads to the church of San Nicola (1459) and the adjoining
monastery, both hewn out of the tufa rock. On your way
down you can choose the road to Forio or Casamicciola.

Looking out over Capri from the Monte Solaro chairlift

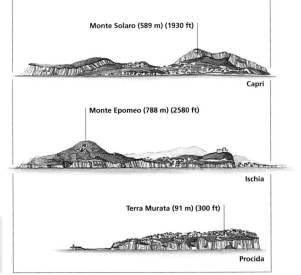

Monte Solaro (589 m) (1930 ft)

Capri

Monte Epomeo (788 m) (2580 ft)

Ischia

Terra Murata (91 m) (300 ft)

Procida

TRAVELLERS' NEEDS

WHERE TO STAY

The fascination and enchantment of Naples and the surrounding countryside have drawn visitors here for many centuries. Kings and queens, revolutionaries in exile, poets, writers and composers are among the host of celebrities who have wintered at the foot of Mount Vesuvius since the 18th century. Hotels and pensioni in the centre of Naples tend to be fairly expensive, but efforts are being

PRESTIGE
hotels

Logo of the Prestige hotels

made to widen the range of facilities available. Along the Amalfi coastline, around Sorrento and on the islands, traditional holidaying areas, the range of accommodation is much wider. Choices on offer cover all price categories, from simple pensioni to a grand luxury hotel with pools and magnificent views along the coast. This section and the lists of hotels on pages 178–87 will help you make your choice.

The 5-star Excelsior *(see p180)* overlooking the seafront

WHERE TO LOOK

Outside Naples there is no lack of choice of hotels, from luxury chains to cheaper, family-run pensions. The latter are clean and comfortable, and often have fine panoramic views. In Naples itself, the range is fairly limited, although more bed and breakfasts are now appearing. Hotels sometimes offer poor value for money. The most exclusive hotels are usually located on hills or on the seafront with superb views.

If you plan to spend a lot of time visiting museums, churches and galleries, it is best to stay in the centre of Naples. You will be within easy reach of the most important sights, and you can go back to your hotel to relax between spells of sightseeing. For those who don't mind the walk, a hotel in the commercial

district is ideal; it may not have the characteristic charm of an older establishment but will be modern and comfortable. The Prestige hotel chain, such as the Grand Hotel Vesuvio, the Excelsior and the Majestic, offer excellent service to an international clientele, and include 42 suites and 22 conference halls. The information bureaux of the Ente Provinciale per il Turismo (**EPT**, the Italian Tourist Board – *see p219*) publishes lists of hotels, pensioni and camp sites. For further information you can also make inquiries at the **Associazione Albergatori Napoletani** (Neapolitan Hotel Owners' Association).

PRICES AND GRADING

Italian hotels are classified by a star-rating system, from one, the lowest, to five stars. Prices including taxes are displayed inside each room. Breakfast is often not

Breakfast on the terrace of the Hotel Executive *(see p179)*

included, and may be an expensive item compared with a coffee and croissant in the nearest local bar. In Naples there is no difference between low and high season, but it is always worth asking about discounts, particularly off season. It is often possible to negotiate special rates for groups or longer stays. On average, single rooms cost two-thirds of the double room rate; rooms without a bathroom may cost up to 30 per cent less. In holiday resorts prices differ in low and high season; during the peak summer months you may be expected to take half-board.

HOTEL FACILITIES

Almost all the middle-range and luxury hotels in Naples underwent refurbishment some years ago and now provide a high level of comfort, including soundproofing. The cheaper hotels (one or two stars) tend to have clean but simple rooms, often with shared bathroom. Hotels outside Naples usually offer better facilities for less money.

The Hotel Pension Pinto Storey *(see p180)*, opened in 1878

◁ San Carlo Theatre, Naples

The elegant foyer in Hotel Parker's *(see p180)*

BOOKING AND PAYING

You should book well in advance if you have special requests such as a room with a good view. During July and August, the peak holiday season, hotels along the coast and on the islands get very full, so once again you must book ahead of time. Naples can also get busy, particularly if there are special events scheduled, and advance booking is recommended. If you do need to find a hotel on arrival, the local tourist offices will advise you.

When booking, you will probably be asked to pay a deposit, which can be done by credit card or international money order. When you arrive at your hotel, the reception will ask for your passport; this is to register travellers with the police, a legal formality. By law, the hotel must give you a receipt when you check out.

Telephone calls from the room and drinks from the mini-bar can be very expensive, so it is advisable to check beforehand.

BUDGET ACCOMMODATION

The **AIG** (Associazione Italiana Alberghi per la Gioventù – Youth Hostel Association) has lists of hostels. In Naples, the **Ostello Mergellina** *(see p219)*, near the Mergellina railway station, is highly recommended. Rooms have washing facilities, and breakfast is included.

There are also inexpensive family-run pensions with clean, basic rooms, but in general bathrooms are communal. Located away from the city, *agriturismi*, or farm properties, are great for families.

Interior of Il Nido hotel in Sorrento *(see p187)*

(see p180) ... *(see p219)* ... *(see p187)* ... *(see p185)*

DIRECTORY

Agriturismo
www.agriturismo.net/campania

AIG
www.aighostels.com

Associazione Albergatori Napoletani
Piazza Carità 32. **Tel** 081 552 02 05. www.napleshotels.na.it

Camping
Camp sites are usually open from April to October. Small brown road signs indicate the nearest site. The one closest to Naples is **Vulcano Solfatara***. Reached by metro (Pozzuoli stop), it has bungalows with 2–4 beds, as well as a restaurant, swimming pool and a minimarket. Along the coast, at Meta di Sorrento, is* **Bleu Village***, while Sorrento offers* **Nube d'Argento***, in the middle of an orange grove, and* **Fortunata Campogaio***, overlooking the sea. On Ischia, try* **Eurocamping dei Pini***, about 1 km (half a mile) from the centre, or* **Mirage***, on Maronti beach.* **Punta Serra** *is a good camp site on Procida.*

Bleu Village
Via Carracciolo 199 (Meta di Sorrento). **Tel** 081 878 65 57. www.bleuvillage.com

Eurocamping dei Pini
Via delle Ginestre 28 (Ischia). **Tel** 081 98 20 69. www.ischia.it/camping

Fortunata Campogaio
Via Capo 39 (Sorrento). **Tel** 081 807 35 79. www.santafortunata.eu

Mirage
Spiaggia dei Maronti (Barano d'Ischia). **Tel** 081 99 05 51. www.campingmirage.it

Nube d'Argento
Via Capo 21 (Sorrento). **Tel** 081 878 13 44. www.nubedargento.com

Ostello Mergellina
Salita della Grotta 23. **Tel** 081 761 23 46. www.ostellonapoli.com

Punta Serra
Via Serra (Procida). **Tel** 081 896 95 19.

Vulcano Solfatara
Via Solfatara 161 (Pozzuoli). www.solfatara.it

View from the terrace of the Hotel Poseidon in Positano *(see p185)*

Choosing a Hotel

The hotels in this guide have been carefully selected for their quality of service and location. They are listed by area. For more detailed information on exact locations in Naples, see the Street Finder on pages 228–43; for towns and islands in the rest of the region, see the Road Map on the inside back cover.

PRICE CATEGORIES
The following price ranges are for a standard double room and taxes per night during the high season. Breakfast is not included, unless specified.

€ Under €80
€€ €80–€140
€€€ €140–€180
€€€€ €180–€260
€€€€€ Over €260

NAPLES

TOLEDO AND CASTEL NUOVO Chiaja B&B

€€

Via Palasciano 17, 80122 **Tel** *081 240 47 55* **Fax** *081 240 47 54* **Rooms** *6 (plus 3 apartments)* **Map** *6 D2*

Opposite Da Dora *(see p195)*, one of the city's finest fish restaurants, this little bed and breakfast has charming rooms, as well as some apartments. A short walk from the Riviera di Chiaia and the seafront, it is owned by a helpful family of sailing aficionados and boat excursions are available. Breakfast on the terrace. **www.chiaiabaiabb.it**

TOLEDO AND CASTEL NUOVO Covo degli Angioini
€€

Via Melisurgo 44, 80133 **Tel** *390 810 14 02 38* **Fax** *081 19 32 36 60* **Rooms** *6* **Map** *7 B2*

Within walking distance of Castel Nuovo and the port of Naples, this modern bed and breakfast offers spacious rooms with king-size beds. The communal lounge has a widescreen TV set, Internet access and a bar. The proximity to the port makes this place ideal for day trips to the Amalfi Coast and the islands. **www.covodegliangioini.it**

TOLEDO AND CASTEL NUOVO Chiaja Hotel de Charme
€€€

Via Chiaia 216, 80121 **Tel** *081 41 55 55* **Fax** *081 42 23 44* **Rooms** *27* **Map** *6 F2, 7 A3*

Set on the first floor of a *palazzo* on the pedestrian shopping street of Via Chiaia, this lovely, intimate hotel is only two minutes' walk from Piazza Plebescito. All rooms are soundproofed and individually furnished with antiques; seven have whirlpool baths. Deservedly popular, with charming and professional staff. **www.hotelchiaia.it**

TOLEDO AND CASTEL NUOVO Hotel Palazzo Alabardieri
€€€€

Via Alabardieri 38, 80121 **Tel** *081 41 52 78* **Fax** *081 40 14 78* **Rooms** *33* **Map** *6 F2*

This hotel was built within the former convent of the church of Santa Maria di Chiaia, just off Piazza dei Martiri, one of the city's most prestigious squares. All rooms are elegant. Superior rooms are spacious and generally have parquet floors. The junior suites are particularly stylish. Private tour guides available for excursions. **www.palazzoalabardieri.it**

TOLEDO AND CASTEL NUOVO Mercure Angioino
€€€€

Via Depretis 123, 80133 **Tel** *081 552 95 00* **Fax** *081 552 95 09* **Rooms** *85* **Map** *7 B2*

Located between the university and the port, the Mercure Angioino is convenient for ferries to the islands and visiting Castel Nuovo. Mainly a business hotel, it provides modern and comfortable facilities. The clean, tastefully decorated bedrooms are soundproofed to block out street noise. Nearby public car park. **www.mercure.com**

SPACCANAPOLI Ginevra
€

Via Genova 116, 80143 **Tel** *081 28 32 10* **Fax** *081 28 32 10* **Rooms** *19* **Map** *4 F4*

Ideal for a short visit or for those on a budget, the Ginevra is conveniently located for the station in a pleasant area – the nearby morning market around Via Nazionale is excellent. All rooms are modern, clean and comfortable, with TVs and phones. Superior rooms have fridges. Friendly staff. **www.hotelginevra.it**

SPACCANAPOLI Hotel Garden

€

Corso Garibaldi 92, 80142 **Tel** *081 28 43 31* **Fax** *081 633 77 35* **Rooms** *35* **Map** *4 E4*

At the far end of Piazza Garibaldi, this is a well-run, moderate-range hotel, with a panoramic roof terrace and a bar. Bedrooms are comfortable, some have balconies. It is within walking distance of the sights of central Naples, and handy for trips to Pompeii, Sorrento and beyond. Several good bars and restaurants are nearby. **www.hotelgardenapoli.it**

SPACCANAPOLI Decumani Hotel de Charme
€€

Via San Giovanni Maggiore Pignatelli 15, 80134 **Tel** *081 551 81 88* **Fax** *081 551 81 88* **Rooms** *22* **Map** *7 B1, 9 C4*

This hotel is situated on one of the narrow alleyways of the historic centre. Once home to local nobility, the building features spacious rooms with antique furniture and typical 19th-century Neapolitan decorations. Guests can linger in the 18th-century reading room. In the summer, breakfast is served on the panoramic terrace. **www.decumani.com**

SPACCANAPOLI Albergo Palazzo Decumani

€€€

Piazza Giustino Fortunato 8, 80100 **Tel** *081 420 13 79* **Fax** *081 790 15 40* **Rooms** *28* **Map** *3 C5, 10 D3*

Located in an early 20th-century Liberty (Art Nouveau) building in the heart of the city, this hotel is a stylish, urban establishment within walking distance of the Archivio di Stato and the convent of Santa Chiara. Rooms are spacious and luxury suites are available. Breakfast may be served in the room. Free Wi-Fi. **www.palazzodecumani.com**

Key to Symbols *see back cover flap*

SPACCANAPOLI Hotel Executive

Via del Cerriglio 10, 80134 **Tel** *081 552 06 11* **Fax** *081 551 90 90* **Rooms** *19*   **Map** *7 B1, 9 C5*

Occupying part of the pretty monastery of Santa Maria La Nova, the Executive enjoys a central location yet is away from the bustle of busy roads. It is managed by a local hotel chain, in an efficient and friendly way. Public rooms are filled with antiques, and bedrooms are attractive too. There is a sauna and a lovely roof terrace. **www.sea-hotels.com**

SPACCANAPOLI Hotel Il Convento

Via Speranzella 137a, 80132 **Tel** *081 40 39 77* **Fax** *081 40 03 32* **Rooms** *14*   **Map** *7 A2*

Standing next to the old convent of Santa Maria di Francesca delle Cinque Piaghe, this central hotel has a fairly modern interior. Bedrooms are airy, decorated in soothing colours, attractively furnished and with balconies. The larger rooms and two suites have their own tiny flower-filled roof terraces. Free Wi-Fi connection. **www.hotelilconvento.com**

SPACCANAPOLI Renaissance Naples Hotel Mediterraneo

Via Nuova Ponte di Tappia 25, 80133 **Tel** *081 797 00 01* **Fax** *081 552 58 68* **Rooms** *223*   **Map** *7 A2*

Part of the Marriott chain, this hotel has a lovely location just off Via Toledo – close to the historical sights, shops, restaurants and port. Bedrooms and suites display an understated elegance and many offer fine views. Breakfast is served in the panoramic roof restaurant. Piano bar and cocktail bar. **www.mediterraneonapoli.com**

SPACCANAPOLI Starhotel Terminus

Piazza Garibaldi 91, 80142 **Tel** *081 779 31 11* **Fax** *081 20 66 89* **Rooms** *173*   **Map** *4 E4*

Moments from the central railway station at Piazza Garibaldi, this large hotel caters mainly for the business market and offers facilities such as Wi-Fi throughout. Bedrooms are stylish and comfortable and there is a charming roof terrace and bar. Executive rooms are designed with business guests in mind. Breakfast is included. **www.starhotels.it**

DECUMANO MAGGIORE Aleph B&B

Via dei Tribunali 309, 80138 **Tel** *081 45 47 93* **Fax** *081 45 47 93* **Rooms** *1*   **Map** *3 C4, 10 D2*

The Aleph combines a B&B with a contemporary art museum filled with pieces by the owner-architect. The en suite room has a balcony overlooking San Lorenzo church. The friendly owners are great with children and always ready to help with planning their guests' time in Naples. Breakfast is included. **www.alephdesign.info**

DECUMANO MAGGIORE Donna Regina

Via Luigi Settembrini 80, 80139 **Tel** *081 44 67 99* **Fax** *081 44 67 99* **Rooms** *3*   **Map** *3 C3, 10 D1*

Formerly the mother superior's quarters in the 14th-century Donna Regina monastery, this lovely bed and breakfast overlooks two churches. It is filled with both heirlooms and modern art (the owner is a painter). Bedrooms are all en suite and utterly charming. Dinner is available on request. **www.discovernaples.net**

DECUMANO MAGGIORE Hotel Neapolis

Via F Del Giudice 13 (Via Tribunali), 81038 **Tel** *081 442 08 15* **Fax** *081 442 08 19* **Rooms** *19*   **Map** *3 B5, 9 C3*

Beside the church of the Pietrasanta, on the ancient Decumano Maggiore, this third-floor hotel is within easy striking distance of all the major sights. It is above a good trattoria that has a lovely patio – great for summer dinners alfresco. Free Internet access is available in the smart, spacious bedrooms. **www.hotelneapolis.com**

DECUMANO MAGGIORE L'Alloggio dei Vassalli

Via Donnalbina 56, 80134 **Tel** *081 551 51 18* **Fax** *081 420 27 52* **Rooms** *5*   **Map** *9 B5*

This appealing bed and breakfast is on the second floor of Palazzo Donnalbina, which dates from the 18th century. Wooden beams, stucco work and antique furniture are among its smart features. All rooms have private bathrooms and DVD players. Next to the hotel there is a day spa. **www.bandbnapoli.it**

DECUMANO MAGGIORE Tribù B&B

Via dei Tribunali 339, 81038 **Tel** *081 45 47 93 or 328 546 12 00* **Fax** *081 45 48 38* **Rooms** *4*   **Map** *3 C4, 10 D3*

Built in the 13th-century Palazzo d'Angiò, Tribù unites Naples' medieval history with modern design. Each of its four light-filled rooms is decorated differently, with pieces made or adapted by its artist/architect proprietors. Guests can gather for wine on the cool courtyard and terrace, where breakfast is also served. **www.tribunapoli.com**

DECUMANO MAGGIORE Costantinopoli 104

Via S Maria di Costantinopoli 104, 80138 **Tel** *081 557 10 35* **Fax** *081 557 10 51* **Rooms** *19*   **Map** *9 B2, 3 B4*

This Liberty (Art Nouveau) villa has beautiful stained glass, a courtyard and a garden with palm trees, a sun terrace and a small pool. It is an oasis from the chaos beyond, located in the historic centre, on a street of antiquarian shops and booksellers. Wi-Fi is available in the rooms and breakfast is included. **www.costantinopoli104.it**

CAPODIMONTE AND I VERGINI Casa Totò B&B

Via Antonio de Curtis 1b, 80137 **Tel** *081 19 70 86 66* **Rooms** *3*   **Map** *3 C3*

This friendly B&B is close to the end of Via Duomo, on the street where Neapolitan comedy legend Totò *(see p37)* was born and lived: his house-museum is nearby. Every room is en suite and has a corner kitchen; guests can relax in the charming garden. Breakfast can be served in your own private kitchen. **www.bnbnapoli.com**

CAPODIMONTE AND I VERGINI Villa Capodimonte Hotel

Salita Moiariello 66, 80131 **Tel** *081 45 90 00* **Fax** *081 29 93 44* **Rooms** *55*   **Map** *3 C1*

Conveniently located near the Capodimonte Museum and Park, this modern hotel looks out over the Bay of Naples. Rooms are airy and comfortable, and the best ones have a terrace with a view of the sea. Breakfast is served on the veranda overlooking the pretty hotel gardens. **www.villacapodimonte.it**

VOMERO Hotel Cimarosa

Via Cimarosa 29, 80127 **Tel** *081 556 70 44* **Fax** *081 578 28 52* **Rooms** *15* **Map** *2 D5*

A step away from the funicular station at Piazza Fuga, from which you can ride down to Via Toledo, this hotel occupies the top floor of a genteel *palazzo*. Rooms are light, spacious and immaculate, with views over the Bay of Naples towards Capri. Some don't have en suite bathrooms. **www.hotelcimarosa.it**

VOMERO San Francesco al Monte

Corso Vittorio Emanuele 328, 80135 **Tel** *081 423 91 11* **Fax** *081 423 94 61* **Rooms** *45* **Map** *2 F5*

Once a Francescan monastery, this hotel has a spectacular roof terrace and pool perched high on Vomero hill, giving views over Naples, Vesuvius and the sea. Each of the rooms – former monks' cells – is beautifully furnished. Bathrooms are luxurious and breakfast is included. Terrace restaurant in summer. **www.sanfrancescoalmonte.it**

VOMERO Grand Hotel Parker's

Corso Vittorio Emanuele 135, 80121 **Tel** *081 761 24 74* **Fax** *081 66 35 27* **Rooms** *83* **Map** *6 D1*

Built by an English marine biologist over a century ago, this imposing pile has an air of hushed luxury. Bedrooms are large and the public rooms are decorated with Neo-Classical furniture and paintings. A beautiful view of the Bay of Naples can be had from the panoramic bar and restaurant. There is also a spa/gym. **www.grandhotelparkers.com**

CASTEL DELL'OVO AND CHIAIA Cappella Vecchia

Vico Santa Maria a Cappella Vecchia 11, 80121 **Tel** *081 240 51 17* **Fax** *081 245 53 38* **Rooms** *6* **Map** *6 F2*

This small guesthouse with modern rooms is in a charming area, on a tiny street off Piazza dei Martiri in Chiaia. Convenient for exploring the city, it is near the Piazza Vittoria bus terminus, the Piazza Amedeo metro station and plenty of shops. The owners are very helpful. Breakfast and free Wi-Fi are included. **www.cappellavecchia11.it**

CASTEL DELL'OVO AND CHIAIA Hotel Ausonia

Via F Caracciolo 11, 80122 **Tel** *081 68 22 78* **Fax** *081 66 45 36* **Rooms** *12* **Map** *5 B3*

The Ausonia occupies a house on the seafront, just steps away from the harbour of Mergellina. A lovely family-owned hotel, it offers nautically-themed rooms and is, appropriately, run like a tight ship. Views are of an internal courtyard. Staff go out of their way to be helpful. Breakfast is included. **www.hotelausonianapoli.com**

CASTEL DELL'OVO AND CHIAIA Hotel Rex

Via Palepoli 12, 80132 **Tel** *081 764 93 89* **Fax** *081 764 92 27* **Rooms** *33* **Map** *7 A4*

One street back from the seafront, this hotel is well located and offers reasonable rates. While facilities are minimal, bedrooms are large and comfortable – ideal for families. Some have balconies with pleasant views. Breakfast is included. Rooms can be noisy as the windows are not soundproofed. **www.hotel-rex.it**

CASTEL DELL'OVO AND CHIAIA Parteno Bed & Breakfast

Via Partenope 1, Lungomare Caracciolo, 80121 **Tel** *081 245 20 95* **Fax** *081 247 13 03* **Rooms** *6* **Map** *7 A4*

Overlooking the Castel dell'Ovo, this bed and breakfast is located at the seafront, surrounded by some of the best restaurants in town and within easy walking distance of downtown Naples as well as the port. Most rooms have views of the sea and balconies. Complimentary Wi-Fi. **www.parteno.it**

CASTEL DELL'OVO AND CHIAIA Pinto Storey

Via G Martucci 72, 80121 **Tel** *081 68 12 60* **Fax** *081 66 75 36* **Rooms** *16* **Map** *6 D1*

This hotel is in an elegant part of town, within walking distance of the seafront, opposite the metro and near the funicular to Vomero. On the fourth and fifth floors of a Liberty (Art Nouveau) villa. The lobby is filled with antiques, while the bedrooms have more modern fittings. Breakfast is included. No reception midnight–7am. **www.pintostorey.it**

CASTEL DELL'OVO AND CHIAIA Miramare

Via N Sauro 24, Via Partenope, 80132 **Tel** *081 764 75 89* **Fax** *081 764 07 75* **Rooms** *31* **Map** *7 B4*

This lovely Art Nouveau hotel, standing on the seafront along from Santa Lucia towards the port, is crammed with antiques and has charming proprietors. There is a beautiful terrace with fine views towards Vesuvius. Bedrooms vary, but all are soundproofed. It pays to upgrade to a room with a sea view. **www.hotelmiramare.com**

CASTEL DELL'OVO AND CHIAIA Palazzo Turchini

Via Medina 21–22, 80132 **Tel** *081 551 06 06* **Fax** *081 552 14 73* **Rooms** *27* **Map** *7 B2*

A venerable institution, this former royal orphanage and music conservatory dates from the 1700s. Facing the Fountain of Neptune and beside the parish church, La Incoronotella, it boasts a roof terrace and a winter garden. Bedrooms have parquet floors and elegant furnishings; some have private terraces. **www.palazzoturchini.it**

CASTEL DELL'OVO AND CHIAIA Royal Continental

Via Partenope 38, 80121 **Tel** *081 245 20 68* **Fax** *081 764 57 07* **Rooms** *400* **Map** *7 A4*

The only hotel on Santa Lucia harbour with a roof-top pool and spa: its 1950s exterior belies its stylish interior. Bedrooms and the restaurant have fine views over Castel dell'Ovo. All bedrooms are smart, but modernists will love the Gio Ponti floor with its 24 rooms conceived by the design pioneer. Breakfast is included. **www.royalgroup.it**

CASTEL DELL'OVO AND CHIAIA Excelsior

Via Partenope 48, 80121 **Tel** *081 764 01 11* **Fax** *081 764 97 43* **Rooms** *136* **Map** *7 A4*

Easily the best located of the cluster of luxury hotels along Santa Lucia, the Excelsior has front and side views of Vesuvius and Castel dell'Ovo. The roof-top terrace is disarmingly beautiful and the restaurant is a real treat, serving excellent food. Comfortable bedrooms and sumptuous decor throughout. Helpful staff. **www.excelsior.it**

Key to Price Guide *see p178* **Key to Symbols** *see back cover flap*

CASTEL DELL'OVO AND CHIAIA Grand Hotel Santa Lucia €€€€€

Via Partenope 46, 80121 **Tel** *081 764 06 66* **Fax** *081 764 85 80* **Rooms** *95* **Map** *7 A4*

Directly facing the harbour of the same name, the Santa Lucia is one of Naples' historic seafront hotels. Built over a century ago, it has elegant Neo-Classical furnishings. Bedrooms are airy, stylish and filled with antiques; the nicest are a good size and have wonderful sea views. Many of the bathrooms have whirlpool baths. **www.santalucia.it**

CASTEL DELL'OVO AND CHIAIA Grand Hotel Vesuvio €€€€€

Via Partenope 45, 80121 **Tel** *081 764 00 44* **Fax** *081 764 44 83* **Rooms** *160* **Map** *7 A4*

Arguably one of Naples' most luxurious hotels, Vesuvio is found in Santa Lucia. The penthouse suite is famously spectacular, the choice of royalty, politicians and footballers. All rooms are sumptuous and full of antiques. Many have a terrace or balcony. Other facilities include a spa, gym and roof-top restaurant. Breakfast is included. **www.vesuvio.it**

POSILLIPO Relais Posillipo €€

Via Posillipo 69, 80123 **Tel** *081 248 31 93* **Fax** *081 575 76 22* **Rooms** *11* **Map** *5 A4*

This glass-walled boutique hotel is set high on Posillipo's prestigious hill, with spectacular views. Spacious rooms are decorated to a blue-and-white scheme; some bedrooms have Jacuzzis and terraces. It is an easy bus ride to the centre and Vomero, while the Parco Virgiliano and Marechiaro are nearby. Breakfast is included. **www.relaisposillipo.com**

POSILLIPO Hotel Paradiso €€€€

Via Catullo 11, 80122 **Tel** *081 247 51 11* **Fax** *081 761 34 49* **Rooms** *72* **Map** *5 A4*

Part of the Best Western chain, this hotel has gorgeous views across the bay and a roof-top bar and restaurant. Rooms are spacious and elegant, with parquet floors. A little isolated for those without their own transport, although it is only a short walk to a funicular, which takes you down to Mergellina port. **www.hotelparadisonapoli.it**

POMPEII & THE AMALFI COAST

AMALFI Hotel Lidomare €€

Largo Duchi Piccolomini 9, 84011 **Tel** *089 87 13 32* **Fax** *089 87 13 94* **Rooms** *18* **Road Map** *D4*

A stylish, old-fashioned and extremely comfortable family-run hotel in the heart of Amalfi. Rooms are large and quiet with majolica-tiled floors, heavy old furniture and modern bathrooms. Some have private balconies with sea views. Breakfast is included. The entrance is tucked away upstairs, down an alley opposite the Duomo. **www.lidomare.it**

AMALFI La Conchiglia €€

Piazza dei Protontini 9, 84011 **Tel** *089 87 18 56* **Fax** *089 87 18 56* **Rooms** *11* **Road Map** *D4*

On the far side of Amalfi, near the sea, this small hotel offers large and airy rooms, some featuring private terraces and sea views. A warm welcome awaits guests, who can also take advantage of a private beach. Excellent value for money. **www.amalfihotelconchiglia.it**

AMALFI Hotel Amalfi €€€

Via dei Pastai 3, 84011 **Tel** *089 87 24 40* **Fax** *089 87 22 50* **Rooms** *40* **Road Map** *D4*

Tucked away in a quiet spot in old Amalfi, this family-run hotel occupies a former pasta factory. From the lovely terrace, there are views of the Duomo across the roof tops. A patio and a bar are also available for guests. Ask ahead for a room with a geranium-decked balcony. Bedrooms are large and comfortable. **www.hamalfi.it**

AMALFI Hotel Antica Repubblica €€€

Vico dei Pastai 2, 84011 **Tel** *089 873 63 10* **Fax** *089 873 63 10* **Rooms** *7* **Road Map** *D4*

This small hotel has a roof terrace where breakfast is served and a bar. Overlooking the main square, it is also close to the seafront. Rooms are cheerful, with terracotta floor tiles and pastel coloured walls with stencilling. Junior suites have whirlpool baths and four-poster beds. Friendly owners. **www.anticarepubblica.it**

AMALFI Grand Hotel Convento di Amalfi 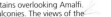 €€€€

Via Annunziatella 46, 84011 **Tel** *089 873 67 11* **Fax** *089 873 67 04* **Rooms** *53* **Road Map** *D4*

This luxury hotel is housed in a 12th-century monastery dramatically set in the mountains overlooking Amalfi. The rooms are elegantly decorated in white and beige, and many have terraces or balconies. The views of the coastline from the bougainvillea-lined walkways and restaurant are spectacular. **www.ghconventodiamalfi.com**

AMALFI Hotel Miramalfi  €€€€

Via S Quasimodo 3, 84011 **Tel** *089 87 15 88* **Fax** *089 87 12 87* **Rooms** *49* **Road Map** *D4*

This getaway boasts a magical setting just outside Amalfi, perched on the cliff side above a sea-water pool and a beach reached by a lift. The facilities are modern, though the decor is a little dated. Each room has its own terrace and is spacious, light and airy. A panoramic terrace restaurant and bar complete the picture. **www.miramalfi.it**

AMALFI Hotel Luna Convento €€€€€

Via P Comite 33, 84011 **Tel** *089 87 10 02* **Fax** *089 87 13 33* **Rooms** *43* **Road Map** *D4*

A beautiful convent building, dating from 1222, houses this hotel on the coastal road leaving Amalfi. A romantic Moresco cloister and a lovely pool and sun terrace built around a Saracen look-out tower are among its charms. Bedrooms, originally monastic cells, are individually styled and there are two suites. **www.lunahotel.it**

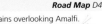
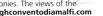

AMALFI Santa Caterina

SS Amalfitana 9, 84011 **Tel** 089 87 10 12 **Fax** 089 87 13 51 **Rooms** 66   **Road Map** D4

In the family since 1880, this luxury hotel is one of the Amalfi Coast's finest. Poised on a promontory high over Amalfi, it has extensive gardens and terracing. Bedrooms and suites are lavish, with antiques, majolica tiles and balconies. Facilities include a spa, a private lido and two restaurants. Breakfast included. **www.hotelsantacaterina.it**

BAIA Agriturismo Il Casolare di Tobia

Via Pietro Fabris 12, Contrada Coste Fondi di Baia, Bacoli, 80070 **Tel** 081 523 51 93 **Rooms** 3   **Road Map** B3

This deservedly popular *agriturismo* provides delicious food and rustic accommodation. It is set amid lush vegetation that thrives in the fertile soils of a 10,000-year-old extinct volcano. The owner will collect guests from Lucrino railway station. The shared kitchenette is ideal for families. Wonderful views and a sun terrace. **www.datobia.it**

CAPRI Hotel La Tosca

Via D Birago 5, Capri, 80073 **Tel** 081 837 09 89 **Fax** 081 837 48 03 **Rooms** 11   **Road Map** C5

Just steps from the Charterhouse of San Giacomo and Gardens of Augustus, this pretty hotel offers charming service and a central location at excellent rates. Rooms are simple and comfortable, many with private terraces and views. Wi-Fi is available throughout the hotel. Breakfast is served on a panoramic terrace.

CAPRI La Reginella

Via Matermania 36, Capri, 80073 **Tel** 081 837 05 00 **Fax** 081 837 91 26 **Rooms** 10   **Road Map** C5

Up in the hills outside Capri Town, overlooking Marina Piccola, La Reginella offers spectacular views over the bay, the Faraglioni islands and Monte Solaro. This family-run hotel has an attractive sitting room, terrace and garden. The restaurant upstairs is air conditioned in the summer. Bedrooms offer old-fashioned comfort. **www.hotellareginella.com**

CAPRI Villa Mimosa Resort

Via Nuova del Faro 48a, Anacapri, 80071 **Tel** 081 837 17 52 **Fax** 081 837 17 52 **Rooms** 6   **Road Map** C5

Not far from the centre of Anacapri, in a lovely spot with sea views, Villa Mimosa has cool, elegant rooms with delightful individual furnishings. Sunny flower-filled terraces adjoin each room. Only a short stroll away from the bus terminal. Friendly hosts make for an intimate, relaxing break. Breakfast is included. **www.mimosacapri.com**

CAPRI Biancamaria

Via G Orlandi 54, Anacapri, 80071 **Tel** 081 837 10 00 **Fax** 081 837 20 60 **Rooms** 25   **Road Map** C5

In the heart of Anacapri, this small family hotel is convenient for exploring the whole island. The decor of the cool, airy rooms is traditional and they are clean and comfortable. Small patios give views to Monte Solaro or the roadside. Rooms at the back are quieter. Breakfast included. Charge for air conditioning. **www.hotelbiancamaria.com**

CAPRI Villa Krupp

Via G Matteoti 12, Capri, 80073 **Tel** 081 837 03 62 **Fax** 081 837 64 89 **Rooms** 12   **Road Map** C5

Built by German industrialist Friedrick Krupp, the villa was once home to Maxim Gorky and a notorious former guest was Lenin. Incredible views are to be had from the terraces, which face the Faraglioni islands and the Roman gardens of Augustus. Meals are served on the terrace. Ask for a room with a sea view. Breakfast included. **www.villakrupp.it**

CAPRI Gatto Bianco

Via V Emanuele 32, Capri, 80073 **Tel** 081 837 04 46 **Fax** 081 837 80 60 **Rooms** 41   **Road Map** C5

Very close to the Piazzetta, this hotel boasts elegant public rooms, charming service and pretty gardens. Furnished with antiques, the bedrooms are cool and spacious; some offer balconies or terraces. A white cat was found during the hotel's construction, hence the name. Beauty treatments available. **www.gattobianco-capri.com**

CAPRI Hotel La Minerva

Via Occhio Marino 8, Capri, 80073 **Tel** 081 837 70 67 **Fax** 081 837 52 21 **Rooms** 18   **Road Map** C5

This pretty five-storey hotel offers flower-filled terraces, sea views and attractive architectural details and is located in a quiet, picturesque spot not far from the centre of Capri Town. Superior rooms have terraces with sea views; deluxe rooms have whirlpool baths and private sea-facing terraces. Breakfast is included. **www.laminervacapri.com**

CAPRI Hotel Villa Brunella

Via Tragara 24, Capri, 80073 **Tel** 081 837 01 22 **Fax** 081 837 04 30 **Rooms** 20   **Road Map** C4/5

This elegant, family-owned hotel stands in lush gardens, with a pool overlooking the bay of Marina Piccola. Bedrooms and suites are decorated in cool, mellow tones, accentuating the space and light. Suites have sitting rooms and terraces. The terrace restaurant is charming and the sun terrace by the pool has magical views. **www.villabrunella.it**

CAPRI Hotel Weber Ambassador

Via Marina Piccola 118, Capri, 80073 **Tel** 081 837 01 41 **Fax** 081 837 88 66 **Rooms** 78   **Road Map** C5

Perched above Marina Piccola, Capri's most spectacular beach, with fine views over the Faraglioni islands, this yellow-painted hotel has flower-filled terraces shaded by blue canopies. There is a roof garden and a lovely terrace for breakfast (expensive, but generous). Sea-view rooms and suites cost more. **www.hotelweber.com**

CAPRI Il Mulino

Via La Fabbrica 9, Anacapri, 80071 **Tel** 081 838 20 84 **Fax** 081 838 21 32 **Rooms** 7   **Road Map** C5

Set in lower Anacapri, down towards the Blue Grotto, is the lovely Il Mulino. It is a 15-minute walk to town or you can take a bus. This former farm has gardens and terraces amid olive groves, citrus trees and tumbling geraniums. Rooms are comfortable, with modern facilities, and each has a terrace. Delicious breakfasts. **www.mulino-capri.it**

Key to Price Guide *see p178* **Key to Symbols** *see back cover flap*

CAPRI San Michele

Via G Orlandi 1–3–5, Anacapri, 80071 **Tel** *081 837 1427* **Fax** *081 837 1420* **Rooms** *60*   **Road Map** *C5*

This delightful rose-coloured villa in central Anacapri is finished in Neo-Classical style and has a timeless family feel. There is a tempting pool and a garden affording wonderful views. Some bedrooms have terraces or balconies with views. Not all have air conditioning. The restaurant terrace is impressive. **www.sanmichele-capri.com**

CAPRI Capri Palace Hotel & Spa

Via Capodimonte 14, Anacapri, 80071 **Tel** *081 978 01 11* **Fax** *081 837 31 91* **Rooms** *77*   **Road Map** *C5*

One of Capri's most beautiful hotels, located in quiet Anacapri. Bedrooms, some with balconies, overlook Monte Solare or the sea. Suites have private terraces and most have private pools. Lovely main pool, spa, gym and beach club. Hotel boats for excursions. Award-winning restaurant, L'Olivo *(see p197)*. **www.capri-palace.com**

CAPRI Punta Tragara

Via Tragara 57, Capri, 80073 **Tel** *081 837 08 44* **Fax** *081 837 77 90* **Rooms** *44*   **Road Map** *C4/5*

In a wonderful quiet position facing the Faraglioni islands, this red-hued hotel combines luxury and design in harmony with nature. Its architect was Le Corbusier and bedrooms are serene, with antiques, art, amazing views and Internet access. There's a beautiful pool and candle-lit dining in the renowned restaurant. **www.hoteltragara.com**

CAPRI Villa Le Scale

Via Capodimonte 64, Capri, 80071 **Tel** *081 838 2190* **Fax** *081 838 2796* **Rooms** *8*   **Road Map** *C4/5*

Perfect for those seeking total hush and relaxation, this award-winning boutique hotel occupies a luxurious and historic private home built by a local baron in the 1800s. The gardens and pool create an enchanted setting outside while a collection of art and antiques adorns the interior. **www.villalescale.com**

CETARA Hotel Cetus

SS 163 for Amalfi, Cetara, 84010 **Tel** *089 26 13 88* **Fax** *089 26 13 88* **Rooms** *37*   **Road Map** *E4*

A fine hotel on the Amalfi Coast road, Cetus has a spectacular setting jutting out from a cliff top and boasts dazzling views through its glass walls. All bedrooms have sea views, as do the restaurant terrace and bar. There is a private beach within short walking distance. The hotel is close to the fishing town of Cetara *(see p161)*. **www.hotelcetus.com**

FURORE Hotel Ristorante Bacco

Via G B Lama 9, 84010 **Tel** *089 83 03 60* **Fax** *089 83 03 52* **Rooms** *20*   **Road Map** *D4*

This 19th-century villa, now a taverna with rooms, borders an olive grove, vineyard and terrace. The individually named bedrooms are simple and whitewashed, with terracotta floors and balconies. Suites have huge glass windows. The excellent restaurant offers its own brand of white wine. Free Wi-Fi in public rooms. **www.baccofurore.it**

FURORE Furore Inn Resort & Spa

Via dell'Amore 1, 84010 **Tel** *089 830 47 11* **Fax** *089 830 47 77* **Rooms** *22*   **Road Map** *D4*

Set on Italy's only fjord, in the lovely village of Furore on the Amalfi coast. Small, luxurious and modern, all rooms have sea views and whirlpool baths; deluxe rooms and suites are especially grand. Excellent restaurant, three pools and a health spa. Boat excursions and cookery lessons are available as is a regular shuttle bus to Amalfi. **www.furoreinn.it**

ISCHIA Hotel Da Raffaele

Via Roma 29, 80077 **Tel** *081 99 12 03* **Fax** *081 99 12 03* **Rooms** *18*   **Road Map** *B4*

Right in the centre of Ischia Porto, this hotel and restaurant offers a welcoming environment and central location near the harbour and the beautiful beach. The rooms are simple and comfortable. The restaurant Da Raffaele *(see p198)* is a popular spot serving local grilled specialities. Breakfast is included. **www.daraffaele.it**

ISCHIA Il Vitigno B&B

Via Bocca 31, Forio d'Ischia, 80075 **Tel** *081 99 83 07* **Fax** *081 99 83 07* **Rooms** *13*   **Road Map** *A4*

This lovely *agriturismo* includes a large vineyard and an estate where you can walk and enjoy nature. Rooms are within the farmhouse and two outhouses – the decor is rustic and all are en suite. Meals are relaxed communal affairs with guests enjoying the farm produce and the local wine. **www.agriturismoilvitigno.it**

ISCHIA Hotel Il Monastero

Castello Aragonese, Ischia Ponte, 80077 **Tel** *081 99 24 35* **Fax** *081 99 18 49* **Rooms** *22*   **Road Map** *B4*

One of the most distinguished addresses on the island belongs to this hotel as it occupies a former convent within Castello Aragonese. It has been refurbished by the art collector owners. The rooms (former cells) are cheerfully decorated and some have terraces. The views are breathtaking. **www.albergoilmonastero.it**

ISCHIA Hotel della Baia

Baia di S Montano, Lacco Ameno, 80076 **Tel** *081 98 63 98* **Fax** *081 98 65 00* **Rooms** *16*   **Road Map** *A4*

This comfortable hotel is ideally placed for the beach at San Montano. It also neighbours the breathtaking gardens of Negombo, established by an Italian nobleman. The gardens contain a thermal spa, to which the hotel's guests receive free entry. The hotel has a panoramic terrace, a restaurant and five suites with gardens. **www.negombo.it**

ISCHIA Park Hotel Miramare

Via Comandante Maddalena 29, Sant'Angelo, 80070 **Tel** *081 99 92 19* **Fax** *081 99 93 25* **Rooms** *52*   **Road Map** *A4*

Overlooking Maronti Bay, one of Ischia's most beautiful, is this elegant beach hotel. It has an excellent spa a short walk from the main building. Rooms have sea views; some have terraces or balconies. Two suites are set in the gardens. Breakfast is included. Sant'Angelo town is picturesque and favoured by Italians. **www.hotelmiramare.it**

ISCHIA Mezza Torre Resort & Spa €€€€€

Via Mezzatorre 23, Forio d'Ischia, 80075 **Tel** *081 98 61 11* **Fax** *081 98 60 15* **Rooms** *57*　　**Road Map** *A4*

A luxury spa hotel set in a pine forest, on a bluff high above the sea between Forio and Lacco Ameno. Some rooms have balconies: comfort rooms have sea views while others overlook the park. Superior rooms and suites are sumptuous; some are in a romantic old Saracen tower. Beautiful pools, restaurant and spa. **www.mezzatorre.it**

ISCHIA Miramare e Castello €€€€€

Via Pontano 5, Ischia Ponte, 80077 **Tel** *081 99 13 33* **Fax** *081 98 45 72* **Rooms** *41*　　**Road Map** *B4*

In a beautiful spot between Ischia Porto and Ischia Ponte, with views of Castello Aragonese and the big blue sea beyond, this lovely family-run hotel dates from the 1950s. Bedrooms are elegantly furnished; prices increase with comfort and for views. Breakfast is served on the exquisite roof terrace. **www.miramareecastello.it**

ISCHIA Regina Isabella e Royal Sporting €€€€€

Piazza S Restuita 1, Lacco Ameno, 80076 **Tel** *081 99 43 22* **Fax** *081 90 01 90* **Rooms** *128*　　**Road Map** *A4*

Built in the 1950s, this is probably Ischia's most luxurious hotel – the choice of Elizabeth Taylor and Richard Burton during filming of Cleopatra. The spa, certainly, is the island's most advanced. Decor is ultra stylish: bedrooms have majolica tiles, antiques and contemporary textiles and most have private terraces or balconies. **www.reginaisabella.it**

MAIORI Reginna Palace Hotel €€

Via C Colombo 1, 84010 **Tel** *089 87 71 83* **Fax** *089 85 12 00* **Rooms** *67*　　**Road Map** *D4*

This charming hotel is located in Maiori, right in the heart of the Amalfi Coast, and boasts a lush Mediterranean garden with a beautiful pool and a private beach nearby. Rooms are warm and welcoming, some featuring balconies overlooking the waterfront. Excursions on the Amalfi Coast can be arranged. **www.hotelreginna.it**

MAIORI Casa Raffaele €€€€

Via Casa Mannini 10, 84010 **Tel** *089 85 35 47* **Fax** *089 854 18 65* **Rooms** *9*　　**Road Map** *D4*

This frescoed house was built and furnished by Raffaele Conforti, a 19th-century lemon merchant. Peaceful and elegant, it is now open as a small hotel in the heart of Maiori. Antique furniture adds to the sense of stepping back in time. The suite has a whirlpool bath under a frescoed ceiling. **www.casaraffaeleconforti.it**

MASSA LUBRENSE La Certosa €€

Via Marina del Cantone 23, 80061 **Tel** *081 808 12 09* **Fax** *081 808 12 45* **Rooms** *16*　　**Map** *C4*

In a lovely spot, right on the beach in the beautiful Baia di Nerano, where Ulysses was bewitched by the Sirens. The hotel partly occupies a 14th-century convent with medieval vaulting and architectural detail carried through into its modern extension. Rooms are simple, colourful and comfortable. Breakfast included. Terrace dining. **www.hotelcertosa.com**

MASSA LUBRENSE Locanda del Capitano €€

Piazza delle Sirene 10, Marina del Cantone, 80061 **Tel** *081 808 10 21* **Fax** *081 808 18 92* **Rooms** *12*　**Road Map** *C4*

Not just a wonderful fish restaurant, but also a small inn overlooking the enchanting bay of Marina del Cantone. The food and wine share the billing here alongside the extraordinary view. The hotel is a pretty white building right on the beach. The stylish bedrooms share the views. Breakfasts are delicious. **www.tavernadelcapitano.it**

MASSA LUBRENSE Piccolo Paradiso €€

Piazza Madonna della Lobra 5, 80061 **Tel** *081 878 92 40* **Fax** *081 808 90 56* **Rooms** *54*　　**Map** *C4*

Set amid citrus trees near the old parish church, close to the centre of Massa Lubrense, this hotel has a pool and fine views. A quiet, comfortable place, it is a pleasant stroll away from the Marina di Lobra below, where you can watch the fishermen at work and sample their catch. Regular buses run to Sorrento. **www.piccolo-paradiso.com**

NERANO Relais Vittoria €€

Via A Vespucci 25, 80061 **Tel** *081 808 22 12* **Fax** *081 808 29 33* **Rooms** *8*　　**Road Map** *C4*

Located in Nerano, at the tip of the Sorrento Peninsula, this luxury B&B is a haven of peace. Rooms are elegant and bright. The panorama from the sea view rooms is worth the extra price. Boat services are available, and a free shuttle runs to a pretty beach nearby. Breakfast is included and served on a terrace with sea views. **www.relaisvittoria.com**

PAESTUM Agriturismo Seliano €€

Via Seliano, Capaccio Scalo, 84047 **Tel** *0828 72 36 34* **Fax** *0828 72 45 44* **Rooms** *14*　　**Road Map** *F5*

Run by the Bellelli family, whose forefathers were famously painted by Edgar Degas, this *agriturismo* is a short drive off the main road between Capaccio Scalo and Paestum. Rooms are in the main house or estate cottages. Pretty gardens, a pool and delicious food. Staying on the buffalo farm is also an option. **www.agriturismoseliano.it**

PAESTUM Hotel Paistos €€€

Via Laura Mare 39, Capaccio, 84040 **Tel** *0828 85 16 83* **Fax** *0828 85 16 61* **Rooms** *15*　　**Road Map** *F5*

This small and comfortable modern hotel with surrounding garden is not far from the beach at Capaccio and around 3.5 km (2 miles) from the temples of Paestum. Bedrooms are simple and most have balconies. There is a good restaurant, with mostly organic dining. Breakfast is included. Closed Dec–Feb. **www.hotelpaistos.com**

POMPEII Hotel dei Misteri €

Via Villa dei Misteri 11, 80045 **Tel** *081 861 35 93* **Fax** *081 862 29 83* **Rooms** *40*　　**Road Map** *D3*

A fine retreat after a dusty day touring Pompeii's ruins or hiking up Vesuvius, this hotel is located close to the Circumvesuviana train and Pompeii's Villa dei Misteri entrance. Motel-style rooms are available near the cooling pool, or you can choose to stay in the main building. Not all rooms have air conditioning. **www.villadeimisteri.it**

Key to Price Guide *see p178* **Key to Symbols** *see back cover flap*

POMPEII Hotel Amleto

Via B Longo 10, 80045 **Tel** *081 863 10 04* **Fax** *081 863 55 85* **Rooms** *26*   **Road Map** *D3*

Family-run, this is a comfortable modern hotel, with elegant decor and well-furnished rooms. In the heart of new Pompeii, it is convenient for the Circumvesuviana train between Naples and Sorrento and a short walk to the ruins. Very pleasant roof terrace. Pompeiian-style frescoes adorn the public areas. Breakfast included. **www.hotelamleto.it**

POSITANO Pensione Maria Luisa

Via Fornillo 42, 84017 **Tel** *089 87 50 23* **Fax** *089 812 23 60* **Rooms** *10*   **Road Map** *D4*

Positano's oldest hotel is a delightfully simple place at Fornillo beach. Unlike luxurious Positano, it has minimal facilities, though some rooms have private terraces. Fridges are provided. Prime views can be savoured from the breakfast terrace. The owner keeps several cats on the premises. **www.pensionemarialuisa.com**

POSITANO Albergo Casa Albertina

Via della Tavolozza 3, 84017 **Tel** *089 87 51 43* **Fax** *089 81 15 40* **Rooms** *20*   **Road Map** *D4*

Above the beach, this lovely hotel, once the haven of Italian playwright Luigi Pirandello, has old wooden doors and airy bedrooms with colourful tiled floors and antiques. Some rooms have whirlpool baths. Overhanging flower-filled terraces provide guests with lovely views. The restaurant is excellent. Breakfast included. **www.casalbertina.it**

POSITANO Hotel California

Via Cristoforo Colombo 141, 84017 **Tel** *089 87 53 82* **Fax** *089 81 21 54* **Rooms** *15*   **Road Map** *D4*

A delightful family hotel in the Palazzo Bruno, a noble residence with a modern annexe. The spacious terrace affords wonderful views. Some of the old bedrooms have 18th-century frescoes; the new ones have whirlpool baths. All have balconies and sea views. Breakfast is included. There is a bus stop nearby. **www.hotelcaliforniapositano.com**

POSITANO Villa La Tartana

Via Vicolo Vito Savino 4/6/8, 84017 **Tel** *089 81 21 93* **Fax** *089 812 20 12* **Rooms** *9*   **Road Map** *D4*

A good value, popular bed and breakfast. Family-run, it is a climb uphill from Piazza Molino, where there is a public car park and a bus stop. The house is on four levels and all rooms have balconies and views. Breakfast is served in a lovely dining room. Porter service. Reasonably close to the beach. **www.villalatartana.it**

POSITANO Hotel Palazzo Murat

Via dei Mulini 23, 84017 **Tel** *089 87 51 77* **Fax** *089 81 14 19* **Rooms** *30*   **Road Map** *D4*

This genteel hotel was once the summer residence of Napoleon's brother-in-law. It is set around an enchanting courtyard with a fine restaurant. Rooms in the 18th-century wing come with wooden beams and frescoes. Those in the elegant modern annexe have air conditioning. Minimum two-night stay at weekends. **www.palazzomurat.it**

POSITANO Hotel Poseidon

Via Pasitea 148, 84017 **Tel** *089 81 11 11* **Fax** *089 87 58 33* **Rooms** *49*   **Road Map** *D4*

A beautiful family-run villa immersed in lush vegetation. All rooms have private terraces, with views over the bay or the garden. Quiet and intimate, the hotel has a renowned spa and an excellent restaurant in a romantic setting. Bedrooms are large and stylish, with tiled floors and antique furniture. **www.hotelposeidonpositano.it**

POSITANO Le Sirenuse

Via Cristoforo Colombo 30, 84017 **Tel** *089 87 50 66* **Fax** *089 81 17 98* **Rooms** *61*   **Road Map** *D4*

With its excellent Swiss-trained management team, Le Sirenuse vies with the San Pietro to be Positano's top hotel. Occupying an 18th-century townhouse, it boasts exquisitely furnished rooms. Guests luxuriate under pergolas, on vine-laden terraces and beside possibly the world's most glamorous pool. Breathtaking views. **www.sirenuse.it**

POSITANO San Pietro

Via Laurito 2, 84017 **Tel** *089 87 54 55* **Fax** *089 81 14 49* **Rooms** *60*   **Road Map** *D4*

This luxurious hideaway in an extraordinary setting 2 km (1 mile) from town is the choice of many celebrities and royals. Built in the 1970s, it nevertheless has a magnificent decor, with Vietri majolica, wrought ironwork and antiques. Privacy is key on the sea-facing terraces leading from the bedrooms. Private beach. **www.ilsanpietro.it**

POZZUOLI La Tripergola

Via Miliscola 165, 80078 **Tel** *081 804 21 20* **Fax** *081 804 21 24* **Rooms** *30*   **Road Map** *B3*

Located in Arco Felice, a short distance from Pozzuoli, this hotel is a great base for exploring the Phlegraean Fields. Rooms with sea views overlook the Bay of Pozzuoli, with Capri in the distance. The excellent hotel restaurant features local specialities and alfresco dining in the summer. Breakfast is included. **www.latripergola.it/hotelnapoli.htm**

PRAIANO Hotel Margherita

Via Umberto I, 70, 84010 **Tel** *089 87 46 28* **Fax** *089 87 42 27* **Rooms** *28*   **Road Map** *D4*

A family home converted into a hotel, with slightly old-fashioned decor but lovely views and a peaceful location. Rooms are extremely comfortable; it is worth paying extra for one with a private balcony. There is a small pool offering hydromassage. Free shuttle from Praiano SITA bus stop. Breakfast is included. **www.hotelmargherita.info**

PRAIANO Onda Verde

Via Terramare 3, 84010 **Tel** *089 87 41 43* **Fax** *089 813 10 49* **Rooms** *25*   **Road Map** *D4*

In a quiet town between Amalfi and Positano, this family-run hotel has a panoramic terrace with a restaurant. Rooms are located within five villas clustered on a cliff top; many have balconies. Breakfast is included. There is a path down to a small sandy beach, beside which is a private lido. Daily boat excursions. Bus connections. **www.ondaverde.it**

PROCIDA Hotel Crescenzo

€€

Via Marina Chiaiolella 33, 80079 **Tel** *081 896 72 55* **Fax** *081 810 12 60* **Rooms** *10*   **Road Map** *B4*

A charming blue-painted hotel with a view over the harbour at Chiaiolella, Crescenzo is also one of the island's finest fish restaurants, so half board is an additional bonus. Rooms are either rear facing and quiet or overlook the harbour. Some have balconies and all are prettily decorated to a blue-and-white nautical theme. **www.hotelcrescenzo.it**

PROCIDA Hotel La Corricella

€€

Via Marina Corricella 88, 80079 **Tel** *081 896 75 75* **Fax** *081 810 17 56* **Rooms** *9*   **Road Map** *B3*

Pastel-coloured houses tumble down to the sea in this picturesque fishing harbour. Part of this scene is the charming pink-and-turquoise Hotel La Corricella, where rooms are calm, airy and spacious and the views are picture-postcard perfect. There is a terrace where guests can sit and admire the view. Closed Dec–Feb. **www.hotelcorricella.it**

PROCIDA La Casa sul Mare

€€€

Via Salita Castello 13, Terra Murata, Corricella, 80079 **Tel** *081 896 87 99* **Rooms** *10*   **Road Map** *B3*

High up beside the Terra Murata, this small hotel boasts views over the harbour of Corricella, where *Il Postino* was filmed. It has elegant public areas and a charming sea-facing garden, where breakfast is served. All bedrooms have their own private terraces. A boat takes guests to the beach at Chiaia every day in summer. **www.lacasasulmare.it**

RAVELLO Da Salvatore

€€

Via della Repubblica 2, 84010 **Tel** *089 85 72 27* **Fax** *089 858 60 00* **Rooms** *6*   **Road Map** *D4*

Six comfortable rooms are available at this inn, which is well-known for its excellent seafood *(see p200)*. They share the same fabulous view as the restaurant upstairs. Each room has a beautifully finished en suite bathroom, as well as a private balcony perfect for sitting out and enjoying the wonderful view. **www.salvatoreravello.com**

RAVELLO Best Western Hotel Marmorata

€€€

Via Bizantina 3, Loc. Marmorata, 84010 **Tel** *089 87 77 77* **Fax** *089 85 11 89* **Rooms** *37*   **Road Map** *D4*

Located on the coast between Minori and Amalfi, this converted 15th-century paper mill is in a prime secluded spot, with perfect sea views and a pool. Bedrooms are stylish. A shuttle bus takes guests up to Amalfi daily, and there is also a local bus stop outside the hotel. Breakfast is included. Good restaurant. **www.marmorata.it**

RAVELLO Hotel Graal

€€€

Via della Repubblica 8, 84010 **Tel** *089 85 72 22* **Fax** *089 85 75 51* **Rooms** *42*   **Road Map** *D4*

Far less grand than the other choices in Ravello, this modern hotel is on the main road entering the upper part of town. Views are wonderful and facilities include a pool, a sun terrace and a restaurant. The tasteful decor includes colourfully tiled floors. Some rooms have whirlpool baths and balconies. Breakfast is included. **www.hotelgraal.it**

RAVELLO Hotel Giordano

€€€€

Via Trenita 14, 84010 **Tel** *089 85 71 70* **Fax** *089 85 70 71* **Rooms** *33*   **Road Map** *D4*

Owned by the local Palumbo family, this pretty hotel has a lovely pool and a central position. Bedrooms are large, airy and whitewashed, with terraces or balconies facing the garden and pool side. A generous breakfast is served out on the terrace. Good parking facilities which is a definite perk in busy Ravello. **www.giordanohotel.it**

RAVELLO Hotel Caruso

€€€€€

Piazza S Giovanni del Toro 2, 84010 **Tel** *089 85 88 01* **Fax** *089 85 88 06* **Rooms** *48*   **Road Map** *D4*

This wonderful place was re-opened by Orient Express in 2005, who spent several years refurbishing it. The result is a stylish hotel offering excellent service. Once popular with the Bloomsbury Group, it has sumptuous bedrooms, gardens restored to their former glory, an exquisite pool and a piano bar. Breakfast included. **www.hotelcaruso.com**

RAVELLO Hotel Palumbo

€€€€€

Via S Giovanni del Toro 16, 84010 **Tel** *089 85 72 44* **Fax** *089 858 60 84* **Rooms** *17*   **Road Map** *D4*

This *palazzo* dating from the 12th century is one of the prettiest hotels in Italy, with romantic Moorish architecture in pale pink stonework. Terraces and gardens, alcoves and intimate corners – elegance and relaxation are the bywords here, as well as old-fashioned family hospitality. Every room is individually decorated. **www.hotelpalumbo.it**

RAVELLO Villa Cimbrone

€€€€€

Via Santa Chiara 26, 84010 **Tel** *089 85 74 59* **Fax** *089 85 77 77* **Rooms** *19*   **Road Map** *D4*

This 12th-century villa has world-famous romantic gardens, set in a citrus grove high on a cliff top. Bought by an Englishman in 1904, it became a haunt of the Bloomsbury Group. Bedrooms have spectacular vaulting, frescoes, majolica tiles, fireplaces and antiques. Lovely restaurant and pool. **www.villacimbrone.com**

SALERNO Hotel Plaza

€€

Piazza Vittorio Veneto 42, 84123 **Tel** *089 22 44 77* **Fax** *089 23 73 11* **Rooms** *42*   **Road Map** *E4*

A central hotel, opposite the train station and within easy walking distance of the port, the old quarter and the regular bus service along the Amalfi Coast. Bedrooms are large, modern, clean and comfortable. There's a bar, and breakfast is included. Secure parking is available nearby. **www.plazasalerno.it**

SORRENTO Hotel Nice

€

Corso Italia 257, 80067 **Tel** *081 878 16 50* **Fax** *081 878 30 86* **Rooms** *28*   **Road Map** *C4*

Perfectly placed for central Sorrento, and for those using the town as a base to explore the area, this small hotel is a step from the train station. It provides simple, clean and comfortable budget accommodation. As it is on a main street, rooms at the back are quieter. Friendly owners. **info@hotelnice.it**

Key to Price Guide *see p178* **Key to Symbols** *see back cover flap*

SORRENTO Hotel Mignon Meuble

€€

Via Sersale 9, 80067 **Tel** *081 807 38 24* **Fax** *081 877 43 48* **Rooms** *24*   **Road Map** *C4*

In the historic centre of Sorrento, near the cathedral and the old walls, this charming *pensione* offers spacious rooms with traditional furniture, tiled floors and good bathrooms. Breakfast is served in guests' rooms, some of which have French windows and small balconies. Limited hotel parking. **www.sorrentohotelmignon.com**

SORRENTO Il Nido

€€

Via Nastro Verde 62, 80067 **Tel** *081 878 27 66* **Fax** *081 807 33 04* **Rooms** *29*   **Road Map** *C4*

A pretty hotel some 5 km (3 miles) outside Sorrento, with fine views over the Bay of Naples to Vesuvius. A shuttle bus runs every hour into town; it is also on a local bus route. Bedrooms are large and airy. The family room has a great view. Wonderful home cooking in the restaurant and helpful owners. Internet access. **www.ilnido.it**

SORRENTO La Magnolia B&B

€€

Viale Caruso 14, 80067 **Tel** *081 877 35 60* **Fax** *081 877 44 12* **Rooms** *7*   **Road Map** *C4*

Set in an old noble palace near Piazza Tasso in the historic centre, this B&B is beautifully decorated with pieces by local artisans, particularly inlaid wooden furniture. The friendly owner Carlo will arrange boat rentals or excursions and happily advise visitors on getting around the Amalfi coast. **www.magnoliasorrento.it**

SORRENTO La Neffola

€€

Via Capo 21, 80067 **Tel** *081 878 13 14* **Fax** *081 807 34 50* **Rooms** *8*   **Road Map** *C4*

These charming apartments, within a stone farmhouse standing in lush gardens, are high on a cliff top above the main harbour. They have great views towards Vesuvius. Guests may make use of the lovely pool, terrace and restaurant of the neighbouring campsite. Kitchens are well equipped and there is a friendly bar. **www.neffolaresidence.com**

SORRENTO La Tonnarella

€€€€

Via Capo 31, 80067 **Tel** *081 878 11 53* **Fax** *081 878 21 69* **Rooms** *24*   **Road Map** *C4*

Perched on a cliff, 3 km (2 miles) outside Sorrento's centre, this hotel was the summer residence of an aristocratic family. Inside, there are majolica floor tiles, Moorish vaulting and antique furniture. With wonderful views, a room with a sea view, balcony or terrace costs more. Good, if tiny, restaurant. Breakfast included. Private beach. **www.latonnarella.it**

SORRENTO Parco dei Principi

€€€€

Via Rota 1, 80067 **Tel** *081 878 46 44* **Fax** *081 878 37 86* **Rooms** *177*   **Road Map** *C4*

A 1960s hotel with a difference, designed by style icon Gio Ponti and with a location that is hard to beat. The gardens, including a pool and a cliff-top terrace, afford incredible views. The interior is filled with quirky nautical motifs and pebble or shell mosaics. Other facilities include a beach, spa and gym. **www.grandhotelparcodeiprincipi.net**

SORRENTO Bellevue Syrene

€€€€€

Piazza della Vittoria 5, 80067 **Tel** *081 878 10 24* **Fax** *081 878 39 63* **Rooms** *50*   **Road Map** *C4*

A grand hotel in every sense, high on a bluff in Sorrento. Established in 1820 and a perennial favourite of royalty and romantic writers, the Bellevue Syrene is sumptuously decorated with frescoes, vaulting, antiques and fine paintings. Built on the foundations of a Roman villa, views of the sea and Vesuvius abound. **www.bellevue.it**

SORRENTO Gran Hotel Cocumella

€€€€€

Via Cocumella 7, Sant'Agnello, 80065 **Tel** *081 878 29 33* **Fax** *081 878 37 12* **Rooms** *53*   **Road Map** *C4*

A former Jesuit monastery in landscaped gardens, this beautiful hotel is found in a quiet suburb of Sorrento. Famous former guests include the Duke of Wellington and Sigmund Freud. Suites are stylish, with fabulous views over the Bay of Naples, while there is a romantic restaurant on the terrace. Classical concerts in summer. **www.cocumella.com**

TORRE DEL GRECO Casa Rossa 1888 al Vesuvio

€€

Via Mortelle 60, 80056 **Tel** *081 883 15 49* **Fax** *081 847 46 02* **Rooms** *30*   **Road Map** *C3*

On the coast road between Naples and Sorrento, near Vesuvius, this is a convenient stopping place if you are driving. Stylish modern spaces are filled with light and art. Bedrooms are large, with balconies and sea views. The food in the restaurant is excellent. Also a private beach of black volcanic sand. Popular at weekends. **www.casarossa1888.it**

VICO EQUENSE Agriturismo La Ginestra

€

Via Tessa 2, S. Maria del Castello, Moiano di Vico Equense, 80069 **Tel/Fax** *081 802 32 11* **Rooms** *8* **Road Map** *D4*

This beautifully positioned pink farmhouse, high above the coast, has spectacular terraces bedecked with flowers. There are splendid walks all around – and down to Positano. Public transport links are via Vico Equense. A delightful place to relax, with an excellent restaurant offering organic food. **www.laginestra.org**

VICO EQUENSE Hotel Capo La Gala

€€€€€

Via L Serio 8, 80069 **Tel** *081 801 57 57* **Fax** *081 879 87 47* **Rooms** *22*   **Road Map** *D4*

A place for gazing at the sea from sunrise to sunset, this hotel is on the Sorrento road just 1 km (0.5 miles) before Vico Equense. Imposing terraces, a pool and a private beach reef offer great views, as do all the rooms. There is a wellness centre with spa treatments. All rooms have Internet and Wi-Fi access. **www.capolagala.com**

VIETRI SUL MARE Lloyd's Baia Hotel

€€€

Via dei Marinis 2, 84019 **Tel** *089 763 31 11* **Fax** *089 763 36 33* **Rooms** *129*   **Road Map** *E4*

Built into the cliffside overlooking the sea, this hotel is conveniently located at the gateway to the Amalfi Coast. Rooms, all with sea views and private balconies, are decorated in a Mediterranean style featuring the town's famous ceramic tilework. Elevators take guests to pools and the private beach. Breakfast is included. **www.lloydsbaiahotel.it**

WHERE TO EAT

Neapolitan pizzeria sign

The region known to the Romans as *Campania felix* (happy country) revels in food, especially the fruit, vegetables and vines that grow in abundance on every available slope. Neapolitan cuisine is well known throughout the world, thanks to the emigrants who took pizza and pasta with them wherever they went. Neapolitans have never given up their passion for good food, and eating is a social occasion here – all important events are celebrated with huge meals that may last half a day. Key elements in Neapolitan cuisine are pasta, olive oil and tomatoes, but all along the coast and on the islands you'll find the freshest seafood and fish dishes, from simple pasta sauces to generous fish stews. This is also the home of ice cream, and delectable cakes and pastries.

TYPES OF RESTAURANTS AND BARS

Naples and the outlying area offer a wide choice of restaurants, trattorias and bars to suit all budgets. A *ristorante* may be smarter (and more expensive) than a *trattoria*, which is less formal. Every part of Campania has its own specialities and similar recipes may be interpreted in quite different ways in different locations. Family-run trattorias usually offer excellent home-style cooking. Many of the best restaurants in Naples are located in the seafront area. In Posillipo the famous restaurants are expensive, but you will enjoy breathtaking views, and the mild climate means you can eat outdoors practically all year round.

The city centre is the place to go for less pretentious and cheaper trattorias and pizzerias with typical Neapolitan food. A pizzeria will offer pasta, meat and fish dishes as well as pizza. In the Spaccanapoli

A Fenestella (see p195) looking out on to the Bay of Naples

and Decumano Maggiore districts there are trattorias known as *vini e cucina* where you can eat quite cheaply. Besides good wine served by the bottle or from the barrel, these are good places for trying genuine Neapolitan home cooking. They are usually family-run and small, located in the popular areas; the interiors may be quite plain, with plastic tablecloths and paper napkins; and the menu will either be written on a blackboard or recited at your table by the waiter.

Vini e cucina are popular with locals and students, so you can also experience authentic Neapolitan life. At *tavole calde* (snack bars), first and second courses are economically priced. The food on sale at street stalls and *friggitorie* (for fried food) is often very

The Da Carmine trattoria (see p193)

good: potato croquettes, fried pizzas *(pizzelle)* and *panzerotti* (ravioli). Bars usually offer filled rolls *(panini)* and sandwiches *(tramezzini)*, as well as cakes and pastries. Many bars also operate as *gelaterie*, with a tempting range of ice creams.

Outside the city, *agriturismi* are family-run farms that make their own wines, grow their own food and offer great meals at affordable prices.

HOW MUCH TO PAY

The average price for a full meal at a trattoria is about €20, and it can be as little as €8 in pizzerias and *vini e cucina*. Restaurants cost from €18–€20 upwards. *Vino sfuso*, or house wine, is often served in jugs and is inexpensive. Fresh fish is usually sold by weight, which can make calculating the cost of your meal difficult. You may find it can be quite expensive.

Eating outdoors, one of the many pleasures of Naples

OPENING HOURS

Restaurants are generally open from 12:30 to 3pm and from 7:30 to 11pm, but this may vary somewhat, especially at weekends and in summer, when you can dine until fairly late. Family-run trattorias have more limited business hours and are usually closed on Sundays and in August, especially around Ferragosto (15 Aug), when many shops in the city are closed for holidays. The restaurants in tourist centres on the islands and along the coast usually close in the winter and open around Easter.

A wood-fired pizza oven

MAKING RESERVATIONS AND PAYING

Restaurants and pizzerias tend to be very crowded on Saturday evening, so it's best to book in advance or arrive early. It is also a good idea to book during the holiday season or on local feast days. Service charges are usually included in the menu prices, but it is customary to leave a tip of around five per cent. The larger restaurants accept major credit cards.

READING THE MENU

A typical Neapolitan menu begins with antipasti, which are so varied and interesting they make a meal in themselves: seafood salad, sautéed clams and mussels, or tomato, pepper and aubergine (eggplant) cooked in various different ways. The first course *(primo)* will depend on the season: spaghetti with seafood, aubergine baked in tomato sauce *(parmigiana di melanzane)* or a simple tomato, mozzarella and basil salad *(insalata caprese)* for lunch at the seaside; pasta and meat sauce or rice cake with meat and mushrooms *(sartù di riso)* for a heartier winter lunch. Among the main courses *(secondi)*, you can choose calamari or squid in tomato sauce, assorted fried fish *(fritto misto)* or grilled fish

QUI 100 ANNI FA
NACQUE LA PIZZA MARGHERITA
1889   1989
BRANDI

Centenary of the Margherita pizza

(grigliata mista), or fried baby mozzarella, artichokes and potato or rice croquettes. Try the vegetable pies; the most famous is made with endive and, in the winter, *friarielli*, a type of broccoli found only in Naples. They are sautéed in a pan with *peperoncino* (hot chilli pepper) and are usually served with sausages.

PIZZERIAS

Naples is the original home of authentic pizza, freshly made and baked in wood-fired ovens. True pizza was originally a peasant dish, made very simply from dough spread with olive oil and tomatoes, and dating from the 18th century. Eaten at any hour of the day in the poorer neighbourhoods of Naples, it was ignored by everyone else until Queen Margherita, wife of Umberto I, decided to try this famous dish. The pizza Margherita, with mozzarella and basil added to create the colours of the Italian flag – red, white and green – was invented in her honour. It is now found in every pizzeria around the world. Neapolitan pizza chefs are famous for their creative flair, and as well as classic pizzas like the Margherita and the Marinara, or Napoletana (with buffalo mozzarella, fresh tomatoes and basil), you may find they offer their own chef's special. Expect to wait for a table at many popular pizzerias.

Inside La Bersagliera restaurant *(see p195)*

The Flavours of Naples and the Amalfi Coast

Juicy red tomatoes, creamy white *mozzarella di bufala* and fragrant green basil, topped with a swirl of olive oil – this is *caprese*, a classic Neapolitan *antipasto*. Its mix of intense flavours and vivid colours is characteristic of a cuisine that reflects the region's sunny Mediterranean climate. Dishes here are generally simple and rely for their success on the freshness that a ready supply of superb local ingredients – grains, pulses, vegetables, fruit, fish and olive oil – can deliver. In Naples' bustling streets, the enticing aromas of freshly picked lemons, fresh herbs and grilling fish mingle with the ever-present tang of sea salt.

Fresh herbs

Locals at one of the many freshly squeezed juice stalls in Naples

NAPLES

Neapolitan cuisine has always owed much to the brooding mass of Mount Vesuvius. The fertile volcanic soil on its lower slopes yields a bumper harvest of fruit and vegetables all year round. The superb local aubergines (eggplant), artichokes, fennel and courgettes (zucchini) are served cooked or preserved in oil or vinegar as *antipasti*. Traditionally, meat has been in short supply and meagre rations of lamb or kid were something to save for special occasions. For many, Sunday is still the day for preparing *braciole*, stuffed rolls of meat that are simmered for hours with wine and tomatoes.

The durum wheat used for pasta was first planted in the the region by the ancient Greeks, but the Neapolitans only became avid pasta-eaters after techniques for making it were introduced by the Sicilians several centuries later. The sunny climate proved perfect for making long strands of *maccheroni*, which were left out to dry in the streets. Spanish rule later brought peppers and tomatoes from South America – and local pasta found its ideal partner.

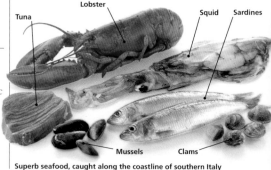

Superb seafood, caught along the coastline of southern Italy

Labels: Tuna, Lobster, Squid, Sardines, Mussels, Clams

LOCAL DISHES AND SPECIALITIES

Rich tomato sauces with herbs, onion and garlic are central to many dishes. Classic examples are *bistecca alla pizzaiola*, beef cooked with tomatoes, garlic and oregano, and *pollo alla cacciatora*, chicken braised in tomatoes, onions, rosemary and red peppers. *Spaghetti alla puttanesca* (literally, prostitute-style spaghetti) probably got its name because the tomato sauce with olives, anchovies and capers would have been quick for a busy, working woman to prepare. *Timballo di maccheroni*, a pie filled with macaroni, wild mushrooms and tomatoes, is a more elaborate local pasta dish. Neapolitans are also noted for being sweet-toothed. One traditional Easter treat – *pastiera napoletana* (candied fruits and ricotta cheese in a pastry case) – is now popular throughout Italy.

Ripe figs

Parmigiana di melanzane
Aubergines (eggplant) are layered with mozzarella, basil, tomato sauce and parmesan.

Making pizzas in an Amalfi restaurant

and *frutti di Mare*, such as clams, mussels, octopus, squid and cuttlefish, are served in dozens of ways, including with pasta.

Until the tourism boom of the 1960s, the islands were mainly home to peasant farmers. Dishes relied on whatever was to hand. A typical meal would be *coniglio all'ischitania* (rabbit stew with white wine, garlic, tomatoes and peppers).

All along the coast, bright yellow lemons grow on the steeply stepped terraces. Amalfi lemons are prized for their almost-sweet, tongue-tingling flavour and feature strongly in local desserts.

The most highly regarded of all local tomatoes is the strongly flavoured, plum-shaped San Marzano. Naples today is ringed by factories producing pasta and canned tomatoes for export, and the city is known the world over as the home of pasta, pizza and ice cream, or *gelati*.

The famous Neapolitan *gelati*, with three coloured layers, originated in the 19th century. Noted makers, such as Tortoni, used chocolate, cherries and pistachios to colour their creations.

AMALFI COAST AND THE ISLANDS

The people of the Amalfi coast and its many islands have always depended on the daily catch. Buying fish fresh from the habour is still part of local life. Traditional

recipes make the most of the readily available fresh anchovies, mackerel and sardines, as well as larger fish which are becoming increasingly rare in these waters. Fish stews are made from whatever is plentiful

Newly picked olives, ready for crushing to extract their oil

WHAT TO DRINK

Vesuvio wines The volcano's vines produce fruity reds and crisp white *Lachryma Christi*.

Fiano di Avellino and **Greco di Tufo wines** Both these dry whites are made from ancient Roman grape varieties.

Taurasi wine This powerful red is made from the local Anglianco grapes.

Ischia wines These include good quality reds, whites and sparkling varieties.

Capri wines Dry and white, these are good with seafood.

Limoncello This lemon liqueur is usually served at the end of a meal.

Pizza Napoletana *This thin-crusted pizza is topped simply with tomato, garlic, oregano, basil and anchovies.*

Pesce spada *In Campania, Puglia and Sicily, swordfish steak is pan-fried or grilled with lemon and oregano.*

Sfogliatella *Paper-thin layers of pastry ooze with butter, sugar, cinnamon, orange peel and ricotta.*

Choosing a Restaurant

The restaurants in this chart have been selected for their high quality of food and value for money. They are listed by price category and district (Naples) or region (outside Naples). See the Street Finder on pages 228–43 for map references in Naples; for those in other areas, see the Road Map on the inside back cover.

PRICE CATEGORIES
The following price ranges are for a three-course evening meal for one, including a half-bottle of house wine, tax and service.

€ Under €20
€€ €20–€30
€€€ €30–€40
€€€€ €40–€55
€€€€€ Over €55

NAPLES

TOLEDO AND CASTEL NUOVO Fratelli La Bufala
€

Via Medina 18, 80133 **Tel** *081 551 04 70*   **Map** *7 B2*

As popular for its pizzas as its meat – and the meat in question is buffalo. The walls of this stylish restaurant feature colourful modern art and service is efficient and friendly. Excellent *mozzarella di bufala* (buffalo mozzarella) and desserts featuring ricotta made from rich buffalo milk. Buffalo steaks, hamburgers and *polpetti* (meatballs in tomato sauce).

TOLEDO AND CASTEL NUOVO Cantina della Tofa
€€

Vico della Tofa 71, 80133 **Tel** *081 40 68 40*   **Map** *7 A2*

In the heart of the Quartieri Spagnoli, Cantina della Tofa offers classic Neapolitan recipes. The choice of vegetable antipasti changes with the season, as do the other dishes. The *parmigiana di melanzane* (baked aubergine (eggplant) with tomato sauce and cheese) is superlative. Good local wines. Closed Sun & Mon dinner, two weeks in Aug.

TOLEDO AND CASTEL NUOVO Ciro a Medina
€€

Via Medina 19, 80133 **Tel** *081 420 60 28*   **Map** *7 B2*

A cheery place with a relaxed feel. At lunch time there is a fixed menu, but a wider choice is available for dinner, including excellent pizzas. Mostly fish-based dishes, with specials such as smoked swordfish with *culatello* (cured pork) sauce and smoked mozzarella, *scialiatelli* (pasta ribbons) with seafood, and *linguine* (pasta) with anchovies and breadcrumbs.

TOLEDO AND CASTEL NUOVO Hostaria Toledo
€€

Vico Giardinetto a Toledo 78a, 80134 **Tel** *081 42 12 57*   **Map** *7 A2*

In the heart of the Quartieri Spagnoli, this *osteria* has been open since 1951 and offers Neapolitan classics. Specials include *ziti al ragu* (pasta with a tomato and beef sauce), *frittura di paranza* (mixed fried fish), *zucchine alla scapece* (courgette gazpacho) and *spaghetti alle vongole* (with clams). Desserts are sublime. Closed Tue dinner.

TOLEDO AND CASTEL NUOVO Osteria Il Garum
€€

Piazza Monteoliveto 2a, 80134 **Tel** *081 542 32 28*   **Map** *7 A1, 9 B5*

This friendly *osteria* sits in the beautiful square of Piazza Monteoliveto, facing the church of Sant'Anna dei Lombardi. It offers superb value and you can choose between a table outside or one in the cosy dining room. Neapolitan cuisine with innovative touches, often using *garum*, an ancient Roman sauce made from fermented fish.

TOLEDO AND CASTEL NUOVO Trianon da Ciro
€€

Via P Colletta 42/46, 80133 **Tel** *081 553 94 26*   **Map** *4 D5, 10 F3*

Serving pizza from a *forno a legna* (wood-burning stove) to Neapolitans since 1923, Trianon is a legendary pizzeria. Although its vast utilitarian space seats more than 300 diners, the restaurant overflows with hungry locals at lunch and dinner time. The pizza with sausage and *friarielli* (a type of broccoli) is excellent.

TOLEDO AND CASTEL NUOVO Amici Miei
€€€

Via Monte di Dio 77/78, 80123 **Tel** *081 764 49 81*   **Map** *6 F2*

A welcoming traditional trattoria in Naples' oldest quarter, where the menu is very much meat orientated. Renowned for its excellent pasta and char-grilled pork, lamb, steaks and game. Try the steak with a *barolo* wine and radicchio sauce. The wine list is excellent as are the desserts. Closed Sun dinner, Mon & Jul–Aug.

TOLEDO AND CASTEL NUOVO Kukai
€€€

Via Carlo de Cesare 55, 80132 **Tel** *081 41 19 05*   **Map** *7 A2*

One of Naples' first sushi bars, Kukai features stylish decor. Aquariums, modern lighting and bar stools surround the glass-walled kitchen, in which Japanese chefs prepare the food before your very eyes. Japanese beer and sake are on hand to wash down the excellent sushi, sashimi and *teriaki*. Trendy and popular, it also does takeaways.

SPACCANAPOLI Da Michele
€

Via C Sersale 1, 80139 **Tel** *081 553 92 04*   **Map** *4 D5, 10 F3*

In existence since 1870, this legendary pizzeria produces only two varieties – *margherita* or *marinara* (tomato, garlic, oregano and basil), washed down with beer and soft drinks. Very cheap and extremely good. Try the *frittura* (fried starters). Queues are long – get a number from the cash desk and wait your turn. Closed Sun & two weeks in Aug.

Key to Symbols *see back cover flap*

SPACCANAPOLI Pizzeria Vesi

 €

Via S Biagio dei Librai 115, 80138 **Tel** *081 55 10 35* **Map** *3 C5 (10 D3)*

Part of a chain, Vesi is a busy pizzeria with wooden tables. Long queues form in the evenings, when regulars jostle for elbow room and service is brisk. Naturally, the pizzas are excellent – try the Neapolitan classic, the *marinara*, or the *rustica* (ricotta, mozzarella and peppers), along with a cold beer.

SPACCANAPOLI Lombardi a Santa Chiara

€€

Via B Croce 58, 80134 **Tel** *081 552 07 80* **Map** *3 B5, 9 C4*

This friendly place is found in the heart of old Naples, close to the lovely church of Santa Chiara. Downstairs, customers perching on stools snack on pizzas and calzoni. Upstairs, there is an elegant dining room, where a huge range of antipasti is served, as well as delicious pasta, pizzas and salads. Very popular so book ahead.

SPACCANAPOLI Mimi alla Ferrovia

 €€€

Via A d'Aragona 21, 80139 **Tel** *081 553 85 25* **Map** *4 E4*

Extremely popular, this oasis of calm off Piazza Garibaldi provides fine food and wine. The decor is Art-Deco elegance and the service refined. Recipes celebrate the *cucina povera* ("peasant cooking") of old Naples and include excellent mozzarella and antipasti and a wide range of pasta, fish and meat dishes, as well as delicious desserts. Closed Sun.

SPACCANAPOLI Palazzo Petrucci

 €€€€

Piazza S Domenico Maggiore 4, 80100 **Tel** *081 552 40 68* **Map** *3 B5, 9 C3*

Built into the former stalls of the Palazzo Petrucci, this elegant addition to Spaccanapoli provides innovative updates to the local *campana* cuisine. There is an abundant tasting menu and the *à la carte* menu is equally tempting, particularly the fresh fish dishes. Desserts are brought in from Scaturchio bakery nearby. Closed Sun dinner, Mon lunch.

DECUMANO MAGGIORE Antica Pizzeria Port'Alba

 €

Via Port'Alba 18, 80010 **Tel** *081 45 97 13* **Map** *3 B3, 9 B3*

Established in 1738 as a street stall, this is where pizza was invented. You can still buy a take-away slice of pizza to enjoy as you wander along the pedestrian road filled with booksellers or you can sit at the rustic tables for a full meal. Try the Napoletana, with buffalo mozzarella and fresh tomatoes, or the Port'Alba, topped with seafood. Closed Wed.

DECUMANO MAGGIORE Di Matteo

 €

Via dei Tribunali 94, 80138 **Tel** *081 45 52 62* **Map** *3 C4, 10 D2*

One of the top pizzerias in Naples' historic centre attracts long queues of locals. While you wait for your pizza or a table, nibble on the delicious fried courgettes (zucchini), artichokes and mozzarella. The pizza dough is wonderful and the toppings are made with the freshest ingredients – try sausage and *friarielli* (a type of broccoli). Closed Sun.

DECUMANO MAGGIORE Sorbillo

 €

Via dei Tribunali 32, 80138 **Tel** *081 44 66 43* **Map** *3 B5, 9 C3*

One of Naples' best pizzerias, this tiny place has a handful of tables and one thing on the menu – pizza. In the family for three generations, its bases are excellent and the finest ingredients are used for the toppings. Service is brisk but friendly. A more upmarket version is further up the same street, but many prefer the original. Worth the queue. Closed Sun.

DECUMANO MAGGIORE Da Carmine

 €€

Via dei Tribunali 330, 80138 **Tel** *081 29 43 83* **Map** *3 C4, 10 D3*

This is a charming, old-style family trattoria, bedecked with sepia pictures of old Naples. Classic Neapolitan cuisine is the order of the day, at bargain prices. The atmosphere is cosy and friendly, the fare is hearty and dishes are freshly prepared. Very close to Napoli Sotterranea and convenient for San Gregorio di Armeno. Closed dinner Sun–Tue.

DECUMANO MAGGIORE Osteria da Carmela

€€

Via Conte di Ruvo 11/12, 80135 **Tel** *081 549 97 38* **Map** *3 B4, 9 B2*

Not far from the Archaeological Museum, this friendly *osteria* features traditional Neapolitan home cooking with innovative touches and a welcoming atmosphere. Try the *pappardelle* pasta with clams and *porcini* (cep mushrooms) or the pasta with white beans and mussels. Excellent wines. Closed Sun.

DECUMANO MAGGIORE Osteria La Chitarra

€€

Rampe San Giovanni Maggiore 1 bis, 80134 **Tel** *081 552 91 03* **Map** *7 B1*

Not far from the University of Federico II, this trattoria only has a few tables. The set lunch menu is a bargain. Try the soups, *parmigiana di melanzane* (baked aubergine (eggplant) with tomato sauce and cheese) and *tubetti* pasta with mussels, *baccalà* (salt cod) and chickpeas. Delicious home-made fruit liqueurs. Closed Sat lunch, Sun & Mon.

DECUMANO MAGGIORE Europeo di Mattozzi

 €€€

Via Marchese Campodisola 4/10, 80133 **Tel** *081 552 13 23* **Map** *7 B1, 9 C5*

A welcoming restaurant near Piazza Borsa with a rustic feel with copper ware and early 20th-century photos hanging from the walls. Delicious and decidedly seasonal Neapolitan fare: antipasti, hearty soups with chickpeas, beans and peas, and excellent pastas. Try the fresh *gragnano* pasta with *genovese* (mince and onion) sauce. Great wine list.

CAPODIMONTE AND I VERGINI Antica Cantina del Gallo

 €

Via Telesino 22, 80136 **Tel** *081 544 15 21* **Map** *2 F2*

Not far from the Fontanelle in the Sanita quarter, this pizzeria-trattoria has been around for 200 years. Set in a *tuffo* (tufa rock) cave, the decor is basic but the good food ensures its popularity. Choose from pizzas, *pizzicotti* (calzoni stuffed with aubergine (eggplant), mozzarella, sausage and broccoli), bean soups and pastas.

CAPODIMONTE AND I VERGINI O' Core 'e Napule €

Via Misericordiella 23/24, 80137 Tel 081 29 25 66   **Map** *9 C1, 3 B3*

Conveniently located near Piazza Cavour and the Museo Archeologico Nazionale, this restaurant and pizzeria prides itself on preserving true Neapolitan cooking traditions. The pizzas are excellent, but also try the pasta and fish dishes, such as the pasta with courgettes (zucchini) and mussels.

CAPODIMONTE AND I VERGINI Pizzeria Starita a Materdei €

Via Materdei 27/28, 80136 Tel 081 557 36 82   **Map** *2 F2*

This is the place to head to for the ultimate Neapolitan pizza experience. This traditional pizzeria has been in the hands of the Starita family since 1901. Film fans might be interested to learn that the utensils framed over the doorway were used by Sophia Loren in the classic film *L'Oro di Napoli*. Closed Sun lunch, Mon.

CAPODIMONTE AND I VERGINI Lombardi €€

Via Foria 12, 80137 Tel 081 45 62 20   **Map** *3 C3*

A stylish trattoria, not far from the *Orto Botanico* (botanic gardens), this is an oasis away from the traffic of Via Foria. While the menu is limited, all dishes are freshly made to order and there are daily specials. Delicious antipasti and good seafood pasta and risotto. There is a little outside terrace, but the street is rather busy. Closed Mon.

VOMERO Acunzo €

Via Domenico Cimarosa 60/62, 80127 Tel 081 578 53 62   **Map** *2 D5*

An unpretentious trattoria and pizzeria offering simple home cooking and a low-key atmosphere. Both the pasta dishes and pizzas are delicious, using well-sourced ingredients. Convenient for the funicular down to Via Roma, it is the perfect pitstop when visiting San Martino or Castel Sant'Elmo. Expect queues in the evening. Closed Sun & Aug.

VOMERO Toto, Eduardo e Pasta e Fagioli €

Corso Vittorio Emanuele 514, 80135 Tel 081 564 26 23   **Map** *2 F4*

Another classic Neapolitan trattoria, with very honestly priced food and a proud history of *cucina genuina* (traditional cooking). The menu features both meat and fish dishes. There is also a wealth of local desserts to tempt you. Choose to eat inside or out on the ample terrace. Good house wine. Closed Mon.

VOMERO La Cantina de Sica €€

Via G Bernini 17, 80129 Tel 081 556 75 20   **Map** *2 D5*

Neapolitan cuisine is to be had here, with a romantic menu on Sundays for couples. Courteous, efficient service and a rustic decor, with a beamed ceiling and wooden tables. Excellent pastas, antipasti and desserts. Try the *parmigiana di melanzane* (baked aubergine/eggplant) or *ziti alla genovese* (pasta with onions and veal). Closed Sun dinner, Mon.

VOMERO Il Gallo Nero €€€€

Via Tasso 466, 80127 Tel 081 64 30 12   **Map** *5 A1*

This stylish restaurant is set in a beautiful Liberty (Art Nouveau) villa, high on Vomero hill, with wonderful views. The menu is limited, but it features Neapolitan classics created using the finest ingredients – freshly caught fish and the best meat from the Campanian hinterland. Eat in the garden in summer. Good wine list. Closed Sun dinner, Mon.

CASTEL DELL'OVO AND CHIAIA Brandi €€

Salita S Anna di Palazzo 1/2, Via Chiaia, 80132 Tel 081 41 69 28   **Map** *7 A3*

Laying claims to the invention of the *pizza margherita*, this historic pizzeria has been in business since 1780. Friendly and very popular, it also serves good pasta dishes and is a fun place to spend an evening. Yet, purists might point out that they are not the best pizzas the city has to offer and prices are a little steep. Closed Mon.

CASTEL DELL'OVO AND CHIAIA Da Ettore €€

Via Santa Lucia 56, 80123 Tel 081 764 04 98   **Map** *7 A4*

A trattoria-pizzeria, with a loyal following and old-fashioned charm. In summer you can choose from the wood-panelled dining room or street-side tables. Excellent antipasti, especially the *mozzarella di bufala*, (buffalo mozzarella) and good pizzas and pastas. Handy for Santa Lucia or Piazza Plebescito. Closed Sun, Aug.

CASTEL DELL'OVO AND CHIAIA Da Pasqualino €€

Piazza Sannazzaro 77/79, 80122 Tel 081 68 15 24   **Map** *5 B3*

Ideally located for the ferry port, the nearby railway station and the seafront at Mergellina, this pizzeria opens onto a pretty but busy square. Here you can watch the locals' driving style from a safe distance and enjoy a bite to eat. Very cheap and cheerful, its pizzas are more than satisfactory, and pasta and fried nibbles are on offer too. Closed Tue.

CASTEL DELL'OVO AND CHIAIA Da Tonino €€

Via Santa Teresa a Chiaia 47, 80121 Tel 081 42 15 33   **Map** *6 E2*

At this *enoteca* and *osteria*, run by the same family for over 100 years, meals are served in a wood-panelled dining room. Portions are generous; at lunch there is a limited menu, but in the evening a more ample one is on offer. Good wine and typical Neapolitan cuisine: pasta with lentils or meat sauce; fish stews. Closed dinner Mon–Thu.

CASTEL DELL'OVO AND CHIAIA La Cantina di Triunfo €€€

Riviera di Chiaia 64, 80122 Tel 081 66 81 01   **Map** *5 C2*

A veritable institution, this is a wine shop by day and a trattoria by night. The long, cool room has an open kitchen, so you can watch your food being prepared. The daily changing menu is limited to two options for each course; the chef uses regional recipes and seasonal ingredients. The house wine is excellent and very good value. Closed Sun.

Key to Price Guide *see p192* **Key to Symbols** *see back cover flap*

CAPRI Le Grottelle

€€€

Via Arco Naturale 13, Capri, 80073 **Tel** *081 837 57 19* **Road Map** *C4/5*

Not far from the Arco Naturale and near the descent to Piazzolungo, Le Grottelle serves simple, no-nonsense meals from land and sea on a sunny panoramic terrace or in caves excavated from the living rock. Grilled meat and fish are the speciality, but the pasta dishes, especially the *ravioli*, are worth a try.

CAPRI Add'O Riccio

€€€€

Via Grotta Azzurra 11, Anacapri, 80071 **Tel** *081 837 13 80* **Road Map** *C4*

A narrow stairway separates this charming restaurant from the famous Blue Grotto. It is a perfect stop-off for those arriving by road. Tables are perched on a wooden platform just above the sea and there is also a lovely lido, which customers can use, so you can make a day of it. Delicious seafood, pasta and fresh fish. Closed Nov–mid-Mar.

CAPRI Da Gelsolmina alla Migliara

€€€€

Via Migliara 72, Anacapri, 80071 **Tel** *081 837 14 99* **Road Map** *C4*

This traditional family-run restaurant is set in a garden with a swimming pool, near a romantic walk to La Migliara, some 20 minutes from Anacapri. The cooking is exemplary: try the delicious pasta with beans or the *ravioli capresi*. Also on offer are "brick-baked" chicken, fresh fish and rabbit. Views over Ischia and beyond. Good wine list.

CAPRI La Columbaia

€€€€

Hotel Quisisana, Via Camerelle 2, Capri, 80073 **Tel** *081 837 07 88* **Road Map** *C4/5*

For romantic dining beside the pool at one of the world's legendary hotels, La Columbaia is hard to beat. Impeccable service is to be expected and the menu offers a good choice of pasta, fish and meat dishes. There is a lunch-time buffet and pizzas are cooked in a wood-fired oven. Open noon–5pm daily (no dinner). Closed Nov–Mar.

CAPRI La Capannina

€€€€€

Via Le Botteghe 12 bis, Capri, 80073 **Tel** *081 837 07 32* **Road Map** *C4/5*

Celebrities and visiting royalty flock here to enjoy the fine cuisine. There is a beautiful veranda and it is just a hop, skip and a jump from the legendary *passeggiata* (evening walk) of the Piazzetta. Romantic candle-lit dining, typical Caprese cuisine and fine house wine. Try to book an outside table.

CAPRI L'Olivo

€€€€€

Capri Palace Hotel, Via Capodimonte 14, Anacapri, 80071 **Tel** *081 978 01 11* **Road Map** *C4/5*

In one of Italy's finest hotels (*see p183*), L'Olivo won two Michelin stars in 2008. The decor is stylish and the service impeccable. Dishes are a feast for both the eyes and the tastebuds, while the wines are superb. Typical fare includes seabream with peach and fennel puree, or a timbale of prawns, asparagus, caviar and apple sauce. Closed Nov–Mar.

CASERTA Gli Scacchi

€€

Via S Rocco 1, 81100 **Tel** *0823 37 10 86* **Road Map** *C2*

In Caserta Vecchia, a beautiful medieval hill-side town, is this restaurant offering wonderful antipasti and dishes using local and seasonal produce such as chestnuts, mushrooms, rabbit, lamb and pork. Try the *cianfotta* (local summer soup) or the fresh pasta. Home-made desserts and good house wine. Generous portions. Closed Mon–Wed.

CASERTA Ristorante Soletti

€€

Largo San Sebastiano 1, 81100 **Tel** *082 332 80 22* **Road Map** *C2*

Just a short walk from the main entrance of the Royal Palace, this restaurant serves traditional pasta and other main courses. In particular, try the delicious *pasta bolognese* (with a tomato and meat sauce) and the excellent mixed grill platter. There are a few tables outside.

CASERTA Le Colonne

€€€

Via G Douhet 7, 81100 **Tel** *0823 46 74 94* **Road Map** *C2*

This elegant family-run restaurant is set inside a villa with a garden. Produce comes from the fertile soil of the *Terra Felix* (Fortunate Earth), as the Romans called Campania. Naturally, cheese and meat dominate, with much use of the fine local buffalo mozzarella and grilled buffalo steaks, but there is also excellent fish. Good wine list.

CETARA Acqua Pazza

€€€

Corso Garibaldi 36/38, 84010 **Tel** *089 26 16 06* **Road Map** *E4*

Renowned for its fish, Cetara has a large fishing fleet and local specialities are celebrated in this delightful restaurant. Try the thinly sliced smoked fish *carpaccio* or the fresh tuna, and the famed *colatura di alici* (fish sauce). Other choices include cuttlefish with cannellini beans, potato and *bottarga* (dried fish roe) puree. Closed Mon (Nov–Jun).

FURORE Hostaria di Bacco

€€€

Via G B Lama 9, 84010 **Tel** *089 83 03 60* **Road Map** *D4*

Set on Italy's only fjord, with its very own microclimate, this hotel (*see p183*) and restaurant is surrounded by vines. Family owned and popular, its excellent cuisine uses local produce from land and sea. Fresh pasta, fish and rabbit may be washed down with the local Furore white DOC wine. Look out for the fjord's prickly pears in season.

FURORE La Volpe Pescatrice

€€€€€

Furore Inn Hotel, Via dell'Amore 1, 84010 **Tel** *089 830 47 11* **Road Map** *D4*

Top-notch cuisine, prepared by a gifted young chef from Amalfi, awaits in this hotel set in a prime position with a spectacular terrace. The restaurant's name means "the fishing fox" and the emphasis is on combining ingredients from land and sea, using local seasonal produce. Try the *fusilli* pasta with seafood and pinenuts. Closed Jan–Feb.

HERCULANEUM (ERCULANO) Viva lo Re

Corso Resina 261, 80056 **Tel** *081 739 02 07*   **Road Map** *C3*

A bar-restaurant (and rooms to rent), with a wonderful regional wine cellar. The feel is rustic but stylish. Try the paccheri pasta with clams and white fish, the courgette (zucchini) flowers filled with ricotta, or the sardine parmigiana. Hearty soups in winter, good local lamb and ricotta with wild strawberries in season. Closed Mon & Sun dinner.

ISCHIA Lo Scoglio

Via Cava Ruffano 58, Serrara Fontana, 80070 **Tel** *081 99 95 29*   **Road Map** *A4*

In a panoramic position perched over the sea beside a pretty cove, seafood is the obvious attraction on the menu at Lo Scoglio. A busy place, popular with locals, it specializes in delicious soups and pastas featuring mussels and other shellfish, as well as just-caught fish. The grilled seabass is especially good. Closed Nov–Easter.

ISCHIA Ristorante Da Raffaele

Via Roma 29, 80077 **Tel** *081 99 12 03*   **Road Map** *B4*

Located on the Via Roma in Ischia Porto, this casual and fun restaurant has been a neighbourhood staple for more than 30 years. The owner, Raffaele, is a charming host, sometimes even serenading guests with his guitar. Try the rabbit, an Ischia speciality, or the grilled fish, steak or lamb.

ISCHIA Zi Carmela

Via Schioppa 27, Forio, 80075 **Tel** *081 99 84 23*   **Road Map** *A4*

This friendly, lively place is big on seafood and popular with the locals. It is colourful, with ceramic plates and copper paraphernalia. In addition to fish, there is good pizza baked in a wood-fired oven. Try the fried mixed fish, or the *pezogne*, a white fish baked with potatoes and aromatic herbs. Good tasting menus on offer. Closed Tue (Sep–Apr).

ISCHIA Da Coco

Piazzale Aragonese 1, Ischia Ponte, 80077 **Tel** *081 98 18 23*   **Road Map** *B4*

With a remarkable location on the side of the causeway between the mainland and the tiny island of the Castello Aragonese, this seafood restaurant serves ultra-fresh fish from the nearby port. It also serves good pasta with shellfish or baby squid. There are warming vegetable soups in winter. Very popular with the locals. Closed Wed (Oct–Mar).

ISCHIA Trattoria Il Focolare

Via Cretajo al Crocefisso 3, Barana d'Ischia, 80070 **Tel** *081 90 29 44*   **Road Map** *A4*

The owners also have a winery, so there are some well-chosen vintages here. Ischitana cuisine *di terra* (of the land), served on a canopied terrace. For a break from fish, try rabbit, snails, mushrooms and fresh pastas flavoured with wild herbs. The honey bread with lavender and rosemary is a must. Closed Wed (Nov–Mar) and lunch (Mon–Thu).

ISCHIA Il Melograno

Via G Mazzella 110, Forio, 80076 **Tel** *081 99 84 50*   **Road Map** *A4*

On the road heading to Citara beach, this popular and stylish restaurant is run by a native of nearby Procida. Under the shade of lime trees, you can eat steamed fish with lentils, goose liver, fish soup with croutons and good home-made pasta. Also fresh daily fish or Tuscan steaks. Excellent wines and special menus are available.

ISCHIA Umberto a Mare

Via Soccorso 2, Forio, 80076 **Tel** *081 99 71 71*   **Road Map** *A4*

Perched over the sea and beside one of the island's loveliest churches, the Chiesa di Soccorso, this restaurant is also a popular hotel. The dining terrace has views over the sea. Local ingredients and recipes are given an innovative touch. Try the octopus with *peperoncino* (chilli), dark chocolate and roast pumpkin.

MAIORI Il Faro di Capo D'Orso

Via D Taiani 48, 84010 **Tel** *089 87 70 22*   **Road Map** *D4*

Just beyond Maiori, immersed in the green of the Capo l'Orso, there are splendid views from this restaurant across to Li Galli islands. Stylish decor includes stone walls, floor-to-ceiling glass walls and fine tiles from Vietri. Fresh *gragnano* pasta, seafood and fish dominate the menu. Excellent wine list. Closed Tue (Nov–Mar).

MASSA LUBRENSE Antica Francischiello da Peppino

Via Partenope 27, 80069 **Tel** *081 533 97 80*   **Road Map** *C4*

Said to be where the local favourite dessert, *delizia di limone* (a kind of lemon cheesecake) was invented, this well-loved restaurant has been in the same family for four generations. With a terrace offering sea views, it is filled with antiques, ceramic plates and rustic implements. All dishes from the vast menu are prepared with care. Closed Wed (Nov–Mar).

MASSA LUBRENSE I Quattro Passi

Via A Vespucci 13n, Loc Marina del Cantone, 80061 **Tel** *081 808 28 00*   **Road Map** *C4*

At this stylish restaurant, the chef interprets traditional local recipes for refined dining. *Linguine* pasta comes with *fiori di zucca* (courgette (zucchini) flowers), ravioli is stuffed with broad beans, and *scapetti* pasta with oysters. Dishes are often served with edible wild flowers. Superb mousses. Closed Tue & Wed dinner (Jan–May), Nov & Dec.

MASSA LUBRENSE/NERANO Taverna del Capitano

Piazza delle Sirene 10, Loc Marina del Cantone, 80061 **Tel** *081 808 10 28*   **Road Map** *C4*

A friendly family, two Michelin star restaurant with rooms also available. It overlooks the enchanting bay of Marina del Cantone. The young and innovative chef produces superb cuisine from traditional recipes. Freshness is key here, from the bread to the pasta to the fish, all prepared with the minimum of fuss. Excellent wine list. Closed Jan–Feb.

Key to Price Guide see p192 **Key to Symbols** see back cover flap

PAESTUM Ristorante Nettuno

€€

Via Nettuno 2, 84047 **Tel** *0828 81 10 28*　　　　　　　　　　　　　　**Road Map** *F5*

Located right on the edge of the archaeological zone of Paestum, this inviting restaurant has fine views of the nearby ancient Greek temples. Most specialities are based on seafood: try the risotto with crayfish, or sample Paestum's locally made buffalo-milk mozzarella and ricotta cheeses. Closed dinner, Mon (in winter).

PAESTUM Nonna Sceppa

€€€€

Via Laura 45, Loc Capaccio, 80147 **Tel** *0828 85 10 64*　　　　　　　　　**Road Map** *F5*

A large family-run restaurant producing tempting cuisine that represents the Cilento region. Artichokes are one of the house specials, cooked in myriad ways, and the fresh *gragnano* pasta is also delicious. The wine list is good and there are delectable local buffalo cheeses. Service is good. Closed Thu.

POMPEII Al Gamberone

€€

Via Piave 36, 80045 **Tel** *081 850 68 14*　　　　　　　　　　　　　**Road Map** *D3*

A stone's throw from Pompeii's cathedral, this seafood restaurant also serves excellent fresh pasta dishes. Prawns – as the name of the place implies – have top billing. Try the prawns flambéed in brandy. In summer the exterior seating area, situated within an orange and lemon grove, is lovely. Closed Tue.

POMPEII Il Principe

€€€€

Piazza B Longo, 80045 **Tel** *081 850 55 66*　　　　　　　　　　　　**Road Map** *D3*

This elegant restaurant is near the ruins of Pompeii and its decor recreates some of the frescoes from the site. Excellent, beautifully presented food is prepared with flair. Fish dominates, often flavoured with *garum*, an ancient Roman fish spice. Family run, the service is charming and attentive. Closed Mon, Sun dinner.

POSITANO Da Vincenzo

€€

Viale Pasitea 172/8, 84017 **Tel** *089 87 51 28*　　　　　　　　　　　**Road Map** *D4*

In the upper reaches of Positano delicious home cooking is served in this simple place, run by a friendly family. Dishes change according to what is available in the market, but all are cooked with aplomb. Try the *panzarotti* (pastry squares with mozzarella and prosciutto), or the delicious stuffed peppers and salads. Very reasonable prices. Closed Nov–Mar.

POSITANO Da Adolfo

€€€

Spiaggia Laurita 40, 84017 **Tel** *089 87 50 22*　　　　　　　　　　　**Road Map** *D4*

Hard to get to and hard to leave, in more ways than one, but well worth it. Boats take you to this little beach, where Da Adolfo serves tasty alfresco food under the shade of a straw canopy. Freshly grilled fish, spaghetti with clams, and squid and potatoes with garlic, as well as good grilled vegetable antipasti. Check the return boat times to avoid a wait.

POSITANO La Tagliata

€€€

Via Tagliata 22, 84017 **Tel** *089 87 58 72*　　　　　　　　　　　　**Road Map** *D4*

High in the mountains above Positano, in the village of Montepertuso, this charming restaurant is worth the drive for the unbelievable views alone. The rustic interior sets the scene for the grilled-meat specialities, all cooked from locally raised animals. Vegetarians can try the simple but divine *spaghetti al pomodoro* (with a tomato sauce).

POSITANO Lo Guarracino

€€€

Via Positanesi d'America 12, 84017 **Tel** *089 87 57 94*　　　　　　　**Road Map** *D4*

Away from the crowds, high on a pathway on the cliff side, this restaurant has a memorable panoramic terrace with sea views. On offer are pizzas baked in a wood-fired oven, delicious seafood pasta and meat dishes. The *linguini ai ricci di mare* (pasta with sea urchin) or the grilled swordfish are worth trying. Closed Nov–Mar.

POSITANO Ristorante Max

€€€

Via dei Mulini 22, 84017 **Tel** *089 87 50 56*　　　　　　　　　　　**Road Map** *D4*

Set within an art gallery, this restaurant is cool and chic, with antique furniture and modern art. Tables are on the first floor, in the basement, or on the terrace upstairs for al fresco dining in summer. There is a vast range of wines to choose from and a good a la carte menu, as well as daily specials of both meat and fish dishes. Closed Nov–Mar.

POSITANO La Buca di Bacco

€€€€

Via Rampa Teglia 4, 84017 **Tel** *089 87 56 99*　　　　　　　　　　　**Road Map** *D4*

At this ever-fashionable address you can eat anything from a light meal to a feast, while surveying the *passeggiata* (evening walk) and gazing at the sea and Li Galli islands beyond. The *arancini* (rice croquettes with mozzarella) are renowned, as is the mussel soup and fresh fish. In season, try the caramelized figs and oranges. Closed Nov–Mar.

POSITANO La Sponda

€€€€€

Via Cristoforo Colombo 30, 84017 **Tel** *089 87 50 66*　　　　　　　**Road Map** *D4*

The bougainvillea-covered pergola at Le Sirenuse *(see p185)*, one of Italy's most elegant hotels, is the ultimate in candle-lit romance. The refined menu, dominated by seafood, combines traditional recipes with creative flair. The fish is ultra fresh: try the shrimp salad or the casserole of fish and crustaceans. Closed Nov–Feb.

POZZUOLI Fattoria del Campiglione

€€€

Via Vicinale Campana 2, 80078 **Tel** *081 526 37 33*　　　　　　　　**Road Map** *B3*

A cheerful restaurant, where for a change meat – not fish – reigns. There are little copper pots for tableware and a fine array of game and meats to choose from: rabbit, *salumi* (cured meats), grilled beef and steaks, lamb and baby kid; even kangaroo, venison and bison. The wine list is huge, incorporating wines from all over the world. Closed Sun dinner.

POZZUOLI Ristorante del Capitano

€€€

Via Cristoforo Colombo 10, 80078 **Tel** *081 526 22 83* **Road Map** *B3*

Il Capitano is a convenient and convivial place for dinner after a visit to Roman Pozzuoli or the Solfatara, or when hopping on or off a boat from Ischia or Procida. This elegant restaurant also has five rooms for those who wish to extend their stay to overnight. Fresh fish and a wide range of seafood pasta dishes. Fine wine list.

POZZUOLI Agriturismo Terra Mia

€€€€€

Via Lago d'Averno 6, 80078 **Tel** *081 866 27 99* **Road Map** *B3*

Overlooking Lake Averno (Virgil's mythical entrance to Hades), this place prepares a wide array of organic dishes from home-grown vegetables. The wine also comes from the local vineyards, which are famous for their fertile volcanic soil. Try the mixed grilled-meat platter. Reservations recommended. Closed Sun dinner, Mon & Wed–Fri lunch, Tue.

PROCIDA Borderó

€€

Via Roma 82, Marina Grande, 80079 **Tel** *081 810 19 19* **Road Map** *B3*

This informal trattoria specializes in seafood pasta and fresh fish. Expect no-nonsense cooking, brisk service and fair prices. There is a traditional dining room, with air conditioning, and a terrace by the bustling port and main drag. Look out for mussels, clams and fish *all'acqua pazza* (cooked in water, tomato, wine and herbs). Closed Tue.

PROCIDA Crescenzo

€€

Via Marina Chiaolella 33, Chiaolella Port, 80079 **Tel** *081 896 72 55* **Road Map** *B3*

A welcoming hotel *(see p186)* and restaurant by the harbour and beach. Arguably Procida's finest culinary experience, the excellent seafood pasta and fish attracts the hordes at weekends and in high season. Tables are in a cool dining room and out on the terrace. In the evenings there is also pizza, prepared with finesse. Book ahead. Closed Nov.

PROCIDA Gorgonia

€€

Via Marina Corricella 50, Corricella, 80079 **Tel** *081 810 10 60* **Road Map** *B3*

Named after a local seaweed, the focus here is firmly on seafood and fresh fish. In the heart of colourful Corricella and facing the Mediterranean, this place offers some of Procida's finest cuisine. Try the delectable spaghetti with sea urchins and the pasta with beans and mussels. Highly recommended Campanian wines. Closed Mon (Sep–Jun).

PROCIDA Sent'Co

€€

Via Roma 167, Marina Grande, 80079 **Tel** *081 810 11 20* **Road Map** *B3*

Old-fashioned and friendly, this trattoria prepares outstanding seafood and fish. Select from the abundance of antipasti, then sample the *orecchiette* with broccoli and shellfish or the spaghetti with *riccio di mare* (sea urchins), the house speciality. The catch of the day is always worthwhile. A small but pleasing wine list. Closed Mon (Sep–Jun).

PROCIDA La Conchiglia

€€€

Via Pizzaco 10, 80079 **Tel** *081 896 76 02* **Road Map** *B4*

Set in a romantic spot overlooking the beach of Chiaia and the dreamy marina of Corricella, La Conchiglia specializes in freshly caught fish and seafood pastas and main dishes. The *antipasto di mare* (seafood antipasto) is a great way to start off, and the restaurant's home-made *limoncello* (lemon liqueur) is the perfect final touch. Closed Nov–Mar.

RAVELLO Da Salvatore

€€

Via delle Repubbliche 2, 84010 **Tel** *089 85 72 27* **Road Map** *D4*

Right beside the bus stop at the entrance to the top of the town, this popular seafood restaurant has a large airy dining room with panoramic windows and a lovely open terrace overlooking the sea. Staff are gregarious and attentive; there is even a friendly resident mynah bird. Fresh fish and seafood pasta. Closed Mon & Feb.

RAVELLO Ristorante Figli di Papà

€€

Via della Marra 7/9, 84010 **Tel** *089 85 83 02* **Road Map** *D4*

Set in a lovely building dating from the late 13th century, this restaurant has vaulted dining rooms and walls lined with modern art. The food served up by the young chef also balances the classic with the creative. The daily tourist menu is highly recommended, or try a taster menu. Good local wines. Closed Jan, Feb, 2 weeks in Nov; Tue (Oct–Mar).

RAVELLO Cumpà Cosima

€€€

Via Roma 44/46, 84010 **Tel** *089 85 71 56* **Road Map** *D4*

Originally a humble wine shop, this trattoria can get very busy. Close to the Duomo, it is run by a formidable lady, who knows all about good home cooking. She uses meat from her family's butcher's shop next door and produce from her own garden. The pasta and meat dishes are the best choices. Charming decor. Closed Mon (Nov–Feb).

RAVELLO Villa Maria

€€€€

Via Santa Chiara 2, 84010 **Tel** *089 85 72 55* **Road Map** *D4*

On the path leading to the Villa Cimbrone, this small hotel and restaurant has gorgeous views over the Vallone di Dragone towards Scala. Set in an elegant house, with a charming garden in the shade of lime trees, there is a balmy terrace and a dining room. The food is excellent: local game, fresh fish and home-made pasta.

RAVELLO Rossellinis

€€€€€

Palazzo Sasso, Via San Giovanni del Toro 28, 84010 **Tel** *089 81 81 81* **Road Map** *D4*

For romantic candle-lit meals and fine food, dine at this Ravello restaurant, which has two Michelin stars. The view is mesmerising and the food, created by young chef Pino Lavarla, originally from Puglia, is a memorable if expensive experience. Only the finest of ingredients and an impressive wine list. Dinner only. Closed Nov–Apr.

Key to Price Guide *see p192* **Key to Symbols** *see back cover flap*

DIRECTORY

TOLEDO AND CASTEL NUOVO

BARS AND CAFES

Antico Caffè Prencipe
Piazza Municipio 20.
Map 7 B2.

Bar Brasiliano
Galleria Umberto I.
Map 7 A2.

Bar Roma
Corso Garibaldi 378.
Map 4 E4.

Caffè Gambrinus
Piazza Trieste e Trento 38.
Map 7 A3.

PASTRY SHOPS AND ICE CREAM PARLOURS

Pintauro
Via Toledo 275.
Map 7 A2.

La Scimmia
Piazza Carità 4.
Map 7 A1 (9 B5).

La Sfogliatella Mary
Via Toledo 66.
Map 7 A2.

TAKE-AWAY FOOD

Tavola Calda L.U.I.S.E.
Piazza dei Martiri 68.
Map 6 F2.

Tripperia Fiorenzano
Via Pignasecca 14.
Map 7 A1 (9 A5).

SPACCANAPOLI

BARS AND CAFES

Bar Nilo
Via San Biagio dei Librai 129/130.
Map 3 C5 (10 D3).

PASTRY SHOPS AND ICE CREAM PARLOURS

Gran Caffè Aragonese
Piazza San Domenico Maggiore 5/8.
Map 3 B5 (9 C3).

Scaturchio
Piazza San Domenico Maggiore 19.
Map 3 B5 (9 C3).

TAKE-AWAY FOOD

Friggi Friggi
Piazzetta Nilo 14.
Map 3 C5 (10 D3).

Timpani e Tempura
Vico della Quercia 17.
Map 3 A5 (9 B4).

DECUMANO MAGGIORE

BARS AND CAFES

Caffè dell'Epoca
Via Constantinopoli 82.
Map 3 B5.

Caffè Mexico
Piazza Dante 86.
Map 3 A5 (9 B3).

Gran Caffè Duomo
Via Duomo 163.
Map 3 C4 (9 D2).

Intra Moenia
Piazza Bellini 70.
Map 3 B5 (9 C3).

Scaturchio
Via Portamedina 22
Map 3 A5 (9 A4).

PASTRY SHOPS AND ICE CREAM PARLOURS

Carraturo
Via Casanova 97.
Map 4 E3.

TAKE-AWAY FOOD

Di Matteo
Via dei Tribunali 94.
Map 3 C4 (10 D2).

Vaco 'e Presse
Piazza Dante 87.
Map 3 A5 (9 B3).

VOMERO

BARS AND CAFES

Arx Café
Via Tito Angelini 20c.
Map 2 E5.

Caffè Mexico
Via Scarlatti 69.
Map 2 D5.

Caffè Scarlatti
Via Scarlatti 211.
Map 2 D5.

Caffetteria Bernini
Piazza Fanzago 9.
Map 2 D4.

PASTRY SHOPS AND ICE CREAM PARLOURS

Bellavia
Via Luca Giordano 158.
Map 1 C4.

Licardo
Via Belvedere 178/180.
Map 1 B5.

Soave
Via Scarlatti 130.
Map 2 D5.

TAKE-AWAY FOOD

Friggitoria Vomero
Via Cimarosa 44.
Map 2 D5.

Gastronomia Ambrosino
Via Scarlatti 49.
Map 2 D5.

Rossopomodoro
Corso Vittorio Emanuelle 84.
Map 5 B1.

CASTEL DELL'OVO AND CHIAIA

BARS AND CAFES

Bar dell'Ovo
Via Partenope 6.
Map 7 A4.

La Caffettiera
Piazza dei Martiri 26.
Map 6 F2.

PASTRY SHOPS AND ICE CREAM PARLOURS

Chalet Ciro
Via Caracciolo.
Map 5 B4.

Chiquito's
Via Mergellina
(opposite the funicular).
Map 5 B3.

Gran Bar Riviera
Riviera di Chiaia 181.
Map 6 D2.

Moccia
Via San Pasquale a Chiaia 21/22.
Map 6 E2.

Remy Gelo
Via Galiani 30.
Map 5 B3.

POSILLIPO

BARS AND CAFES

Gran Caffè Cimmino
Via Petrarca 147.
Map 5 A4.

PASTRY SHOPS AND ICE CREAM PARLOURS

Augustus
Via Petrarca 81.

Bilancione
Via Posillipo 238/b.

TAKE-AWAY FOOD

Elettroforno Giulia
Via Nicolardi 141.

SHOPS AND MARKETS

Shopping in Naples is an excellent way to explore the labyrinth of this fascinating city. Expensive boutiques line the main streets such as Via Toledo and Via Chiaia, where good quality, stylish clothes, shoes and jewellery can be bought. However, don't limit yourself to the fashionable areas, but wander around the alleyways in the old town to discover the small specialist shops and artisan workshops. Here visitors can find authentic and handmade souvenirs.

Nativity figure

These streets often bear the name of the trade practised there, such as Piazza degli Orefici (Goldsmiths' Square).

Perhaps the most enjoyable way to shop is to follow the example of most Neapolitans and buy from the numerous markets and stalls along the roadside. These *bancarelle* sell everything from clothes to kitchenware, and children's toys to jewellery. Common items are cheap seconds from the manufacturer or imitation designer labels.

Coral jewellery in a shop window

OPENING HOURS

Shops are open from 10am to 2pm and from 4pm to 8pm. They are closed on Sundays and Monday morning in winter, Saturday afternoon and Sunday in summer. Food shops and markets are shut on Thursday afternoons. Before holiday periods like Christmas, many places are open on Sundays and extend their weekly opening hours. In summer most shops close for two weeks around 15 August (Ferragosto).

HOW TO PAY

Major credit cards are accepted in most boutiques and department stores. Make sure you are given the receipt (*ricevuta fiscale*) for your purchase. By law the police can make a spot check outside the shop and if you are without a receipt, you may be fined. Artisans are not required to issue receipts.

SALES

From early July to early September and early January to mid-March, sales are held in Naples. You can find excellent bargains with discounts of up to 50 per cent and sometimes as much as 70 per cent. It is a good idea to check goods before you leave the shop as a refund is unlikely.

FASHION AND ACCESSORIES

The exclusive shops are concentrated in Via dei Mille and Via Calabritto, in the elegant Chiaia district. Here the great fashion designers, such as **Emporio Armani**, **Prada** and **Mario Valentino**, have their stores. A jewellery shop, **Bulgari**, has also opened here. In Riviera di Chiaia, **Magazzini Marinella** sells ties that are worn by many VIPs.

The shop window of the elegant Livio de Simone boutique

Fine accessories for men, such as silver cufflinks, are found at **Argenio**, while **Talarico** specializes in hand-carved umbrellas and canes.

At **Eddy Monetti** the emphasis is on elegant and classical fashion. Clothes with an innovative touch are offered by **Barbaro** in Galleria Umberto I, while more avant-garde men's and women's wear is sold by **Maxi Ho. Livio De Simone**, who is a native of Naples, offers stylish clothes in bright Mediterranean colours, while **Amina Rubinacci** is known for her woollen and soft cashmere jumpers. Naples also has a **Max Mara** boutique.

Clothing at somewhat more accessible prices is sold at **Stefanel** and **Motivi**. Young people have no lack of choice with clothes from the well-known **Benetton** outlets, as well as from **Mango** and **Zara**, which have stores in Via dei Mille and Via Toledo respectively.

The **Prénatal** chain caters for mothers-to-be and small children. Handbags, belts and other accessories, which are mostly made by local craftsmen, are sold in the **Tramontano** store.

In the old centre between San Biagio dei Librai and Via degli Orefici there are many jewellers' and goldsmiths' shops. The age-old tradition of engraving and cameo work is still practised in many of these shops.

Interior of the Colonnese bookshop in Via San Pietro a Majella

Ascione Coralli, a coral and cameo atelier, is open by appointment. **Caso Agostino** has superb coral jewels, and other jewellery shops such as **Ventrella** stock original and attractive designs.

DEPARTMENT STORES AND SHOPPING CENTRES

Most Neapolitans on the whole prefer the smaller, specialist shops, where the service is more personal. However, some of the department stores, in particular **Coin**, offer a good variety of products ranging from quality clothes, cosmetics and perfumes to household goods and crockery. If you are looking for those stores that specialize in household and kitchen goods, try the **Croff** chain, which also sells a very wide variety of modern furnishings. The large chain stores, such as **Upim** and **Oviesse**, are, as you would expect, generally cheaper and feature average-quality cosmetics, lingerie, household articles and clothes.

The shopping centres, **Galleria Vanvitelli** and the elegant **Galleria Scarlatti** can be found in the Vomero district of the city, and the extremely smart 19th-century Galleria Umberto I, off Piazza Trieste e Trento, is an attractive arcade of numerous elegant shops.

Coin
Via Scarlatti 98/100.
Tel 081 578 01 11.

Croff
Galleria Vanvitelli 16–23.
Tel 081 578 96 98.

Galleria Scarlatti
Via Scarlatti.

Galleria Vanvitelli
Piazza Vanvitelli.

Oviesse
Via A Doria 40.
Tel 081 239 63 60.

Upim
Via Nisco 11.
Tel 081 41 75 20.

ART, ANTIQUES AND INTERIOR DESIGN

Naples is renowned for its many fascinating antique and second-hand shops. The best-known antique dealers can be found in Via Domenico Morelli: for instance, **Brandi** and **La Florida** are specialists

in 18th-century furniture and paintings. Shops that stock historic objects include **Antichità Gargiulo**, **Antichità Ciro Guarracino** and **Affaitati** in Via Costantinopoli. Old engravings, prints and lithographs, picture frames and other *objets d'art*, are on sale at **Bowinkel**, which is the oldest shop in Piazza dei Martiri. Items such as rare books, prints and gouaches are sold at the **Casella** and **Regina** antiquarian booksellers, while the **Colonnese** bookshop stocks what can be described as traditional Neapolitan articles. **Maestranze Napoletane** sells exquisite antique marblework, as well as

The traditional craft of making and restoring string instruments

original marble objects made by the owner.

Examples of Naples art galleries that generally have interesting work on show include **Galleria Navarra**, **Lia Rumma** and **Studio Trisorio**.

Leading interior design shops in the city include **Antica Galleria d'Arte**, in the

Neapolitan second-hand dealer with goods on display in the street

Attractive display of traditional nativity scene dolls

Spaccanapoli area, and **Novelli**, featuring the latest styles in home furnishings. Avant-garde modern art pieces by local and foreign artists are available at **Galleria Raucci/Santamaria**, near Capodimonte.

HANDICRAFTS

The many workshops and second-hand shops in the historic centre offer a varied choice of articles, from the kitsch to the well-designed. In Via San Gregorio Armeno is the workshop of the famous nativity scene artisan **Giuseppe Ferrigno**, while in Via San Biagio dei Librai is the **Ospedale delle Bambole** (hospital for dolls) where porcelain dolls, marionettes and puppets are repaired and restored. Nearby at **La Smorfia**, artisans make hand-crafted terracotta statuettes for nativity scenes and collectors. At the **Liuteria Calace**, they make and restore violins, violas, mandolins and lutes, while **Statuaria Sacra di Vincenzo Castaldo** sells religious articles and artifacts. **Nel Regno di Pulcinella** is a workshop dedicated entirely to the making of Neapolitan masks.

Elegant objects made from handmade Amalfi paper make **Legatoria Artigiana di Napoli** a fascinating place. If you are interested in ceramics, it is worth having a look at **Il Cantuccio della Ceramica**.

FOOD, WINE AND SPIRITS

Two of Naples' leading delicatessens are **La Botteghina** and **Gastronomia L.U.I.S.E.**, both of which sell a fantastic variety of local specialities. **Gay Odin** has the finest chocolate in Naples, including the delicious *Vesuvio* chocolate which is made with rum. The old-fashioned **Scaturchio** sells excellent cakes and sweets, as well as ice cream. A good selection of wines is to be found at both the **Enoteca Dante** and the **Enoteca Belledonne**.

OPEN-AIR MARKETS

Street stalls and markets set up in the early morning and usually pack up after midday. Food stalls selling seasonal fruit and vegetables generally have fresher and less expensive produce than the shops. Clothes and household items will be cheap and, although they may not be designer quality, they are perfectly good. Bargaining is not usually done when buying food, but for clothes and other items try asking for a discount *(sconto)*.

Market at Sant'Antonio Abate

Fiera Antiquaria Napoletana
Villa Comunale. ◻ *8am–2pm third Sat & Sun of month.* Antiques market: silverware, jewellery and ornaments.

Mercatino di Antignano
Piazza degli Artisti. ◻ *8am–1pm Mon–Sat.* Clothing, shoes, household articles, fabrics.

Mercatino della Maddalena
Via Santa Candida. ◻ *8am–1pm Wed–Mon.* Clothes, shoes, music.

Mercatino della Pignasecca
Via Pignasecca. ◻ *8am–2pm & 4–8pm Mon–Sat.* Mainly food.

Mercatino di Poggioreale
Via Nuova Poggioreale. ◻ *8am–2pm Fri–Sun.* Clothes, antiques.

Mercatino della Torretta
Viale Gramsci. ◻ *8am–2pm Mon–Sat.* Food and clothing.

Mercato del Casale
Posillipo. ◻ *8am–2pm Thu.* Clothes, accessories, household articles.

Mercato di Porta Nolana
Via S Cosmo. ◻ *8am–6pm Mon–Sat (8am–2pm Sun).* Fresh fish and seafood.

Mercato di Sant'Antonio
Via Sant'Antonio Abate. ◻ *9am–8pm daily.* Food market.

The inviting entrance of the famous Scaturchio *pasticceria*

Directory

FASHION AND ACCESSORIES

Amina Rubinacci
Via dei Mille 16.
Tel 081 41 54 86.

Argenio
Via Filangieri 15e.
Tel 081 41 80 35.

Ascione Coralli
Piazzetta Matilde Serao
19 (2nd floor).
Tel 081 42 11 11.
Open by appointment.

Barbaro
Galleria Umberto 44.
Tel 081 41 12 84.
One of many branches.

Benetton
Via Toledo 253–255.
Tel 081 423 87 11.

Bulgari
Via Filangieri 40.
Tel 081 40 95 51.

Caso Agostino
Piazza San Domenico
Maggiore 16.
Tel 081 552 01 08.

Eddy Monetti
Via dei Mille 45a/b/c.
Tel 081 40 47 07.

Emporio Armani
Piazza dei Martiri 61–62.
Tel 081 42 58 16.

Livio De Simone
Via D Morelli 15.
Tel 081 764 38 27.

Magazzini Marinella
Via Riviera di Chiaia 287.
Tel 081 245 11 82.

Mango
Via dei Mille 62.
Tel 081 42 53 29.

Mario Valentino
Via Calabritto 10.
Tel 081 764 42 62.

Max Mara
Piazza Trieste e Trento 51.
Tel 081 40 62 42.

Maxi Ho
Via Luca Giordano 28.
Tel 081 578 04 39.

Motivi
Via Toledo 157.
Tel 081 551 06 47.

Prada
Via Calabritto 7.
Tel 081 764 13 23.

Prénatal
Via Roma 332.
Tel 081 42 12 22.
One of many branches.

Stefanel
Via Toledo 300.
Tel 081 40 63 35.

Talarico
Via Toledo 329 (inside).
Tel 081 40 19 79.

Tramontano
Via Chiaia 142/143.
Tel 081 41 48 37.

Ventrella
Via C Poerio 11.
Tel 081 764 31 73.

Zara
Via Toledo 210–213.
Tel 081 423 80 60.

ART, ANTIQUES AND INTERIOR DESIGN

Affaitati
Via Costantinopoli 18.
Tel 081 44 44 27.

Antica Galleria d'Arte
Via B Croce 4.
Tel 081 551 70 36.

Antichità Ciro Guarracino
Via V Gaetani 26.
Tel 081 764 69 12.

Antichità Gargiulo
Via C Poerio 32.
Tel 081 764 38 54.

Bowinkel
Piazza dei Martiri 24.
Tel 081 764 43 44.

Via S Lucia 25.
Tel 081 764 07 39.

Brandi
Via D Morelli 9–11.
Tel 081 764 38 82.

Casella
Via C Poerio 92e/f.
Tel 081 764 26 27.

Colonnese
Via S Pietro a Maiella
32/33. *Tel 081 45 98 58.*

La Florida
Via Merliani Giovanni 12.
Tel 081 556 97 21.

Galleria Navarra
Piazza dei Martiri 23.
Tel 081 764 35 95.

Galleria Raucci/Santamaria
Corso Amedeo di Savoia
190.
Tel 081 744 36 45.

Lia Rumma
Via V Gaetani 12.
Tel 081 19 81 23 54.

Maestranze Napoletane
Via Conte di Ruvo 7/8.
Tel 081 544 88 36.

Novelli
Via Vetriera 20.
Tel 081 1956 29 50.

Regina
Via Costantinopoli
51/103.
Tel 081 29 09 25.

Studio Trisorio
Riviera di Chiaia 215.
Tel 081 41 43 06.

HANDICRAFTS

Il Cantuccio della Ceramica
Via B Croce 38 (inside).
Tel 081 552 58 57.

Giuseppe Ferrigno
Via S Gregorio Armeno 8.
Tel 081 552 31 48.

Legatoria Artigiana di Napoli
Calata Trinità Maggiore 4.
Tel 081 551 12 80.

Liuteria Calace
Via San Domenico
Maggiore 9.
Tel 081 551 59 83.

Nel Regno di Pulcinella
Vico San Domenico
Maggiore 9.
Tel 081 551 41 71.

Ospedale delle Bambole
Via S Biagio dei Librai 81.
Tel 081 20 30 67.

La Smorfia
Strada dell'Anticaglia 23.
Tel 081 29 38 12.

Statuaria Sacra di Vincenzo Castaldo
Via S Biagio dei Librai 76.
Tel 081 554 11 01.

FOOD, WINE AND SPIRITS

La Botteghina
Via Orazio 106.
Tel 081 66 05 16.

Enoteca Belledonne
Vico Belledonne a
Chiaia 18.
Tel 081 40 31 62.

Enoteca Dante
Piazza Dante 18–19.
Tel 081 549 96 89.

Gastronomia L.U.I.S.E.
Piazza dei Martiri 68.
Tel 081 41 77 35.

Gay Odin
Via Toledo 214.
Tel 081 40 00 63.

Scaturchio
Piazza San Domenico
Maggiore 19.
Tel 081 551 69 44.

Shops and Markets along the Coast

Every town and village in the region, from the islands to the coast, offers typical local handicrafts such as ceramics or glassware, as well as foods and wines associated with the history and culture of each place. Wandering through the narrow streets in these lovely seaside spots, you will discover all kinds of customs.

FASHION AND ACCESSORIES

Besides shops with designer wear, there are still several old local fashion houses. You can find the top names in Italian and foreign fashion at places such as **Adario & Mario**, who have a shop at Sant'Agata sui due Golfi, or **Loro Piana** in Ischia. **Capricci**, also in Ischia, sells designer lingerie and swimwear. The shopping street in Capri, Via Camerelle, boasts the elegant **Amina Rubinacci** boutique, known for top-quality cashmere pullovers. Other cashmere luxuries are the speciality of **Le Farella**, also in Capri. Two top jewellers in Capri are **La Campanina** and **Chantecler**, both sited in Via Vittorio Emanuele, who stock precious stones in every colour as well as diamonds and coral necklaces of very fine quality.

Fashion styles in Positano are famous for their originality. Among the town's leading houses is **Maria Lampo**, who are well known for making their articles quickly (*lampo* meaning "in a flash"). Top designer wear as well as handmade patchwork clothing and quilts are sold at **Nadir**, while **La Bottega di Brunella** and **La Tartana** are distinguished for their fine fabrics and original patterns. If you want the bikini of your dreams, go to **Susy e Mimi** on Capri, where you can order swimwear made to measure. For custom-made Capri pants, head for **La Parisienne** in Capri.

Sorrento, Positano and Capri are famous for their handmade sandals; to have a pair made especially for you, go to **Siniscalchi** in Sorrento, **Costanzo Avitabile** in Positano, the imaginative **Canfora** in Capri or Antonio Viva's shop at Anacapri, aptly called **L'Arte del Sandalo Caprese**. For the best in high fashion, **Mariorita**, Capri's luxury department store, stocks the finest Italian and international clothing brands and luxury goods.

ART AND HANDICRAFTS

By exploring the craftsmen's shops in the towns and villages outside Naples you can really get to know the heart of a place, and discover its cultural and artistic traditions. The boats known as *gozzi* are built by the **Apreamare** company in Sorrento, and are world-famous. The ancient tradition of marquetry in the Sorrento peninsula is carried on by craftsmen such as **Salvatore Gargiulo**, **Peppe Rocco** and **Giliberto Attardi**. Also in Sorrento is **Gargiulo & Jannuzzi**, with its three floors of ceramic crockery, pottery and embroidered lace.

Vietri sul Mare is famous for its decorated ceramics; the **Solimene** factory employs at least 40 craftsmen who, despite a large output, make fine handmade products. In Maiori, **Fes Ceramiche** produces ceramic tableware and decorative tiles with geometric motifs. Other high-quality ceramics are produced by **Keramos d'Ischia** in Ischia and **Ceramiche d'Arte** in Ravello, while **La Bottega dell'Arte** in Capri – thanks to the well-known ceramicist Sergio Rubini – now has over 200 outlets in the United States alone. Also in Capri, **Carmelina** offers classic naive painting.

In Amalfi, visit the **Cartiera Amatruda** mill, where fine quality paper is produced. As a souvenir of Capri there are the **Carthusia** perfumes, sold only on the island (you can also visit their laboratories at No. 2 Via Parco Augusto). Lastly, the **Emporio Scialò** at Ischia sells raffia dolls and Pulcinella puppets, all made by hand.

FOOD, WINE AND LIQUEURS

Many fine dairy products such as cheese come from the area around Naples. In Sorrento you can visit the **Apreda** dairy and buy fresh plaits of *fiordilatte*, a type of mozzarella made from cow's milk, in the nearby shop. The **Fattoria Terranova** is also worth a visit to stock up on olive oil, preserves and jams. For gourmets, **Capannina Piu'** in Capri offers a mouth-watering array of local food and wines, as does **Anastasio Nicola**, in Amalfi, whose shop is filled with hanging hams, local cheeses, chocolate and more. For the sweet-toothed, Ischia's **Caffè Calise** has orange *sfogliatelle* and at Positano the **La Zagara** pastry shop has delicious fruit tarts called *crostate*. While in Amalfi, try the delightful lemon pastries at **Andrea Pansa**.

Some wine shops also sell local products such as jam, honey and spices: **Piemme** at Sorrento, **Ischia Sapori** on Ischia and **Gusti e Delizie** in Ravello. Good ranges of wine are on sale at **La Valle dei Mulini** in Amalfi. **Limoncello di Capri** is the most famous source of limoncello, or lemon-flavoured liqueur. **Profumi della Costiera** and **I Giardini di Ravello** also stock a good range.

MARKETS

There are numerous markets in the outlying areas. The most important in size and tradition is the second-hand market in Resina at Ercolano (Herculaneum), where you will find used clothes and accessories. It is half an hour from the central railway station in Naples: take the Circumvesuviana line and get off at Ercolano.

DIRECTORY

FASHION AND ACCESSORIES

Adario & Mario
Via Nastro Azzurro 1–3
(Sant'Agata sui Due
Golfi).
Tel 081 878 00 65. One
of two shops.

Amina Rubinacci
Via V Emanuele 13
(Capri).
Tel 081 837 72 95.

**L'Arte del Sandalo
Caprese**
Via G Orlandi 75
(Anacapri).
Tel 081 837 35 83.

**La Bottega di
Brunella**
Via Pasitea 72 (Positano).
Tel 089 87 52 28.

La Campanina
Via V Emanuele 18
(Capri).
Tel 081 837 06 43.

Canfora
Via Camerelle 3
(Capri).
Tel 081 837 04 87.

Capricci
Via Roma 37
(Ischia Porto).
Tel 081 98 20 63.

Chantecler
Via V Emanuele II 51
(Capri).
Tel 082 351 34 20.

Costanzo Avitabile
Piazza A Vespucci 1–5
(Positano).
Tel 089 87 53 66.

Le Farella
Via Fuorlovada 21c
(Capri).
Tel 081 837 52 43.

Loro Piana
Via Camerelle 45–47
(Capri).
Tel 081 838 82 21.
One of two shops.

Maria Lampo
Via Pasitea 12–16
(Positano).
Tel 089 87 50 21.

Mariorita
Via Capodimonte 4/8/12
(Anacapri).
Tel 081 837 14 26.

Nadir
Via Pasitea 44
(Positano).
Tel 089 87 59 75.

La Parisienne
Piazza Umberto 7
(Capri).
Tel 081 837 77 50.

Siniscalchi
Corso Italia 203
(Sorrento).
Tel 081 878 30 65.
One of two shops.

Susy e Mimi
Via Le Botteghe 61
(Capri).

La Tartana
Via della Tartana 5
(Positano).
Tel 089 87 56 45.

ART AND HANDICRAFTS

Apreamare
Via Terragneta 72,
Torre Annunziata.
Tel 081 53 78 41.

La Bottega dell'Arte
Via Catena 2–4
(Anacapri).
Tel 081 837 18 78.

Carmelina
Via Roma (Capri).

Carthusia
Via Capodimonte 26
(Anacapri).
Tel 081 837 36 68.
One of two shops.

Cartiera Amatruda
Via delle Cartiere 100
(Amalfi).
Tel 089 87 13 15.

Ceramiche d'Arte
Via Roma 22 (Ravello).
Tel 089 85 85 76.

**Ceramiche
Artistiche Solimene**
Via Madonna degli
Angeli 7 (Vietri sul Mare).
Tel 089 21 02 43.

Emporio Scialò
Corso Umberto I, 21
(Forio d'Ischia).
Tel 081 99 75 92.

Fes Ceramiche
Via Roma 24,
Minori (Vietri sul Mare).
www.fesceramiche.com

Gargiulo & Jannuzzi
Viale Enrico Caruso 1
(Sorrento).
Tel 081 878 10 41.

Giliberto Attardi
Via Padre R Giuliani
45–49 (Sorrento).
Tel 081 878 12 91.

Keramos d'Ischia
Via d'Aloisio 89,
Casamicciola Terme
(Ischia).
Tel 081 333 01 42.

Peppe Rocco
Via San Nicola 12
(Sorrento).
Tel 081 878 48 74.

Salvatore Gargiulo
Via Fuoro 33 (Sorrento).
Tel 081 878 24 20.

FOOD, WINE AND LIQUEURS

Anastasio Nicola
Via Lorenzo d'Amalfi 36
(Amalfi).
Tel 089 87 10 07.

Andrea Pansa
Piazza Duomo 40
(Amalfi).
Tel 089 87 10 65.

Apreda
Via del Mare 20
(Sorrento).
Tel 081 878 13 34.
One of two shops.

Caffè Calise
Via A Sogliuzzo 69
(Ischia Porto).
Tel 081 99 12 70.

Capannina Piu'
Via delle Botteghe 39
(Capri).
Tel 081 837 07 32.

Fattoria Terranova
Piazza Tasso 32 (Sorrento).
Tel 081 878 12 63.

I Giardini di Ravello
Via Civiltà 14
(Ravello).
Tel 089 87 22 64.

**Gusti e
Delizie**
Via Roma 28–30
(Ravello).
Tel 089 85 77 16.

Ischia Sapori
Via Gianturco 1
(Ischia Porto).
Tel 081 98 44 82.

Limoncello di Capri
Via Roma 85 (Capri).
Tel 081 837 55 61.

Piemme
Corso Italia 374
(Sant'Agnello).
Tel 081 532 21 99.

**Profumi della
Costiera**
Via Trinità 37 (Ravello).
Tel 089 85 81 67.

**La Valle
dei Mulini**
Via Lorenzo d'Amalfi 11
(Amalfi).
Tel 089 87 26 03.

La Zagara
Via dei Mulini 8/10
(Positano).
Tel 089 87 59 64.

ENTERTAINMENT

Naples knows how to entertain: demanding emperors, kings, residents and travellers have enjoyed its delights for over 2,000 years. Once a major European capital, Naples still revels in shows, games, banquets, and horse races, plus newer diversions like opera and football. Perhaps Italy's most energetic city, Naples buzzes with activity. The nightlife is dynamic, the cafés, nightspots and cultural venues are always open late, and just about every taste is catered for. Music and theatre performances take place throughout the year, bolstered by some important international festivals in summertime, mostly held in the holiday resorts. For film buffs there are two main multiplexes as well as some arthouse cinemas. During the week people usually go to the cinema or out to eat; at weekends the piazzas are bustling with life, as it is customary for Neapolitans to meet up to have a drink before going on to nearby nightspots. Clubbers get going after midnight, perhaps winding down at dawn with coffee and a hot brioche at an all-night bar.

Ballet dancer

Night-time illuminations in a city that is happy to party until dawn

INFORMATION AND BUYING TICKETS

Naples' daily newspaper *Il Mattino* has the most complete listings for the city, but the national newspapers also carry Naples listings in their local editions.

A monthly guide to events in Naples is published by the tourist office. Visit www. inaples.it to check it out online. Alternatively, pick up a copy of the magazine *Qui Napoli* *(see p218)*, which is available free from most tourist information offices and hotels.

Tickets for performances can generally be bought at the door on the day. They may be more difficult to obtain for operas at the San Carlo, popular shows at the Diana and Bellini, premieres and special events. The two main booking offices are **Concerteria** and **Box Office**.

THEATRE, OPERA AND DANCE

Naples is one of Italy's leading cities for theatre. It hosts international and national touring productions, as well as prestigious local companies. The main season is from October to May, though some theatres put on extra programmes and there are special events year-round.

Neapolitans are proud of their dialect, so don't be surprised if it features in some theatrical productions. **Teatro Sannazaro**, a 19th-century theatre staging traditional Neapolitan comedy, is the venue where Eleonora Duse, Eduardo Scarpetta and the De Filippo brothers starred. The **Mercadante**, home of Teatro Stabile di Napoli, sometimes stages plays by Eduardo De Filippo *(see p37)* in English.

Teatro Cilea, founded in the 1970s, focuses on traditional Neapolitan theatre. Italian classic drama and Neapolitan musicals are on at the **Bellini**. **Teatro Trianon** bills itself as "the Theatre of Neapolitan Song". The **Augusteo** hosts musicals and concerts, while the **Totò** puts on variety shows, and the **Teatro Bracco** focuses on comedies.

The **Sancarluccio** is a venue where small companies stage performances in Italian or English. Fringe and experimental theatre are on offer at **Galleria Toledo** and **Nuovo Teatro Nuovo**.

Teatro San Carlo *(see p37 and p53)* is one of Italy's top three opera houses. It also serves as the city's leading ballet venue and hosts an important symphony season. A premiere here is a great social occasion. The San Carlo stages performances designed to appeal to young people through its Programma Scuole.

An opera at the Teatro San Carlo

Performance at a city music venue

NIGHTLIFE

La Movada is the Spanish term Neapolitans use to describe their moveable nightlife – snacks here, drinks there, live music somewhere else – in places that stay open until the small hours of the morning. *La Movada* shifts around according to what venues are popular or trendy at any particular time, but favourite streets in the Vomero neighbourhood are Via Giotto, Via Ruoppolo, Via Chiaia and Via Piccinni. Piazza dei Martiri sees plenty of action, and Piazza Bellini is also lively, with cultural associations that host a range of interesting exhibitions and events.

Intra Moenia *(see p78)* is a magnet in Piazza Bellini. It's a large bar-café-book-shop that appeals to a lefty intellectual crowd with its recorded fusion and jazz music. An alternative crowd that is into dance music favours **Kestè**, located near the Orientale University. There's a DJ and, at week-ends, live jazz on a tiny stage.

Via Chiaia, a famously upmarket shopping area by day, attracts a similarly smart set in the evening. Multiple use is in vogue here, with several venues doubling up as bars in the day and as clubs at night. Head to **Chandelier** for the traditional evening *aperitivo* and stay on for a night of house, pop and R&B tunes. If your idea of an enjoyable evening is appreciating a fine wine in a relaxed environment, **Enoteca Belledonne** has an extensive list of Italian and international wines. Also in Chiaia are **Fusion Bar 66**, with its exotic Turkish feel and occasional live bossa nova acts, and **S'move**. *Aperitivo* is served here from 7pm until 9pm to the sounds of acid jazz, electro and funk.

Piazza Santa Maria la Nova draws a younger crowd to chug beer at its stands and cafés; however, it also plays host to the rather grown-up **Aret'a'palm**, a jazz and blues bar with a fine wine list. Look out also for openings at contemporary art galleries clustered around **MADRE** (Museo D'Arte Contempo-ranea Donna Regina Napoli; *see p84*) and **PAN** (Palazzo delle Arti Napoli).

Naples is home to a famous symphony season at the **Teatro San Carlo**, while **Teatro Bellini** sometimes offers chamber music concerts.

Be aware that phone numbers for venues often change, so don't rely on them. A good hotel concierge should be able to provide up-to-the-minute advice – or you can simply head out, follow *La Movada* and see where it takes you.

CINEMA

Most foreign films are dubbed into Italian; however, some movies are occasionally shown in their original language. If this is the case, newspaper listings will bear the words *versione originale* next to the show times. **Plaza Multisala** shows original version films on Tuesdays. Some foreign language institutes, such as the **Institut Français de Naples "Le Grenoble"**, also show films in their original language.

For around ten days in June, the **Napoli Film Festival** highlights international cinema.

The **Filangieri Multisala** screens both mainstream and arthouse movies, while the **Modernissimo** and the **Plaza Multisala** have multiple screens and show childrens' films. **Teatro Augusteo** hosted the 10th Artecinema, an international festival of films about contemporary art.

Some cinemas in the city show new films for half price on Wednesdays. Summertime brings outdoor screenings in squares and at historic sites. Outside Naples there are also some drive-in cinemas *(see p212).*

Festival logo

Fireworks, a popular tradition in Naples and the Campania region

Orchestra playing at the Ravello Festival

CHILDREN'S ENTERTAINMENT

Edenlandia is the main amusement park in Naples, with over 200 attractions, including the World of Fables, Walt Disney favourites, models of sets from Disney stories and theme merry-go-rounds. **Magic World** combines fun rides with a large water park featuring slides and pools. **Bowling Oltremare** has table tennis, football and virtual golf, as well as bowling. For computer-mad kids, Internet terminals are available at **Opus Informatica**.

Carousel at the Edenlandia funfair

SPECTATOR SPORTS

Stadio San Paolo (see p42) hosts *calcio* (football), the sporting event that most fires the passion of Neapolitans. Usually games are held on Sundays and tickets always sell out quickly. Newer to Naples is *basket*: its basketball team is Carpisa Napoli.

The **Ippodromo di Agnano** race track lies in a splendid natural location. Every April it hosts the famous Gran Premio trotting races.

Canoe polo teams, active since the late 1980s, compete in the Coppa Italia di Canoa Polo; check *Il Mattino* sports section for information. If you are lucky enough to

come across a match, don't miss the chance to enjoy a unique experience.

Swimming, diving and, especially, water polo are extremely popular in Naples. All are practised at the **Piscina Scandone**, the city's public swimming pool.

Trotting races at Agnano

OUTSIDE NAPLES

Festivals of classical music in the Amalfi Coast region are often eagerly anticipated annual events. Because of their popularity, it is best to book tickets in advance. Concerts at the Estate Musicale Sorrentina, which are held in the cloister of the church of San Francesco in Sorrento,

are often in demand. The **Ravello Festival** (see p41), which runs from early July until mid September, includes chamber music, orchestral concerts, film, dance and art exhibitions.

Pompei di Notte offers guided evening visits to the remains of Pompeii (see pp146–9) from May to October. One choice includes a light show, with music by Italian composer Ennio Morricone, and has proved popular with Neapolitans and tourists alike.

Settimana della Cultura, an annual week of cultural events held in April, offers visits to archaeological sites in Campania. Some of these sites are not generally open to the public. Others stage special events or entertainment: from art exhibitions to architectural or archival displays; and from film and theatre to sports.

Benevento, Santa Maria Capua Vetere and Caserta all have theatres staging plays, and Pozzuoli and Caserta have drive-in cinemas.

The Phlegraean Fields area has many nightspots, bars and discos. South toward Licola, and on the Sorrento peninsula, the beach bars convert to beach discos on summer evenings. In Capri, after a stroll around La Piazzetta you could try **Number Two** for a night of energetic dancing. On Ischia, dancers at **Valentino** party until well into the night. It is open year round, though in winter only at weekends.

Outdoor café nightlife, La Piazzetta, Capri

DIRECTORY

INFORMATION AND BUYING TICKETS

Box Office
Galleria Umberto I 17.
Map 7 A2.
Tel 081 551 91 88.
www.boxofficenapoli.it

Concerteria
Via M Schipa 23.
Map 5 B2.
Tel 081 761 12 21.

THEATRE, OPERA AND DANCE

Galleria Toledo
Teatro Stabile
D'Innovazione,
Via Concezione a
Montecalvario 34.
Tel 081 42 58 24.
www.galleriatoledo.org

Mercadante, Teatro Stabile
Piazza Municipio 64.
Map 7 B2.
Tel 081 551 33 96.
www.teatrostabilenapoli.it

Nuovo Teatro Nuovo
Via Montecalvario 16.
Map 7 A1.
Tel 081 40 60 62.
www.nuovoteatro
nuovo.it

Teatro Augusteo
Via Toledo 263
(Piazzetta Duca d'Aosta).
Map 7 A1.
Tel 081 41 42 43.
www.teatroaugusteo.it

Teatro Bellini
Via Conte di Ruvo 14.
Map 3 B4.
Tel 081 549 12 66.
www.teatrobellini.it

Teatro Bracco
Via Tarsia 40.
Map 3 A5 (9 A3).
Tel 081 564 53 23.
www.teatrobracco.it

Teatro Cilea
Via San Domenico 11.
Map 1 A5.
Tel 081 714 18 01.

Teatro San Carlo
Via San Carlo 98f.
Map 7 A2.
*Tel 081 553 45 65 or
393 955 3146.*
www.teatrosancarlo.it
Programma Scuole
Tel 081 40 40 64.

Teatro Sancarluccio
Via San Pasquale a
Chiaia 49. **Map** 6 E2.
Tel 081 40 50 00.

Teatro Sannazaro
Via Chiaia 157.
Map 7 A3.
Tel 081 41 17 23.

Teatro Totò
Via Cavara 12.
Map 4 D3.
Tel 081 564 75 25.
www.teatrototo.com

Teatro Trianon
Piazza Calenda 9.
Map 4 D5.
Tel 081 225 82 85.

NIGHTLIFE

Aret'a'palm
Piazza Santa Maria
La Nova 14.
Map 7 B1 (9 C5).
Tel 339 848 6949.

Chandelier
Vico Belledonne
a Chiaia 34–35.
Map 6 E2.
Tel 333 252 8177.

Enoteca Belledonne
Vico Belledonne
a Chiaia 18.
Map 6 E2.
Tel 081 40 31 62.

Fusion Bar 66
Via Bisignano 58.
Map 6 E2.
Tel 081 41 50 24.

Intra Moenia
Piazza Bellini 70.
Map 3 B5.
Tel 081 29 09 88.

Kestè
Largo San Giovanni
Maggiore Pignatelli 26–7.
Map 7 B1.
Tel 081 551 39 84.

MADRE (Museo D'Arte Contemporanea Donna Regina Napoli)
Via L Settembrini 79.
Map 3 C3.
Tel 081 29 28 33.

PAN (Palazzo delle Arti Napoli)
Via dei Mille 60.
Map 6 E2.
Tel 081 795 86 05.

S'move
Vico dei Sospiri 10a.
Map 6 E2.
Tel 081 764 58 13.

Teatro Bellini
*See listing under Theatre,
Opera and Dance.*

Teatro San Carlo
*See listing under Theatre,
Opera and Dance.*

CINEMA

Filangieri Multisala
Via Filangieri 43–7.
Map 6 F2.
Tel 081 251 24 08.

Institut Français de Naples "Le Grenoble"
Via Crispi 86. **Map** 6 D2.
Tel 081 66 96 65.

Modernissimo
Via Cisterna dell'Olio 23.
Map 3 A5.
Tel 081 580 02 54.

Napoli Film Festival
Tel 081 423 81 27.
www.napolifilm
festival.com

Plaza Multisala
Via Kerbaker 85.
Map 2 D4.
Tel 081 556 35 55.

Teatro Augusteo
*See listing under Theatre,
Opera and Dance.*

CHILDREN'S ENTERTAINMENT

Bowling Oltremare
Viale JF Kennedy.
Tel 081 62 44 44.

Edenlandia
Viale JF Kennedy.
Tel 081 239 40 90.

Magic World
Via S Nullo, Giugliano.
Tel 081 804 71 22.
www.magicworld.it

Opus Informatica
Piazza Cavour 140.
Map 3 B3.
Tel 081 29 88 77.

SPECTATOR SPORTS

Ippodromo di Agnano
Via R Ruggiero.
Tel 081 735 711.

Piscina Scandone
Viale Giochi del
Mediterraneo.
Tel 081 570 26 36.

Stadio San Paolo
Piazzale Tecchio
(Fuorigrotta).
www.sscnapoli.it

OUTSIDE NAPLES

Number Two
Via Camerelle 1
(Capri).
Tel 081 837 70 78.

Pompei di Notte
Advance bookings:
www.scavidipompei.it

Ravello Festival
Information
Tel 089 85 84 22.
Advance credit card
booking
Tel 199 10 99 10.
www.ravellofestival.com

Settimana della Cultura
www.beniculturali.it/
settimanacultura

Valentino
Corso V Colonna 97
(Ischia).
Tel 081 98 25 69.

SPECIALIST HOLIDAYS AND OUTDOOR ACTIVITIES

Naples and the Amalfi Coast offer a variety of cultural and sporting activities as well as beautiful and arresting landscapes. You can learn to cook regional dishes and discover wines made from grapes unique to the area, some descended from those of Ancient Greece. Walks can be through small medieval towns, rolling hills, along dramatic cliff tops or over active volcanic

The grape harvest at a local winery

terrain. Horse rides pass mountains, vineyards and ancient temples. Some of the world's most spectacular coastline beckons with its water sports and caves. Those interested in archaeology can join university projects at ancient sites. Alternatively, you can relax at thermal baths, the best of which are on the island of Ischia. Most guided activities are in Italian, unless noted otherwise.

CULINARY COURSES

Cookery courses are run close to Paestum (*see pp162–3*) by **Azienda Agrituristica Seliano**. The courses focus on cuisine derived from ancient Greek and Roman traditions and are held at Agriturismo Seliano (*see p184*), a working farm that can provide room and board. The farm raises buffalo, which produce milk for the best mozzarella. Courses usually last three to five days, but can be flexible.

Il Principe (*see p199*), a restaurant within walking distance of the ruins of Pompeii (*see pp146–51*), offers cookery lessons in ancient or modern Neapolitan cuisine. The ancient Roman recipes were devised in collaboration with the Archaeological Service of Pompeii. *De Gustibus*, a recipe booklet fine tuned by the restaurant's award-winning chef, describes how the Romans prepared their food. Courses last from one to five days, but a short lesson after a meal is also possible.

Pastafest, with tastings and demonstrations, is a five-day fair held in October in Torre Annunziata (*see p141*).

WINE COURSES AND TASTING

Vitignoitalia is an annual wine trade show and tasting experience that began in 2005. For three days in late spring participants visit wine makers, taste wines and enrol at sessions to learn more

about single-varietal wines (those made from only one type of grape), most of which are from southern Italy.

Mastroberardino, a winery founded in 1878, has a joint project with the Archaeological Service of Pompeii to research the grapes and growing systems used in Pompeii at the time of the AD 79 eruption. It holds various wine tasting courses and tours of its cellar.

Feudi di San Gregorio is one of the region's larger wine makers and has a modern *cantina* (cellar) of architectural interest designed in 2002 by Hikaru Mori. It runs wine-tasting events and offers guest accommodation.

WALKING AND HORSE RIDING

Hiking through the glorious countryside is a popular activity. Free maps with suggested routes are available

at EPT offices (*see p219*), which also have details of guided tours.

The Pozzuoli/Solfatara metro stop is recommended as a starting point for exploring Pozzuoli (*see pp136–7*). You can walk to the Temple of Serapis and then on to the Solfatara (*see p137*), with its volcanic phenomena such as fumaroles and bubbling mud.

Naples WWF runs the Cratere degli Astroni nature reserve on Vesuvius' crater. To get there take the Agnano exit on the *tangenziale* (bypass). Paths through the woods lead to stretches of water inhabited by herons and other birds. **Presidio Vulcano Vesuvio** leads guided tours in the park around Vesuvius and up to the crater.

Azienda Agrituristica Seliano in Paestum offers horse riding. It is also worth checking with tourist offices for equestrian centres and other *agriturismi* with horses.

Horse riding, an ideal way to appreciate the region's scenery

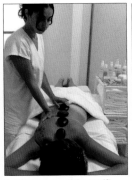

Treatment at one of the Amalfi Coast's spa resorts

SPA HOLIDAYS

The Amalfi Coast's thermal waters attracted the likes of the Roman emperor Tiberius. Unlike those in northern Italy, the region's spas draw few crowds and charge reasonable prices. Ischia has the best facilities. **Grand Hotel Punta Molino Terme** has a thermal pool and spa, as do **Giardini Poseidon Terme** and **Hotel Grazia Terme**. Thermal waters are also to be found at Lacco Ameno, Casamicciola Terme, Telesia near Benevento and Villamaina near Avellino. Note that many spas close in winter.

WATER SPORTS AND EXCURSIONS BY BOAT

Many Neapolitans head to Capri or Ischia on the ferry *(see p226)* for the day.

Scuba lessons and excursions are available at **Lucibello** and (in English as well as Italian) at **Centro Immersione Massa Lubrense**. For diving at Capri and Ischia, contact the **Capri Sea Service** and **Ischia Diving Center** respectively.

Naples' seafront clubs are reserved for members, but your hotel may be able to sponsor you as a guest. Many marinas offer sailing. Weekly yacht rentals (2–5 cabins), with or without a skipper, are available year-round at **Eva**

Mare in Salerno. *La canoa polo* (canoe polo) grew in popularity in Italy in the 1980s and **HyppoKampos Resort** in Castel Volturno organizes both lessons and rentals.

The **Centro Sub Campi Flegrei** offers regular dives as well as guided underwater excursions to the archaeological park of Baia *(see p137).*

ARCHAEOLOGICAL PROJECTS

Each summer, the **Fieldwork Anglo-American Project in Pompeii** offers paying volunteers from around the world an opportunity to join its summer field school, where they investigate a complete block of the ancient city.

SPELUNKING

Those who fancy having a go at cave exploring can experience it in the **Grotte dell'Angelo** (Angel Cave), a trek suitable for amateurs.

DIRECTORY

CULINARY COURSES

Azienda Agrituristica Seliano
Via Seliano, Paestum.
Tel 082 872 36 34.

Pastafest
www.pastafest.it

Il Principe
Piazza Bartolo Longo, Pompeii.
Tel 081 850 55 66.

WINE COURSES AND TASTING

Feudi di San Gregorio
Loc Cerza Grossa, Sorbo Serpico (Avellino).
Tel 082 598 66 86.
www.feudi.it

Mastroberardino
Via Manfredi Altripalda 78/81 (Avellino).
Tel 082 561 41 11.
www.mastroberardino. com

Vitignoitalia
Tel 081 410 45 33.
www.vitignoitalia.it

WALKING AND HORSE RIDING

Azienda Agrituristica Seliano
See Culinary Courses.

Naples WWF
Tel 081 560 70 00.

Presidio Vulcano Vesuvio
Via S Vito 151, Ercolano.
Tel 081 777 57 20
or *337 942 249.*
www.guidevesuvio.it

SPA HOLIDAYS

Giardini Poseidon Terme
Via G Mazzella 87, Ischia.
Tel 081 908 71 11.
www.giardiniposeidon.it

Grand Hotel Punta Molino Terme
Lungomare Cristoforo Colombo 23, Ischia.
Tel 081 99 15 44.
www.puntamolino.it

Hotel Grazia Terme
Via Borbonica 2, Lacco Ameno, Ischia.
Tel 081 99 43 33.
www.hotelgrazia.it

WATER SPORTS AND EXCURSIONS BY BOAT

Capri Sea Service
Via Cristoforo Colombo 64, Capri.
Tel 081 837 87 81.
www.capriseaservice.com

Centro Immersione Massa Lubrense
Marina della Lobra, Via Fontanelle 18, Massa Lubrense.
Tel 081 808 90 03.

Centro Sub Campi Flegrei
Via Napoli 1, Pozzuoli.
Tel 081 853 15 63.
www.centrosub campiflegrei.it

Eva Mare
Via Porto 12, Salerno.
Tel 089 258 30 67.
www.evamare.it

HyppoKampos Resort
Via Fiumitello II, Castel Volturno. *Tel 082 376 46 28.* www.hkresort.it

Ischia Diving Center
Via Iasolino 106, Ischia Porto. *Tel 081 98 18 52.* www.ischiadiving.net

Lucibello
Via del Brigantino 9, Positano. *Tel 089 87 50 32.* www.lucibello.it

ARCHAEOLOGICAL PROJECTS

Fieldwork Anglo-American Project in Pompeii
Apply through University of Bradford, Bradford BD7 1DP, UK. *Tel 01274 232 323.* www.brad.ac.uk

SPELUNKING

Grotte dell'Angelo
Petina or Polla exit from A3, then SS19 and follow signs to the cave.
Tel 097 539 70 37.
www.grotte dellangelo.sa.it

SURVIVAL GUIDE

PRACTICAL INFORMATION

Naples is a lively if somewhat chaotic city. It may seem bewildering at first, but after experiencing its vibrant street life and rich historic and artistic wealth, it is hard not to be won over by Naples' gritty charms. The city has undergone something of a rebirth, with more monuments open at regular hours and a reorganization of its major museums, making the most of their world-class collections. Improved facilities and new pedestrian areas have revived public spaces, and cultural and social activities abound. The city has its frustrating aspects, such as crippling bureaucracy at banks and public offices, and it is wise to be on the lookout for petty crime, keeping money and valuables well out of view. However, visitors need only a few simple guidelines and some forward planning to make the most of this fascinating city and its treasures.

ITALIA

ENTE NAZIONALE
ITALIANO PER IL TURISMO

The ENIT logo

Castel Sant'Elmo, on Vomero hill

IMMIGRATION AND CUSTOMS

European Union (EU) residents and visitors from the United States, Canada, Australia, New Zealand and Japan do not need a visa for stays of up to three months, but they must have one for a longer stay. Non-EU citizens must carry a valid passport with them at all times, while for EU citizens an ID card will suffice.

Non-EU citizens can bring in 400 cigarettes, 100 cigars, or 500 grams of tobacco; 1 litre of spirits or 2 litres of wine; and 50 grams of perfume. There is no limit for EU citizens. Non-EU citizens can also claim back sales tax (IVA) on purchases in excess of €155. For further details on customs allowances, contact your embassy or consulate.

TOURIST INFORMATION

It is possible to organize your itinerary before your trip to Naples via the **ENIT** (Italian tourist board) office in your home country. Once in Italy, the network of local tourist offices known as **EPT** (Ente Provinciale per il Turismo) can provide useful information about accommodation, guided tours and excursions in Naples and the surrounding area. EPT offices can be found at key arrival points such as the airport and the main railway station, as well as in the city centre.

The **Azienda Autonoma di Soggiorno, Cura e Turismo** has offices in Naples and the main tourist resorts. They are good sources of information and will provide free maps and guide books. Smaller towns will also have an information office, called a Pro Loco, often based in the town hall.

OPENING HOURS AND ADMISSION PRICES

Shops in Naples tend to be open 8:30am–1pm and 4:30–8:30pm Monday to Saturday. In the centre, however, many stay open throughout the day. Museums and archaeological sites alternate their closing days between Tuesdays and Wednesdays; smaller museums close on Mondays, while church opening hours vary depending on staff schedules and availability. Always check opening times before visiting.

Entrance to most sights is free for EU citizens under the age of 18 or over 65, and half-price for those aged 18–25 (with ID). Churches are generally free but may charge for some areas. The Campania Artecard (www. artecard.it) offers discounts on archaeological sites, museums and even public transport.

Museo Archeologico Nazionale

TRAVELLERS WITH SPECIAL NEEDS

Naples can be a challenge for travellers with disabilities. Progress is being made, but cobbled streets, chaotic traffic and limited parking make movement difficult for visitors in wheelchairs, the partially sighted or those with hearing impairments. The website **Turismo Accessible** has information on accessible hotels, restaurants, monuments and churches in the city. It is wise to call the establishments you plan to visit in advance to check for accessibility.

Steep hillsides and stone steps make travelling in a wheelchair rather difficult on the Amalfi Coast. The centre and waterfront of Amalfi town are the most wheelchair-

◁ Fishing boats at Marina Grande, Sorrento

friendly areas here. Local tourist offices have information on accessible public transport and accommodation.

If you need assistance when travelling by train, contact customer services at the **Stazione Centrale** 24 hours before your train's departure.

STUDENT TRAVELLERS

Students and people under 26 can obtain discounted air, rail and ferry tickets at the **Centro Turistico Studentesco (CTS)**. Membership (€30) includes the International Student Identity Card (ISIC) and the Italian Carta Giovani; both can also be purchased separately (€10 each). The ISIC can be used for reduced entry at museums and archaeological sites, while the Carta Giovani offers discounts at theatres and bookshops. CTS has a 24-hour telephone helpline and can also help with cheap car hire.

The **Associazione Italiana Alberghi per la Gioventù (AIG)** (Italian Youth Hostelling Association) operates hostels for members of the YHA (Youth Hostel Association). Membership (€18) can be purchased at any hostel. In Naples, the **Ostello Mergellina** is conveniently located and open all year round; for hostels outside Naples, contact the AIG.

LISTINGS INFORMATION

The free monthly magazine *Qui Napoli*, available from most hotels and information offices, lists events in and around Naples. Each issue has up-to-date information in Italian and English on local exhibitions, theatre

performances and concerts. More detailed information on lectures, seminars, sports and entertainment can be found in the national magazines or in the relevant supplements of newspapers. *Il Mattino*, Naples' daily newspaper, lists museum opening hours and events, as well as ferry and train schedules.

ITALIAN TIME

Italy is 1 hour ahead of Greenwich Mean Time (2 hours ahead in the summer). London is therefore 1 hour behind Italian time and New York 6 hours behind; Tokyo is 8 hours ahead, and Sydney 10 hours ahead.

RESPONSIBLE TOURISM

Visitors can help preserve the beauty of this area by respecting the environment and supporting local businesses. Buying local foods and wines helps farming communities throughout the region. In Naples, shop at the open-air markets *(see p206)*, including the daily Mercatino della Pignasecca, near Via Toledo. Outside of the city, visit **Tenuta Vannulo**, a certified organic water-buffalo farm promoting sustainable agriculture. Take a tour of the mozzarella factory or relax in the café serving buffalo-milk products.

The ethos of **ICNOS Adventures** is captured in the acronym of its name (Italian Culture, Nature, Outdoor, Sustainability). This tour operator specializes in non-damaging tourism that preserves the cultural heritage and natural beauty of the Amalfi Coast and Campania.

DIRECTORY

TOURIST INFORMATION

Azienda Autonoma di Soggiorno, Cura e Turismo
Naples
Via Marino Turchi 16. **Map** 7 A4.
Tel 081 245 74 75.
Piazza del Gesù. **Map** 9 B4.
Tel 081 551 27 01.
Via San Carlo 9. **Map** 7 A3.
Tel 081 40 23 94.
www.inaples.it
Sorrento
Via Luigi De Maio 35.
Tel 081 807 40 33.
www.sorrentotourism.com

ENIT

United Kingdom
Tel 020 7408 1254.
www.italiantouristboard.co.uk
United States
Tel 212 245 56 18.
www.italiantourism.com

EPT

Piazza dei Martiri 58. **Map** 6 F2.
Tel 081 410 72 19.
www.eptnapoli.info

TRAVELLERS WITH SPECIAL NEEDS

Stazione Centrale (Customer Services)
Tel 081 567 29 91.

Turismo Accessibile
www.turismoaccessibile.it

STUDENT TRAVELLERS

Associazione Italiana Alberghi per la Gioventù (AIG)
www.aighostels.com

Centro Turistico Studentesco (CTS)
Via Scarlatti 198. **Map** 1 C5.
Tel 081 558 65 97. **www**.cts.it

Ostello Mergellina
Salita della Grotta 23. **Map** 5 A3.
Tel 081 761 23 46/12 15.
www.ostellonapoli.com

RESPONSIBLE TOURISM

ICNOS Adventures
Via Mazzini 107, Vietri sul Mare.
Map 2 F3. **Tel** 089 21 24 89.
www.icnosadventures.com

Tenuta Vannulo
Via G Galilei 10, Capaccio Scalo, Salerno. **Tel** 0828 72 78 94.
www.vannulo.it

Fruit and vegetables on display at one of Naples' many open-air markets

Security and Public Services

While most areas outside Naples do not pose particular problems, petty crime is quite widespread in the city itself. However, by taking a few simple precautions, you will be able to protect yourself from pickpockets and purse-snatchers. Don't wear valuable jewellery or watches; handbags are easy targets, so hold on to them tightly, and carry your money in your pockets or in a money belt. If possible, keep cameras and video cameras hidden from sight. It's best to be wary in Naples, but don't let apprehension ruin your trip.

Officers of the *polizia*

POLICE AND SECURITY

In Naples there are several types of police force, each one serving a particular role. The state police, or *polizia*, wear blue uniforms and handle most crimes. The military-trained *carabinieri* wear black uniforms with red-striped trousers. They deal with offences ranging from organized crime to traffic violations, and they also conduct random security checks. The *vigili urbani* are the municipal traffic police, dealing with traffic and parking offences. Officers from any of these forces will be of assistance in an emergency.

WHAT TO BE AWARE OF

Do not carry large sums of money on you while walking around the city; leave it in your hotel safe. Make photocopies of vital documents like passports, or at least make a note of the number. Report any loss or theft to the police; lost or stolen credit cards and traveller's cheques should be immediately reported to the issuing bank. If you are travelling by car, always park in supervised car parks, and do not leave items visible inside the vehicle. In crowded public areas or on public transport, be on your guard against pickpockets; purse-snatchers on mopeds prefer to take jewels and handbags from strolling pedestrians. The train station is best avoided at night, and it is not advisable to walk around alone after dark.

IN AN EMERGENCY

For any police or medical emergency service, including ambulances, dial 113 *(Soccorso Pubblico di Emergenza)*. The *carabinieri* emergency number is 112. To call an ambulance, dial 118. For the *Vigili del Fuoco* (fire brigade), dial 115; and for roadside assistance *(Soccorso Stradale)*, dial 116.

MEDICAL MATTERS

EU nationals with a European Health Insurance Card (EHIC; www.ehic.org.uk) receive reduced or free medical care, although you may find you first have to pay for the medical attention and reclaim the money later. Not all treatments are covered by the card, so it is a good idea to arrange medical cover before travelling. Non-EU citizens should try to arrive in Italy with comprehensive medical insurance.

If you should need urgent medical assistance, call the **Pronto Soccorso** (casualty department) of the nearest hospital. All pharmacies have a list of branches open at night and on public holidays *(farmacia di turno)* posted on their door. The **Farmacia Alma Salus** is open all night every night from 8pm.

BANKS AND BUREAUX DE CHANGE

Opening hours for banks are usually 8:30am–1:20pm Monday to Friday; some are also open 2:45–3:45pm. Identification, such as a passport, is required for any transaction. Banks often offer the best exchange rates, but you can also exchange currency at post offices or private exchange offices. Larger hotels will also offer this service, often at a slightly higher rate.

CURRENCY

The Italian currency is the euro. Euro banknotes have seven denominations. The €5 note (grey in colour) is the smallest, followed by the €10 note (pink), €20 note (blue), €50 note (orange), €100 note (green), €200 note (yellow) and €500 note (purple). The euro has eight coin denominations: €1 and €2; 50 cents, 20 cents, 10 cents, 5 cents, 2 cents and 1 cent. The €2 and €1 coins are both silver and gold in colour. The 50-, 20- and 10-cent coins are gold. The 5-, 2- and 1-cent coins are bronze.

Euro notes

DEBIT AND CREDIT CARDS

Major credit cards such as **VISA**, **MasterCard**, **American Express** and **Diners Club** are accepted by most larger businesses and restaurants. However, since some smaller restaurants, shops and bars do not take credit cards, it is advisable to carry some cash with you. Credit and debit cards are the most convenient way to access euros, and you can use either at ATMs (*Bancomat*), which display the logos of the cards they accept. Note that you may be charged for using your debit or credit card at some ATMs; check with your bank for more information. To avoid the inconvenience of international transactions blocking your card, contact your bank before travelling, and alert them to your travel dates and destinations.

A public telephone on the street

PUBLIC TELEPHONES

The widespread use of mobile phones in Italy means that many of Naples' payphones have been neglected or vandalized. Most of them require a phonecard (*scheda*), which can be purchased from tobacconists, newsagents or bars. Some phone boxes also take credit cards, but be wary: some unscrupulous companies stick official-looking 0800 numbers on public phone boxes and charge high rates for international calls. To be on the safe side, use an international calling card, also available at tobacconists or newsagents.

International call shops all over the city offer competitive rates for international calls, while making calls from hotel telephones can be very expensive. For the international operator, and to have your calls charged to your home phone bill, dial 170.

The area code for Naples is 081. Note that in Italy you always need to dial the area code before the number, even when making a call within the same town or city.

MOBILE PHONES

Travelling with, or even acquiring, a mobile phone (*telefonino*) in Italy is easy. If your mobile is a GSM, dual- or tri-band phone, check if it can be unlocked. If so, consider purchasing an Italian SIM card (about €10), which gives you an Italian mobile number and access to a pre-paid service. Visit a **Vodafone**, **TIM** or **Wind** store and ask for a *SIM prepagato* (pre-paid SIM).

INTERNET

Many Internet cafés in Naples are located around the train station and on the side streets west of Via Toledo. Access costs from €2 to €5 per hour. Many hotels in the city and the surrounding areas include Internet access in their rates. Call ahead for details. Cafés and bars offering a Wi-Fi service to their customers are also on the increase. If you are travelling with your laptop and need frequent mobile Internet connection, you can purchase an Internet key (*chiavetta*) at mobile phone shops like Vodafone, TIM or Wind.

POST OFFICES

Post offices in Naples are open from 8:30am to 1:15pm Monday to Friday, 8:30am to noon Saturday and until noon on the last day of the month. The main office, **Posta Centrale**, is open from 8am to 6:30pm Monday to Friday (to 12:30pm on Saturdays). Post office branches are located all over the city, in the railway stations and at Capodichino airport. Stamps can be bought at tobacconists (*tabaccai*), as well as in the post office itself.

DIRECTORY

POLICE AND SECURITY

Ambulance
Tel 118.

Fire
Tel 115.

General Emergencies
Tel 113 or 112.

Police (Carabinieri)
Tel 112.

Police Headquarters
Via Medina 75. **Map** 7 B1.
Tel 081 794 11 11.

Traffic Police
Tel 081 595 41 11.

MEDICAL MATTERS

Farmacia Alma Salus
Piazza Dante 71. **Map** 9 B3.
Tel 081 549 93 36.

Pronto Soccorso Ospedale Cardarelli
Via Cardarelli 9.
Tel 081 545 33 33.

Ospedale dei Pellegrini
Via Portamedina 41. **Map** 9 A4.
Tel 081 254 21 11.

Ospedale San Paolo
Via Terracina 219.
Tel 081 254 82 11.

CREDIT CARDS AND TRAVELLER'S CHEQUES

MasterCard/VISA
Tel 800 819 014.

American Express
Tel 067 22 82 or 800 91 49 12.

Diners Club
Tel 800 86 40 64.

MOBILE PHONES

TIM
www.tim.it

Vodafone
www.vodafone.it

Wind
www.wind.it

POST OFFICES

Posta Centrale
Piazza Matteotti. **Map** 7 B1.
Tel 081 551 14 56.
www.poste.it

TRAVEL INFORMATION

aples' only airport is Capodichino, which is conveniently
close to the city and used for
domestic, European
and charter flights; the
nearest intercontinental
airport is located in
Rome, to the north. The
fastest means of reaching Naples
by land is by train, since there are
few long-distance coach connections
with European cities, and driving is
far from ideal because of traffic

Alitalia logo

problems and parking restrictions. The
city also has a large maritime passenger
terminal with ferry connections to the
various islands in
the Bay of Naples.
Moving within the city
and its surrounding
area is getting easier as
Naples is working to improve its metro
system and to create an efficient
transport network. Three underground
lines, buses and funiculars link all the
main sights in the city of Naples itself.

Check-in desk at Capodichino airport, Naples

ARRIVING BY AIR

Daily flights to Naples from
London, Paris, Frankfurt and
Munich are operated by the
Italian state airline **Alitalia**,
Air One and foreign carriers
such as **Air France** and **British
Airways**. Numerous budget
and charter airlines also offer
flights to Naples; these include
easyJet, which has direct
flights from London and Paris.
Gesac, the airport authority,
has a website with a useful
facility for finding flights into
Naples from foreign cities.

Naples' Capodichino airport
is fairly small, even though it
is the only international one
in the region. Travellers from
outside Europe will probably
transfer to a connecting flight
to Naples in Rome, although
Eurofly (operated by
Meridiana) offers direct
flights from New York
between June and September.

To get from the airport
to the city centre, take the
Alibus. Run by the **Azienda
Napoletana Mobilità (ANM)**, it
goes to Napoli Centrale train
station and Piazza Municipio
every 20 minutes (€3). From
Napoli Centrale, you can then

pick up the Circumvesuvian
railway *(see pp226–7)* to travel
to Pompeii and the coast.
Piazza Municipio is within
walking distance of Molo
Beverello *(see opposite)*,
where you can take ferries to
the islands. The ANM-3S also
runs to Piazza Garibaldi from
the airport. Additionally,
every 90 minutes a **CTP**
bus travels to Caserta.

If you want to travel by
taxi, make sure you go to
the airport's official rank and
that the meter is on. There
are set tariffs for journeys
such as the one from the
airport to the centre (€12.50–
€20); these should be clearly
displayed. The trip lasts
about 20 minutes.

ARRIVING BY TRAIN

Trains in Italy are run by
Trenitalia. There are three
main railway stations in
Naples: **Napoli Centrale**, in
Piazza Garibaldi; **Mergellina**;

on the seafront; and **Campi
Flegrei**, at Fuorigrotta. Napoli
Centrale is also the main
interchange for the city's
public transport systems.
Access to the underground
(metropolitana) and the
Circumvesuviana *(see pp226–7)*
is from inside the station,
while the square in front of
the station is the main
terminal for city and suburban
buses, as well as for buses
heading to southern Italy.

The high-speed Frecciarossa
service runs between Rome
(Roma Termini) and Naples
(Napoli Centrale), with a
travel time of just 1 hour
and 10 minutes. Other train
services running several times
each hour include the Euro-
star (ES) trains, the InterCity
(IC) trains and the regional
services, which are generally
very slow. Train connections
are extensive and frequent
throughout Italy. Salerno
is a convenient station for
reaching the Amalfi Coast.

The elegant Campi Flegrei railway station

Heavy traffic in Naples city centre

ARRIVING BY CAR

Should you decide to travel to Naples by car, be prepared for stressful driving conditions, heavy traffic congestion and parking difficulties. A car may be convenient for visiting other towns in the region, but in Naples itself it is wise to use the public transport system or walk.

The **Automobile Club d'Italia (ACI)** provides road maps and a towing and repair service to its members and members of affiliated foreign associations. Tolls are charged on the *autostrada* (motorway) and can be paid in cash or with a magnetic Viacard, which can be purchased from tobacconists *(tabaccai)* or at an ACI agency. Emergency telephones can be found at regular intervals along the motorway.

The A1 motorway exits into the highway that runs through Naples *(Tangenziale–A56)*, which then takes you quickly to the centre of the city and out to the Phlegraean Fields, including Pozzuoli and Cumae. For the coastal resorts, follow signs for the A3 *autostrada*, signposted Salerno; then take the SS145 into Sorrento. The SS163 runs the length of the Amalfi coastline.

ARRIVING BY BOAT

The main maritime passenger terminal used by cruise ships that come into Naples while touring the Mediterranean is the Molo Angioino, located opposite Piazza Municipio.

Ferries and hydrofoils for connections to the various islands in the Bay of Naples and the Sorrento Peninsula depart from the adjacent Molo Beverello *(see also pp226–7)*.

The **Tirrenia** ship line provides direct connections between Naples and several ports in Sardinia and Sicily. **Siremar** operates the route from Naples to the Aeolian Islands, off the northeast coast of Sicily. **SNAV** and **AliLauro** run high-speed hydrofoil services to and from the Aeolian Islands, Ponza and Ventotene. Be aware that some of these routes operate only in the summer months.

Passenger ferry at the Naples seaport

DIRECTORY

ARRIVING BY AIR	CTP	Mergellina	ARRIVING BY BOAT

ARRIVING BY AIR

Air France
www.airfrance.com

Air One
Tel 199 20 70 80.

Alitalia
Tel 06 22 22.
www.alitalia.com

Azienda Napoletana Mobilità (ANM)
Tel 800 639 525 or 081 763 11 11. www.anm.it

British Airways
Tel 0844 493 07 87 (UK).
www.britishairways.com

CTP
www.ctpn.it

easyJet
www.easyjet.com

Gesac
Tel 081 789 61 11.
www.gesac.it

Meridiana
Tel 89 29 28.
www.meridiana.it

ARRIVING BY TRAIN

Campi Flegrei
Piazzale Vincenzo Tecchio 1.

Mergellina
Corso Vittorio Emanuele 4. **Map** 5 B2.

Napoli Centrale
Piazza Garibaldi 69.
Map 4 F4.

Trenitalia
Tel 89 20 21.
www.trenitalia.com

ARRIVING BY CAR

Automobile Club d'Italia (ACI)
Piazzale Vincenzo Tecchio 49d. *Tel* 80 31 16 (emergencies). www.aci.it

ARRIVING BY BOAT

AliLauro
Tel 081 497 22 38.
www.alilauro.it

Medmar
Tel 081 333 44 11.
www.medmargroup.it

Siremar
Tel 89 21 23.

SNAV
Tel 081 428 55 55.
www.snav.it

Tirrenia
Tel 02 26 30 28 03 or 89 21 23. www.tirrenia.it

Getting Around Naples

A scooter can beat the traffic

Naples' transport system is slowly improving, but the main thoroughfares in this densely populated city are often blocked with traffic. Driving is not recommended, while travelling by bus or tram can be a slow affair at busy times, and taxis can be expensive when traffic is heavy. It will often be faster to travel around the centre on foot. The funicular railways offer a convenient link to the Vomero district. The main central squares have display panels that indicate the main bus, tram and metro stops.

GREEN TRAVEL

The main focus in Naples is on improving and expanding the public transport network. While this goes on, green initiatives are not a priority. Using the public transport system not only makes sense in Naples but is also the only way to travel in an environmentally friendly way.

The city centre and many of the key sights are easily accessible on foot or by public transport, so there is no need to rent a car. Although bus and tram services in Naples can be slow due to traffic, they are far-reaching.

Many popular destinations outside Naples – including Pompeii and Herculaneum,

Mount Vesuvius, the Amalfi Coast, the Sorrento Peninsula and the islands in the Bay of Naples – can be easily reached by train, bus or ferry.

CITY RAILWAYS

Naples' rail system is confusing because many non-connecting lines run through the city. Construction of a comprehensive metro (Metropoliana) system has been under way for several years, but lack of funds and archaeological finds keep stalling the project.

There are three main metro lines. **MetroNapoli** runs Linea 1, or the hill metro (Collinare), which goes from Piazza Dante through the main areas of Naples, Vomero

and beyond, to the Chiaiano and Secondigliano quarters. It runs from 6:30am to 11:45pm, with departures every 7–15 minutes. MetroNapoli also runs the short Linea 6, which links the Fuorigrotta area with Mergellina.

Trenitalia (see p223) runs Linea 2, which goes from Gianturco to Pozzuoli, with stops at Piazza Garibaldi, Piazza Cavour (where it intersects with Linea 1), Montesanto, Piazza Amedeo, Mergellina, Piazza Leopardi, Campi Flegrei, Cavalleggeri, and Bagnoli. It runs from 5:30am to 11pm, with departures every 10–20 minutes.

There are also two aboveground railway lines, the Circumflegrea and the Cumana, that go through the city and into the Phlegraean Fields (see p226).

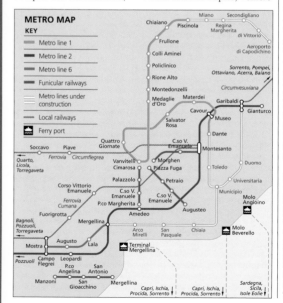

Modern funicular at a station

FUNICULAR RAILWAYS

There are four funicular routes in Naples, all run by MetroNapoli. Funicolare Centrale, Funicolare di Montesanto and Funicolare di Chiaia connect the city centre with the Vomero district. The fourth funicular, Mergellina, links the seafront area (Via Mergellina) with Via Manzoni. The funiculars are reliable and fast, and they run every 10 minutes from 6:30am until 10pm. The Centrale line from Piazza Fuga, operates until 12:30am at weekends.

BUSES AND TRAMS

In Naples, bus and tram journeys take time because of the heavy traffic; in addition, these means of transport are often crowded. Be aware of pickpockets, and keep your valuables tucked away. The bus and tram networks are run by the ANM. The red bus lines R1, R2, R3

METRO MAP

KEY

▬▬	Metro line 1
▬▬	Metro line 2
▬▬	Metro line 6
▬▬	Funicular railways
▬▬	Metro lines under construction
▬▬	Local railways
⚓	Ferry port

and R4 pass by key sights in the city centre; they run every 7–16 minutes from 5:30am to 11:30pm. The electric buses E1 and E3 serve the old town and the Quartieri Spagnoli.

TICKETS AND FARES

Naples' transport network runs under the Uniconapoli system (www.unicocampania. it), whereby one ticket is valid for all local buses, trams, funiculars, the *metropolitana* and the Cumana and Circum-flegrea train lines. Available from stations, newsagents and tobacconists, a single Unico-napoli ticket (€1.10) is valid for 90 minutes. An all-day ticket is €3.10, a weekend ticket €2.60 and a monthly pass €36.70. Validate your ticket before departure by stamping it in a machine. If you change to a different form of transport within your 90-minute journey, you must revalidate it.

The Unico 3T (also at www.unicocampania.it) and Campania Artecard (*see p219*) are popular tourist passes.

WALKING

Pedestrianized areas allow visitors to enjoy Naples in relative peace and quiet. For traffic-free shopping, head to Via Chiaia, Via Toledo and Via Scarlatti, in the Vomero area. On Sundays, part of Via Partenope is also closed to traffic, enabling you to admire Vesuvius and Castel dell'Ovo. However, be very careful crossing the road elsewhere: drivers often ignore traffic lights and zebra crossings, and fast-moving scooters appear from nowhere.

Walking down an alley in Naples' historic centre

GUIDED TOURS

Citysightseeing Napoli runs a hop-on, hop-off service with three routes: two covering the main city sights, and one along the Bay to Posillipo. The main stop is outside Castel Nuovo.

Visits to underground Naples are organized by **LAES La Napoli Sotterranea** (Thu, Sat, Sun and hols) and **Napoli Sotterranea** (daily). For a good introduction to Naples, hire a local tour guide via the tourist information offices (*see p219*) or by inquiring at your hotel reception desk.

TAXIS

If you take a taxi, make sure it is from an official rank. The meter should read €3 at the start of the ride. The minimum fare is €4.50 (double for out-of-town trips), and rides from the airport to the centre cost €12.50–20. There is an extra charge of €2 at weekends and public holidays; €2.50 from 10pm to 7am; and €0.50 for each item of luggage.

You can find taxis in the official ranks at the train and metro stations, and in the main squares. If you phone for a taxi, the fare starts when it responds to your call.

DRIVING AND PARKING

Traffic in Naples is a challenge even for experienced drivers, and parking is a problem. Designated parking areas are marked with blue lines and cost €0.70–1.50 per hour, with a maximum stay of 1 or 2 hours. For cheaper parking, head to **Parcheggio Brin**, a multilevel parking garage that is connected to the city centre by bus lines. Avoid areas with yellow lines; they are reserved for residents.

SCOOTER AND MOPED HIRE

Mopeds and scooters can be hired at some car-hire agencies (*see p227*) or at **Rent Sprint**, which specializes in scooters. **Penisola Rent** is a convenient starting point for exploring the Sorrento Peninsula and Amalfi Coast by scooter.

DIRECTORY

GREEN TRAVEL

Azienda Napoletana Mobilità (ANM)
Tel 800 639 525 or 081 763 11 11. www.anm.it

CITY RAILWAYS

MetroNapoli
www.metro.na.it

GUIDED TOURS

Citysightseeing Napoli
Tel 081 551 72 79.
www.napoli.city-sightseeing.it

LAES La Napoli Sotterranea
Tel 081 40 02 56.
www.lanapolisotterranea.it

Napoli Sotterranea
Tel 081 29 69 44.
www.napolisotterranea.org

TAXIS

Cotana
Tel 081 570 70 70.

Napoli
Tel 081 556 44 44.

Partenope
Tel 081 556 02 02.

DRIVING AND PARKING

Colli Aminei
Via Pietravalle (corner of Via Colle Aminei). Tel 081 763 22 52.

Grilli
Via G Ferraris 40. Map 4 F5.
Tel 081 26 43 44.

Mergellina
Via Mergellina 112. Map 5 B4.

Parcheggio Brin
Via B Brin. Tel 081 763 28 55.

Supergarage
Via Shelley 11. Map 7 A2.

Turistico
Via A De Gasperi 14. Map 7 B2.
Tel 081 552 54 42

SCOOTER AND MOPED HIRE

Penisola Rent
Corso Italia 259, Sorrento.
Tel 339 293 05 67.
www.penisolarent.com

Rent Sprint
Via Santa Lucia 36. Map 7 A4.
Tel 081 764 13 33.
www.rentsprint.it

Travelling Outside Naples

SEPSA coaches logo

Even if you are based in Naples, it is not difficult to reach ancient sites such as the Phlegraean Fields, Pompeii and Herculaneum, the towns on the Amalfi Coast (Amalfi, Positano and Ravello) and the enchanting islands of Capri, Ischia and Procida. Most places are easily accessible by local train, bus or ferry, and excursions are organized by bigger hotels and local travel agents.

A Circumvesuviana train from Naples to Sorrento

LOCAL TRAINS

The **Circumvesuviana** commuter train service connects Naples with various towns around Mount Vesuvius (including ancient Pompeii and Herculaneum) and those on the Sorrento Peninsula. The main terminus is in Corso Garibaldi, with the next stop in Piazza Garibaldi (underground).

The Circumvesuviana has five routes: San Giorgio–Napoli–Via Centro Direzionale; Napoli–Sorrento; Napoli–Pompei–Poggiomarino; Napoli–Ottaviano–Sarno; and Napoli–Nola–Baiano. There are three types of train: the *accelerato* (ACC), which stops at all stations en route; the *diretto* (DIR), stopping only at the main ones; and the *direttissimo* (DD), stopping at even fewer stations. Services run from 5am to 10pm (to midnight in summer for the Napoli–Sorrento line), with trains departing roughly every 20 minutes. You may want to avoid travelling late at night, because trains are infrequent and there are fewer people around. At all times, be sure to stay alert for pickpockets.

From April to October, there is also a service, run by the Funivia di Monte Faito cableway, starting from Castellammare di Stabia on the Circumvesuviana line. This takes you up to the top of Monte Faito, which is one of the most scenic viewpoints overlooking the Bay of Naples (*see p152*), Mount Vesuvius and the islands of Capri, Ischia and Procida.

To reach the various towns on the Phlegraean Fields and the coast, take the **Ferrovia Cumana**, while the **Ferrovia Circumflegrea** serves the region's interior. The main station for both Cumana and Circumflegrea is located in Piazza Montesanto (near Piazza Dante and Via Toledo), and the service is fast and efficient. The Cumana service runs from 5:21am to 10:30pm, with departures every 10 minutes for Bagnoli and every 20 minutes for Pozzuoli.

The main stops on the Circumflegrea line are Montesanto, Soccavo, Quarto, Licola and Torregaveta. Departures are every 20 minutes (5:52am–9:43pm). Several trains per day stop at Cumae and Lido Fusaro. Another useful train is the one departing every half-hour from Napoli Centrale to Caserta (*see pp164–7*).

JETS AND FERRIES

Various shipping lines offer frequent high-speed jet crossings from Naples to the islands in the bay. The Sorrento Peninsula and the towns of Positano and Amalfi can also be reached by boat. In Naples, most companies operate from Molo Beverello (*see p223*). From the port of Pozzuoli, the crossing to Procida and Ischia is shorter and cheaper; you can also take your car on board, but check on available space beforehand. The **Caremar** line operates a ferry to Procida, Ischia and Capri that departs from the Molo Beverello, and to Procida and Ischia from Pozzuoli. **Medmar** is the only company that still runs ferries. They offer a service to the island of Ischia from Molo Beverello, which is also the departure point for the **SNAV** high-speed jet service to Procida, Ischia and Capri, and for **AliLauro**'s ferry services to Ischia, Sorrento and Capri. Jets run by **Navigazione Libera del Golfo** depart from Molo Beverello for Capri, Sorrento and the Amalfi Coast. For daily departures, check the local newspaper *Il Mattino* or visit the local tourist office.

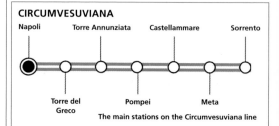

CIRCUMVESUVIANA

Napoli	Torre Annunziata	Castellammare	Sorrento

Torre del Greco   Pompei   Meta

The main stations on the Circumvesuviana line

One of Sita's distinctive blue coaches

TRAVELLING BY COACH

You can also reach towns and resorts in the region by coach. Local companies depart from the coach terminus in Piazza Garibaldi or from Capodichino airport.

The bus company **CTP** serves the town of Caserta, with departures every 20 minutes on weekdays and every 40 minutes on Sundays and public holidays. **SEPSA** covers the towns in the Phlegraean Fields area (Baia and Bacoli), while the blue **Sita** coaches travel to various towns and resorts on the Sorrento Peninsula, the tourist sites on the Amalfi Coast (Amalfi, Maiori, Minori, Positano, Ravello and others) and Salerno. The main Sita terminus is located in the central Via Pisanelli, near Piazza Municipio. There are two departures daily.

CAR HIRE

Hiring a car in Italy is quite expensive. In addition, driving in Naples is a highly stressful experience and not recommended. However, if you are determined to drive, it is wise to make reservations prior to your arrival.

While public transport is the best option in Naples, reaching the Amalfi Coast by train or coach can be inconvenient and tiresome, especially after a long flight or train journey. Driving the Amalfi Coast road is a thrill and a challenge, but it is wise to contact your hotel in advance to make sure parking is available.

Be aware that you must be over the age of 21 to rent a car. You will also be asked to supply a credit card number as a deposit.

RULES OF THE ROAD

Driving in Naples requires strong nerves. Always stay alert, especially for scooters, which will zip past you at breakneck speed. Drive on the right, and give way to traffic from the right. Seat belts are compulsory for all passengers. Motorcyclists must wear helmets. Heavy fines are levied for using a mobile phone while driving. Headlights must be turned on even during the day on motorways and outside built-up areas. The speed limit in urban areas is 50 km/h (30 mph); outside urban areas it is 110 km/h (70 mph) on dual carriageways and 90 km/h (56 mph) on other secondary roads. On motorways the limit is 130 km/h (80 mph) for vehicles over 1100cc, 110 km/h (70 mph) for those under 1100cc.

The dramatic Vallone di Furore bridge, on the Amalfi Coast

DIRECTORY

LOCAL TRAINS

Circumvesuviana
Corso Garibaldi 387. **Map** 4 E4.
Tel 800 053 939.
www.vesuviana.it

**Ferrovia Circumflegrea/
Ferrovia Cumana**
Piazza Montesanto. **Map** 3 A5.
Tel 800 181 313. www.sepsa.it

JETS AND FERRIES

AliLauro
Molo Beverello. **Map** 7 B3.
Tel 081 497 22 38.
www.alilauro.it

Caremar
Molo Beverello and Pozzuoli.
Map 7 B3. *Tel* 89 21 23.
www.caremar.it

Medmar
Tel 081 333 44 11.
www.medmargroup.it

**Navigazione Libera
del Golfo**
Tel 081 552 07 63.
www.navlib.it

SNAV
Tel 081 428 55 55.
www.snav.it

TRAVELLING BY COACH

CTP
Via Sannio 19.
Tel 800 482 644. www.ctpn.it

SEPSA
Via Cisterna dell'Olio 44.
Map 3 B5 & 9 B4. *Tel* 081 735
41 11. www.sepsa.it

Sita
Via Pisanelli 3–7. **Map** 3 B4 &
9 C2. *Tel* 089 386 67 11.
www.sitabus.it

CAR HIRE

AVIS
Via Partenope 13. **Map** 6 F3.
Tel 081 240 03 07.
Capodichino Airport.
Tel 081 780 57 90.

Hertz
Via G Riccardi 5 (Napoli Centrale
station). *Tel* 081 20 62 28.
Capodichino Airport.
Tel 081 780 29 71.

NAPLES STREET FINDER

The page grid superimposed on the *Area by Area* map below shows which parts of Naples are covered by this Street Finder. The map references given for the restaurants, hotels and sights in Naples refer to the maps in this section. Central Naples has been enlarged on map pages 9 and 10 to make it easier to read. Sights in this area will give both map references. A complete index of the street names and major sights in the city follows on pages 230–33. The key on the opposite page shows the scales of the maps and explains the symbols. All the main sights in the city are clearly indicated in pink so they are easy to find.

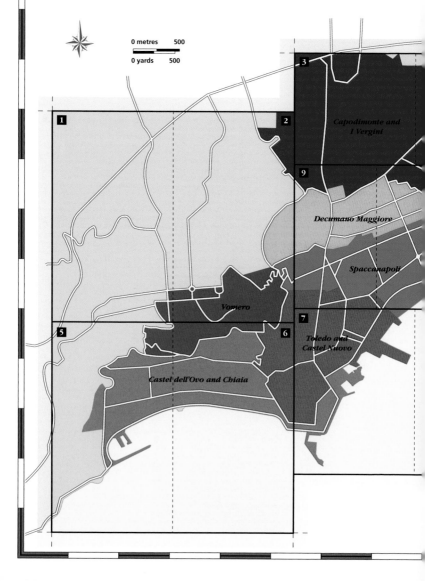

0 metres 500

0 yards 500

1

2

3 Capodimonte and I Vergini

9 Decumano Maggiore

Spaccanapoli

Vomero

5

6 Toledo and Castel Nuovo

7

Castel dell'Ovo and Chiaia

HOW TO USE THE MAPS

The first number corresponds to the Street Finder map.

Gesù Nuovo ❸

Piazza del Gesù Nuovo. **Map** 3 B5 (9 B4). **Tel** 081 551 86 13. ◯ 7am–12:30pm, 4–7:30pm daily.

The letters and numbers form the map coordinates. Letters are along the top, numbers are along the sides.

The map continues on page 7 of the Street Finder.

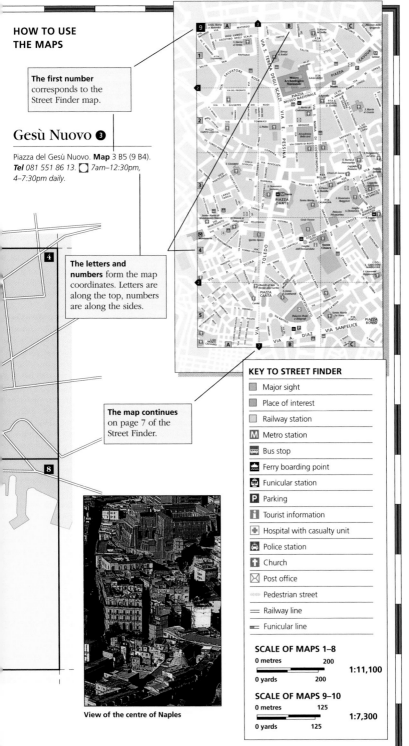

View of the centre of Naples

KEY TO STREET FINDER

🟧	Major sight
🟩	Place of interest
⬜	Railway station
Ⓜ	Metro station
🚌	Bus stop
⛴	Ferry boarding point
🚠	Funicular station
🅿	Parking
🛈	Tourist information
✚	Hospital with casualty unit
🚓	Police station
✝	Church
⊠	Post office
⋯	Pedestrian street
═	Railway line
▬	Funicular line

SCALE OF MAPS 1–8

0 metres   200
0 yards   200   **1:11,100**

SCALE OF MAPS 9–10

0 metres   125
0 yards   125   **1:7,300**

Street Finder Index

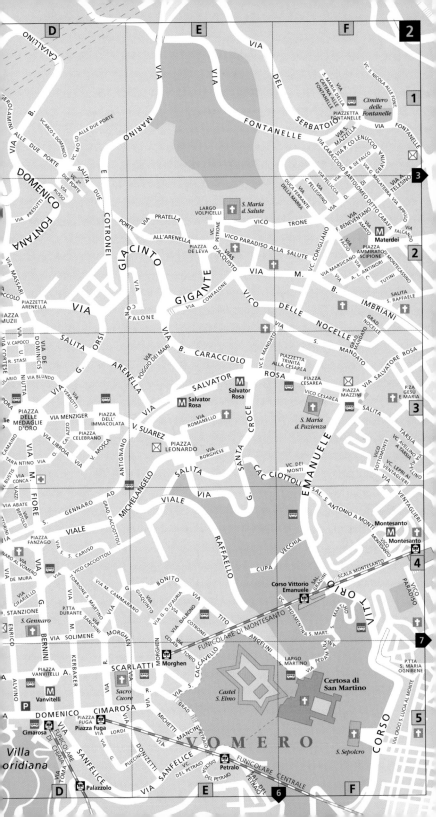

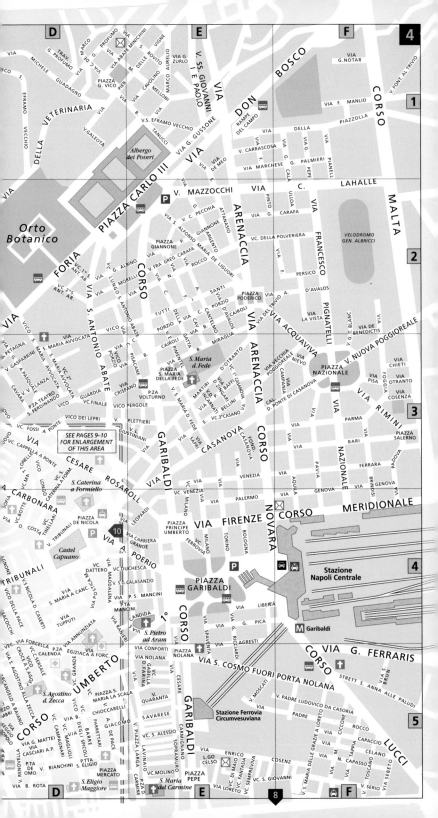

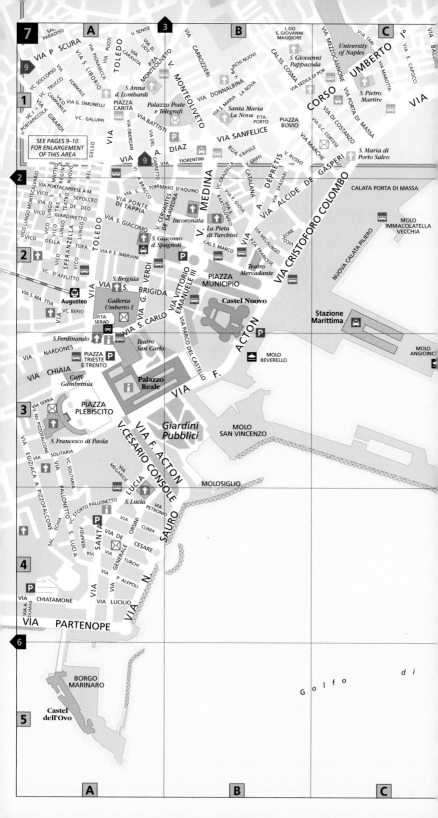

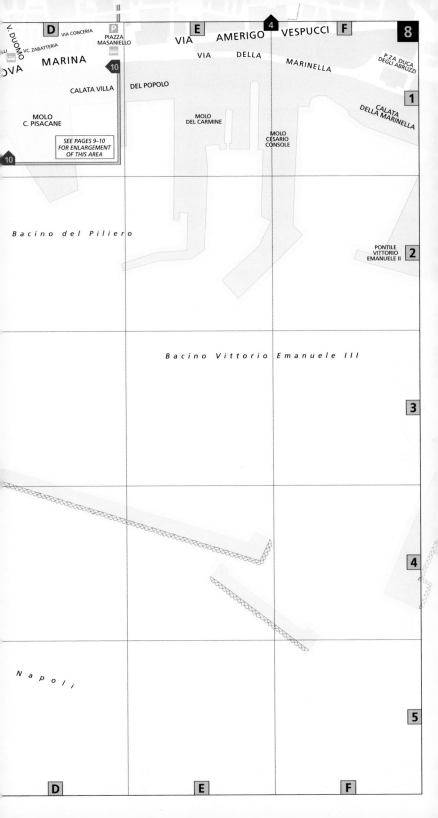

D | VIA CONCERIA | **P** PIAZZA MASANIELLO | **E** | VIA AMERIGO | **4** | VESPUCCI | **F** | **8**

V. DUOMO | VC. ZABATTERIA

LLI

OVA | **MARINA** | **10**

VIA | DELLA | MARINELLA

P.ZA DUCA DEGLI ABRUZZI

CALATA VILLA | DEL POPOLO

MOLO C. PISACANE

MOLO DEL CARMINE

CALATA DELLA MARINELLA | **1**

MOLO CESARIO CONSOLE

SEE PAGES 9–10 FOR ENLARGEMENT OF THIS AREA

10

Bacino del Piliero

PONTILE VITTORIO EMANUELE II | **2**

Bacino Vittorio Emanuele III

3

4

Napoli

5

D | **E** | **F**

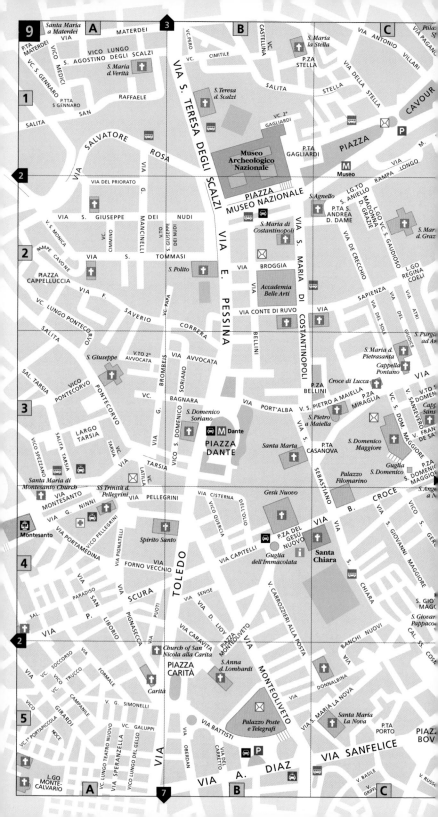

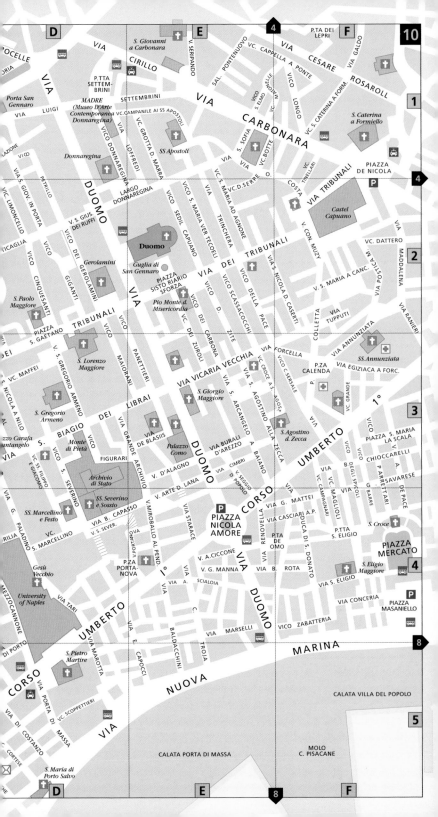

General Index

Acknowledgments

Dorling Kindersley would like to thank the following people whose contributions and assistance have made the preparation of this book possible: Guido Bevilacqua, Luigi Consiglio, Diana Georgiacodis, Costantino Pantano, Adriana Sandrini Maione. Dorling Kindersley would also like to thank all the museums and tourist information offices, too numerous to mention individually, for their assistance and kind permission to photograph at their establishments.

Editorial and Design Assistance
Gillian Allen, Riccardo Baldini, Marta Bescos, Julie Bond, Cooling Brown, Michelle Crane, Felicity Crowe, Vivien Crump, Emer FitzGerald, Anna Freiberger, Annette Jacobs, Felicity Laughton, Jude Ledger, Georgina Matthews, Ferdie McDonald, Jane Oliver-Jedrzejak, Giorgio Padovani, Catherine Palmi, Katie Parla, Ellen Root, Sands Publishing Solutions, Sargasso, Meredith Smith, Julie Thompson, Ingrid Vienings, Dora Whitaker.

Additional Contributors
Sima Belmar, Judy Edelhoff, Julius Honnor, Leonie Loudon, Barbara Zaragoza.

Additional Photography
Demetrio Carrasco, Ian O'Leary, Barbara Zaragoza.

Picture Credits

Key: t = top; tl = top left; tlc = top left centre; tc = top centre; trc = top right centre; tr = top right; cla = centre left above; ca = centre above; cra = centre right above; cl = centre left; c = centre; cr = centre right; clb = centre left below; crb = centre right below; cb = centre below; bl = bottom left; br = bottom right; b = bottom; bc = bottom centre; bcl = bottom centre left; bcr = bottom centre right.

Every effort has been made to trace the copyright holders. The publisher apologizes for any unintentional omissions and would be pleased, in such cases, to add an acknowledgment in future editions. All the photographs reproduced in this book are from the Overseas S.r.l. Milano picture library except for the following:

4CORNERS IMAGES: SIME/Mastrorillo Massimo 206t; Giovanni Simeone 130–131. ADNKRONOS COMUNICAZIONE: 212tl. ALAMY IMAGES: AA World Travel Library 190cl; CuboImages srl 210br; CuboImages srl/Alfio Giannotti 224cr; culliganphoto 85t, 123tl; Danita Delimont 154tl; Adam Eastland 154bl; Peter Forsberg 219bl; Christopher Griffin 227tl; Peter Horree 2–3, 216–217, 221cl; Ilianski 210tc; Lonely Planet Images/Dallas Stribley 220cla; Pangea Images 155tl; Sergio Pitamitz 174–175; Rolf Richardson 153tr; Vittorio Sciosia 211br. ALITALIA: 222tc. ASSOCIAZIONE CULTURALE ARCHIVIO PARISIO, NAPLES: 24br, 26c, 26bl, 27tl, 28bc, 42tr, 55cl, 85cl, 129c, 131c, 135cra, 143cr. CIRCUMVESUVIANA srl: 226cla; CORBIS: Jonathan Blair 27bl, 191tl; Owen Franken 191c; Mimmo Jodice 46. IL DAGHERROTIPO: Roberto Della Noce 10cl, 28–29, 120clb, 122bl, 123br, 123c, 124, 153bl, 154cr. GETTY IMAGES: AFP/Stringer 222cla; Richard Ellis 218cl; Picavet 225bl. GIUSEPPE AVALLONE, NAPLES: 1, 21cr, 23cr, 29cr, 31bl, 33tl, 35tl, 38cl, 38br, 41tl, 41br, 55cr, 60, 63tl, 65tc, 76tr, 77bc, 89bl, 92br, 102, 124, 128, 134bc, 134cl, 135br, 140cl, 144cl, 157tr, 157b, 158tl, 160tr, 161tr, 161bl, 169tl, 171b, 172b, 205cl, 206c, 210cl. GRAND HOTEL PARKER'S: 177tl. GRAND HOTEL PUNTA MOLINO: 215tl. GRAZIA NERI: Stefano Cellai 11bc; Toty Ruggeri 211tl; M. Sestini fotogiornalismo/M. Tramonte 29br; Francesco Vignali 153cr. FORNASA S.A.S., PORTICI (NAPOLI): 206tl. HOTEL IL NIDO: 177c. IMAGE BANK, MILAN: 2–3, 12–13, 30–31, 32tr, 32cl, 38tr, 38tl, 39cl, 40cr, 42br, 44–45, 105cl, 107tl, 112, 115c, 117b, 130–131, 135tl, 136bc, 136cl, 137ca, 143bl, 146tr, 149tl, 156tr, 156br, 158tr, 159tr, 159cl, 162cl, 165cl, 165tr, 166tl, 168tl, 169bl, 169br, 170cl, 170bl, 171tl, 171cr. LONELY PLANET IMAGES: Stephen Saks 227bc. MIMMO JODICE, NAPLES: 40tc, 68bc, 80tr, 96bc. MARKA, MILAN: Danilo Donadoni 122tr; D. Donati 62bc; Nunzio Mari 11tr; L. Sechi 223cr. NAPOLI FILM FESTIVAL: 211cr. NEWIMAGE s.r.l: Sandro Battaglia 214ca; Ronaldo Fabrini 214br. LUCIANO PEDICINI, NAPLES: 21tc, 68c, 69tl, 71c, 81c, 84c, 84bl, 151br, 162tr, 163cl, 163tr, 163tc, 166bl, 167cr. PHOTOLIBRARY: Tommaso Di Girolamo 218cr. REUTERS: Str Old 83crb. SCALA GROUP S.P.A: 72tl, 86bc. SUPERSTOCK: Hemis.fr 223tl.

Jacket

Front – AWL IMAGES: Demetrio Carrasco. Back – ALAMY IMAGES: David Askham bl; Cairney Down cla; F1online digitale Bildagentur GmbH/Bowman tl; David Sutherland clb. Spine – AWL IMAGES: Demetrio Carrasco t. Front Endpapers – CORBIS: Mimmo Jodice.

Phrase Book

In Emergency

Help!	Aiuto!	eye-yoo-toh
Stop!	Fermo!	fair-moh
Call a	Chiama un	kee-ah-mah oon
doctor.	medico.	meh-dee-koh
Call an	Chiama un'	kee-ah-mah oon
ambulance.	ambulanza.	am-boo-lan-tsa
Call the	Chiama la	kee-ah-mah lah
police.	polizia.	pol-ee-tsee-ah
Call the fire	Chiama i	kee-ah-mah ee
brigade.	pompieri.	pom-pee-air-ee
Where is the	Dov'è il telefono?	dov-eh eel teh-leh-
telephone?		foh-noh?
The nearest	L'ospedale	loss-peh-dah-leh pee-
hospital?	più vicino?	oo vee-chee-noh?

Communication Essentials

Yes/No	Sì/No	see/noh
Please	Per favore	pair fah-vor-eh
Thank you	Grazie	grah-tsee-eh
Excuse me	Mi scusi	mee skoo-zee
Hello	Buon giorno	bwon jor-noh
Goodbye	Arrivederci	ah-ree-veh-dair-chee
Good evening	Buona sera	bwon-ah sair-ah
morning	la mattina	lah mah-tee-nah
afternoon	il pomeriggio	eel pom-eh-ree-joh
evening	la sera	lah sair-ah
yesterday	ieri	ee-air-ee
today	oggi	oh-jee
tomorrow	domani	doh-mah-nee
here	qui	kwee
there	là, lì	lah, lee
What?	Che?	keh?
When?	Quando?	kwan-doh?
Why?	Perchè?	pair-keh?
Where?	Dove?	doh-veh?

Useful Phrases

How are you?	Come sta?	koh-meh stah?
Very well,	Molto bene,	moll-toh beh-neh
thank you.	grazie.	grah-tsee-eh
Pleased to	Piacere di	pee-ah-chair-eh dee
meet you.	conoscerla.	coh-noh-shair-lah
See you later.	A più tardi.	ah pee-oo tar-dee
That's fine.	Va bene.	va beh-neh
Where is/are ...?	Dov'è/Dove sono...?	dov-eh/doveh soh-noh?
How long does	Quanto tempo ci	kwan-toh tem-poh
it take to get to ...?	vuole per	chee voo-oh-leh pair
	andare a ...?	an-dar-eh ah ...?
How do I	Come faccio per	koh-meh fah-choh
get to ...?	arrivare a ...?	pair arri-var-eh ah...?
Do you speak	Parla inglese?	par-lah een-gleh-zeh?
English?		
I don't	Non capisco.	non ka-pee-skoh
understand.		
Could you speak	Può parlare	pwoh par-lah-reh
more slowly,	più lentamente,	pee-oo len-ta-men-teh
please?	per favore?	pair fah-vor-eh?
I'm sorry.	Mi dispiace.	mee dee-spee-ah-cheh

Useful Words

big	grande	gran-deh
small	piccolo	pee-koh-loh
hot	caldo	kal-doh
cold	freddo	fred-doh
good	buono	bwoh-noh
bad	cattivo	kat-tee-voh
enough	basta	bas-tah
well	bene	beh-neh
open	aperto	ah-pair-toh
closed	chiuso	kee-oo-zoh
left	a sinistra	ah see-nee-strah
right	a destra	ah dess-trah
straight on	sempre dritto	sem-preh dree-toh
near	vicino	vee-chee-noh
far	lontano	lon-tah-noh
up	su	soo
down	giù	joo
early	presto	press-toh
late	tardi	tar-dee
entrance	entrata	en-trah-tah
exit	uscita	oo-shee-ta
toilet	il gabinetto	eel gab-bee-net-toh
free, unoccupied	libero	lee-bair-oh
free, no charge	gratuito	grah-too-ee-toh

Making a Telephone Call

I'd like to place a	Vorrei fare	vor-ray far-eh oona
long-distance call.	una interurbana.	in-tair-oor-bah-nah
I'd like to make	Vorrei fare una	vor-ray far-eh oona
a reverse-charge	telefonata a carico	teh-leh-fon-ah-tah ah
call.	del destinatario.	kar-ee-koh dell dess-
		tee-nah-tar-ree-oh
Could I speak to...	Potrei parlare con...	po-tray par-lah-reh con
I'll try again later.	Ritelefono più	ree-teh-leh-foh-noh
	tardi.	pee-oo tar-dee
Can I leave a	Posso lasciare	poss-oh lash-ah-reh
message?	un messaggio?	oon mess-sah-joh?
Hold on.	Un attimo,	oon ah-tee-moh,
	per favore.	pair fah-vor-eh
Could you speak	Può parlare più	pwoh par-lah-reh
up a little please?	forte?	pee-oo for-teh?
local call	telefonata locale	te-leh-fon-ah-tah
		loh-cah-leh

Shopping

How much	Quant'è,	kwan-teh
does this cost?	per favore?	pair fah-vor-eh?
I would like ...	Vorrei ...	vor-ray...
Do you have ...?	Avete ...?	ah-veh-teh... ?
I'm just looking.	Sto soltanto	stoh sol-tan-toh
	guardando.	gwar-dan-doh
Do you take	Accettate le	ah-chet-tah-teh leh kar-teh
credit cards?	carte di credito?	dee creh-dee-toh?
What time do	A che ora apre/	ah keh or-ah
you open/close?	chiude?	ah-preh/kee-oo-deh?
this one	questo	kweh-stoh
that one	quello	kwell-oh
expensive	caro	kar-oh
cheap	a buon prezzo	ah bwon pret-soh
size, clothes	la taglia	lah tah-lee-ah
size, shoes	il numero	eel noo-mair-oh
white	bianco	bee-ang-koh
black	nero	neh-roh
red	rosso	ross-oh
yellow	giallo	jal-loh
green	verde	vair-deh
blue	azzurro	ah-tsee-roh

Types of Shop

antique dealer	l'antiquario	lan-tee-kwah-ree-oh
bakery	il forno/	eel forn-oh/
	il panificio	eel pan-ee-fee-choh
bank	la banca	lah bang-kah
bookshop	la libreria	lah lee-breh-ree-ah
butcher	la macelleria	lah mah-chell-eh-ree-ah
cake shop	la pasticceria	lah pas-tee-chair-ee-ah
chemist	la farmacia	lah far-mah-chee-ah
delicatessen	la salumeria	lah sah-loo-meh-ree-ah
department store	il grande	eel gran-deh
	magazzino	mag-gad-zee-noh
fishmonger	il pescivendolo	eel pesh-ee-ven-doh-loh
florist	il fioraio	eel fee-or-eye-oh
greengrocer	il fruttivendolo	eel froo-tee-ven-doh-loh
grocery	l'alimentari	lah-lee-men-tah-ree
hairdresser	il parrucchiere	eel par-oo-kee-air-eh
ice cream parlour	la gelateria	lah jel-lah-tair-ree-ah
market	il mercato	eel mair-kah-toh
newsstand	l'edicola	leh-dee-koh-lah
post office	l'ufficio postale	loo-fee-choh pos-tah-leh
shoe shop	il negozio di	eel neh-goh-tsioh dee
	scarpe	skar-peh
supermarket	il supermercato	eel su-pair-mair-kah-toh
tobacconist	il tabaccaio	eel tah-bak-eye-oh
travel agency	l'agenzia di viaggi	lah-jen-tsee-ah dee
		vee-ad-jee

Sightseeing

art gallery	la pinacoteca	lah peena-koh-teh-kah
bus stop	la fermata	lah fair-mah-tah
	dell'autobus	dell ow-toh-booss
church	la chiesa/	lah kee-eh-zah/
	la basilica	lah bah-seel-i-kah
closed for	chiuso per le	kee-oo-zoh pair leh
holidays	ferie	fair-ee-eh
garden	il giardino	eel jar-dee-no
library	la biblioteca	lah beeb-lee-oh-teh-kah
museum	il museo	eel moo-zeh-oh
railway station	la stazione	lah stah-tsee-oh-neh
tourist	l'ufficio	loo-fee-choh
information	turistico	too-ree-stee-koh

Staying in a Hotel

Do you have any vacant rooms?	Avete delle camere libere?	ah-veb-teh deleb kab-mair-eh lee-bair-eh?
double room	una camera doppia	oona kab-mair-ah dob-pee-ah
with double bed	con letto matrimoniale	kon let-toh mab-tree-mob-nee-ab-leb
twin room	una camera con due letti	oona kab-mair-ab kon doo-eb let-tee
single room	una camera singola	oona kab-mair-ah sing-gob-lah
room with a bath, shower	una camera con bagno, con doccia	oona kab-mair-ab kon ban-yob, kon dot-chab
porter	il facchino	eel fab-kee-noh
key	la chiave	lab kee-ab-veh
I have a reservation.	Ho prenotato.	ob preb-nob-tab-toh

Eating Out

Have you got a table for ...?	Avete una tavola per ... ?	ah-veb-teh oona tab-vob-lab pair ...?
I'd like to reserve a table.	Vorrei riservare una tavola.	vor-ray ree-sair-vab-reb oona tab-vob-lab
breakfast	colazione	kob-lab-tsee-ob-neb
lunch	pranzo	pran-tsoh
dinner	cena	cheb-nab
The bill, please.	Il conto, per favore.	eel kon-toh pair fab-vor-eb
I am a vegetarian.	Sono vegetariano/a.	sob-nob veb-jeb-tar-ee-ab-noh/nah
waitress	cameriera	kab-mair-ee-air-ah
waiter	cameriere	kab-mair-ee-air-eb
fixed price menu	il menù a prezzo fisso	eel meb-noo ab pret-soh fee-soh
dish of the day	piatto del giorno	pee-ab-toh dell jor-no
starter	antipasto	an-tee-pass-tob
first course	il primo	eel pree-mob
main course	il secondo	eel seh-kon-doh
vegetables	il contorno	eel kon-tor-nob
dessert	il dolce	eel doll-cheb
cover charge	il coperto	eel kob-pair-tob
wine list	la lista dei vini	lab lee-stab day vee-nee
rare	al sangue	al sang-gweb
medium	al puntino	al poon-tee-nob
well done	ben cotto	ben kot-toh
glass	il bicchiere	eel bee-kee-air-eb
bottle	la bottiglia	lab bot-teel-yab
knife	il coltello	eel kol-tell-ob
fork	la forchetta	lab for-ket-tab
spoon	il cucchiaio	eel koo-kee-eye-ob

Menu Decoder

l'acqua minerale gassata/naturale	lab-kwab mee-nair-ab-leb gab-zab-tah/ nab-too-rah-leb	mineral water fizzy/still
aceto	ah-cheb-toh	vinegar
aglio	al-ee-ob	garlic
l'agnello	lab-niell-ob	lamb
al forno	al for-nob	baked/roasted
alla griglia	ah-leb greel-yab	grilled
l'aragosta	lab-rah-goss-tab	lobster
arrosto	ar-ross-tob	roast
basilico	bab-zee-lee-koh	basil
la birra	lab beer-rah	beer
la bistecca	lab bee-stek-kab	steak
il brodo	eel brob-doh	broth
il burro	eel boor-ob	butter
il caffè	eel kab-feb	coffee
i calamari	ee kah-lah-mab-ree	squid
i carciofi	ee kar-choff-ee	artichokes
la carne	la kar-neb	meat
la cipolla	la chip-ob-lab	onion
i contorni	ee kon-tor-nee	vegetables
le cozze	leb cob-tzeb	mussels
i fagioli	ee fab-job-lee	beans
il fegato	eel fay-gab-toh	liver
il finocchio	eel fee-nok-ee-ob	fennel
il formaggio	eel for-mad-job	cheese
le fragole	leb frab-gob-leb	strawberries
il fritto misto	eel free-tob mees-tob	mixed fried dish
la frutta	la froot-tab	fruit
frutti di mare	froo-tee dee mab-reb	seafood
i funghi	ee foon-gbee	mushrooms
i gamberi	ee gam-bair-ee	prawns
il gelato	eel jeb-lab-tob	ice cream
l'insalata	leen-sab-lab-tab	salad

il latte	eel labt-teb	milk
lesso	less-ob	boiled
la melanzana	lab meb-lan-tsab-nab	aubergine
la minestra	lab mee-ness-trab	soup
l'olio	lob-lee-ob	oil
il pane	eel pab-neb	bread
le patate	leb pab-tab-teb	potatoes
le patatine fritte	leb pab-tab-teen-eb free-teb	chips
il pepe	eel peb-peh	pepper
la pesca	lab pess-kab	peach
il pesce	eel pesb-eb	fish
il polipo	eel pob-lee-pob	octopus
il pollo	eel poll-ob	chicken
il pomodoro	eel pob-mob-dor-ob	tomato
il prosciutto cotto/crudo	eel pro-shoo-tob kot-tob/kroo-dob	ham cooked/cured
il riso	eel ree-zob	rice
il sale	eel sab-leb	salt
la salsiccia	lab sal-see-cbab	sausage
le seppie	leb sep-pee-eb	cuttlefish
secco	sek-kob	dry
la sogliola	lab soll-yob-lab	sole
i spinaci	ee spee-nab-chee	spinach
succo d'arancia/ di limone	soo-koh dab-ran-chah/ dee lee-moh-neb	orange/lemon juice
il tè	eel teb	tea
la tisana	lab tee-zab-nab	herbal tea
il tonno	eel ton-nob	tuna
la torta	lab tor-tab	cake/tart
l'uovo	loo-ob-vob	egg
vino bianco	vee-nob bee-ang-kob	white wine
vino rosso	vee-nob ross-ob	red wine
il vitello	eel vee-tell-ob	veal
le vongole	leb von-gob-leb	clams
lo zucchero	loh zoo-kair-ob	sugar
gli zucchini	lyee dzoo-kee-nee	courgettes
la zuppa	lab tsoo-pab	soup

Numbers

1	uno	oo-nob
2	due	doo-eb
3	tre	treb
4	quattro	kwat-rob
5	cinque	cbing-kweb
6	sei	say-ee
7	sette	set-teb
8	otto	ot-tob
9	nove	nob-veb
10	dieci	dee-eb-chee
11	undici	oon-dee-chee
12	dodici	dob-dee-chee
13	tredici	tray-dee-cbee
14	quattordici	kwat-tor-dee-cbee
15	quindici	kwin-dee-cbee
16	sedici	say-dee-cbee
17	diciassette	dee-cbab-set-teb
18	diciotto	dee-cbot-tob
19	diciannove	dee-cbab-nob-veb
20	venti	ven-tee
30	trenta	tren-tab
40	quaranta	kwab-ran-tab
50	cinquanta	ching-kwan-tab
60	sessanta	sess-an-tab
70	settanta	set-tan-tab
80	ottanta	ot-tan-tab
90	novanta	nob-van-tab
100	cento	chen-tob
1,000	mille	mee-leb
2,000	duemila	doo-eb mee-lab
5,000	cinquemila	ching-kweb mee-lab
1,000,000	un milione	oon meel-yob-neb

Time

one minute	un minuto	oon mee-noo-tob
one hour	un'ora	oon or-ab
half an hour	mezz'ora	medz-or-ab
a day	un giorno	oon jor-nob
a week	una settimana	oona set-tee-mab-nab
Monday	lunedì	loo-neb-dee
Tuesday	martedì	mar-teb-dee
Wednesday	mercoledì	mair-kob-leb-dee
Thursday	giovedì	job-veb-dee
Friday	venerdì	ven-air-dee
Saturday	sabato	sab-bab-tob
Sunday	domenica	dob-meb-nee-kab

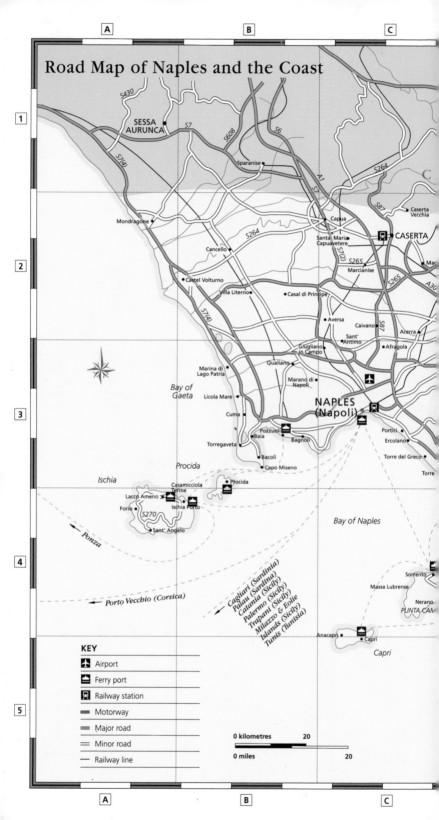